ERNIE K-DOE
EMBER
SHIRLEY'S TUFF
E-1075
Minit
45 R.P.M.
604
MAKE YOU LOVE ME
K-DOE
LOVE YOU THE BEST
ERNIE K-DOE
BEATING LIKE A TOM TOM
ERNIE K-DOE
MOTHER-IN-LAW
039
ERNIE K-DOE
INSTANT
RECORDS
BABY SINCE I MET YOU
ERNIE K-DOE
3260
INSTANT
RECORDS
REAPING WHAT I SOW
ERNIE K-DOE
3264
DANCIN' MAN
DUKE
ERNIE K DOE
DON'T KILL MY GROOVE
DUKE
ERNIE K-DOE
UNTIL THE REAL THING COMES ALONG
DUKE
ERNIE K. DOE
Sansu
HOTCHA MAMA
ERNIE K-DOE
LET ME LOVE YOU
SYLA
JUMP INTO YOUR LOVE
MR. ERNIE K-DOE

ERNIE K-DOE: *The R&B Emperor of New Orleans*

The Louisiana Musicians Biography Series, a complement to the Louisiana Artists Biography Series, exemplifies The Historic New Orleans Collection's commitment to preserving and celebrating the region's unique culture.

ALSO IN THE SERIES

Unfinished Blues: Memories of a New Orleans Music Man
by Harold R. Battiste Jr. with Karen Celestan

winner of the Black Caucus of the American Library Association's
Award for Excellence in Scholarship

A DAPPER YOUNG K-DOE
ca. 1953
Courtesy Antoinette K-Doe

ERNIE
The R&B Emper

K-DOE

or of New Orleans

Written by
BEN SANDMEL

With a foreword by
PETER GURALNICK

Published by
THE HISTORIC NEW ORLEANS COLLECTION
2012

The Historic New Orleans Collection is a museum, research center, and publisher dedicated to the study and preservation of the history and culture of New Orleans and the Gulf South region. The Collection is operated by the Kemper and Leila Williams Foundation, a Louisiana nonprofit corporation.

Library of Congress Cataloging-in-Publication Data

Sandmel, Ben.
Ernie K-Doe : the R&B emperor of New Orleans / by Ben Sandmel ; edited by Sarah Doerries.
p. cm. -- (The Louisiana musicians biography series)
Discography: p.
Includes bibliographical references and index.
ISBN-13: 978-0-917860-60-7
ISBN-10: 0-917860-60-8
1. K-Doe, Ernie. 2. Rhythm and blues musicians--United States--Biography. I. Doerries, Sarah R. II. Title.
ML420.K04S36 2012
782.421644092--dc23
[B]
2011040576

533 Royal Street
New Orleans, Louisiana 70130
www.hnoc.org

Second printing. 2,500 copies

Printed by Imago

Priscilla Lawrence, Executive Director
Jessica Dorman, Director of Publications
Sarah R. Doerries, Senior Editor, editor of the Louisiana Musicians Biography Series

Book design by Alison Cody
Printed and bound in Singapore for Imago

K-DOE, KING OF KREWE DU VIEUX
2001
Photo by Pat Jolly

Ernie K-Doe's
Lounge

ERNIE K-DOE
oil on canvas
2011
By Francis Pavy

Dedicated to Jimmy Johnson, a wise teacher of blues music and the ways of its world, and Dr. Portia K. Maultsby, who got me started writing about music. And to the memory of Ernie and Antoinette K-Doe, Herman Ernest, Mary Herczog, Gilbert Hines, Bernard "Bunchie" Johnson, Tad Jones, Elemore Morgan Jr., Louis Nugent, and Sunnyland Slim.

I'M COCKY
BUT I'M GOOD!
... ERNIE K-DOE
NEW ORLEANS, L A

TABLE OF CONTENTS

ERNIE K-DOE
"I'M COCKY BUT I'M GOOD"
BOXER SHORTS

K-DOE

FOREWORD: *The Once and Future Emperor*

Every so often a book, or a film, or a piece of music will come along that you just want to savor. Part of you wants desperately to slow down, you want to take in every element and prolong the aesthetic pleasure of the moment—but the impact of the work itself simply will not permit you to. And as you inevitably find yourself swept up by the headlong tide, you make a promise to yourself that you will return to this narrative passage, you will revisit that turn of phrase, you will save your full appreciation for a second (or third) read.

That was my experience with this book.

I could call it elegant and ironic (although not, of course, in the hipster but in the *humanist* sense), except this would not even begin to suggest the sheer gusto and unqualified appetite for all the vagaries of the human experience that Ben Sandmel's genuinely offbeat appreciation for this most offbeat of subjects contains on almost every page. Even its most bizarre episodes are recounted with such affectionate indulgence that you feel a sense of privilege to be present when K-Doe captures the *New York Times* reporter, a frisson of existential recognition when K-Doe's effigy (the statue posthumously produced by sculptor Jason Poirier) takes its place as an honored guest in the New Orleans social ramble.

Anyone who ever visited K-Doe's eponymous Mother-in-Law Lounge (its name deriving, it goes without saying, from the song its creator called one of the "two songs that will stand the test of time, until the end of the world," the other being "The Star Spangled Banner") will know immediately what to expect—the Mother-in-Law Lounge could well have substituted for a fully accredited course in surrealism, to which I can attest on the basis of a minimal amount of personal experience. There was the night, for example, when Ben took me to what might under any other circumstances have passed for an ordinary occasion—a birthday party. K-Doe's wife, Antoinette, was cueing her husband from behind the bar over her taxicab dispatcher's mic; inveterate keyboard-tinkerer Rico Watts was doing his best Elvis impersonation with "Suspicious Minds" or "It's Now or Never"; and K-Doe, of course, was the imperturbably whirling center of it all—but what I will always remember is the arrival of a somewhat bedraggled lady of the night who to all appearances had ducked in out of the rain, just in time for K-Doe's introduction of his honored academic guest by his full doctoral title. That was all it took, as the woman made a beeline for this PhD in anthropology and folklore, a well-known radio host, and

K-DOE PERFORMING AT HIS OWN TRIBUTE CONCERT, THE MOTHER-IN-LAW LOUNGE
March 25, 2000
Photo by Scott Saltzman

FOLLOWING PAGES
K-DOE CHARMS THE AUDIENCE AT TIPITINA'S, NEW ORLEANS
1977
Photo by Michael P. Smith
©The Historic New Orleans Collection, 2007.0103.1.651

graphically described her symptoms. Yet another example of the brash talent, uninhibited self-advocacy, and boundless self-belief that marked the good-hearted spirit of Ernie K-Doe's world.

The Mother-in-Law Lounge is gone, but its spirit lives on—in music, in memory, and in the indelible portraits etched in this book. What I think is so unique about *Ernie K-Doe: The R&B Emperor of New Orleans*—well, Ernie K-Doe himself is, of course, the ultimate source of its uniqueness, but what's so unique about Ben Sandmel's *book* is the undisguised relish Ben takes in his rambunctious subject, the delightful shivers of irony, affection, and appreciation that are abundantly juxtaposed with a seriousness of purpose and lightness of touch that so rarely go hand in hand.

What Ben Sandmel has done, like all great cultural reporters—like A. J. Liebling or Joseph Mitchell or Murray Kempton in another guise—is to set out on an unmapped journey of exploration, to throw caution and preconception to the winds for the sheer "life-enhancing" thrill, as Kempton wrote, of "going around," and then to come back with a *story*. And what is so wonderful about the story is that, while it is filled with people and events immediately recognizable to both the idle observer and the active participant, at the same time it gives shape to those events, it gives shape to the random universe we all inhabit, in a manner and style that allow us to fully take in its many variegated and tragicomic turns.

Brevity being the soul of wit, it is a brief tour, relatively speaking. Emperor of the Universe? Who is to say? K-Doe lived in a rich tradition of grandiosity that encompasses not just New Orleans (though New Orleans may be its most striking contemporary manifestation) but the equally capacious worlds of Rabelais, Don Quixote, and Tristram Shandy. Eccentricity is all very well as far as it goes, but it is *humanity* that remains at the heart of the creative experience—and Ben Sandmel has given us Ernie K-Doe in all of his flawed glory, an emperor stripped bare for all to see and acknowledge, not on the basis of so paltry a thing as blind fealty to the crown, but out of recognition of our shared, tattered humanity.

—Peter Guralnick

K-DOE RESTING INSIDE AN RV BEFORE A PERFORMANCE AT THE NEW ORLEANS JAZZ AND HERITAGE FESTIVAL
May 6, 2001
Photo by Tabitha Haggerty

© EBET ROBERTS

CHAPTER 1: *The Importance of Being Ernie*

I don't need your little paper!"

Such withering scorn is rarely directed at the *New York Times*. It's an impolitic outburst for an aging rhythm and blues singer who yearns to jump-start his career—especially if he shouts it at an admiring *Times* critic just after an interview. Particularly if his harsh words accompany harsher actions: halting a song midverse to accuse the critic of secretly taping his performance. Demanding the surrender of the critic's microcassette machine. Calling 911 to report a robbery in progress. Locking everyone inside his tiny nightclub so that patrons and critic become a truly captive audience. Instructing a burly employee to execute kung fu moves by the door to discourage thoughts of escape.

But a veteran New Orleans rhythm and blues singer named Ernie K-Doe committed all these major breaches of professionalism. It went down at the Mother-in-Law Lounge, K-Doe's self-adoring shrine to his big hit from 1961. When cops arrived with guns drawn—ready to quash an armed robbery but powerless to stop an alleged theft of intellectual property—the critic, Neil Strauss, explained that he'd come to the lounge to write an article that would "let more people know about Mr. K-Doe." But Mr. K-Doe didn't perceive Strauss's visit as a rare chance for high-profile coverage, because Mr. K-Doe had barely heard of Strauss's employer. There was no reason why K-Doe would—or should—have been familiar with the *New York Times*. Virtually none of "all the news that's fit to print" has relevance in New Orleans's music community, where the cell-phone grapevine prevails. K-Doe's accusation of aural thievery didn't come completely from left field, either. There is a niche market for live albums, especially overseas, where an odd concept of authenticity often favors low-fidelity recordings.

The police eventually settled matters, the hostages were all set free, and Strauss was released with the tools of his trade intact. So was *Times* photographer Ebet Roberts, whose cameras K-Doe had tried to confiscate. Both felt stunned by the dispute, which was quite unprecedented in their professional experience. Even so, in a classic case of lemons-to-lemonade, the despised "little paper" gave Ernie K-Doe a half page of favorable, bemused coverage, accompanied by a flattering photo. On May 17, 2000, under the wry headline THE MOTHER-IN-LAW OF ALL VISITS, Strauss generously encouraged readers to see the lounge for themselves (despite, he acknowledged, his probably being banished for life). Instead of crucifying K-Doe in revenge, the *Times* scribe made light of a harrowing experience.

K-DOE AT THE MOTHER-IN-LAW LOUNGE
May 2000
Photo by Ebet Roberts

Meanwhile, scores of better-behaved musicians searched in vain for their names in print.

When such egregious acts beget such great press, some powerful mitigating forces must be at work. In this case the saving graces were the personal charisma of Ernie K-Doe and the considerable charm of his club. K-Doe, who passed away in 2001, was an adored elder statesman of New Orleans music, a larger-than-life character, and usually an amiable host. The Mother-in-Law Lounge, which thrived in K-Doe's image until 2010, was a place that filled visitors with giddy wonderment. Their delight ensued from the lounge's welcoming environment and the surreal sensory overload that walloped all who crossed the threshold. This physical entrance doubled as the conceptual portal into Ernie K-Doe's eccentric parallel universe—a festive, Fellini-esque realm where shameless idolatry and unfettered happiness reigned supreme. ("There's a lot of love in here" was a frequent, typical reaction of first-time visitors.)

These intriguing enticements inspired many to bring their friends to the Mother-in-Law Lounge, for the pure fun of watching the newcomers' enthrallment with this joyous, quirky little bar. The lounge's hybrid ambience combined elements of a juke joint, a mosh pit, an R&B museum, and a cinematic set from *Satyricon*. It attracted a similarly eclectic clientele. Well-dressed, middle-aged black people bellied up to the bar alongside white street kids with torn jeans and bizarre piercings. Joining them were politicians seeking cultural credibility, off-duty cops, laborers in dirty work clothes, and fanatical R&B fans on pilgrimages to hallowed music sites around the South. A busload of blue-haired suburban ladies might turn up at any minute, stopping in for a nightcap after a casino-gambling excursion. Birthday celebrants might likewise arrive en masse, sporting all manner of outrageous costumes. Derelicts and winos wandered in at times, receiving the same respect as well-heeled customers. The harmonious interactions of these diverse patrons affirmed them in the tradition of Huey P. Long's credo "Every Man a King." Or, as Ernie K-Doe often put it, "All you got to do is just keep the faith in what you are doing. You set your goal line, and don't let nobody change you. You know what you say when people tell you you can't do something? *Fool, shut your mouth up*!"

This resolute stance helped propel Ernie K-Doe through years of scuffling before "Mother-in-Law" hit the top. It also helped sustain him through the long, lean years after his star had faded. He nurtured himself during these tough times with glorious memories of May 1961, when "Mother-in-Law" became the best-selling record in America. The best-selling record in two Americas, actually—white and black—as delineated by *Billboard* magazine's separate sales charts for pop and R&B. "Mother-in-Law" topped both charts, ruling pop's Hot 100 for a single week and dominating the R&B survey for five. In pop it unseated Del Shannon's "Runaway" and was in turn replaced by Ricky Nelson's "Travelin' Man." (No other New Orleans artist, not even Fats Domino, had ever reached this peak with a song recorded in New Orleans. Domino, in fact, despite his frequent lofty chart positions and astronomical sales, never had a number-one record.) On the R&B side,

"Mother-in-Law" displaced Ray Charles's "One Mint Julep" and was bumped by Ben E. King's "Stand by Me." (Charles and K-Doe would compete again at the Grammy Awards, when Charles's "Hit the Road Jack" was voted best R&B recording of 1961, leaving "Mother-in-Law" as an also-ran.)

Compared to these hits and most others of the day, in both pop and R&B, "Mother-in-Law" has very blunt lyrics:

> The worst person I know, Mother-in-Law, Mother-in-Law.
> She worries me so, Mother-in-Law, Mother-in-Law.
> If she leaves us alone, we would have a happy home.
> Sent from down below, Mother-in-Law, Mother-in-Law,
> Mother-in-Law, Mother-in-Law.
>
> Satan should be her name, Mother-in-Law, Mother-in-Law.
> To me they're about the same, Mother-in-Law, Mother-in-Law;
> Every time I open my mouth, she steps in, tries to put me out.
> How could she stoop so low? Mother-in-Law, Mother-in-Law,
> Mother-in-Law, Mother-in-Law.
>
> I come home with my pay, Mother-in-Law, Mother-in-Law.
> She asks me what I make, Mother-in-Law, Mother-in-Law.
> She thinks her advice is a contribution, but if she will leave that will be the solution,
> And don't come back no more, Mother-in-Law, Mother-in-Law,
> Mother-in-Law, Mother-in-Law.

Tame as these lines are by contemporary standards, they raised eyebrows in the early '60s, especially overseas. The English music weekly *Melody Maker* opined that "Mother-in-Law" "has made a big showing in the States—more, we feel, on account of its simple melodic appeal and rocking beat than the libellous sentiments it contains." But London's *New Musical Express* praised the song as "a cute comedy number in which Ernie tells his mother-in-law a few home truths about herself."

If K-Doe's disdainful sentiments in "Mother-in-Law" flirt with libel, his terse and deceptively cool delivery belie its caustic message. In New Orleans speak, this state of obvious annoyance—which, as alert observers realize, could imminently escalate into fireworks—is often telegraphed with the warning "You are working my last single nerve!" K-Doe's ominously understated, last-single-nerve delivery is complemented by the sparse, less-is-more arrangement of producer Allen Toussaint. Toussaint, a New Orleans rhythm and blues savant who emerged as a major creative figure in American popular music, also plays piano on "Mother-in-Law." His lilting solo echoes the Afro-Caribbean-influenced styles of such seminal New Orleans pianists as Jelly Roll Morton (Ferdinand LaMothe) and

Professor Longhair (Henry Roeland Byrd). A century before "Mother-in-Law," the same folk traditions had inspired the classical compositions of native son Louis Moreau Gottschalk.

"Mother-in-Law" was so popular that it inspired two "answer songs": "Son-in-Law," by the girl group the Blossoms, also recorded by Louise Brown ("the other day he even hocked her wedding ring"), and "Brother-in-Law (He's a Moocher)," by rockabilly artist Paul Peek ("He's lazy, won't work, never had a job—get out of my house, you big fat slob"). "Mother-in-Law" is still considered a classic of overlapping genres, including R&B, pop, rock, and the loosely defined "beach music" of the Carolina coast. It has been reissued on at least a hundred anthologies and continues to get significant airplay on such diverse programs as *Theme Time Radio Hour with Your Host Bob Dylan* and *American Routes* with Nick Spitzer, and numerous oldies shows on R&B and pop stations. A multitude of new renditions continue to be recorded, including several Spanish-language versions, commonly titled "La Suegra." In New Orleans, where the borders between musical genres are extremely porous, bands of every sort are asked to play "Mother-in-Law." They're expected to know it, along with K-Doe's regional hits "T'aint It the Truth," "Hello My Lover," "Te Ta Te Ta Ta," and "A Certain Girl." None of these other fine songs achieved national success comparable to that of "Mother-in-Law," but all are perpetual Gulf Coast favorites. Collectively they established the reputations of Ernie K-Doe and Allen Toussaint as masters of New Orleans rhythm and blues.

This was no small achievement at a time when that field was quite crowded. A vast surge of creativity and commercial success energized the Crescent City from the late 1940s to the early '60s, an era later dubbed the golden age of New Orleans rhythm and blues. A cursory list of its other luminaries includes Fats Domino, Professor Longhair, Shirley and Lee, Smiley Lewis, Irma Thomas, Lee Dorsey, Lloyd Price, Art Neville, Aaron Neville, Huey "Piano" Smith, Frankie Ford, and Clarence "Frogman" Henry. The Meters and Dr. John, who emerged in the late '60s, and the Neville Brothers (with siblings Aaron, Art, Charles, and Cyril), who formed a decade later, also stand in that illustrious number. So do the musicians who accompanied these artists on many of their records: saxophonists Lee Allen and Nat Perrilliat, drummers Earl Palmer and Smokey Johnson, bassists Frank Fields and Lloyd Lambert, and guitarists Roy Montrell, Justin Adams, and "Deacon" John Moore, to name but a few.

Ernie K-Doe felt thrilled when "Mother-in-Law" reached the top. He felt gratified decades later by its staying power. But he never ever felt surprised. "There ain't but two songs that will stand the test of time," K-Doe often declared. He would then pause at considerable dramatic length before naming them: "The first song is 'The Star Spangled Banner,' and the second song is 'Mother-in-Law.' Because people gonna have a mother-in-law until the end of the world."

If K-Doe exaggerated his song's importance, he did not overstate its broad, perpetual appeal. Negative depictions of mothers-in-law date back at least to the Roman satirist Juvenal: "Give up all hope of peace so long as your mother-in-law is alive." Countless comedians, Henny Youngman for one, have echoed Juvenal's sentiments: "I bought my mother-in-law a chair. Now they won't let me plug it in." And men are not alone in alleging persecution. The website www.motherinlawhell.com was created for "the daughter-in-law sisterhood . . . you are not alone. stop suffering in silence." In an article entitled "Women's Studies and Popular Music Stereotypes," B. Lee Cooper mentioned K-Doe's hit while proposing that "ideas about hateful maternal relatives . . . need to be tempered." But such mellowing entails an arduous slog through dense cultural attitudes. Emotional issues factor in, too, including the fear of dominant personalities.

Ernie K-Doe did not fear his mother-in-law. Au contraire, he bragged about throwing her out: "My first wife's mother's name was Lucy—but it should have been *Lucifer*! . . . She used to wake up six o'clock in the morning to bring me daytime nightmares. . . . She was staying at my house, eating up all my grub and talking her noise. I took her outside in the pouring rain. I said, 'You know something—when a boil comes to a head, you ain't got to squeeze it, it busts itself, and you done busted that boil now. I want you out of my house!' I told her, 'This street run to the left, and this street run to the right—NOW PICK ONE!' I walked back inside and my first wife said, 'Where Mama?' I said, 'Come look out the window—I can *show* you better than I can *tell* you!'" But in other moods K-Doe assessed their relationship with the aggrieved tone of a victim who felt a desperate need for immediate escape: "Have you ever found a love, somebody that you need? Seem like to me that I can remember the day, and I can remember it well, when I first fell in love. But what took me out of love was the time I met my mother-in-law. I thought I was Superman or Captain Marvel, [flying] out of my own house!" There were also times when K-Doe's tone was begrudgingly conciliatory: "I had a mother-in-law at one time, and in one way she really did help me, she caused me being able to go all over the United States."

K-Doe's son Ernest Kador Jr. offered a more nuanced, myth-busting explanation: "My father exaggerated about a lot of things. Because I can honestly say—and not because he was my daddy—but as God is my witness, him and my grandmother Lucy got along. She *would* give him a hard time about taking care of her daughter. And she was upset because my mom and dad supposedly were cousins. I don't know what kind of cousins—first cousins, third cousins, whatever—but supposedly they were cousins, and they fell in love but they kept my grandmother in the dark about their relationship for so long, until they got married. But with all that, when my dad went to my grandmother's house, they would kiss, and they would hug. They wasn't to where they would shout at each other."

Absent the personal strife that K-Doe perceived, however, he might not have sung "Mother-in-Law" with the convincing quality that catapulted him to the peak of his profession. When the song hit number one, Ernie K-Doe became a respected peer of his R&B idols. He began performing at prestigious venues around America and in the Caribbean. He cast a significant shadow of musical influence over Europe, especially the nascent world of the British Invasion; in the UK his songs were covered by the likes of the Yardbirds and Herman's Hermits. And he created a substantial and lasting legacy of top-notch rhythm and blues recordings.

But such heady success ended by the mid-'60s, and Ernie K-Doe plummeted into chronic alcoholism. ("I do not mess with no drugs," he said truthfully, "but me and Brother Jack Daniels—we got something goin'!") He spent years trudging in torment through many a lonesome valley, scraping by with bottom-rung gigs and low-selling records. He ran marginal businesses, such as Ernest Kador's Hauling Service—his slogan, "You Load and Unload," probably cost him some customers. The Ernie K-Doe Mother-in-Law Shoe Shine Stand, set on a rough corner in New Orleans's Tremé neighborhood, was not likely lucrative.

Some two decades passed before K-Doe rose to prominence again, and his second act was no chastened plea for approval. Still drinking—although still quite entertaining, up to a point—K-Doe regained fame in the 1980s as a ranting, raving disc jockey who shattered every notion of professional radio protocol. The *Ernie K-Doe Show* found K-Doe spinning his old records while screaming over them about his prodigious talent: "Louis Armstrong, Fats Domino, and Ernie K-Doe—the best things that have ever happened to the city of New Orleans: THEM THREE!" Listeners loved these loopy broadcasts on New Orleans's community-sponsored station, WWOZ-FM, and Tulane University's WTUL-FM. But exasperated station managers couldn't handle K-Doe's over-the-top pronouncements and his penchant for plugging questionable businesses owned by his friends: "Doctor O. J.—he's a doctor just for ladies. . . . And once you see Doctor O. J. on Jackson Avenue and Liberty, then you don't have to worry about that anymore!"

By the early 1990s K-Doe's radio days were over too. Further disillusioned, he sank even deeper—into abject dereliction. He seemed destined to die in the gutter. And then, at a critical juncture, Ernie K-Doe was saved by love, in the form of Antoinette Dorsey Fox. In 1995 she opened the Mother-in-Law Lounge so that K-Doe would always have a place to perform. The next year they got married. Antoinette turned Ernie's life around, both personally and professionally. "Didn't He Ramble" is the title of a favorite song in deep New Orleans tradition, and ramble K-Doe certainly had, living hard and wreaking havoc. Now he had a home, a convivial safe haven where he could mingle with his colleagues and hold court with his fans. What's more, Antoinette helped Ernie cut back dramatically on his drinking. This constituted a huge accomplishment because they had moved in above the lounge and a whole bar's worth of temptation. Once K-Doe finally found stability, contentment, and a new sense of purpose, he started making consistently good music again.

Upon regaining his balance, K-Doe also managed to integrate two conflicting personality traits: his meticulous professionalism and his irrepressible, loose-cannon charisma. The result was an effective new persona: a cherished elder statesman, albeit a bit crazed at times, whose musicianship still commanded respect. K-Doe's next strategic maneuver combined a logical step with a quantum leap. In 1998 he christened himself Emperor of the World. Once renamed, K-Doe began dressing the part, in flowing robes, profuse plumage, and a succession of crowns. He thus emerged as a flamboyant figurehead of New Orleans's rich tradition of grassroots surrealism.

The late 1990s saw K-Doe continue to regain lost ground on the New Orleans R&B circuit, and to expand his following. Among K-Doe's new admirers was a young bohemian audience that began to lionize him as patriarch of the city's Ninth Ward alt-rock scene. His star rose again in the national arena too: K-Doe received a lifetime achievement award from the Rhythm and Blues Foundation in 1998, performed for a vast crowd at the foot of the Washington Monument in 1999, and hosted a feature-film shoot at the Mother-in-Law Lounge in 2000. (He also appeared in the movie, *Happy Here and Now*, released in 2002.) K-Doe's comeback was gaining ever more momentum when he died, of esophageal cancer, on July 5, 2001, aged sixty-five. Throughout his terminal illness he continued to hatch new schemes for a bright future, never disclosing that anything was amiss.

K-Doe's demise amplified both his own legend and the stature of the Mother-in-Law Lounge. Until the lounge's closure in 2010, he was memorialized there with florid trappings à la Elvis Presley and Graceland. Presley's 1977 death inspired many singers to become full-time Elvis impersonators. (In similar fashion, the Chicago blues scene was flooded with Howlin' Wolf impersonators after that popular artist passed away in 1976.) No flesh-and-blood performers presumed to impersonate Ernie K-Doe, but he was dramatically represented by a life-size statue fashioned from a mannequin. It stood on display in the lounge and made frequent appearances around town. In one extreme case, K-Doe was even deified in an online "Prayer to Ernie." No wonder artist Jason Poirier, who crafted the statue, referred to it as "a divine manifestation."

Even as an idol, however, Ernie K-Doe's feet of clay were amply evident. Adversity, foible, and failure all figure prominently in his saga, along with faith and—finally—sweet redemption. K-Doe's hero-outlaw odyssey would not be complete without Antoinette, his heroine. She stood by her man, helped him to stand tall again, and dedicated her widowhood to honoring his memory. K-Doe's story is also the story of his colleagues, talented men and women who have made vast contributions to one of the world's most vibrant music scenes. Their resilient creativity continues to flow in a city that has long straddled a line between whimsy and violence, erupting from human nature and Mother Nature alike. Even in death, Ernie K-Doe remains a beloved icon and a work in progress. His legacy continues to inspire creative expression, in words, music, and art.

A chronicle of such cosmic complexity does not lend itself to strict linear exposition. Especially not in profoundly illogical New Orleans, a city set on a bend of the Mississippi so that the sun rises over the river's west bank. This geographic quirk explains the moniker "the Crescent City" and the fact that New Orleanians do not use conventional compass points. In place of north, south, east, and west they refer instead to lake (denoting Lake Pontchartrain), river, downtown, and uptown. Not that such mundane matters of orientation ever fazed Ernie K-Doe. "What's cold is *hot*," he often expounded, "and them what say they are gone, don't always be gone." Accordingly, this telling of K-Doe's tale begins where the tale, in fact, ended.

ERNIE K★DOE
Mother-In-Law
Lounge

THE MOTHER-IN-LAW LOUNGE
March 5, 2009
Mural by Daniel Fuselier
Photo by Melissa Carrier

TEENAGE ANTOINETTE YOU CAN'T BREAK HER YET!!!
SWAMP
KREWE du VIEUX
I'M COOKY BUT I'M GOOD!!
152

CHAPTER 2: *An Emperor's Home Is His Castle*

Close by New Orleans's French Quarter, an elevated highway casts shadows upon North Claiborne Avenue. Old men play checkers in the gloom below, seated on milk crates and abandoned car seats. Steely-eyed teens cruise restlessly on children's bicycles three sizes too small, their knees pumping high above the handlebars. People flinch at sudden loud noises, fearing they may be gunshots, which are not infrequent.

North Claiborne was once a lovely tree-lined boulevard, home to a bustling commercial district. Then the majestic oaks were razed in the 1960s, and Interstate 10 rose up to block the sun. Stretches of this erstwhile main drag of New Orleans's black community are now shabby shells, where sparsely stocked stores display more bullet-proof glass than merchandise. Its decline worsened in the ongoing aftermath of Hurricane Katrina. On the streets where Bush and Brownie did such a heck of a job in 2005, the process of recovery remains uneven seven years later. Meticulous renovations sit next to storm-abandoned buildings that rot from neglect. Curbside signs touting HOUSE DEMOLITION stand cheek by jowl with ads for bulk discounts on custom-made funeral T-shirts.

Much like the rescuers who battled Katrina's rancid muck, New Orleans's mental health professionals are still digging through a toxic ooze of post-traumatic stress and depression. The 2008 evacuation for Hurricane Gustav exacerbated the citizenry's stress with collective flashbacks. But in this ravaged city, on the ravaged North Claiborne strip, a walled oasis once beckoned. Its outer perimeter was a parade of claw-foot bathtubs, painted and lined up end-to-end. This porcelain parapet suggested an esoteric art installation. But its primary function was to block drunk drivers from crashing through the wall of the inner sanctum: the small, two-story building that housed the Mother-in-Law Lounge and the K-Does' upstairs apartment. Antoinette K-Doe passed away in 2009, the tubs are gone now, and the lounge is closed, but at this writing its impressive murals remain. There are no plans to paint over them, although the designs and imagery may change.

Every external inch of the building is covered by a swirling mural that hits the eye like a train bedecked with graffiti. Many murals have come and gone since the lounge first opened in 1995. One of the most memorable incarnations, commissioned by Antoinette, emblazoned the lounge in 2000. It featured the work of artist David "LEBO" LeBatard. A frenzied freeze-frame centered on Ernie K-Doe, who sported a flashy suit, gold cape, and some seriously big hair. His gaudy combo of coif and couture suggested the dandified love child of James Brown and the Marquis de Lafayette. K-Doe held a microphone in a pose of vocal passion, while appearing to leap forth from a bright-blue background festooned with stars and musical notes. No opportunity for ornamentation was missed; the AC window units and burglar bars were adorned with metallic gold paint.

In a city rife with distinctive decor and architecture, the lounge stood out significantly. Likewise, in a city where excess and idiosyncrasy are adored, the late Ernie K-Doe still

THE MOTHER-IN-LAW LOUNGE
March 5, 2009
Murals by Daniel Fuselier
Photos by Melissa Carrier

occupies a niche as a supremely outré character. Had K-Doe lived during the late nineteenth century, his exploits would likely have been covered by Lafcadio Hearn, whose florid reportage often depicted the exotic side of New Orleans. Conversely, had Hearn lived during the late twentieth century, he would likely have hung out at the Mother-in-Law and written about its parade of picaresque patrons. K-Doe and Hearn, it may further be conjectured, would have hit it off famously—unless, perhaps, they were too much alike. The following description of Hearn, by his friend Dr. Rudolph Matas, could have applied equally to the Emperor: "I never judged him by conventional standards. I listened to the brilliant, erratic, intemperate outpourings of his mind, aware of his eccentricities without allowing them to blind me to the beauty and value of his really marvelous nature."

K-Doe flourished as a real-life eccentric who would have fit perfectly in the pages of John Kennedy Toole's mid-twentieth-century comedic masterpiece of New Orleans fiction, *A Confederacy of Dunces.* ("Fiction" is an advised term, because Toole's depiction of his hometown is fanciful by only the thinnest of margins.) Long after Ernie K-Doe's musical fame had peaked, he came to attract a cult following comparable to that of Toole's novel. And like Toole's absurdist leading man, Ignatius J. Reilly, Ernie K-Doe made many statements that were endearingly delusional: "Whoever think they can beat me dancing, beat me singing, doin' splits, kickin' the microphone, rollin' off them stages, making them women tear my clothes off—come see me now, 'cause the boy-child ain't been born yet! Gomer Pyle ain't gonna be able to stop me, and them Duke boys of Hazzard cannot hold me down! Burn, K-Doe, burn!" And "I'm leading the people of New Orleans out of bondage, just like Moses led the Hebrew children out of Egypt. The pope couldn't do it, Martin Luther King couldn't do it, the mayor can't do it, but *I'm going to do it*!" And the ultimately immodest and oft-repeated "Ernie K-Doe, how great thou art!"

Many of these self-absorbed pronouncements were aptly made within the bastion of the Mother-in-Law Lounge. After Ernie and Antoinette's 1996 wedding, which was held on the premises, the K-Does hosted periodic reenactments of their vows "for the fans." For the newlyweds, meanwhile, living over the lounge seemed to blur the boundary between professional and personal life. This led Ernie to run, or run amok, with the idea that a man's home is his castle. Like any self-respecting lord of the manor, he often dressed the part, donning his regal clothes upstairs and down-, onstage and off-, whether the lounge was open or closed. All of his ornate outfits were designed and handmade by his wife, who explained that she was "a seamstress by trade. I learned from my grandmother. When I was a little girl, I never played outside with all the other children. I was sitting at that old Singer sewing machine with her."

Antoinette quickly turned the Mother-in-Law Lounge into a treasure trove of Ernie-phernalia, maintained with loving care and fastidious attention to detail. With a curatorial flair worthy of the Louvre, she rotated her exhibits, debuting as-yet-unseen treasures and returning some artifacts to the vault of her apartment. Like an autobiographical docent, K-Doe would gladly expound at length upon the significance of these relics. Some of his

TOP
ERNIE AND ANTOINETTE'S WEDDING, THE MOTHER-IN-LAW LOUNGE
1996
Photo by Paula Burch-Celentano

BOTTOM LEFT
FIRST-ANNIVERSARY REENACTMENT OF ERNIE AND ANTOINETTE'S WEDDING, THE MOTHER-IN-LAW LOUNGE
1997

BOTTOM RIGHT
SECOND-ANNIVERSARY REENACTMENT OF ERNIE AND ANTOINETTE'S WEDDING, THE MOTHER-IN-LAW LOUNGE
1998
Photos by Syndey Byrd

PEG LEG MOFFET

commentary was purely factual—"Here I am getting a big award up in New York"—but guests were often treated to rants and embellishments that might start at any moment: "Some folks said I had lost my voice and all that kind of crap. Well, I showed them people in New York that Ernie K-Doe HAVE NOT LOST *NOTHIN'!*" And he once described a bundle of cotton batting jumbled among Antoinette's sewing supplies as "white mink."

Antoinette wisely hauled the whole collection, ermine or ersatz, upstairs when Katrina's floodwaters began seeping under her door. Although the ground floor of the lounge was ruined, she gamely did much of the repair work herself and resourcefully found philanthropic funding—plus a host of volunteers—to help. Work finished in time for a grand reopening on August 29, 2006, the first anniversary of Katrina. Once again a rotating series of historic photographs stood watch over the lounge's two small rooms, marking K-Doe's journey from cradle to grave: as a toddler, a schoolboy, a star posing for publicity shots, and lying in state at his celebrity funeral.

Tellingly, K-Doe's ever-changing photo gallery also embraced such inspirational figures as Malcolm X, Martin Luther King, Muhammad Ali, and K-Doe's childhood idol, the heavyweight boxing champion Joe Louis. Glossy publicity photos of various R&B peers looked on too: Fats Domino, Sam Cooke, Jackie Wilson, James Brown, Joe Tex, and a singing amputee from Georgia named Peg Leg Moffett. An inspired if obscure vocalist whose best-known song was "The Shocker," Moffett graced K-Doe's wall of fame in a publicity shot that was a composite of several performance images. Close inspection of his poses reveals the curious migration of his prosthesis from his left leg to his right and back again. The factual reason for this phenomenon, of course, is simply a reversed negative. But in the phantasmagoric confines of the Mother-in-Law Lounge, such marvels somehow seemed plausible.

One of the most striking photos on display featured K-Doe dressed in Native American garb, striking the proud stance of a warrior. This was no random, generic Halloween snapshot, however; it captured K-Doe as a Mardi Gras Indian. In New Orleans groups of black men parade—on Mardi Gras Day, St. Joseph's Day, "Super Sundays," and other occasions—chanting, drumming, and engaging in mock battles while sporting elaborate hand-sewn Native American costumes. Though the tradition has deep Afro-Caribbean roots, it also honors the fact that some Native Americans in Louisiana gave shelter to runaway slaves. Each New Orleans aggregation gives itself the name of an imaginary Native American tribe—the Creole Wild West and the Yellow Pocahontas, for example—and the act of participation is known as masking Indian. K-Doe masked Indian for twelve years with the still-extant Young Sons of Geronimo, and, in keeping with custom, he did so at considerable expenditure of both time and money. K-Doe's first cousin, R&B guitarist and singer Walter "Wolfman" Washington, recalled that "K-Doe would sew with the Indians. . . . I remember the day after carnival he had already made a cape and a crown. That man had everybody in the family sewing. I'd go to school, come back, and jump on the sewing again!" This labor of love, undertaken by all Mardi Gras Indians, is

TOP LEFT
PEG LEG MOFFETT PROMOTIONAL PHOTO
ca. 1966
Courtesy Antoinette K-Doe

TOP RIGHT AND BOTTOM
K-DOE MASKING INDIAN WITH THE YOUNG SONS OF GERONIMO
mid-1950s
Courtesy Antoinette K-Doe

celebrated in the songs "Sew, Sew, Sew" by the White Cloud Hunters and "New Suit," a perennial Mardi Gras favorite, by Bo Dollis, the "big chief" of the Wild Magnolias.

Ernie K-Doe's "new suit" is long gone—as are most of his other outfits that Antoinette would use to dress the statue. Many were sold after she died, and a few have been acquired by museums. Many can still be admired in two dimensions, in photos of the Emperor. They include a black ensemble with gold trim that he wore when receiving his award from the Rhythm and Blues Foundation, in New York; a thematically appropriate Uncle Sam costume—including a stars-and-stripes stovepipe hat—from a July Fourth concert in Washington, DC; and a white outfit with black trim he sported when riding as the king of a Mardi Gras parade.

Images of these career highlights exploded from the walls of the lounge, alongside various proclamations, award certificates, and laminated newspaper articles. For a time such evidence of accomplishment shared space with a spurned recording contract, posted in outrage because K-Doe found the terms unacceptable. It was difficult to share his indignation, however, because the pages were randomly tacked up along the walls in both rooms. Reading them all in order entailed a zig-zag processional—akin to saying prayers at nonsequential Stations of the Cross—that made the legal verbiage even harder to absorb.

Paper stars and streamers dangled from every inch of the ceiling, creating the atmosphere of a perpetual party in progress. There were many aural flourishes as well. The jukebox was programmed to play "Mother-in-Law" every twenty minutes. K-Doe loved to stand behind the bar and sing along with the music, karaoke style. Croaking valiantly through a horribly distorted cab-dispatcher's microphone, he would exhort himself through thick static and intermittent drop-out with such mantras as "I'm cocky but I'm good!" "Burn, K-Doe, burn!" and "Go ahead, K-Doe, with your bad, bad self!"

Sometimes K-Doe would leave his post behind the bar to perform across the room, usually on Sunday evenings, on the small bit of floor that served as the lounge's bandstand. On these occasions he was accompanied by a dapper man named Rico Watts. An accomplished Elvis impersonator, Watts played a cheesy-sounding synthesizer and reinforced his rhythm with a programmable drum machine. Ostensibly programmable, that is, because it broke down frequently, like an unreliable old car. The de facto first set of all K-Doe and Watts's shows consisted of their attempts to coax coherent beats from this temperamental gizmo. Forty-five minutes would pass while they twisted knobs, plugged in cords and then yanked them out again, like old-fashioned telephone operators. This exercise in frustration was punctuated by deafening squeals of feedback, random appeals to the audience for help, and fits of imperial pique from K-Doe. When they finally got the drum machine working, Rico Watts would perform a lengthy warm-up set, despite the late start. Most Sundays this climaxed with a dramatic rendition of "It's Now or Never," Elvis Presley's homage to one of his idols, the operatic pop singer Mario Lanza.

And then, finally, it was star time! K-Doe usually opened his headlining segment with the unlikely old standard "(Won't You Come Home) Bill Bailey," followed by a relatively

TOP LEFT
K-DOE BEHIND THE BAR AT THE MOTHER-IN-LAW LOUNGE
May 1999
Photo by Warren J. Woods

TOP RIGHT
K-DOE PERFORMING WITH RICO WATTS AT THE MOTHER-IN-LAW LOUNGE
December 31, 2000
The Historic New Orleans Collection, 2009.0232.31
Courtesy Betty Ann Fox

BOTTOM
ANTOINETTE'S SEWING STATION IN THE MOTHER-IN-LAW LOUNGE
March 5, 2009
Photo by Keely Merritt

CHANGE
Coke

ensoniq
Roland

offBEAT
SOUL OF
RAY
HOUSE OF BLUES
NEW ORLEANS JAZZ
& HERITAGE
FESTIVAL
2006

ERNIEK-DOE
NEW ORLEANS JAZZ & HERITAGE FESTIVAL
$35

new original song, "Short Dress." Simple yet catchy, its lone verse was "Wear those short dresses just for me, / wear those short dresses just for me, / wear those short dresses just for me— / but don't bend over, just don't bend over!" The last line's edict preemptively absolved K-Doe of any lustful acts that such bending over might incite. In a somewhat surprising transition, these lines were followed by a chorus that took the form of a travelogue, recalling James Brown's "Night Train": "New York City—SHORT DRESS! Atlanta, GA—SHORT DRESS! Washington, DC—SHORT DRESS!" Whipped into a soft-core frenzy, the audience had attained sufficient sonic lubrication for "Mother-in-Law" and K-Doe's other early '60s hits, each introduced with the exaggerated claim "Here's another one that sold a million for Ernie K-Doe!"

When K-Doe sang with Rico Watts, Antoinette took over the microphone behind the bar. She had no qualms about using it liberally—to advertise secret-recipe cocktails such as the Burn, K-Doe, Burn, or to castigate chintzy patrons who didn't put money in the battered old brass spittoon that doubled as a tip jar. And, should her husband disseminate any misinformation—say, garbling the date for an upcoming appearance—Antoinette would mash down the mic's talk button to interrupt him with literal and figurative static: "No, Ernie, you are wrong! People, he is playing there on the *fifth*. Not the fourth. Next Saturday is the *fifth*, Ernie!" With the world-weary grimace of the perpetually hen-pecked, K-Doe would aggrievedly tell the audience, "There goes my old echo chamber!"

CHAPTER 3: *Ernie, You Are So Hard-Headed!*

Death barely stilled the spectacle that is Ernie K-Doe, thanks to the statue. Still extant, although no longer on public display, its limbs could be adjusted to reenact various dramatic bandstand poses. Its similitude could be further enhanced by an ever-alternating series of stage outfits, which Antoinette would change periodically, drawing on the vast wardrobe she had designed and assembled for her husband. She also affixed artificial nails to the statue's fingers. Once a week the hands were unscrewed for a disembodied trip to the manicurist. At one point the statue was rigged with a continual taped loop of K-Doe-isms, which issued from a concealed speaker. Although the distorted dispatcher's mic was not utilized, it might as well have been, because the sound quality was similarly, gloriously atrocious. The tape was also hooked up to a transmitter that broadcast on 1500 on the AM radio dial, for a range of some two hundred feet. The numerology of these call letters was hardly random, since the address of the Mother-in-Law Lounge was 1500 North Claiborne. While sitting in a car outside the lounge, perhaps nursing a cocktail (perhaps a Burn, K-Doe, Burn), or continually circling the block, anyone could enjoy a unique programming concept: all K-Doe, all the time.

ANTOINETTE WITH THE K-DOE STATUE
2003
Photo by Cheryl Gerber

Antoinette brought the statue to gatherings around town, sometimes with the help of sculptor Jason Poirier. Such appearances prompted an interview with Poirier in the

Times-Picayune, New Orleans's daily newspaper. Man-about-town columnist Chris Rose asked the sculptor if he ever felt strange carrying the effigy. "When I have to grab him in the crotch to lift him, yes, it's a little weird," Poirier told Rose. "But I just say, 'OK, Ernie, cough!'" One notable soiree visited by the statue was the Mourning Glory Ball, a yearly benefit for the Friends of New Orleans Cemeteries. (Since much of New Orleans lies several soggy feet below sea level, conventionally buried caskets can wash away in rising water. Interment, therefore, often takes place in above-ground tombs. Many of these have considerable historic significance, and the city's cemeteries are championed by preservationist groups.) The 2002 Mourning Glory Ball took place at Saint Alphonsus Catholic Church in the Lower Garden District, the real-life scene of several fictional episodes in Anne Rice's novel *The Witching Hour.*

Although decommissioned as a place of worship and then reinvented as an arts center, Saint Alphonsus kept its full array of Catholic statuary in place. This holy horde looked on as the Madame Tussaud–esque K-Doe was plunked down in its sacred midst. A bodyguard named Cisco accompanied Ernie's effigy. He stood stock-still by his charge's side lest anyone should feel prone to K-Doe kleptomania. But almost everyone else at the church was in frenetic motion. A zydeco band set up in front of the altar and cranked out upbeat two-steps and slow, low-down blues. This irresistibly danceable blend inspired the cemeteries' more extroverted friends to twirl, bump, and grind by the baptismal font, with their Lestat costumes and Goth garb all a-flutter. At evening's end Antoinette disassembled and packed up the statue—like all mannequins, it is sectional—with the disarming comment, "I'm just working poor Ernie to *death*!" Then, struggling to angle the limbless torso through a door, she muttered, "Hurry up, Ernie—you are so hard-headed!"

When Ernie was alive, his and Antoinette's appearances at such events had often landed them in the Living section of the *Times-Picayune*. Photos of the happy couple—beaming beneath matching hairdos and dressed to the nines in matching outfits—were jauntily juxtaposed among "Big Easy Partying Shots" of dowagers and debutantes, muscle-bound sports heroes in too-tight suits, wealthy patrons of the arts, itinerant writers on book tours, and various aspiring scene makers. Not long after the statue's public debut, photographs of the widow with her new companion began to appear, breezily captioned "The statuesque Ernie K-Doe and Antoinette." *Times-Picayune* photographer Steven Forster explained his fascination with the pair:

> I first became aware of K-Doe when I was a kid. To me he was an established New Orleans icon; I mean, who didn't know "Mother-in-Law"? It was on the radio all the time. I can't imagine what New Orleans would have been like without all those great R&B songs, and K-Doe was such a powerful part of that tradition. So by the time I was working at the *Times-Picayune*, covering events, K-Doe was about as big a star as anybody I could ever think of. I would hightail

THE K-DOE STATUE OUT ON THE TOWN
"Big Easy Partying Shots"
Times-Picayune
TOP
July 20, 2003
BOTTOM
August 22, 2004
Photos by Steven Forster

Richwell Ison and Esquizito

THE BEAT WILL GO ON

◀ **Harold Brown, Rico Watts, Michael Buchanan** and **George 'Red Bean' Wroten** took in the Musicians Tomb Benefit at Rock'N'Bowl. The Friends of New Orleans Cemeteries rocked the house.

▲ John Blancher, Antoinette K-Doe, Anna Ross and Heather Twichell

Antoinette K-Doe with statuesque Ernie K-Doe and birthday boy Rob Florence

WE WAS ROBBED!

Author **Rob Florence** celebrated his birthday at St. Alphonsus Art and Cultural Center, with **Ruthie** the Duck Lady sharing the first dance with the honoree. Also seen: **Hazel Washington, Ronnie Virgets, John Grimsley** and **Rick Delaup.**

around town to get shots of him because I knew that there were readers who would be so excited to see K-Doe's picture.

I never knew that some people dismissed the latter-day K-Doe as a kook or an outsider—to me he was an insider, and any week that I had him on the page, I had a star! Over the years I've had photos of Mikhail Gorbachev and Aretha Franklin and Ray Charles when they came to town, but K-Doe was even more exciting to me because he was New Orleans, and he was almost the last of his breed. To me he was a treasure.

As for the statue, after K-Doe died people really missed him. So when Antoinette had the statue made, I just felt, Well, yeah! The statue will be a great memory! It was so fun, in the spirit of Ernie, and it was interesting too, the way people wanted to pose with it. I wanted to help keep that memory going, and I hope on some level that the page is educational about our heritage.

In many cities, Antoinette and the statue might have been seen as a macabre couple—she with a pulse, he made of plaster—but many New Orleanians embraced the idea. Indeed, the statue cemented K-Doe's position in a metaphysical Crescent City pantheon, alongside the diverse likes of voodoo queen Marie Laveau, the pirate Jean Lafitte, the fictional Blanche DuBois from *A Streetcar Named Desire*, and the aforementioned Ignatius J. Reilly. Former Louisiana governors Earl K. Long and Edwin W. Edwards also qualify for this amorphous monument, native New Orleanians though they are not. It matters little whether these conceptual K-Doe cohorts are real or imaginary, serious or silly, still living or long, long dead. In New Orleans such distinctions are blurry at best and ultimately quite irrelevant.

CHAPTER 4: *You Won't Find That in Webber's Dictionary*

Ernie K-Doe was born Ernest Kador Jr., on February 22, 1936, at New Orleans's Charity Hospital. During Hurricane Katrina, Charity gained notoriety as a scene of both horror and heroism. For K-Doe, however, it represented a place of great pride, equivalent to a certain manger in biblical-era Bethlehem. He repeatedly—and publicly—proclaimed his joy in being a "Charity baby." K-Doe's tributes to Charity Hospital were heard most widely during the 1980s, when he sat in the announcer's chair at New Orleans listener-supported radio station WWOZ.

During the two decades that followed K-Doe's hit with "Mother-in-Law," most New Orleanians regarded him as just one of the city's many conventional R&B singers; few knew of his rambunctious, eccentric side. But this image changed dramatically in 1983, when K-Doe debuted as an 'OZ DJ and began displaying his wild verbal skills. Any program named for its host is inherently egocentric, but the *Ernie K-Doe Show* supercharged this concept. As New Orleanians are wont to say when describing extreme behavior, K-Doe's repartee was "totally out the box": "You been listening to the one and only Burn, K-Doe, Burn, WWOZ, 90.7 on your radio dial! You been listening to the number-one DJ coming out the city of New Orleans on anybody's radio station, and that's with a period behind it! I tell you one thing: any other station in the city or in the state that can beat us, come on and check me out, honey! 'Cause I will come to your own radio station and you won't stand a possible chance!"

K-Doe's genius, he immodestly claimed, was due in no small part to his birthplace: "If I was born somewhere else, at another hospital—I'm not trying to put down any other hospital, but I tell you one thing—I might not have been this smart as I am today!" K-Doe further maintained that his brilliance was apparent from the instant his mother went into labor. Though he obviously couldn't recall this moment, that didn't deter him from recounting it with considerable panache: "On the second month, the twenty-second day, nineteen and thirty-six, eight-fifteen in the morning time, Charity Hospital went to rumblin' and a-grumblin'! The building started to bendin', the walls started shakin', and the doctors said, 'What's wrong? What's happening?' The people told them doctors, 'A boy-child is being born on the third floor, at this particular time!' And I believe about that time the doctor had done finished what he had to do, and the nurses had done washed this beautiful body of mines down and brought it to my mother, and I believe my mother looked up at my father and said, 'Huh! What we gonna name the boy this morning?' And my father looked down at my mother and said, '*Hush*! You can't name him nothin' but one thing, that's Ernie K-Doe Jr., and he's gonna be a bad motor scooter!'"

In many renditions of this stock soliloquy, which K-Doe would recite at the drop of a hat—on request, unsolicited, or even when specifically asked *not* to—he would often pause for breath, and then continue: "Some people ask me, 'Ernie K-Doe, why you brag on Charity Hospital? *Why* do you brag on Charity Hospital?' 'Fool, Charity Hospital is the one that got me here!'" He might time-travel even further back, to another event he could not possibly have observed—his conception: "Daddy shot me. Yes he did. He fired his pistol, and he fired it good. That's the reason why I'm here today! Mama carried me in her oven for nine long months! I don't know what day it was, I ain't worried about what time or moment it was when my mother and father got together. But I'm glad that they dug each other." Here K-Doe might go deep into New Orleans–speak: "And I'm glad that they *likeded* each other and *loveded* each other, 'cause they got this body of mine here. You see, my mother, she came from Centreville, Mississippi. And then again my father, he came from the one and only, I'm talkin' 'bout the town of False River, Louisiana. Ernest and Loree. I believe my mother must have told my father, 'Uh, uh, uh, uh, Ernest, *What you got? What you fittin' to do?*' And I believe my daddy must have looked at mother and told her, '*I got a little red rooster!*' And then I believe my mother must have told my daddy, '*I know that rooster ain't too lazy to crow for a day!*' It make me feel so good that I'm alive today to say that I had a mother and a father, and that I'm a Charity Hospital baby!"

While Ernie K-Doe created a uniquely personal verbal repertoire, he also drew on a vast trove of African American folklore and traditional wordplay. Such traditions are often expressed in vernacular speech patterns that differ significantly from mainstream English. This was certainly true in K-Doe's case. His use of language in no way defined him as ignorant; to the contrary, he was a man of keen intelligence. Dialects, accents, and colloquialisms—and even deliberate foolishness, performed for effect—should never be conflated with stupidity. Nevertheless, the *Ernie K-Doe Show* took some criticism as a demeaning vestige of minstrelsy. One colleague who articulated this view was the veteran guitarist and singer John Moore. The leader of Deacon John and the Ivories, a band that has thrived in New Orleans since the '50s, Moore became president of the New Orleans chapter of the musicians' union—the local 174-496—in 2006. His résumé also includes session credits on numerous early '60s New Orleans R&B classics. Moore explained his perspective: "Some black people in New Orleans were offended and embarrassed by K-Doe's radio show. . . . [T]here was a feeling that K-Doe was perpetuating a negative stereotype of black people as loud, ignorant, and speaking in an uneducated dialect because they couldn't learn standard English. And I think that some people who listened to K-Doe's show were laughing *at* him, not with him. There is still a lot of racism in New Orleans, including racist perceptions about black musicians, and racist treatment of black musicians."

Such racial bias, with all its complex emotional contradictions, inevitably extends to some white people who sincerely love K-Doe's music. The line between laughing *with* and laughing *at* can be thin and hazy indeed. Elitism and condescension doubtless prompted some of the amusement with K-Doe's '80s radio shows and the scene at the Mother-in-Law Lounge too. But Ernie K-Doe never pandered to any such sentiments. Subservience was simply not in his nature. As Cyril Neville, a famously outspoken observer of racial politics, observed, "Ernie K-Doe was definitely not an Uncle Tom. No way. Never! K-Doe was all about making black people believe in themselves."

K-Doe's style recycled elements of the macho "bad man" tales of Stagger Lee, the folktales of symbolic fictional characters such as the Signifying Monkey, the rhyming recitations known as toasts, the competitive insults of "the dozens," and DJ trash talk. This twentieth-century tradition was quite well established in New Orleans, thanks to such local jocks as Okie Doke, Papa Stoppa, Dr. Daddy-o, Jack the Cat, and Ernie the Whip. Long before and after Ernie K-Doe, countless black musicians and comedians—from Cab Calloway to Kanye West, from Moms Mabley to Dave Chappelle and beyond—have tapped into this collective memory and enriched it with their own new interpretations. Some such entertainers—Richard Pryor, for one—came to be viewed as heroes, outlaws, or both. And some, including Ernie K-Doe, unabashedly conferred such status upon themselves.

In doing so, K-Doe elicited comparisons to then-contemporary heroes with far more renown than his. "K-Doe was like Muhammad Ali in the boxing ring," commented Harold Battiste—saxophonist, writer-arranger, producer, educator, entrepreneur, and a true renaissance man of jazz and R&B. "The shit that K-Doe used to talk," Battiste said, "is a big part of what made him great. But not everyone dug it. K-Doe was a cocky cat and he drove some people nuts. Muhammad Ali drove some people nuts too. That's how it was, that's how they came on. But, like Muhammad Ali, K-Doe could back it up."

Numerous other New Orleans musicians have invoked the K-Doe-Ali comparison. Ernie K-Doe's egotistical oratory was more free-form than Ali's neatly structured couplets. Ali was famous for maintaining, "I am the greatest"; about opponent Sonny Liston, he taunted, "To prove I'm great, he will fall in eight!" But there is a striking similarity in many of K-Doe's assertive themes, not to mention his vocal cadences:

> I'm here, and I'm back! The big K! You know what the "K" stands for? The king of kings of kings of KINGS! I am back, honey, and ain't nobody gonna beat me! . . . I'm so bad I got to pinch myself in the morning to see if I'm still alive! I'm so slick grease gotta come ask me how to be greasy! . . .
>
> Do you know what bragging means? I want you to get you a pencil and a piece of paper—now I ain't sayin' you are dumb, but if you got somebody close around you, ax them to write it down for you what it is I'm saying, so you will have the definition of bragging. Bragging is when you say you're gonna do something and then don't do it. But when you tell a person what you gonna do, and then you do it—get you a dictionary and look in there, they can tell you what bragging is: when you can't perform your job! But when a man—and I'm talking about a whole lot of people put legs in pantses ain't got to be no man—I'm talking about a real man—when he say what he gonna do, and do it, that wasn't no braggin'!

Ernie K-Doe loved words. He loved to string them together, often in puzzling combinations, and to imbue them with startling new definitions. Consider "Naugahyde," the brand name of a synthetic leather touted by its manufacturer as "the real performance fabric." In K-Doe-speak, "Naugahyde" referred to a quite different combination of "performance" and "fabric," namely his self-proclaimed prowess between the sheets. Besides functioning as a celebratory term for sexuality—principally his own, yet everyone else's too—"Naugahyde" was also used to convey a general joie de vivre. K-Doe embellished this code word with additional syllables, referring to himself as "Mr. Ma-Naugahyde" or "Mr. Ma-Naugahyde-Thuh." (An apocryphal tale states that the manufacturers of Naugahyde served K-Doe with a cease and desist order for alleged trademark infringement.) Just how or why K-Doe came up with the Naugahyde concept remains a mystery; when asked to elucidate, he would cryptically reply, "You won't find that in Webber's dictionary." Or, compounding the enigma: "The dictionary says 'Ma-Naugahyde,' but Ernie K-Doe, a Charity Hospital baby, says 'Ma-Naugahyde-*Thuh*.'" This explanation utilized another of K-Doe's favorite rhetorical devices: self-reference in the third person.

Perhaps the closest K-Doe ever came to a precise explanation of "Naugahyde" was this: "The woman got the hyde, the man got the Nauga—you put 'em both together you got 'Ma-Naugahyde-Thuh'!" Or, in long form: "I want all the Naugahydes under the sound of my voice—burn, K-Doe, burn!—to have a very Merry Christmas and a very Happy New Year. Oh, it's so good to say that you have a Naugahyde that you can call on! I love diamonds, clothes, and money, I love that! But my Naugahyde beat all that! When I get to achin' in my body, my Naugahyde, she puts her hands on my body. Anything that's ailin' me, she takes care of it very well. I think every man and woman in the world ought to have a Naugahyde that say, 'This is mines, and mines alone. You want to make me mad? Let me catch you messin' with my Naugahyde! It's something about my Naugahyde, I just, I get disturbed, and when the K-Doe get disturbed, he really is *disturbed*, you hear what I'm sayin'? So I'm gonna say like this, wherever you may be—Opelousas! Port Allen! Baton Rouge! Lake Charles! Shreveport! Let me tell you one thing, I'm gonna do it some more, I'm gonna do it to you 'til it comes through your ear hole, cause you got to hear what I'm saying—burn, K-Doe, burn!"

Always the egalitarian, K-Doe gladly included other people in his private lexicon. Even if they didn't get exactly what he meant, the general drift was obvious, as in this on-air telephone conversation with a fan:

[K-Doe:] I'll play that record for you. All right BAY-bee! Are you a good Ma-Naugahyde-*Thuh*?
[Caller:] Yes, indeed!
[K-Doe:] Are you sure you is?
[Caller:] I'm positive!
[K-Doe:] Are you bonafide or qualified?
[Caller:] I'm both of them!
[K-Doe:] Oh my goodness gracious, girl, go ahead with your bad self!

"Naugahyde" was K-Doe's favorite redefined word, but there were others. For instance, he used "address" or "address book" as synonyms for "ass." Many performers of K-Doe's generation would never swear or make overt sexual references onstage. "I do not like the cursing and the strong language in rap music," K-Doe once stated; "I don't agree with it." Double entendres and euphemisms were employed instead, and "ass" was one such proscribed word, mild though it is by contemporary standards: "When I hit that stage, I'm hittin' that stage for one reason: to kick some *add*resses! I don't need no *add*ress book 'cause simply why I don't need no *add*ress book, because them people didn't check with *me* about *they add*ress book that I done *kicked* they *add*ress book. Burn, K-Doe, burn!" In New Orleans-speak, such abstruse eloquence may elicit the equally vague affirmation, "What *he* said!" This deceptively simple phrase confers gravitas, conveys respect, and recognizes the profundity of good sense that initially appears to make no sense.

Even people who knew Ernie K-Doe well were sometimes floored by his use of language. One of those was Milton Batiste—trumpeter, entrepreneur, leader of the long-standing Olympia Brass Band, and, for a time, K-Doe's manager and producer—who was a frequent guest on the *Ernie K-Doe Show*, especially during WWOZ fund drives. Batiste had known K-Doe for years. He was accustomed to Mr. Ma-Naugahyde's quirky locutions and had clearly heard all of his stories innumerable times. For the most part he humored K-Doe with autopilot acknowledgments in a distinct "Yes, dear" tone. But one night even Batiste couldn't take it. K-Doe had ended yet another account of his amazing birth at Charity Hospital and launched straight into a new monologue, using a preacher's cadence: "I remember one time, and I remember it well. I remember it so well, it put chill bumps on my *bot*-tee. Let me say it again—it put chill bumps on my *bot*-tee." As K-Doe raved on, Milton Batiste could be heard in the background, incredulously muttering, "'*Bot*-tee'? How do you even *say* that?"

The Emperor also loved assigning esoteric nicknames to the various New Orleans R&B artists whose records he would play: "That was Geronimo, better known as Mr. Fats Domino. Boy he can pluck on that piano! Can he pluck that piano! Yes, indeed!" And one of K-Doe's most bizarre touches was his penchant for having on-air conversations with himself—over the records he was playing and sometimes in response to them. Apropos of nothing, K-Doe would veer into two-part dialogue with no announcement of his suddenly bifurcated role. In the nonvisual medium of radio, narrative clarity depends, of course, upon aural identification of the characters. But Ernie K-Doe, with the blithe disregard of an open-mouthed ventriloquist, would play both protagonists with precisely the same voice and intonation. Such conversations almost always took the form of a mock argument, settled with the threat of corporal punishment:

> **[K-Doe 1:]** Play that git-tar, boy!
>
> **[K-Doe 2:]** I told you, fool, that's a *spit*-tar, that ain't no *git*-tar. And don't say it no more!
>
> **[K-Doe 1:]** I just slipped that time—*git*-tar!
>
> **[K-Doe 2:]** Didn't I tell you before? I'll slap you upside your head! Shut up!
>
> . . .
>
> **[K-Doe 1:]** I want to know, is it good to you? Is it good to you, baby? Baby, I will pop something on you that you ain't never had!
>
> **[K-Doe 2:]** What is that, K-Doe?
>
> **[K-Doe 1:]** Ain't none of your business, fool, don't you ask! 'Cause I'll go upside your head and stay three hundred and sixty-five days! You don't want your eyes dislocated, you better turn 'em another way!

This Gemini repartee could end as quickly as it began, but it might reappear at any moment. Or some other equally odd tangent might materialize; K-Doe's penchant for free association allowed him to completely ignore the need for logical transition. As records ended he often resumed his DJ patter with a segue from the fading song's title, but then wandered far afield—as he did after spinning Eddie Floyd's "Knock on Wood": "That's what I say, I think I better knock on wood this evening. You know, sometime you can have it, and then again sometime you cannot get it. But it makes you feel so good when you holding the one that you love in your arms, and you say 'I feel good.' Then the one you love look at you and say, '*You* feel good—what do you think about *me*?'"

While listeners likely struggled to find a thread—perhaps murmuring, "What *he* said!" with bemused admiration—K-Doe continued: "I wonder what Jack and Jill went up the hill to do. I often wondered about it, because they never did find that pail of water. I wonder what made Humpty Dumpty sit up on the wall. And Humpty Dumpty had a —a very great fall. They never did tell what Humpty did. I wonder why they couldn't say what Humpty did? Humpty might have had something that he just couldn't handle. Maybe he needed somebody, like somebody standin' next to him, to handle it—but at that time, they just was just a little too slow. And Humpty Dumpty grabbed ahold to it and said, *'I'm not Tarzan! And then again, I don't have no Jane! But what I got, I'm gonna do the best that I can!' Burn, K-Doe, burn!"*

Many such recitations centered upon Humpty Dumpty, Jack and Jill, Tarzan and Jane, and the Lone Ranger and Tonto. K-Doe also made frequent references to a mysterious couple known as Grandma Hemline and Papa Dickie, whom he mentioned with a casual familiarity that assumed his listeners knew them well—though no additional information was ever divulged. Animals might wander on the set at any moment too: "Oh, that made dog look like a cat and a cat look like a dog—I wonder who gonna say 'bow-wow' and who gonna say 'meow'!"

At times K-Doe's fascination with nursery rhymes popped up on his records. Jazz and R&B artists, and even rappers, have long drawn on this folk tradition, from Ella Fitzgerald's "A Tisket, a Tasket" to Louis Jordan's "School Days" to Run-DMC's "Peter Piper." But Ernie K-Doe did not devote entire cohesive songs to this playground theme; instead he introduced kiddie couplets from far left field, midsong. His great but little-known song from 1986, "Jump into Your Love," for instance, begins as a generic declaration of macho sexual ambition—and then swerves into a preschool consciousness: "Jack be nimble, Jack be quick, / Jack jump over the candlestick / I wish I could, I wish I might— / Get some of your good lovin' tonight!"

Even with this premise established, who would then expect to encounter the poster girl for curds and whey? "Little Miss Muffin / Sittin' on her tuffin / Eatin' her favorite pie; / I was the black spider / Who laid down beside her / And drove Miss Muffin away!" In keeping with the song's title, K-Doe jumped right into the intense arrangement, a mid-1980s swirl of funky horns, wild guitar leads, and thumb-popping bass lines. His masterful performance demonstrates his command of settings far more modern than those on his early-'60s hits. (Fats Domino, in marked contrast, never reacted to any stylistic

K-DOE AND BILLY DELLE, WWOZ-FM
May 1990
Photos by Paula Burch-Celentano

trends whatsoever; his music stayed absolutely unchanged for decades, much to his fans' delight.)

Little Miss Muffet was not the only fictional female to be invoked in "Jump into Your Love." K-Doe also sang, "Hey, around the roses, / A pocket full of toeses, / Ride me, Sally, ride me / 'Til you dry my weeping eyes!" The last two lines are based on a child's play song, "Little Sally Walker," dating back at least to nineteenth-century Britain: "Little Sally Walker, / Sittin' in a saucer, / Ride, Sally, ride, / Wipe your weepin' eyes." In the New World this song from Anglo-American tradition was adapted by the African American community. There, its varying lyrics are still used in jump-rope rhymes, traditional blues songs, and commercial R&B. The most famous example of the latter is heard on Wilson Pickett's 1966 hit rendition of "Mustang Sally": "All you want to do is ride around, Sally—ride, Sally, ride / . . . One of these early mornin's, gonna be wipin' your weepin' eyes."

The unheralded appearance of these folkloric characters may well have confused some listeners. But it all made perfect sense to Ernie K-Doe, "the number-one DJ coming out the city of New Orleans on anybody's radio station, and that's with a period behind it!" On the *Ernie K-Doe Show*, "Jump into Your Love" was played in heavy, heavy rotation.

CHAPTER 5: *Some Other Kind of a Man*

Many people loved the *Ernie K-Doe Show*, abrupt Mother Goose references and all. Some loved it precisely because of the numerous non sequiturs and generally anarchic ambience. New Orleanians recorded K-Doe's shows off the radio and sent copies around the world, spawning a cultlike following that thrives yet today. Sound bites are still played on WWOZ, especially during fund drives, underscoring K-Doe's pervasive iconic stature. But such high regard was—and is—not unanimous. A contrasting school of thought perceived K-Doe's broadcasts as the nostalgic maunderings of a pathetic has-been. Comparisons have been made between K-Doe and the characters in Bruce Springsteen's "Glory Days," who do nothing but boast of long-faded accomplishments. (This 1985 hit coincided with the peak of K-Doe's radio era, and the parallel seemed obvious in certain circles.) K-Doe's program elicited a dismissive, "We are not amused" response among some listeners, and some people in New Orleans still view him with considerable disdain. They were quite repulsed by the K-Doe statue and found neither mirth nor merit in the Emperor's après-funeral antics.

The *Ernie K-Doe Show* irritated some of K-Doe's R&B colleagues, such as Mac Rebennack, on a personal level. Rebennack launched his career in the mid '50s as a teenage prodigy on the New Orleans studio scene. He started out playing guitar but switched to piano as his primary instrument after suffering a gunshot wound to his left hand. Between recording sessions and club dates, Rebennack worked with virtually everyone on the New Orleans R&B and rock scenes before moving to Los Angeles in 1963. There, in the late '60s, he created his alter ego, Dr. John, a character based on a nineteenth-century voodoo priest. As Dr. John the Night Tripper, whose first albums were produced by Harold Battiste, Rebennack brought south Louisiana music and voodoo references to the world of psychedelic rock. In 1973 he hit the national top ten with "Right Place, Wrong Time," produced by Allen Toussaint with accompanists including the Meters.

"I don't know how many people called me," Rebennack said with a roll of his eyes, "and told me, 'Mac, you won't believe this shit that K-Doe is talkin' on the radio!' And I thought, 'Oh Lawd, boy, he done really went overboard this time.' He sounded like he was runnin' for president. You had to be in the mood for it. You see, when K-Doe would get deep into his shit it would overwhelm motherfuckers—I mean cats who was *used* to his shit would get overwhelmed. James Booker called me up and told me about it, and he was considered to be way out there himself." "Way out there" is an understated description of the late Booker, the "Piano Prince of New Orleans," who is justly revered as one of the most inventive and able pianists in a city that has burst with such talent for centuries. He was known to conclude his shows by announcing, "You have just been entertained by the great Eartha Kitt!"

During the decades before K-Doe went on the air, he had already worked Rebennack's last single nerve, leaving little room for further foolishness: "I was at K-Doe's gig one time, and he started talking all this shit about 'Here's Dr. John, he played on all my sessions!' and I didn't play on any of them. I'm pretty sure I never recorded with him at all. K-Doe used to bug me, too, when he'd say, 'James Brown got all his steps from me,' because I thought that James Brown actually got all his steps and mic-stand tricks from Joe Tex. All the cats in New Orleans really dug Joe Tex." Tex, whose prolific hits include such originals as "Hold What You Got," and "Skinny Legs and All," is an oft-mentioned and respected figure among New Orleans R&B veterans. A native of Texas—hence his stage name—Joseph Arrington Jr. frequently played in New Orleans and environs. Tex's vocal range and style bore a striking resemblance to K-Doe's. The two were close friends and collaborative songwriters. But Rebennack doubted K-Doe's claim that it was he who "invented all those steps and those mic tricks." Rebennack pointed out that

> there was definitely some weird sides to some of K-Doe's stuff. On a gig he'd come out of a bag on you, but when he wasn't on the set he was more like a regular cat—well, for him, that is. At times I had a lot of kicks with K-Doe. . . . It was when K-Doe did the radio show that I was avoiding him. I was not anxious to see K-Doe then. But I also remember, a lot of times, when someone passed, K-Doe would sing at their funeral service. I liked that about him. Seeing that side of the picture meant something. I always felt that his heart was with the cats. [But] I saw K-Doe once at Jazz Fest when he ran his set overtime, and I knew that he knew he was doing that. I don't know whether he was pissed off at

[festival producer] Quint Davis, or whether he was doggin' someone's time, but he was known for doggin' into other people's time. Herman Ernest, my drummer, he told me this funny story about how K-Doe got hired to play up in Alabama for some very square people. A wedding reception or some shit like that. A buddy of me and Herman's named Chilly Billy got K-Doe this gig. K-Doe showed up with all his K-Doe shit on—I mean he was deep into his shit—and when K-Doe walked in, all these old redneck people saw some shit that they was not ready to see. And K-Doe kept hittin' up Chilly Billy for more money. Chilly paid him in advance and then K-Doe split, and the band didn't get they cake, didn't get paid, 'til way later. But the ones who really knew K-Doe and dug him, they'd overlook that. I know people who he did that shit to—club owners, friends of mine—they'd put up with K-Doe's shit because K-Doe was special. Anybody who believes in that shit to the point of where he took it is amazing. Anybody who believes in they own thing to that point has got to be some other kind of a man.

Outgoing and boisterous, K-Doe loved to laugh and make others laugh too. He acted a fool at times—to his detriment in certain cases. But in other instances K-Doe used ostensible foolishness as a canny ploy. He knew that an outrageous facade served him well in public. During the summer of 1999, for instance, his repertoire of stock phrases—uttered completely at random—included "They're fixin' to put my picture on a box of Wheaties!" and "I'm ready to accept the Nobel Prize!" As percussionist and producer Kenneth "Afro" Williams observed, "K-Doe and his crazy act: he could turn it off and turn it on, he knew when to do it, and it worked for him, absolutely. That's why we're talking about him right now. If he had just been a normal cat, everybody would've forgotten about him. But at the same time I liked when it was just me and him in the studio and he didn't feel no pressure to act like K-Doe. He'd calm down a little bit. He'd be a totally different cat."

But put K-Doe in front of an audience—onstage or on the air—and he was off to the races. He was especially notorious for launching into long, preachy monologues on the bandstand, where his loquaciousness was rarely well received. K-Doe's talkative tendencies inspired Peter "Chuck" Badie—the veteran jazz and R&B bassist who played on "Mother-in-Law"—to christen K-Doe with an apt sobriquet: "We were in some joint and K-Doe was on the bandstand, talking like a Baptist preacher. I told him, 'Lighten up, Pastor!' and that nickname, 'Pastor,' stuck." It stuck so well, in fact, that several other New Orleans musicians also claim credit for bestowing it. Sanctimonious nicknames aside, K-Doe's irrepressibly silly side was rarely far beneath the surface. "Oh, I'm gonna cornflake it up tonight!" he would shout, snapping out of a quasi-sermon with sudden, infectious exuberance. "I'm gonna Kellogg cornflake it up tonight!"

K-DOE ONSTAGE AT THE NEW ORLEANS JAZZ AND HERITAGE FESTIVAL
2000
Photo by Ebet Roberts

K-Doe's childhood friend, Reverend Samson "Skip" Alexander, offered an insightful explanation of K-Doe's overcompensating behavior: "Some people thought K-Doe was obnoxious, but you know what? That's all we black people had back then. You had nothing, and all you could do is imagine that you was gonna be somebody." Irma Thomas similarly discerned the core of goodness behind K-Doe's clamoring for attention. "K-Doe and I appeared on various shows together," recalled the Grammy winner known as the Soul Queen of New Orleans, whose early '60s hits include "It's Raining" and the K-Doe composition "I Done Got Over It." "K-Doe was a good singer, a good entertainer, when he would actually sing. But often he would get up there and just talk and talk and talk, and people didn't want to hear it. K-Doe's arrogant personality worked to his advantage sometimes, but it could work to his disadvantage too. He really was a very nice guy, bighearted as he could be—but just arrogant, that's all."

The history of New Orleans music is full of similarly shameless egotists. One especially extreme example is Jelly Roll Morton, the great pianist, singer, and composer-arranger. "All styles are Jelly Roll," Morton once announced; he also claimed that he "personally originated jazz in New Orleans in 1902." Although Morton overstated his case, his contributions to the genre were profound nonetheless. But, as the folklorist Alan Lomax put it, Morton's "epic self-praise antagonized even his admirers." Ditto for Ernie K-Doe, and then some. With all his big talk on the air and onstage, could K-Doe still back it up, twenty years—and then thirty, even forty—after "Mother-in-Law" hit? Perhaps not on the level of his '60s heyday, as the gulf between his self-image and actual abilities continually widened. But Ernie K-Doe possessed more than enough talent to allow him to recede from the top ten respectably. After all, he had performed at the Apollo Theater—the mother church of rhythm and blues in Harlem, then the epicenter of African American culture. He'd also played such comparably prestigious venues as the Regal in Chicago, the Royal in Baltimore, the Uptown in Philadelphia, and the Howard in Washington, DC, and participated in a package tour of Jamaica, where a concert in Kingston was billed as "so big it bulges at its entertainment seams!"

Ernie K-Doe had prospered in the merciless milieu of early R&B, where competitors scrutinized his every move for signs of weakness. The least lapse in showmanship or appearance invited ruin. Survival depended on solid interpersonal skills, infinite patience, no small amount of psychology, and, when necessary, mental and physical toughness. Getting paid could be dicey, prompting the apt advisory, "Don't start explaining, just give me my money!" Scam artists and imposters were everywhere, poised to fleece performers, ruin their reputations, or worse. As Charles Neville recalled, "K-Doe and my brother Aaron were really popular at the same time in the early '60s. They recorded for the same label, Minit, and they were often cobilled. In those days the black artists weren't seen on TV, so people didn't know what the hell they looked like. I was on the road with a band somewhere in Florida and I saw a poster for a show with Aaron and Ernie, so I went to the club that afternoon. The band was setting up. I saw a couple of cats that I knew from New Orleans, and I told one of 'em, 'I'm lookin' for Aaron Neville and Ernie K-Doe.' And this cat whispered, 'Hey man, be cool, don't blow our shit—*'I'm* Aaron Neville tonight!' And the other guy was pretending to be K-Doe!"

FOLLOWING PAGES
ALLEN TOUSSAINT'S BIRTHDAY PARTY, TIPITINA'S FRENCH QUARTER: (FROM LEFT) K-DOE, TOUSSAINT, AND BRIAN "BREEZE" CAYOLLE
1998
Photo by Michael P. Smith
©The Historic New Orleans Collection, 2007.103.8

The rigors of touring were even worse for black musicians, who also had to contend with segregation. Basic services—such as rooms and meals—were off-limits in many cases, and random police harassment was a constant concern. These combined strains would all take their toll on Ernie K-Doe, but not before he'd proven himself in the biggest of big leagues, and he always held some of that star power in reserve. Despite age, illness, and goofy self-indulgence, Ernie K-Doe made the best of every situation and always gave 100 percent. He remained masterful, in his own way, obvious flaws and all. K-Doe lost much of the vocal range he'd once had—which, at its best, had not been not especially broad—and his fleet-footed dancing slowed down into what he proudly called the K-Doe walk ("they're doing it all over the world!"). His between-song patter was prone to increasingly lengthy and irrelevant digressions. At times he worked with rag-tag musicians who didn't know his material, if he worked with musicians at all; more than once K-Doe determinedly sang karaoke to the wrong prerecorded accompaniment, resulting in excruciating renditions of "Mother-in-Law" to the clashing tune and chord changes of, say, "Stand by Me." Many singers would have instantly aborted such mismatched melodies, but K-Doe, ever stubborn and single-minded, would grind it out until the track finished, no matter how long this took. And at the end he would close with a dramatic flourish as if he were headlining at the Apollo.

K-Doe's manic energy and pure love of music never faltered. Adoring audiences responded to his commitment, intensity, and indeed his rough edges, at venues ranging from the Mother-in-Law Lounge to the New Orleans Jazz and Heritage Festival, the Rhythm and Blues Foundation's annual awards banquet, and even an indie-rock event in North Carolina called Sleazefest 2000. And when K-Doe was backed by good musicians who really knew his material—such as Allen Toussaint's band or a group from Houma, Louisiana, called the Blue Eyed Soul Revue—he could still be magnificent. "I'm just like a rabbit," K-Doe once said, seemingly on the verge of another endless, cryptic monologue. Then he succinctly explained, "When you throw that rabbit in the briar patch, that's exactly where he wants to be. And that's me onstage. I'm happy then, and I'm making others happy too."

CHAPTER 6: *Two Wings and a Chinchilla Cap*

Although Ernie K-Doe loved to rant about his conception and birth, he was markedly less garrulous about the rest of his childhood. His disruptive upbringing might explain this atypical reticence, and the resulting insecurities may have fueled K-Doe's need to brag and embellish. K-Doe never lived with his father, and resided with his mother only sporadically—in Baton Rouge, New Orleans, and, for a brief time, Chicago. K-Doe was raised primarily by his maternal aunts, Marie Washington, Walter "Wolfman"

Washington's mother, and Susie Johnson, whom everyone in the family called Aunt Red. "It's a strange story," his cousin Adrianna Cador explained. (Some family members spell the surname with a "C" rather than a "K.") "But you know how life is and how people are—sometimes they have kids from the outside, and Ernie was an outside child. Reverend Ernest Kador Sr., Ernie K-Doe's father, he was married to a woman named Eula. They lived in Erwinville, in West Baton Rouge Parish. I was raised there too." Reverend Kador also spent a lot of time in adjacent Pointe Coupee Parish, where he had another church. In K-Doe's fanciful birth narratives, he always raved that his father hailed from the Pointe Coupee town of False River.

Kador and Cador—the phonetic spelling "K-Doe" was devised in 1959 by a record company—are fairly common surnames around Greater Baton Rouge and Pointe Coupee Parish. Located some forty miles upriver from Baton Rouge, about a hundred miles upriver from New Orleans, and primarily rural, Pointe Coupee lies nestled between two rivers, the Mississippi to the east and the Atchafalaya to the west. Defined by a large oxbow lake called False River, the parish's descriptive French name means "the point that was cut off."

"So Ernest [Kador] Sr.," Adrianna Cador said, "was married to Eula, but they had not had any children yet. Then this lady Loree [Williams] came along, she was in the mix, and she got pregnant by Ernest Sr. When Loree had Reverend Kador's baby boy, she named him Ernest Kador Jr. even though she wasn't married to Ernie's father, and even though she knew that Reverend Kador already had a wife." Loree bore another child for Reverend Kador—a boy named Melvin. Adrianna Cador continued:

> Loree was from Baton Rouge, and I guess that's where Ernest Sr. met her. I don't know how long of a relationship they had; I think it lasted awhile. I can tell you that they never lived together, though, because Reverend Kador was already married. But Reverend Kador didn't seem to object to his outside child having his name. And then Eula bore Reverend Kador four children in wedlock. The oldest was Ernie's half brother Eugene. Then a daughter named Lenora. Then a son named Huey, although everyone called him Pete. And then I guess Eula decided, "Hey, that's my husband, and I been married to him, I don't care"—so she named her last son Ernest Kador Jr. too. Everybody called that boy "June," and everybody called Ernie K-Doe "Ernie," so there was never a problem with them having the same name.
>
> Ernie and Eula got along great. Eula was a sweet, sweet woman, one of the sweetest people you'd ever want to meet, and she took everything just as it was. She accepted Ernie as hers, right along with her own children, regardless of the circumstances. But Ernie never lived with them in Pointe Coupee. He stayed in New Orleans, or sometimes in Baton Rouge with his mother and her people.

TOP LEFT
YOUNG ERNIE
ca. 1938
TOP RIGHT
ERNIE'S MOTHER, LOREE WILLIAMS (RIGHT), AND FRIEND
mid-1950s
BOTTOM LEFT
ERNIE'S AUNT MARIE, WALTER "WOLFMAN" WASHINGTON'S MOTHER, AT HER SISTERS' HOUSE IN NEW ORLEANS
mid-1950s
BOTTOM CENTER
K-DOE SCHOOL PORTRAIT
1948–49
BOTTOM RIGHT
WALTER "WOLFMAN" WASHINGTON
ca. 1949
All photos courtesy Antoinette K-Doe and Betty Ann Fox

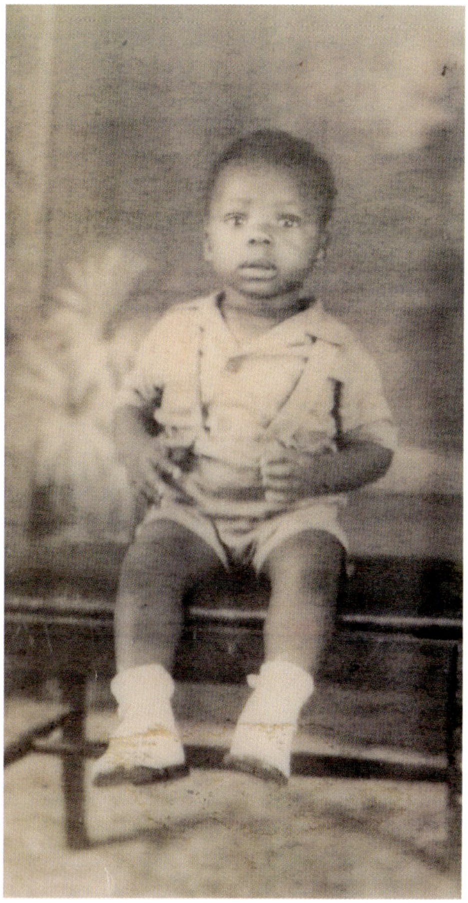

2419

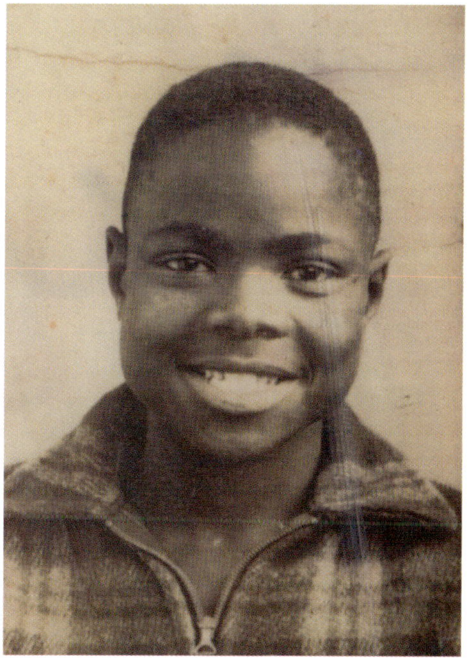

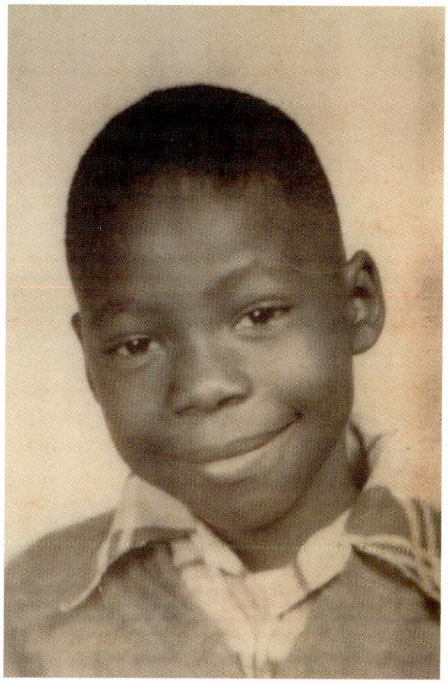

Mary Kador, Ernie K-Doe's aunt, painted an equally rosy picture: "Reverend Ernest Kador was my brother, and I knew Loree, K-Doe's mother. She would come around sometimes, and we all got along, it wasn't no problem. Everything was just fine, it was like family, nobody cared about anybody's past history, not at all. We all are the same and we all are God's children. In that time segregation hadn't passed [ended] yet, and we only had each other. The people they all stuck together, no matter what. If they had any animosity this morning, before the day was out and the sun had set, everything was fine." The bond between the Williams and Kador families was further strengthened when Loree's sister Carrie married Major Kador, Mary and Reverend Ernest's brother.

If the family situation was harmonious, Eugene Kador still felt strongly that it put his half brother at a disadvantage:

> K-Doe didn't live with us. He would just visit. I study my Bible, and a boy needs a dad. A woman can raise a girl—but with a boy, a woman can't tell him nothing. He needs that man instinct. The difference between me and Ernie is that he was raised loose and I was raised tight. Ernie wasn't with my dad, he didn't have a man to teach him, and that crippled him a bit. Ernie did the best he could on his own, but he'd have done better if he would've lived with us. My dad worried about Ernie; he would say, "Oh, that boy, that boy. . . ."
>
> My dad would help Ernie all he could. My dad wasn't educated so he couldn't help him with business, but he could teach Ernie the old way. He had wisdom like you get from old folks, mother wit. He had all these sayings, like, "A man without a word, he ain't a man." He meant that you have to do what you tell people you gonna do. And he'd say, "When you speak a word, watch what you say because once you put it out you can't put it back in." People would say, "Boy, your daddy crazy, why he say all that stuff?" But Ernie would listen. He respected my dad.
>
> Ernie's mother, Loree, had a temper. She was nice, but she was air-ish—high-class, we called it. My mother was humble-like, down to earth. Now, if Ernie was air-ish, he never brought it around us. He was outspoken, now, but it's alright to be outspoken when you know what you talkin' about. Ernie and I were very close and I learned a lot from him. I learned to stand up on my own, stand my ground. That's why I went to preaching, which is what I really wanted to do.

After Loree's relationship with Reverend Kador ended, she lived for a time with the popular Baton Rouge blues guitarist and singer Lightnin' Slim (Otis Hicks). Hicks's raucous, rural sound remains popular today via such '50s hits as "Rooster Blues" and "Hoodoo Man Blues." He shone as a leading light of the rich blues scene that has long flourished in Louisiana's capital city.

"Lightnin' Slim was sort of like Ernie's step-daddy," K-Doe's cousin Wade Williams explained, "even though Ernie spent most of his time in New Orleans. Musicians like Slim Harpo would come by our house here all the time. Right here on North Thirty-Eighth Street, he sure would." Wade's sister Jackie Williams added, "Our Aunt Carrie and Uncle Major had a little nightclub called Kador's Bar and Lounge on Capitol Avenue. Lightnin' Slim and his harmonica player, Lazy Lester, would play there. My aunt and uncle lived over the club, so when we'd stay with her we'd hear all that music coming up through the ceiling. And when I say 'we' I mean Ernie, too, when he visited us. But Ernie didn't live with us, no, and he didn't live with his parents. That's just how it was; I don't know why. And with my Aunt Red you did *not* ask questions. She was tough."

Mary Kador visited frequently too: "I practically lived there over my brother Major's club! I was too young to go inside the club, but I could visit my family. And even when I was grown I never went in, and I never did see K-Doe perform. I liked Ernie, and I was happy and proud that he was successful. But I am a church person. I am not a nightclub person. I didn't like to go places where it was violence goin' on, guns, the people in them places wouldn't consider it fun unless there was some kind of violence. Although I don't consider Ernie's music to be wicked music; I enjoyed it all! 'Cause, you see, you got to deal with the bad as well as the good to know which one is what."

Thanks in part to his Baton Rouge family connections, the influence of traditional blues is quite evident in K-Doe's work, more so than in the music of most other New Orleans R&B artists. The best-known Baton Rouge blues alumnus to date is guitarist Buddy Guy, who made his name in Chicago in the 1960s. His brother Phil Guy often played with K-Doe in Louisiana in the '60s and '70s before moving to Chicago himself. But the most commercially successful blues artist to stay in Baton Rouge was James Moore, aka Slim Harpo. (Moore played harmonica, also known as the mouth harp—hence his stage name.) In 1966 Slim Harpo scaled the national record charts (reaching number one in R&B, number sixteen on the Hot 100) with "Baby Scratch My Back." Such unvarnished blues songs rarely made the pop charts, but Harpo wrote catchy lyrics, and his sultry sound proved irresistible.

Be it time spent in Baton Rouge, Pointe Coupee, New Orleans, or Chicago, K-Doe divulged few details about his childhood in interviews or on the radio. His devotion to his parents was obvious just the same: "Some people say, 'Why you like to talk about your mother and father?' Fool, you are crazy! Did you hear what I say? Fool, you are crazy! Any time that you don't love to talk about your mother and father, you are crazy—and better still, you pass *ree*tardation. Because your mother and father is the ones who are responsible for you being here today. And you're going to tell me, call me on the radio and ask me why I talk about my mother and father? *You* are crazy, and you pass retardation. One thing I want to say under the sound of my voice this evening, if you have a mother that's living, be thankful. If you have a father that's living, be thankful. Because some people don't have them."

If K-Doe said little regarding his youth, he made a strong statement nonetheless by following his father into gospel music. Like many R&B and blues artists (and country singers too) Ernie K-Doe first found his voice in church. "Everyone in the family was either in music or preaching," as K-Doe's half brother Eugene pointed out, and Reverend Ernest Kador Sr. was in both. As a child K-Doe always sang in church, whether he was visiting Pointe Coupee or living in Baton Rouge or New Orleans. In New Orleans, K-Doe and his cousin Walter "Wolfman" Washington would sing at the New Home Missionary Baptist Church. "If you ever been to a Baptist church," K-Doe said, "and you heard when they take up the collection march, you will hear the music of Ernie K-Doe." Over the years K-Doe told many journalists that, as a teen, he joined a popular New Orleans ensemble called the Golden Chain Jubilee Singers. Reverend James Parnell, the group's leader, dismissed this notion with no small degree of hauteur: "I knew of Ernie K-Doe," Parnell said, seemingly pained by the idea, "but he was a rock and roll singer. Therefore, *he* would not have performed with *us*." The reverend's dismissal was summarily rejected by Jo "Cool" Davis, an ebullient gospel singer and beloved figure on the New Orleans music scene. "Parnell don't know like I know!" Davis declared emphatically. "I been singin' gospel in New Orleans since 1963, and I can tell you that Ernie K-Doe *did* sing with the Golden Chain Jubilees. You're talking about one of my heroes, now!"

Gospel singers were heroes to K-Doe, too, and he went to hear them whenever possible. He felt especially drawn to those who concocted their religious messages with flamboyant showmanship. No one delivered this potent combination better than Reverend Utah Smith of the Two-Wing Temple, which K-Doe visited often in his youth. "There used to be a church called the Two-Wing Temple," K-Doe told music historian Jeff Hannusch, "and all the gospel groups played the Two-Wing Temple when they came to New Orleans. The Rocks of Harmony, the Highway QCs, Sister Rosetta Tharpe, Mahalia Jackson, the Soul Stirrers, the Five Blind Boys of Mississippi—I saw them all." The temple took its name from the song "I Want Two Wings," a traditional song recorded by Smith and many other gospel artists. Smith dramatized this number by attaching a huge set of faux wings to his preacher's robe. On occasion he even tried to simulate celestial soaring à la Broadway productions of *Peter Pan*. (Art Neville reported that "one time he tried to fly on wires and he almost killed himself!") Smith accompanied himself on an electric guitar that, during live performances, was tethered to the amp by a long cord that allowed him to roam at will throughout the temple. If so moved by the spirit, Smith could expand this Pentecostal promenade by playing out in the street. His crowd-pleasing routine was soon adapted by secular artists in New Orleans, most notably Guitar Slim (Eddie Jones), whose 1954 hit "The Things that I Used to Do" became one of the biggest-selling blues records of all time.

Smith's intensity and showmanship made a big impression on K-Doe, but his favorite singer per se was Archie Brownlee, lead vocalist for the Blind Boys of Mississippi. Using his forceful, decisive voice like a musical instrument, Brownlee stretched one-syllable

TOP

THE BLIND BOYS OF MISSISSIPPI (FROM LEFT) LAWRENCE ABRAMS, LLOYD WOODARD, PERCELL PERKINS, AND ARCHIE BROWNLEE

BOTTOM

UTAH SMITH PLAYING HIS ELECTRIC GUITAR IN THE AISLE OF THE TWO-WING TEMPLE
between 1950 and '53
Photo by Ralston Crawford
Courtesy Hogan Jazz Archive, Tulane University

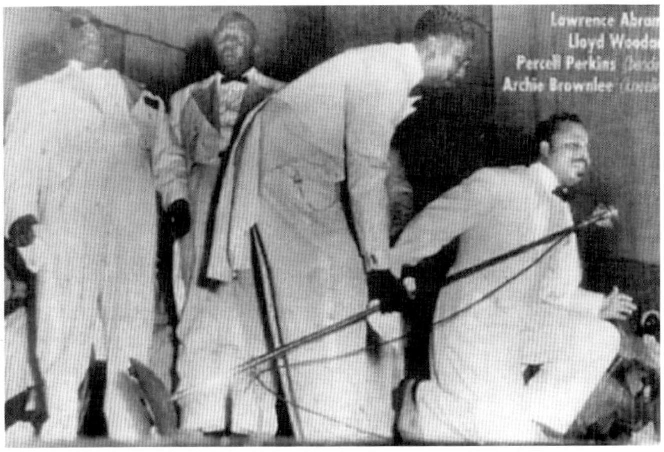
Lawrence Abram
Lloyd Wood
Percell Perkins
Archie Brownlee

words into long, powerful bent-note phrases that wrung out every possible drop of emotion. This intense, impassioned style can be heard on classic numbers such as "Leave You in the Hands of the Lord." Ira Tucker of the Dixie Hummingbirds told gospel expert Tony Heilbut that "Archie started that scream you hear all the soul singers do." Brownlee is considered a seminal influence on James Brown, Ray Charles, and many of their contemporaries—as a riveting performer as well as a vocalist. His influence on Ernie K-Doe can be plainly heard on such lesser-known yet excellent songs as "Waiting at the Station" and "There's a Will, There's a Way." "When you hear me sing," K-Doe once stated with great admiration, "you're hearing [Brownlee's] voice come over my body." He told music historian Rick Coleman, "When I came out of church [to sing R&B], I didn't change my style; just the words changed." When recording songs such as "Mother-in-Law," Allen Toussaint persuaded K-Doe to adopt a style more conversational than fervent. But in live performance K-Doe would emulate the no-holds-barred approach of Archie Brownlee and Utah Smith.

Though Ernie K-Doe loved gospel music, he gravitated equally toward blues and R&B. Many gospel singers, both black and white, condemn secular material as "the Devil's music," but K-Doe kept one foot firmly in the R&B camp. As he explained to writer and '60s activist John Sinclair, "See, I was staying on Derbigny between First and Second, and the Rhythm Club—better known as the Club Rock-It [also Club Rocket]—was on the corner of Derbigny and Jackson . . . [W]e used to go upstairs . . . and look at the band and look at the people. . . . I used to see Count Basie, Duke [Ellington]. . . . I was lookin at what the band was doing, what the artist was doing. That's the first time I ever saw Billy Eckstine in my life. And I appreciated him." K-Doe chose an eclectic bunch of singers and dancers as his secular music heroes: the forceful blues singer Big Joe Turner; doo-wop groups Billy Ward and the Dominoes, from Detroit, and the Spiders, from New Orleans; and a little-known R&B doo-wop vocalist from K-Doe's neighborhood named Issacher "Izzicoo" Gordon. "Izzicoo could outsing us all," K-Doe said with respect; by "us" he meant Art Neville, Aaron Neville, and other young musicians from the area. K-Doe's love of dancing stemmed in part from seeing a live show by the future Hollywood star Sammy Davis Jr., who was working the vaudeville circuit as a teenage song-and-dance artist called "Little Sammy." Peter "Champ" Clark—a school teacher, author, sportscaster, and prominent figure in the black community—encouraged K-Doe to channel his athletic prowess into artistic footwork. Clark served as a father figure to many young people. "Champ Clark inspired me," K-Doe said, "when I didn't know what it was to be inspired."

By his early teen years, K-Doe was singing gospel music in church and belting out blues, R&B, and doo-wop in teen clubs and on street corners. "We used to have water poured on us," he told Rick Coleman, "and people used to put red brick [powder] on their front steps to keep us from sitting there and singing. . . . Everybody would sing and give different opinions—'No, you're doing this wrong, you ought not sing it like that, you should do it this way.'" This experience taught K-Doe a lifelong lesson in staying connected with his roots: "You have to be a corner young man . . . you got to get out on the street and get to walking, and listen to what the children are saying and how they feel . . . [If] you behind a desk, how do you know? And half of the record industry, you would never see them standin' on a corner, 'cause they just can't bring themselves down to do this."

K-Doe did his share of corner hanging but also spent lots of time in the gym. Skip Alexander recalled that "back around 1948, 1950, or so, K-Doe used to come to the YMCA on Dryades Street. That was the Y for black people, back in segregation. He wanted to be a basketball player, and when he'd play ball he'd start singing. The man who ran the Y told him, 'Man, you can't sing a lick!' But K-Doe proved him wrong when he won a talent contest on the radio, on WMRY, singing Big Joe Turner's 'Chains of Love.' He was only fifteen. Soon after, K-Doe started going to sock hops at the teen recreation center on the corner of Jackson and Simon Bolivar. Lots of hot New Orleans bands would play there, like the Cha-Paka-Sha-Wees—they made 'No One to Love Me'—and Shirley and Lee. K-Doe liked Shirley and Lee because they'd always let him come up and sing a number." Shirley and Lee were best known for the hits "Let the Good Times Roll" and "Feels So Good." Although they had no real-life love connection, Shirley Goodman and Leonard Lee were marketed as the Sweethearts of the Blues. Aladdin Records hyped the release of each new single like a soap-opera sequel. This cute-couple fantasy obscured the exquisite R&B craft that went into the duo's music. In 1974 Shirley Goodman, working solo and using her full name, climbed the charts again with the disco hit "Shame, Shame, Shame."

K-Doe was buoyed by Shirley and Lee's encouragement, but despite his brash passion for the limelight, he experienced some growing pains: "When I first started, I had stage fright. It happens to everyone when they first adventure off into that field." K-Doe also had to choose where to focus his talent. A photo from the mid-1950s shows him playing guitar, an instrument he quickly set aside. Some three decades later, on WWOZ, K-Doe discussed his brief flirtation with the instrument. He broached the topic by posing a rhetorical question to his guest, the singer King Floyd, best known for the 1971 hit "Groove Me."

[K-Doe:] Who do you think discovered Ernie K-Doe?

[King Floyd:] I think *Ernie K-Doe* discovered Ernie K-Doe!

[K-Doe:] I want everybody to have this on their tape, I'm going to tell you who really discovered Ernie K-Doe. Some people don't like you to tell who discovered them, they want to keep that in the background, but *I want the whole world to know* who discovered the Almighty Dancing Singer Performer and Dresser, all on the one! He stay in the Lower Ninth Ward, he's a saxophone player who made a record that sold a million for him, "Barefootin'"—Mr. Robert Parker! As I look back on my life, Robert really did me a very good favor, 'cause I didn't really want to sing at all. I just wanted to get up there and dance and play guitar, like Guitar Slim.

Robert Parker confirmed K-Doe's claim: "That's true. I am the one put the mic in Ernie's hand." Parker recalled an incident in the early '50s when he was playing at a New Orleans club called the Tiajuana:

> I led the house band there for about ten years, I imagine, and a lot of guys hung around there tryin' to get a start. And K-Doe used to come around every night; he wanted to sing. He was around fifteen years old—young, we was all young then. I'd let him get up there and run through a few numbers, and he showed me good potential. He'd sing the latest numbers that were out at the time, numbers by Roy Brown, Gatemouth Brown, Wynonie Harris—blues, you know, the rockin' blues. So I told him, "Hey, man, I think you can do it," and so on and on and on, and he kept comin' around.
>
> At first K-Doe was playin' the git-tar—he'd bring one with him—but mostly I would let him get up there and sing; he'd sit in with the band and try to figure out things. He was doing so good singing—he had a good voice, and I could hear it—so I told him, "I believe you should go on and concentrate on that." And he never did get back to the git-tar. He learned to dance at the Tiajuana too. He was a good dancer and he could really cut a rug. K-Doe was very, very active. He was never a shy type of fellow, he wanted to *do it*! I was not surprised when he had those hits like "Mother-in-Law" later on, no indeed! And when he did, I went on the road with him.

When he was seventeen, Ernie K-Doe and his mother moved briefly to Chicago. Though still a minor, K-Doe managed to sit in at such popular nightspots as the Crown Propeller Lounge and Club Bagdad. He hustled up his own gigs too. The *Chicago Defender*, the city's venerable black-community newspaper, lists "Ernest Kado" performing at Jimmie's New Apex on Veterans Day, 1953, cobilled with a troupe of shake dancers. On the Chicago R&B circuit, K-Doe met such seminal doo-wop bands as the Five Blazes, the Moonglows, and the Flamingos. Decades later K-Doe claimed to have recorded with these groups, specifically taking credit for the lead vocals on the Flamingos' hit rendition of "I Only Have Eyes for You." Although completely unsubstantiated and almost certainly untrue, repetition of this assertion has made it an established article of K-Doe folklore. He further embellished the tale by claiming to have toured with his own private tutor.

Indisputably, one "Ernest Kador" did make his first recordings in the Windy City, on November 30, 1953. At that time Chicago was a haven for the raucous, rural-tinged blues of such southern émigrés as Howlin' Wolf (Chester Burnett) and Muddy Waters (McKinley Morganfield). Their classic work—with its aggressive vocals and tight interplay between stinging guitars and wailing harmonicas—is often cited as exclusively defining the city's

TOP LEFT
K-DOE PLAYING GUITAR
mid-1950s
Courtesy Antoinette K-Doe

TOP RIGHT
AD FOR A SHOW FEATURING "ERNEST KADO"
Chicago Defender
November 12, 1953
Courtesy Robert Pruter

BOTTOM
AD FOR THE CLUB TIAJUANA
Louisiana Weekly
September 1, 1956
Courtesy Amistad Research Center, Tulane University

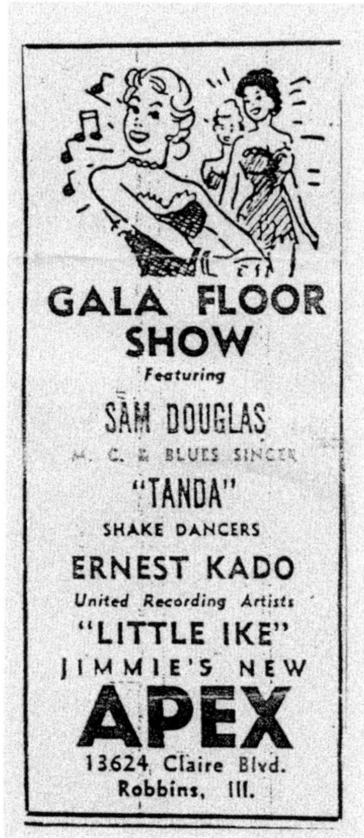
GALA FLOOR SHOW
Featuring
SAM DOUGLAS
M. C. & BLUES SINGER
"TANDA"
SHAKE DANCERS
ERNEST KADO
United Recording Artists
"LITTLE IKE"
JIMMIE'S NEW
APEX
13624 Claire Blvd.
Robbins, Ill.

2-SHOWS-2 Nitely
TIAJUANA
1207 S. Saratoga
featuring
DOTTIE CASSANDRE
ERNEST CATO
plus
Robert Parker's Ork
And Others

blues style. But as Jerry Butler, the suave R&B crooner known as the Ice Man, pointed out, "You can't talk about a single Chicago sound—in R&B or blues or soul. There were many different styles going on in the city back then, and there still are today." Instead of catering to Howlin' Wolf's and Muddy Waters's audience of rural expatriates, the material Ernest Kador cut for United Records was aimed at fans of a more urbane, crooning sound, à la Nat "King" Cole and Charles Brown.

Though Ernie K-Doe always sang with great feeling, he did not possess a truly great voice. His range was average. His timbre tended to get somewhat thin at times, especially at faster tempos, although he could luxuriate on sensual, slow material. In terms of technique only, his forte was ballads. But K-Doe's main strength as a singer was versatility. He could inhabit a song and fully convey the mood at hand—be it joy, romance, heartbreak, yearning, lust, or anger. He also leaned heavily on several effects, most notably his famous double grunt, which sounded something like "Ack! Ack!" It came to be considered one of K-Doe's trademarks.

The most striking among K-Doe's debut numbers is "Process Blues," an ode to the perceived benefits of straightened hair:

> You can call me bully wooly, 'cause my hair looks so bad,
> But someone invented process, Lord you know I'm glad.
> I pulled off that chinchilla cap, all the girls say I'm lookin' good.
> Now I can have my choice of any girl in the neighborhood.
> I don't need no pocket full of money, no long black Cadillac,
> Don't need to sit on the bar, baby, and try to rack 'em back.
> When I step out the House of Process and the sunlight hit my hair,
> All the girls flock around me, willin' to take me anywhere!

The process hairdo—also known as a conk—was all the tonsorial rage in the African American community at this time. In his autobiography Malcolm X memorably describes getting his first conk, a painful procedure that entailed rubbing caustic chemicals into his scalp. By the late '60s, due to the political consciousness that Malcolm X helped elevate, the processed pompadour had morphed into a badge of low self-esteem and assimilationist shame. Its full-bodied opposite, the Afro, came into vogue instead. Years later there was a curious little postscript to this aspect of K-Doe's first recording session, at the annual awards banquet of the Rhythm and Blues Foundation. As usual, the Emperor's show included frequent exclamations of "I'm cocky but I'm good!" A music journalist in attendance misheard and became confused. "Why does K-Doe keep talking about conking?" this scribe inquired. "His hair isn't processed."

CHAPTER 7: *Blue Diamonds and Morphodites*

United Records did not issue "Process Blues." Record companies often produce far more material than they actually release, and many factors besides quality—current trends, internal politics, mere whim—can dictate which sides come to market and which stay in the vault. Perhaps a seventeen-year-old's debut session seemed too risky for a company with a roster of successful artists such as singing blues pianists Roosevelt Sykes and Memphis Slim, and soul-jazz saxophonists Gene Ammons, Jimmy Forrest, and Tab Smith. Whatever the case, "Process Blues"—along with the equally good "Talking to the Blues," "Too Drunk to Drink," and "Get Out of Here, Woman"—languished under a chinchilla cap of anonymity for fifty years. These early tunes finally appeared on a posthumous CD anthology in 2003.

Undaunted, K-Doe returned to New Orleans and sat in with bands wherever he could. Decades later guitarist Irving Banister, then with the Cha-Paka-Sha-Wees, still shook his head in amazement at the ambitious youngster's overeagerness: "K-Doe had a tendency that when some big artist came into the Tiajuana, K-Doe would start singin' that artist's number! Lloyd Price comes in and K-Doe starts singin' 'Lawdy Miss Clawdy'! I told him, 'Hey, man, why the fuck you gonna sing that man's number—supposing *he* wants to sing it?' K-Doe did the same thing with Fats Domino—Fats walks in, here goes K-Doe with 'Blueberry Hill'! But K-Doe would always do that; he wanted that attention."

K-Doe also raised the eyebrows of the masterful songwriter Earl King. Besides his own signature tunes, including "Trick Bag" and "Those Lonely, Lonely Nights," King penned such New Orleans anthems as "Big Chief" ("chief" denoting a Mardi Gras Indian leader) for Professor Longhair. King also stood out as an expressive, urgent singer, a charmingly chaotic guitarist, and a beloved raconteur. "Musicians would stand in line to go on the road with Earl," said Eddie Bo, the pianist, singer, arranger, and live-wire performer of such New Orleans R&B gems as "Check Your Bucket" and "Hook and Sling." "They'd go with Earl," Bo continued, beaming with affection, "just to hear Earl tell stories. They'd ride all the way to Detroit—didn't care about the money—just so they could sit there and listen to Earl. And Earl would talk the whole time, and talk all the way back too. For a while Earl even published a little newspaper with all the gossip from the Dew Drop. It was called the *LaSalle Street Strip*."

As King told music historian David Kunian, "They used to have talent shows at the Tiajuana Club. Believe it or not, the guy who ran the talent show was Ernie K-Doe. Ernie K-Doe wouldn't let nobody sing on that talent show except for the ones that he thought would be miserable up there. . . . Like, Chris Kenner, myself, and all those other guys? K-Doe wouldn't let *anyone* of *us* sing. He would run out of time or something like that. K-Doe wouldn't let us on, no."

Fortunately for K-Doe, his colleagues did not retaliate with similar rivalry. Eddie Bo laughed at the memory: "I led the house band at a place called the Golden Leaf, on South

Rampart. This was, say, 1955. K-Doe used to come around and sit in. He always had a woman with him. He'd walk past the bandstand, real casual-like, and whisper, 'Hey, Bo, hey man, call me up there!' and then he'd go back and sit down. So I'd make an announcement, introduce him, say, 'Ladies and gentlemen, we have a very special guest in the house, he's going to join us to sing a few songs. Let's welcome Mr. Ernest Kador!' And he'd put on this whole act—'God-*damn*, man, I can't go out anywhere to just relax and have a drink without people asking me to sit in! Oh, well, *if you insist . . .*' I thought it was hilarious the way he did it, acting all reluctant, and of course after all that then the people wanted to hear him sing even more. And K-Doe could sing! He was a good entertainer. He'd cover whatever was popular on the jukebox then, songs by Roy Brown or whoever, and he'd do it well. The people would clap for him and try to get him back up there again when he was through."

In hopes of gaining more notice, K-Doe began fronting a band called the Blue Diamonds. By this time the golden age of New Orleans R&B was in full swing, thanks in large part to the success of Lloyd Price's "Lawdy Miss Clawdy" and Fats Domino's "The Fat Man." These songs' ascent of the R&B charts inspired national labels to record in New Orleans with the city's best studio musicians and best audio engineer, Cosimo Matassa. (The self-effacing Matassa always downplayed his talent and his innovative contributions to the art of recording: "Pioneer?" he told journalist Todd Collins. "That's a guy with an ass full of arrows.") Record labels such as Atlantic, Imperial, Specialty, and Chess could easily have worked at less expense in the major cities where they were based. But they opted instead for New Orleans, where Matassa and the session players at his studio were thought to possess an intangible feel that guaranteed commercial success. This hunch had already been proved right on hits such as Big Joe Turner's "Honey, Hush" and Guitar Slim's "The Things that I Used to Do" (featuring a young Ray Charles on piano), and later in the '50s on Little Richard's "Tutti Frutti" and "Long Tall Sally," among others.

Among the corporations that made the pilgrimage to New Orleans was Savoy Records, from Newark, New Jersey, which signed K-Doe and the Blue Diamonds in 1954. Savoy's diverse roster included the dynamic R&B saxophonist "Big" Jay McNeely and gospel singer Clara Ward. Such weighty talent may have left Savoy with little patience for developing new artists. The Blue Diamonds got just one chance to prove themselves, on the single "Honey, Baby," which was coupled with "No Money" and released on both 45 and 78 rpm formats.

"No Money" is clearly the better of the two songs, in terms of both material and performance. Still searching for a vocal style of his own, Ernie K-Doe did not reprise the understated approach he'd tried so effectively on "Process Blues." Instead, on "No Money" K-Doe mimics the quasi-operatic sound of Roy Brown. Brown had risen to fame in 1948 when his "Good Rockin' Tonight" became the first big R&B hit recorded in New Orleans. The song remained hugely popular six years later. A few months after K-Doe imitated Brown, in fact, Elvis Presley cut a fine cover version of "Good Rockin' Tonight" for Sun Records, in Memphis. Roy Brown's dramatic style was also a major influence on the extraordinary '60s R&B singer Jackie Wilson, as heard on such classics as "Baby Work Out."

On "No Money" K-Doe plugs right into Brown's soaring approach. K-Doe lacked Brown's extensive range, but on "No Money" he effectively blends a teenager's hormonal passion with a deft poise that belies his youth. The Blue Diamonds back K-Doe with equally adept doo-wop harmony, reflecting the local influence of the Spiders. His accompanists play in similarly fine form. Billy Tate, the house guitarist at the Tiajuana, tosses in a wildly exciting solo—including a sly quote from the gospel tune "Down by the Riverside"—that might have spun out of rhythmic control without the solid grounding of bassist Frank Fields and drummer Earl Palmer.

Fields and Palmer constituted the A-team rhythm section at Matassa's studio, locking in the beat on dozens of great New Orleans R&B records. Their tight interplay epitomized the old bandstand adage that "bass and drums is one instrument played by two people." Palmer eventually got fed up with the segregation and limited career opportunities in New Orleans; he moved to Los Angeles in 1957 and quickly became one of the music industry's preeminent session drummers. Palmer's departure from New Orleans created a gaping void on the local scene. Even today, more than half a century later, some older New Orleans musicians refer to the chronological milestone "after Earl left." Frank Fields stayed in New Orleans, reigning for decades as one of the city's first-call R&B and traditional-jazz bassists.

"No Money" also features a young pianist named Huey Smith, who would soon make waves leading his own band, the Clowns. Several raucous hits by Smith—"Rockin' Pneumonia and the Boogie-Woogie Flu," "High Blood Pressure," and the exquisitely silly "Don't You Just Know It"—remain perpetual favorites in New Orleans. So does singer Frankie Ford's "Sea Cruise," which features Smith and the Clowns' accompaniment. But despite all this stellar talent behind K-Doe—"lots of spirit here," *Billboard* noted, while dismissing the song itself as "just so so"—"No Money" was largely ignored, with a self-fulfilling title.

The flip side, "Honey, Baby" is a weak, cobbled together spin-off of two then-recent hits, Lloyd Price's "Lawdy Miss Clawdy" and Smiley Lewis's "Tee Nah Nah." To make matters worse, the Blue Diamonds sing backup in a different key than K-Doe's lead, even though "No Money" proves that they certainly knew better. The only strong moment on "Honey, Baby" comes midsong, when K-Doe and the Blue Diamonds sing the melody to "Tee Nah Nah" in doo-wop unison, a moment *Billboard* praised as "an unusual gimmick which should get deejay attention." Otherwise, the magazine aptly opined, "Honey, Baby" was a "Routine Reading of a Routine Blues."

So much for Savoy; K-Doe left the Blue Diamonds when he landed a solo deal with Specialty Records. "A lot of recording executives," Robert Parker recalled, "would come by the Tiajuana trying to find talent. There was a guy named Bumps Blackwell who worked for Specialty. He produced Little Richard. Bumps heard K-Doe and he liked his singing, so Bumps signed K-Doe up." For a skilled producer with keen commercial instincts and high artistic standards, Blackwell chose surprisingly weak material for K-Doe, who recorded for Specialty as Ernest Kador. "Eternity" sounds lively enough, fueled by the trendy pattern of repeated triplets. (This insistent, catchy pattern superimposes three quick little beats over each of the four beats per measure that anchor most R&B, pop, and rock songs, as heard on "Lawdy Miss Clawdy" and many Fats Domino songs.) "Kador sends this one through with lots of pressure," *Billboard* acknowledged. Even so, "Eternity" closely resembles dozens of other mid-'50s R&B songs in terms of its tune and arrangement, while its trite, generic lyrics do not compare favorably.

"Do Baby Do" is not a fully formed song so much as a repeated riff with ultrasimplistic lyrics set to a fast "church beat." This tempo—also known as a sanctified rhythm and used on secular songs such as Muddy Waters's "Got My Mojo Working"—would bring the Isley Brothers great success with "Shout" in 1959. But the Isleys' number also features a middle passage with a catchy rhythm change, intricate doo-wop backup vocals, and lyrical substance. Even working with so little, however, K-Doe maximized what he had on "Do Baby Do," singing full-tilt and using the gospel-tinged setting to emulate his idol Archie Brownlee. K-Doe also presaged his future forays into anarchy by launching into another verse just as the band tried to end the song. Spirited but not the least bit catchy, "Eternity" and "Do Baby Do" went nowhere. But even if they had been really strong songs, it is likely that Specialty still would have focused its marketing and promotional efforts on Little Richard's groundbreaking hit "Tutti Frutti," which was recorded at Cosimo Matassa's studio during the same week in September 1955.

K-Doe's short tenure with Specialty also included the generic "So Glad You're Mine" and the distinctive "You Never Miss a Good Woman," a powerful song that was heavily influenced by Guitar Slim's "The Story of My Life." Although bursting with hit potential, "You Never Miss a Good Woman" was not released at the time it was recorded. It appeared years later, without fanfare, on a compilation LP. If a hit remained elusive, however, Ernest Kador was gaining rapid acclaim as a powerhouse performer. "K-Doe knew how to work a house," Mac Rebennack commented, adding, "and to me that was one of the high points of what he contributated to New Orleans music. But not only his showmanship; there was a certain group of guys in New Orleans who shifted the old funk into the new funk, and K-Doe was part of that. He was there at the advent of when the drumming shifted gears into the new funk. After Earl [Palmer] left, you had drummers like John Boudreaux coming in, the cat who played on 'Mother-in-Law.' K-Doe came up at the end of one era, especially in terms of drumming, and he helped bring things into the later era."

Allen Toussaint likewise praised K-Doe's performance skills: "I have never seen someone with that much energy and ambition who commanded the stage so well. I saw K-Doe early on at a show at the Municipal Auditorium with Bobby Bland and some other folk. Everyone came out and sang their blues and it was nice, but when K-Doe got out there he covered every inch of that stage!" K-Doe's name and photo began to appear frequently in the *Louisiana Weekly,* where he was captioned as "Ernest Kador, the handsome crooner." He also began performing for pay—instead of just sitting in—principally at the Tiajuana and also at the bigger and better-known Dew Drop Inn. Both clubs were located in Central City—the Tiajuana at 1207 South Saratoga, the Dew Drop at 2836 LaSalle—not far from K-Doe's childhood home on Derbigny Street. These appearances led to even more visibility for the up-and-coming star via the *Louisiana Weekly*'s display ads.

The Dew Drop represented an especially prestigious gig for an ambitious young singer. "The Dew Drop was *the* place to be in New Orleans," Bobby Bland stated emphatically. The veteran blues star and road warrior explained: "*Everyone* played there. If you didn't play the Dew Drop, you weren't happening—simple as that. They should make a museum from that place." Touring headliners at the Dew Drop included Bland, Big Joe Turner, Solomon Burke, Little Willie John, Clarence "Gatemouth" Brown, Little Richard, Joe Tex, Lavelle White, Etta James, and innumerable others, both famous and obscure. These artists toured the loose aggregation of southern R&B clubs known as the Chitlin' Circuit. Visiting luminaries such as Duke Ellington, Ella Fitzgerald, and Lionel Hampton might be seen at late-night jam sessions after performing at bigger venues. "Ain't no tellin' who would walk in," Eddie Bo said, "because Frank Painia, the owner, had an open-door policy for musicians who wanted to come by when they finished playing downtown. Oftentimes they'd sit in too."

Such guest appearances could be challenging for resident musicians. Trumpeter Porgy Jones recalled that "[i]f you were in the house band, it was very highly possible that you'd have to play with people without ever having a chance to practice. Most of those name artists expected you to be familiar with their material automatically. They tended to have an attitude, and they'd say, 'Hey man, I'm so and so, and you're 'sposed to know my shit! What? *You don't know my shit*? What's wrong with you?'"

Besides performing at the Dew Drop, touring musicians often stayed there too, in the hotel–rooming house upstairs. "Frank Painia took care of you," Bobby Bland said, echoing the appreciative sentiments of many others, including singer Gerri Hall. Hall—known for her local hit "I Cried a Tear" and for her vocal accompaniment of both Huey Smith and Ray Charles—told music historian Jonathan Foose, "It was like a family. Mr. and Mrs. Painia were ma and pa to me and the other girls that lived there. It was really a two-family thing that you had with the Painias, and . . . the other people who lived around you in the hotel. You had to be screened by Frank. . . . Everyone had concern for each other's welfare, and you did not violate the trust that was given by the Painias."

The Dew Drop played a crucial role in nurturing the New Orleans R&B scene. From the mid-1940s through the early '70s, Painia's enterprise presented a virtual Who's Who of local R&B artists, including Allen Toussaint, Earl King, James Booker, Art Neville—and of course Ernie K-Doe. Even musicians who didn't live upstairs were apt to hang around constantly, since "the Drop" was the hub. "If you needed to hire a musician," Porgy Jones said, "you just went by the Dew Drop and you'd always find somebody who was great at whatever instrument you were looking for. If you were looking for a gig, just go by the Dew Drop too—next thing you know you'd be hired. You might get a good gig in town, or you might be on your way to New York right then and there." A good gig in town might mean studio work, as it did for "Deacon" John Moore, who recalled, "One night I was playing at the Dew Drop with my band . . . and Allen Toussaint came in. Allen said he liked my playing, and would I be interested in recording? The next day I was at Cosimo's recording with Ernie K-Doe. And that led to lots more session work with Allen."

The Dew Drop pulsed as a place of great spectacle and showmanship, significantly influencing Ernie K-Doe's dynamic stage act. Frank Painia augmented his rich musical lineup with X-rated ventriloquists such as Chester Calhoun and his dummy Society Red (who released an album titled *Doctor Dickem*); an amputee tap dancer named Peg Leg Bates; novelty artists such as Iron Jaw Harris, who climaxed his show by "dancing with three tables in his mouth"; plus scores of dancing girls, some of whom were also strippers—and some of whom were actually men. Indeed, the Dew Drop was as renowned for its bevy of female impersonators as for its musical roster. The master-mistress of ceremonies was one Patsy Vidalia (Irving Ale), the charismatic leader of the Powder Box Revue. Guitarist Tabby Thomas recalled that "when Patsy brought your ass on, he'd build you up so big that if you didn't come out there and really put on a show, you'd look like *shit*!" Vidalia flirted and danced with many a male patron, "and then," Irving Banister said with a wry smile, "somebody would tell one of these poor guys, 'Do you know that's a man you been after all night, with your nose open?' Sometimes they'd get mad; mostly they just had to laugh. But Patsy Vidalia turned some of those guys out, too."

Bobby Marchan, lead singer for Huey "Piano" Smith and the Clowns, doubled as one of the Dew Drop's spiffy cross-dressers. He also pursued a solo music career. Marchan's hits include "There Is Something on Your Mind," a remake of an instrumental by saxophonist "Big" Jay McNeely, to which Marchan added an outrageous monologue. As a member of Huey Smith's band, Marchan did not flaunt his transvestite tendencies, but he did pose proudly in drag for many of his own publicity photos, festooned with a blond wig. Among his most treasured memories, Marchan once divulged, was the night in 1954 when "Little Richard gave me my first evening gown!" As opposed to K-Doe's mantra, "I'm cocky but I'm good," one of Marchan's favorite refrains was "If you got a little girl and she don't treat you right, throw the bitch out and get you a morphodite!"

The entrepreneurial Marchan's career continued long after the Dew Drop closed. In the 1980s he recorded a remake of Clarence Carter's "Strokin'." Marchan also helped pioneer New Orleans's nascent rap, hip-hop, and bounce-music scenes by starting his own label, Manicure Records, a name more evocative of morphodites than rappers. His early recordings of local artists paved the way for such famous New Orleans rappers as Master P and, later, Lil' Wayne, Big Freedia, and Katey Red. Marchan the businessman and Marchan the

BOBBY MARCHAN (LEFT) AND PATSY VIDALIA (FAR RIGHT) PERFORMING AT THE DEW DROP INN
ca. 1954
Photo by Ralston Crawford
Courtesy Hogan Jazz Archive, Tulane University

performer coexisted in surprising ways at times. Telephoning the Manicure office could be disconcerting, because Marchan used radically different speaking voices within the space of a single sentence. He usually answered in the squeakiest of falsettos and then abruptly dropped into a deep growl, like a mouse transformed into a bear. Equally startling was Marchan's penchant, as a popular emcee at '80s R&B shows, to greet well-dressed, middle-aged audiences with such flip opening lines as "Fuck it, we all grown! Who's got the biggest dick in the house?" At the Theater of the Performing Arts, this line prompted a flurry of raised hands from people dressed as men and women alike. Few eyebrows were raised among Marchan's fans, however, because one of the emcee's other blunt slogans was "I'm not a woman, I'm not a man, I'm BOBBY MARCHAN!"

Marchan's outfit-de-soir—a dress? a suit?—indicated which gender would prevail on any given evening. Be it male or female, however, he always dressed impeccably. "Bobby Marchan was flamboyant," Deacon John commented, "but he had that quiet elegance about him too. Ernie K-Doe was more of a street guy." And although K-Doe was decidedly and exclusively heterosexual, Mac Rebennack noted that "there was a certain Dew Drop-ness about K-Doe's flamboyant side. Not in the same way as Little Richard or Bobby Marchan—now Bobby was an *original*. Not like Esquerita, the cat with the big hair whose real name was Eskew Reeder; Little Richard got a lot of his style from Esquerita. Ernie K-Doe wasn't in that direction, he wasn't to that extreme, but he had something about him. Early on, from when I first saw K-Doe, he already had his star thing on, even when all he had was just some little local hit record."

CHAPTER 8: *Bubbling Under*

In his continuing quest to make the world appreciate his "star thing," the artist whose name was now being spelled "Ernie Kado" took another shot at cutting a hit record. The New York–based Ember Records released "My Love for You," backed with "Tuff-Enuff," in 1959. Al Silver, Ember's owner, hired saxophonist Lee Allen for the session with the idea that Allen would produce K-Doe as well as accompany him. But the great sax soloist was not up to this expanded role, and so the up-and-coming pianist Allen Toussaint ably stepped in. This pairing marked the beginning of K-Doe's association with Toussaint as his producer. Just twenty years old when these songs were recorded, Toussaint was naturally trying out various approaches in search of his own style. For this session he chose a well-crafted, generic sound—perky, pop-tinged R&B supported by female backup singers with a stylized sound à la Ray Charles's Raeletts. It differed significantly from the distinct New Orleans feel that would soon establish Toussaint's reputation.

Similarly, K-Doe's singing on "My Love for You" lacks the distinctive stamp of personality that enlivens his best records. But it does present him as a suave, soulful, and adaptable professional. The up-tempo flipside, "Tuff-Enuff," shows considerably more spark. Lee Allen matches K-Doe's enthusiasm with a sax solo reminiscent of his full-tilt work with Fats Domino and Little Richard. Allen was K-Doe's labelmate on Ember at the time and had recently enjoyed a hit of his own with the instrumental "Walkin' with Mister Lee."

"Tuff-Enuff" was the first of two songs in which K-Doe literally sang the praises of his first wife, Shirley, whom he had married on May 12, 1956. (The second such tribute would be "Wanted, $10,000.00 Reward," released in 1961.) "Tuff-Enuff" did not take off nationally, but it significantly raised K-Doe's profile as a regional performer. On Memorial Day weekend, 1959, for instance, "Ernest 'Tuff Enuff' Kador" headlined at Lincoln Beach, an amusement park on the south shore of Lake Pontchartrain patronized exclusively by a black clientele. K-Doe's warm-up act was the Hawketts, famed for the perennial local favorite "Mardi Gras Mambo," featuring Art Neville on lead vocals and keyboard. K-Doe's burgeoning reputation and career potential had also netted him a well-connected manager, Larry McKinley. Even so, Mr. Tuff-Enuff had to take a day job washing cars at the Stephens Chevrolet dealership in downtown New Orleans. He had entered fatherhood—his first son, the identically named Ernest Kador Jr., was born on July 30, 1959—and music alone could not pay the bills.

K-Doe washed cars near the office of A-1 Record Distributors, at 628 Baronne Street. A-1 sold a lot of R&B material—released by many different labels—to retail stores all around New Orleans. Promotional copies of the latest releases were always on hand, and K-Doe often stopped by on his lunch break to listen to them. He thus made the acquaintance of A-1's owner, Joe Banashak, who had just decided to start a record label in partnership with Larry McKinley. This joint venture, called Minit Records, paired two of the most savvy and ambitious figures on the local scene. Banashak brought decades of experience in many aspects of the record business, acquired through hard work around the nation. In addition, his ownership of A-1 solved one of the biggest problems typically faced by record labels: erratic cash flow. "I had an advantage," Banashak explained to Jeff Hannusch. "I could sell A-1 one thousand records, and A-1 could issue a check to our label immediately so that we'd be able to have capital to do something else."

Minit had another strong advantage in Larry McKinley's powerful stature in the radio industry. (Until Hurricane Katrina, McKinley's instantly recognizable voice was ubiquitous in local radio and TV advertising, most notably on spots for the New Orleans Jazz and Heritage Festival.) He was the program director at the popular radio station WMRY—"which beams at Negro audiences," as *Billboard* put it in contemporaneous parlance—and was "probably the hottest jock in the city," according to Banashak. To say the least, this boded extremely well for local airplay. "Of course I knew that Larry was going to play the records," Banashak stated. McKinley also exerted considerable national influence, to the degree that major labels sought his approval in breaking new releases. The executives at Atlantic, for example, felt that McKinley played a crucial role in the huge success of Ray Charles's "What'd I Say" in 1959.

After McKinley and Banashak had committed to recording Ernie K-Doe, they held a mass audition to decide who else to sign. Attendees included singers Benny Spellman, Jessie Hill, Irma Thomas, Aaron Neville, and a vocal group called the Del Royals. Allen Toussaint accompanied many of them. That evening on his way out, Toussaint asked Banashak and McKinley to please keep him in mind for session work. The two had hoped that Harold Battiste would handle creative duties for their new label, but Battiste was already committed to Specialty Records. And so Toussaint—the R&B wunderkind singer, pianist, songwriter, arranger, producer, and bandleader—auspiciously took the helm. "They saw me as being able to do what Harold would do," Toussaint told journalist Giacomo Friedman; "they wanted me to pinch-hit until he could come in." But Toussaint quickly progressed from pinch-hitting to the regular lineup, and that full-time spot gave him a great opportunity to hone his skills. The convergence of talent and acumen in the association of Toussaint, Banashak, and McKinley constituted a collective milestone—for Ernie K-Doe, Toussaint, the label's other artists, New Orleans R&B in general, and, by extension, American popular music. In its heyday Minit released many classic records, including Irma Thomas's "It's Raining" and "I Done Got Over It" (the latter written by K-Doe); Aaron Neville's "Over You," "Wrong Number," and "Let's Live"; Benny Spellman's "Lipstick Traces" and "Fortune Teller"; and Jessie Hill's "Ooh Poo Pah Doo" and "Whip It On Me."

Toussaint's first production assignment for the fledgling company was to work with Ernest Kador. "Larry McKinley and I held auditions for Minit," Toussaint said, "but K-Doe was automatically in. He was already establishing himself, plus Larry was his manager. We were all glad about that, because with K-Doe's enthusiasm we all felt that he was a star already—just as he did! K-Doe was very energetic, and he was in great shape; he used to go the gym just about daily, that was religion to him. K-Doe always knew that he was a star, he was just waiting for the rest of us to find out. And he would remind us—*not* occasionally."

Toussaint didn't record this sure-to-be-stellar artist, however, until Minit tweaked his last name so the public would know which syllable to emphasize: both. "We put a 'K,'" K-Doe explained to journalist Bill Griggs, "put a dash, and put 'DOE,'—and they had to say '*K-Doe*'! People on the radio had a problem pronouncing my name. You see, my name is French and Creole." With the possible exception of ? and the Mysterians, the '60s rock band of "96 Tears" fame, few musicians have focused so intently on the punctuation marks within their monikers. Even fewer have delighted in public declarations of these punctuation marks in the course of shouting out the spelling of their stage names. And surely none has done so with more flair than "Kay-Dash-Dee-Oh-Eee, *a bad motor scooter*!"

Joe Banashak attributed this bad motor scooter's first record, "Make You Love Me," simply to "K-Doe," with no first name on the label. "The reason I did it," Banashak told Rick Coleman, "is because everyone called him 'K-Doe'; they didn't call him 'Ernie.' Banashak also recalled that Dick Clark, the highly influential host of the national television program *American Bandstand*, was both impressed and puzzled by this sobriquet. "I remember Dick Clark saying, 'K-Doe? What is that? . . . I don't know what it is but we'd better listen to the record and see.' And it wasn't long he had a [single name like] 'Fabian' after that. It really stuck with [Clark], the one name." Despite Clark's interest, the one-name approach lasted for K-Doe's first record only, although Banashak looked back on his decision to add the first name "Ernie" with some regret: "I should have left it like that. I think there was a little more mystery."

When Minit was formed, Allen Toussaint still lived at his parents' house, where Minit artists would gather to rehearse: "We had a group of guys, and a girl, Irma Thomas, and we often spent the day together at my family's house on College Court in Gert Town," Toussaint recalled. "From the time I woke up, there were guys and a couple of girls sitting on the front porch waiting for me. I'd get up, freshen up, and let the guys in and we'd get in the front room of my parents' house and jam all day long. . . . [My parents] were at work. And when they would come in they would come through the back door and just not even bother us." Toussaint explained that the material was evaluated quickly: "We'd try one song after another, and if it didn't come off right away we would move on. We were having so much fun, and we were impatient about trying things over and over." The close-knit group supported each other, as K-Doe told filmmaker Stevenson J. Palfi: "At Minit we helped out each other . . . we workeded together so hard. . . . And maybe that's why we came out with hits—we realized that, in the company, wasn't nobody a star; everybody was working and that's the only way we made it." Aaron Neville also belonged to this close-knit team:

> We were all like a big family, over there rehearsing at Allen Toussaint's folks' house—me, Irma Thomas, and K-Doe. I had already met K-Doe when I was growing up. My family had moved into the Calliope Housing Project, and he lived close by. K-Doe and I used to run together in the projects. We would both be hanging around the Rosenwald Gym, and we would get together and sing; K-Doe was a great singer. When I hooked up with Minit in 1960, K-Doe was already signed with them. I sang backup on some of K-Doe's records—I couldn't tell you which ones—and he sang on some of mine. . . .
>
> I did a lot of live gigs with K-Doe then too, like at the ILA Hall, the longshoremen's union. It was a great time in my life when I was doing those gigs with K-Doe. I was working my records like "Waiting at the Station," "Over You," and "Wrong Number," and of course K-Doe had his hits like "A Certain Girl" and "Mother-in-Law." We'd play sock hops, school dances, fraternity parties—me, K-Doe, Benny Spellman, and Irma. K-Doe and I were good friends. With him being a little older, I looked up to him, especially when he became a big-name cat, a star—he had a number-one record and he was doing shows with Sam Cooke, and James Brown! K-Doe was a *singin'* dude back in the day.

The
FLAMINGOS

> I used to do some of his songs, like "Hello My Lover" and "T'aint It the Truth." K-Doe played a big part in my life. Everybody loved K-Doe. And regardless of how cocky he was, K-Doe was a cool guy.

K-Doe's first Minit single—just the third record issued by the label—was "Make You Love Me," released in late 1959. It didn't make any noise, to use music-business jargon, but it showed that K-Doe and Toussaint had grown extremely well matched as artist and producer, and that they made significantly more distinctive music when they emphasized their New Orleans roots. The new song also demonstrated the subtle, deceptive simplicity of Toussaint's maturing production skills, as he developed an uncluttered approach that in this case drew on traditional New Orleans jazz. Many R&B and pop producers of the day sought to hook the record-buying public with lavish instrumentation and elaborate backup vocals that at times suggested choral singing. This slick, histrionic approach characterized many R&B hits of the day, Lloyd Price's "Stagger Lee" for one. Toussaint sought comparable commercial success, no doubt, but he had learned to place his artists squarely at the aural forefront. As he told music historian Tad Jones, "In an arrangement there would be a few things to pay attention to, rather than crowding it with a whole lot of garbage."

For "Make You Love Me" Toussaint crafted a churning foundation of percussive piano, punchy brass, and one of the syncopated, push-and-pull rhythmic patterns known locally as a second-line beat. The term "second line" can function variously as an adjective, noun, or verb. Besides denoting a rhythm—of which there are many variants—it refers to the people who follow the brass bands at street parades and jazz funerals; the gatherings where brass-band jazz is played; and the solo dance steps—"second-lining"—that such music inspires. Some of the more boisterous moves are referred to as buck jumping, or popping gators, the latter involving crawling on all fours. At jazz funerals such wild steps occur only after the burial and are accompanied by traditional upbeat songs such as "I'll Fly Away" and "I'll Be Glad When You're Dead, You Rascal You." En route to the grave, the pace is appropriately funereal, accompanied by dirges including "Just a Closer Walk with Thee" and "What a Friend We Have in Jesus."

Toussaint called on drummer John Boudreaux to nail down the second-line feel on "Make You Love Me" and many other Minit records that would follow. "Allen wrote out everything, all the parts, for all the rest of the guys," Boudreaux recalled, "but not for the drummer. But still he was very specific about what he wanted from me: a hard backbeat and then maybe some deviations with the bass drum. I had more freedom with my foot than I had with my hands." This description neatly encapsulates a fundamental principle of New Orleans drumming. In most genres and stylistic schools, drummers provide a solid pulse with their bass-drum foot and play more complex patterns with their drumsticks. In New Orleans this process is often reversed; the sticks hold down the groove while the bass drum adds fills and dynamics. "K-Doe's music felt good," Boudreaux said

THE FLAMINGOS: ALLEN TOUSSAINT ON PIANO, RALPH JOHNSON ON SAX, SNOOKS EAGLIN ON GUITAR, JAMES "FESS" JACKSON ON DRUMS, FRANK MORTON ON CLARINET
ca. 1954
Courtesy Hogan Jazz Archive, Tulane University

with enthusiasm. “It was ghetto inspired, in a good way. I was used to that because I was brought up in the Sixth Ward, the Tremé section, and all we had around there was soulful people.”

The soulful, pulsing accompaniment to “Make You Love Me” left ample sonic space for the K-dashing young artist to tear into the song’s quirky, confident lyrics:

> I’m going to take me a plane down to New Orleans,
>   buy me a lucky charm;
> I’m going to find one of them old gypsy queens,
>   make you come back home;
> You going to see my face on your TV screen;
> You’re gonna sit and wonder why you treated me so mean;
> I’m gonna worry you with every little trick that’s good
> To make you love me like you should.

Perhaps to illustrate the breadth of K-Doe’s stylistic range, “Make You Love Me” was paired with “There’s a Will, There’s a Way.” This pensive song recalls Ray Charles’s gospel-tinged ballad “Drown in My Own Tears,” particularly in its use of a first verse with sixteen bars. It also bears the stylistic imprint of Archie Brownlee, an effect further enhanced by Toussaint’s gospel-tinged piano accompaniment.

Both sides on K-Doe’s next Minit release scored hits on the Gulf Coast. Nat Perrilliat’s sax intro kicks off the sly, slinky “Hello My Lover.” It makes the contrite plea: “If you come back, my dear, there’ll be some changes made; / I will humble myself in every way.” After this declaration of remorse, K-Doe promises a specific course of amends, both tender and erotic: “I’m gonna make a brand-new policy, / I’m gonna teach you a lesson in love-ology.” “Hello My Lover” uses the “Ack! Ack!” grunts, squeals, and laughs that became one of K-Doe’s most identifiable, endearing trademarks—and, with overuse, one of his saddest self-caricatures during his lost years. It was paired with Toussaint’s “T’aint It the Truth,” a pithy phrase of affirmation that joined other song titles—Fats Domino’s “Ain’t That a Shame,” Huey Smith’s “Don’t You Just Know It,” and, several years later, Aaron Neville’s “Tell It Like It Is”—as popular expressions on the streets of New Orleans.

K-Doe explained that “T’aint It the Truth” “tells a story. A young lady during that period of time, we had a relationship of being with each other and I enjoyed it and I know she enjoyed it. But now it’s all over, you know, I don’t know what made her walk out on me or why she left me, and really at this particular time I can’t let that bother me. And that’s what I was saying—‘T’aint It the Truth.’ Like the song says, ‘She was the best girl that I ever had’—but that don’t say that I will never find another young lady in my life to take her place.”

With the regional success of “Hello My Lover” and “T’aint It the Truth”—not to mention the titillating appeal of love-ology—K-Doe reached another significant new level in his career: performing as a warm-up act for national headliners. A case in point was the Shower of Stars, which rolled into New Orleans's Municipal Auditorium on August 3, 1960, and then toured the South for several weeks. Singers Sam Cooke and Dakota Staton headlined this traveling package show, which featured a host of New Orleans R&B artists. Notable among them was the blind guitarist Snooks Eaglin, a figure of comparably K-Doevian eccentricity in terms of both his persona and his unorthodox yet brilliant musical technique. If Eaglin found his audience unresponsive to a dazzling solo, for instance, he might harangue them with midsong shouts of "Wake up, goddamn it, this ain't no funeral parlor!" Eaglin likewise expected his bandmates to let loose, and he would spur them on to rowdy self-liberation by shouting, "Don't play it pretty—play it RAGGED!" On this show Eaglin was billed as "Lil" Ray Charles, thanks to his expert mimicry of Charles's hits. Deceptively, the name "Ray Charles" was in letters four times the size of the qualifier.

The Shower of Stars found Eaglin, Earl King, K-Doe, Cooke, and company all accompanied by Dave Bartholomew's orchestra. In the history of New Orleans R&B, the multitalented Bartholomew—trumpeter, songwriter, arranger, producer, and bandleader—stands tall as a major creative figure. Trained as a young child by Peter Davis, the same music teacher who mentored Louis Armstrong, Bartholomew is best known for shaping Fats Domino's sound. It was Bartholomew who brought Domino to Imperial Records, and Bartholomew who arranged and produced the recording sessions that resulted in Domino's numerous hits, many of which the two men wrote together. Bartholomew also crafted great records by Shirley and Lee, Lloyd Price, and Smiley Lewis, possibly the single most powerful vocalist in all of New Orleans R&B. Bartholomew himself was a strong singer, too, whose classic songs include a scathing indictment of human nature, "The Monkey." This serious tone was balanced by such light-hearted numbers as "Who Drank My Beer While I Was in the Rear?" and the original version of the risqué "My Ding-a-Ling," later popularized by Chuck Berry.

Despite Bartholomew's reputation as a stern bandleader not prone to giving extraneous praise, he viewed Ernie K-Doe with great respect: "K-Doe believed in himself. I don't care where we'd go, he'd say all that stuff like, 'I am the greatest,' *but he'd always do a hell of a job.* And if someone else came up onstage after K-Doe had performed, they was gonna catch hell. We toured together for about a month, and the people who came out to the shows really came there to see Sam Cooke. K-Doe was more-or-less unknown. But he'd win over that audience. And by the time those people left, *they knew* who K-Doe was. K-Doe was definitely up there with all the great artists of New Orleans." K-Doe likewise spoke well of Bartholomew, who he felt had taught him a valuable lesson: "I'm proud of Dave Bartholomew. He tricked me. But he tricked me in a good way. . . . If you tell a person that they are not good, they do better. . . . I'll tell anyone today that I thank Dave Bartholomew for telling Ernie K-Doe, 'Say, man, you ain't gonna make a hit record—you can't dance.'"

The Shower of Stars was aggressively promoted in the *Louisiana Weekly*, with a flashy display advertisement that took up almost a full page—but not quite. In a striking juxtaposition of glamour and utilitarian tedium, the ad for the concert ran next to a small and rather stodgy notice directed exclusively at the food-service industry: "Restaurants: Please call John Allen Owens regarding your potato requirements." But such mundane matters, with their implications of day-gig drudgery, held no interest for the ambitious young Ernie K-Doe. Cosimo Matassa fondly remembered "when they used to have big R&B package shows at the Municipal Auditorium, and K-Doe was opening for someone really famous—I think it was Clyde McPhatter. K-Doe was standing in the wings waiting to go on, and he told me, 'When I come off, Clyde McPhatter ain't gonna want to go on the stage!' And you know what? K-Doe was right! In a sentence: Ernie K-Doe invented confidence."

Porgy Jones experienced this bravura firsthand while playing in K-Doe's band: "Working with K-Doe could be kind of strange, in a way. It got monotonous listening to him talk all that shit. It didn't bother me; I knew he was using that talk to market himself, just like Muhammad Ali. If K-Doe didn't talk all that shit, then he would not have seemed like himself, so we accepted that persona. I remember Allen Toussaint saying, 'K-Doe is always onstage, even when he's offstage.' . . . Now, when it was time to go work, K-Doe would go to *work*! We'd play a long set and I'd whisper to him, 'Hey, man, let's take a break,' and K-Doe would say, 'No, wait, man, I ain't finished with them yet. I'm gettin' 'em there, *but I gotta kill 'em*!' He meant knock out the audience. So I'd tell him, 'OK, Pastor, go ahead on and kill 'em!' *Kill, 'em, Pastor*!' And then the rest of the cats in the band would get mad at me!"

By the spring of 1961, K-Doe's lethal stagecraft earned him cobilling on an "Entertainment Extravaganza" at the longshoremen's union hall. The lineup was extravagant indeed. Hometown heroes included Patsy Vidalia, presumably resplendent in a beautiful gown; Irma Thomas, appearing on the heels of the success of "You Can Have My Husband, But Please Don't Mess with My Man"; Allen Toussaint, already a seasoned veteran at twenty-three; the great Earl King; the expert crooner Danny White, soon to be acclaimed for "Kiss Tomorrow Goodbye" and "Loan Me a Handkerchief"; Benny Spellman; Johnny Adams, a singer whose five-octave range, according to K-Doe, would make "the wind and the trees start dancing by themselves"; and James "Sugar Boy" Crawford, who had blended Mardi Gras Indian chants with R&B accompaniment to craft a local hit with "Jock-A-Mo" in 1954. (In 1965 the Dixie Cups reached a national audience by reprising the same traditional Mardi Gras Indian lyrics under the title "Iko Iko.")

The Entertainment Extravaganza also featured several New Orleanians who had already attained national renown: Huey "Piano" Smith, Clarence "Frogman" Henry (whose sobriquet came from the lyrics "I have a voice, I love to sing; / I sing like a girl, and I sing like a frog!"), and Lee Dorsey. Dorsey boasted a minor hit with "Lottie Mo" and would soon have a huge one with "Ya Ya," plus many more to follow. In mid-March 1961 Ernie K-Doe was still considered a local performer, not on the same plane with these headliners. But in two short months, all that would change.

LEFT
AD FOR THE FIRST NATIONAL TOURING SHOW WITH K-DOE ON THE BILL
Louisiana Weekly
August 3, 1960

RIGHT
AD FOR ONE OF K-DOE'S LAST LOCAL PERFORMANCES BEFORE "MOTHER-IN-LAW" MADE HIM A NATIONAL ACT
Louisiana Weekly
March 18, 1961

MUNICIPAL AUDITORIUM
WEDNESDAY
AUG. 3rd
8:00 P. M. AND 10:15 P. M.
Admission: $1.75 - $2.50 - $3.00
Tickets On Sale: WERLEIN'S - DOOKY CHASE - ONE STOP - CAFE ROUX
SHOWER OF STARS
FEATURING
SAM COOKE
DAKOTA STATON
PLUS SPECIAL ADDED ATTRACTION
"LIL" RAY CHARLES
(FORD EAGIN)
WITH...
DAVE BARTHOLOMEW
AND HIS ORCHESTRA
PLUS 5 BIG ACTS
A CAST OF 25 TALENTED RECORDING ARTISTS
ERNIE K-DOE
THE SPIDERS
EARL KING

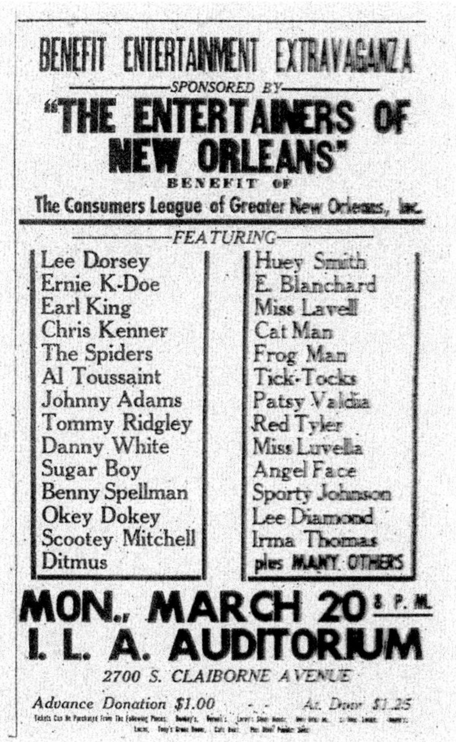
BENEFIT ENTERTAINMENT EXTRAVAGANZA
SPONSORED BY
"THE ENTERTAINERS OF NEW ORLEANS"
BENEFIT OF
The Consumers League of Greater New Orleans, Inc.
FEATURING
Lee Dorsey
Ernie K-Doe
Earl King
Chris Kenner
The Spiders
Al Toussaint
Johnny Adams
Tommy Ridgley
Danny White
Sugar Boy
Benny Spellman
Okey Dokey
Scootey Mitchell
Ditmus
Huey Smith
E. Blanchard
Miss Lavell
Cat Man
Frog Man
Tick-Tocks
Patsy Valdia
Red Tyler
Miss Luvella
Angel Face
Sporty Johnson
Lee Diamond
Irma Thomas
plus MANY OTHERS
MON., MARCH 20 8 P. M.
I. L. A. AUDITORIUM
2700 S. CLAIBORNE AVENUE
Advance Donation $1.00
At Door $1.25

Chapter 9: *There Ain't but Two Songs that Will Stand the Test of Time*

Ernie K-Doe recorded "Mother-in-Law" on April 25, 1960. But the song that would become his signature tune sat on the shelf for nearly a year before its release, and it almost wasn't recorded at all. Accounts of the genesis of this epic number diverge on several key points. For the most part, K-Doe claimed to have written "Mother-in-Law" himself, referring to his grim experience with his own mother-in-law Lucy (or Lucifer, as he called her) as ample proof of authorship. Sometimes he simply cited Allen Toussaint as the writer, acknowledging, "There wouldn't be no Ernie K-Doe if there wasn't no Allen Toussaint." In a third, more complex version, K-Doe claimed to have originated the concept and then coached Toussaint on how to get it down on paper; K-Doe described this sequence of events somewhat confusingly, in both the third and first person: "During that time Allen wasn't even much married, was not even thinking about getting married. . . . Allen did not really write 'Mother-in-Law.' Ernie K-Doe sat down and explained 'Mother-in-Law' to Allen, because I was thinking about my mother-in-law. 'Mother-in-Law' is not just my true story . . . that is *my life*! I'm branded like a cow! Some things will never be put in the background, some things you can never forget! I cannot forget being married at nineteen years old. That caused me a nightmare until now, in the '90s. I can never forget this, I can never forget that I paid two-fifty for the license, ten dollars for the preacher, a hundred and fifty for the wedding reception, and it cost me sixty-three thousand to get rid of all this nightmare! I can never forget it, as long as I live."

Toussaint's recollection includes no such collaboration, nor any real-life experience, on either K-Doe's part or his own. "It was odd," he told journalist Steve Wildsmith, "because I wasn't married at the time, so I had no mother-in-law. It was just a joke used on television a lot in those days—'Take my mother-in-law . . . please!' [The song] was such a huge success, but it came from such an odd place." Huge popularity meant repeated dissemination of its lyrics. This troubled Toussaint's paternal grandmother, as he explained to Billy Delle, music historian and beloved host of *Records from the Crypt* on WWOZ: "She called me at home one day and asked me, how could I write such a terrible song? Didn't I realize that she is my mother's mother-in-law? Had I considered that? I said, 'Of course not.'"

Toussaint did, indeed, write "Mother-in-Law." K-Doe's varying attributions of authorship had only a minor effect, if any, on his long friendship with Toussaint. Not even when K-Doe would sometimes rail against all of his Minit associates en masse: "I was in with a bunch of snakes, but too young to realize it." Tony Owens, a talented R&B singer who started out as K-Doe's protégé, recalled, "Sometimes K-Doe would talk like he was mad with Allen Toussaint, and I explained to him, 'You get confused about things that went on in your life because for part of that time, you was out of it.' We'd talk at length, and I'd tell him, 'Look, man, I don't see where Allen ever did anything but write you some hit songs. Allen didn't handle your money.'" For his part, Toussaint's public statements about K-Doe remained unfailingly positive, respectful, and affectionate.

Everyone involved with recording "Mother-in-Law" agreed that Toussaint hastily scrapped the song when K-Doe didn't take to it immediately. Beyond this point of agreement, the narrative road quickly forks again. Toussaint has repeatedly stated that singer Willie Harper retrieved the song from the trash and persuaded Toussaint to try it again. K-Doe, of course, credited himself; who else would have had the prescience to rescue the creased and crumpled lead sheet from the wastebasket? "Don't you never think," K-Doe raved, "that I don't know what I'm doing. I could make 'em or I could break 'em, I could throw 'em in the trash can and dig 'em out again like I did 'Mother-in-Law'! Oh, that was a blessed day, that day I dug 'Mother-in-Law' out the trash can! It made Ernie K-Doe all over the world, and that's why I'm Ernie K-Doe today!" Toussaint, with typical tact and forbearance, offered this differing account:

> The story that "Mother-in-Law" had gone in the trash is not fiction. But who pulled it *out* is fiction. We were at my parents' house, rehearsing for a session. "Mother-in-Law" just wasn't working at all with K-Doe. I knew I could write many other songs so I didn't waste time with it. I just balled it up and threw it away—I did that a lot in those days. Willie said, "Oh, not this time, man, let's try it again." . . .
>
> You see, when I first began writing for K-Doe, he used to want to do that real aggressive kind of holler like Archie Brownlee. K-Doe liked that a lot, and he wanted to go that route. I thought it might be better suited for us to find a different medium, a vocal style more similar to the singing of a guy named Danny White, who was very popular in New Orleans at that time. Danny had a more unhurried style. I was interested in working with Danny White and writing for Danny White, but I couldn't do that because Danny White was not signed to Minit. So at first I wrote for K-Doe with Danny White's voice in my head, even though I knew that K-Doe would actually sing it. "Mother-in-Law" was a prime example of a song in a Danny White bag.
>
> We used to record four songs per session. The day we did "Mother-in-Law" we also cut "T'aint It the Truth," "Wanted, $10,000.00 Reward," and "Hello My Lover." We thought "Hello My Lover" was the hit song from that session. K-Doe was much too aggressive for the song "Mother-in-Law" in the beginning—not just in terms of his rendition, but his whole *life*. Even though we'd worked it out in rehearsal, the first time K-Doe tried to record "Mother-in-Law," the tempo was too fast. Joseph Banashak, who was head of the company, he and Larry McKinley asked could we slow it down a little bit. We did, and it really worked out. I immediately knew—we all knew—that it was better. Of course, even when it was really fast it was never too fast for K-Doe. We never got it fast enough for him.

A surviving partial outtake of "Mother-in-Law," way uptempo, reveals K-Doe and the studio band sounding quite cocky and comfortable at the higher speed. Perhaps this faster rendition would have sold well too. But the slower pace gives listeners more time to savor the sardonic lyrics.

The flip side of "Mother-in-Law" gushes with romantic enthusiasm. "Wanted: $10,000.00 Reward" is K-Doe's second tribute to his first wife: "Have you seen my baby, have you seen my girl? / I'm talking 'bout Shirley, the one I told you I loved." Its release prompted the reissue of "Tuff-Enuff" with a new title—"Shirley's Tuff"—and a new spelling of the singer's name—Ernie K-Doe. Since everyone at Minit expected "Hello My Lover" to hit big, "Mother-in-Law" was essentially ignored for quite some time after it was recorded. Chuck Badie, the bassist on the session, certainly didn't foresee a hit:

> No, I didn't think much about "Mother-in-Law" when I cut it. No. We all was hungry then, and we hung around the studio trying to make two or three sessions a week. That's why I tell all the young cats today, "Get you a day job, boy, don't be dependin' on this shit!" "Mother-in-Law" was just another session, like when we cut "Ooh Poo Pah Doo" with Jessie Hill.
>
> Toussaint hired me to play on "Mother-in-Law"; that was Toussaint's session, not K-Doe's. Me and Nat Perrilliat—he played sax—we was regulars in that studio by Matassa. I recorded with K-Doe, but I didn't gig with him much. I was into straight-ahead jazz. I worked with Dizzy Gillespie and Lionel Hampton; I'm known as a jazz musician. The only time I played more-or-less rhythm and blues or rock and roll was traveling with Roy Brown, way back when Roy was bigger than Fats Domino. All my life I preferred contemporary and modern jazz. But I play all types of music, and when you're hungry you'll play the dipsy-doo—bein' in the baddest group in the city don't put no pots on the stove! I am not saying I don't like rhythm and blues, but I prefer jazz.
>
> Now let me tell you about how I met Ernie K-Doe. When I first seen K-Doe was in a club at Toulouse and Bourbon, [in] 1957. One night my girlfriend was there, the woman I eventually married. This was back in segregation, and she wasn't allowed to sit in the audience, so she was sitting over by the bandstand, near me. K-Doe walked in and started rappin' to her—and right quick I told him, "*Hold up, little brother, that's my lady, yeah!*" We laughed about it later, but K-Doe was serious. See, he had that aggressive thing, and you had to stop him.

Chuck Badie was just one of many New Orleans R&B session greats who found their bread-and-butter work unchallenging. As Earl Palmer told music historian Tony Scherman, "Guitar Slim . . . one of the stunts he'd do, he had a long cord where he'd run out on the street and keep playing. While he was outside we'd unplug his amp. [He'd] come back in, we were playing bebop, [and he'd say,] 'Who pulled my cord out! I'll cut his throat!' Kind of a wild guy, Slim; when he said, 'I'll cut his throat,' he looked like he meant it."

Defining themselves as modern-jazz musicians, several entrepreneurs within this studio cadre, including Badie and Harold Battiste, formed their own record label. AFO (All For One) Records released adventurous jazz material by the likes of pianist Ellis Marsalis, clarinetist Alvin Batiste, drummer Ed Blackwell, and saxophonists Alvin "Red" Tyler and Nat Perrilliat; many musicians still refer to Perrilliat as the John Coltrane of New Orleans. To generate the cash needed to fund such projects, the company first recorded a batch of expertly crafted New Orleans R&B. AFO's first local R&B hit was "She Put the Hurt on Me" by Prince La La (Lawrence Nelson). Then, in 1962, AFO soared to the national top ten with "I Know" by singer Barbara George. Mac Rebennack analyzed this song's vast if unsung importance: "Melvin Lastie's cornet solo on 'I Know' influenced the brass sound on every record for the next fifteen years." Commercial success proved bittersweet, however. Selling records on paper is far different from actually collecting payment for them while bills continue to pile up. Caught in a cash-flow crunch that has crippled many small labels before and since, AFO went under in 1963.

Minit would eventually disappear too, although its demise was caused by corporate machinations rather than a lack of liquidity. But that fate seemed inconceivable when "Mother-in-Law" reached the national number-one position on May 21, 1961. Many factors, aesthetic and commercial, contributed to its success. For starters, the opening notes of "Mother-in-Law" make a very strong hook—that special moment on a record that instantly catches listeners' interest and impels them to rush out and buy it. Background vocalist Benny Spellman provides this hook for "Mother-in-Law" by singing the title phrase in an unaccompanied deadpan basso profundo, which the English magazine *Melody Maker* described as "vocal interjections of guttural conviction." Spellman reprises the a cappella line three more times, at the end of each verse. In New Orleans, the mere mention of Ernie K-Doe or "Mother-in-Law" usually inspires someone to launch into Spellman's intro. K-Doe's musical peers around the nation often respond similarly. K-Doe's lead vocal, in marked contrast, is rarely referenced with the same familiarity.

After the song is launched by Spellman, background singers Willie Harper and Calvin LeBlanc repeat the title phrase in a higher register, just a second after the band comes in. Then K-Doe cuts right to the chase with his opening line, "The worst person I know." From there, Minit release number 623 saunters along at a danceable midtempo pace. It feels thoroughly fresh—even though the rendition chosen for release was the studio's eleventh take. Many singers cannot deliver their best on such repeated attempts. Disinterest or frustration often ensues, and each effort yields increasingly diminishing returns. (In the occupational folklore of recording studios, many singers adopt the boastful nickname "One Take" and tell the engineer, "Cut me now, while I'm hot!") Such repetition did not faze Ernie K-Doe, who tended to start sessions in a hyper state, requiring several takes to settle down. On "Mother-in-Law" what he settled down into was smoldering rancor.

Allen Toussaint had written "Mother-in-Law" in a light and off-the-cuff vein, inspired in part by television comedians. Many listeners found the song hilarious. The music industry regarded "Mother-in-Law," in part, as a comedic hit à la the Coasters' ribald "Charlie Brown" and Ray Stevens's "Harry the Hairy Ape." Humor certainly contributed significantly to the record's success. But Ernie K-Doe—a man who, in general, loved to make people laugh—brought no cute contrivances or implied winks to his performance. He sounds flat-out fed up. His candor puts "Mother-in-Law" across just as much as its perceived levity does. So does the vicariously liberating experience it offers; as England's *New Musical Express* noted, "a hen-pecked husband can spin it while his wife's mother is in the room and hammer home a few things he wouldn't dare say himself!"

Comedic, cathartic, or both, "Mother-in-Law" also succeeded because of an important business move made the year before its release. In 1960 Joe Banashak signed a distribution deal with a major label, Imperial Records. Banashak had worked for this Los Angeles–based company before venturing out on his own, and he had a long-standing relationship with its owner, Lew Chudd. Imperial's marquee artists at the time included such top sellers as Fats Domino, teen idol Ricky Nelson, and country artist Slim Whitman. Working with Imperial meant that Minit's releases were marketed, promoted, and primed for airplay in the top echelons of the record and radio industries coast to coast. Imperial also licensed its hit songs to various labels in Europe, South America, and Australia, where they tended to sell well too. For Minit, the Imperial deal represented an absolute quantum leap for a small regional company. It still stands as one of the most significant advances of fortune in the annals of New Orleans music—even though it would end badly. Without the Imperial connection, it is infinitely less likely that "Mother-in-Law" would have hit number one.

When that momentous event occurred, K-Doe was ecstatic; Walter "Wolfman" Washington fondly remembered his cousin "yelling and running all through the house." One person did not share K-Doe's joy, however: Benny Spellman. Spellman felt that he had made "Mother-in-Law" a hit. He demanded retroactive top billing and additional compensation, but K-Doe disagreed. Fisticuffs ensued when next they met at Cosimo Matassa's studio. "Benny was kind of disappointed that he wasn't the star," Matassa chuckled. "He felt he wasn't being properly 'propped.'" As for the altercation, Matassa said, "Just kids at play." Deacon John cracked up at the memory: "Benny and K-Doe started duking it out in the vocal booth. So Allen canceled that day's session and sent them both home to cool off." The dispute was all forgotten a year later when Benny Spellman had a hit of his own with "Lipstick Traces." This time, Spellman sang the hook line ("Don't leave me no more!") and the lead vocal too—and, most importantly, it was *his* name on the label.

The success of "Mother-in-Law" sent K-Doe's already healthy ego into overdrive. He embarked on several years of touring, traveling with the biggest names in R&B and the closely related style becoming known as soul music. According to Chicago R&B singer Jerry Butler, K-Doe was soon working the last single nerve of these top-tier stars:

"MOTHER-IN-LAW" SHEET MUSIC
ca. 1961
Courtesy Jurgen Koop

ERNIE K-DOE PUBLICITY PHOTO
ca. 1961
Courtesy Antoinette K-Doe

> A promoter named Henry Wynn, who had an agency called Supersonic Attractions, put a bunch of us on the road together. We would all use the same backup band because we couldn't afford to hire our own musicians. The best we could do was to bring our own guitarist or pianist, and we usually chose a guitarist because most of the pianos we encountered were way out of tune. We'd all ride on the bus together, and, to use the vernacular of the street, Ernie K-Doe would talk a whole lot of shit! He was a nice guy, people liked him, but he was driving us nuts.
>
> One night we were in Charlotte, North Carolina. We checked into one of those hotels where the black minor-league ballplayers, the black truck drivers, the black performers all had to fight each other to reserve rooms, because the supply was so limited before integration. The Coasters were with us, and of course they had already had *lots* of hits—"Searchin'," "Charlie Brown," "Yakety Yak," "Young Blood," "Poison Ivy." They were established. But K-Doe was talking all this shit to them, like, "'Mother-in-Law' is the biggest record ever, I sold two or three million already and I haven't even got started yet!"
>
> One of the Coasters was named Cornell Gunter; he was a great big guy with a barrel chest but very effeminate at the same time. Just a hoot and a hilarious guy. He sang tenor. And he told K-Doe, "Will you cut all that shit out? You ain't got no hit record, and I'll tell you something else—talk to me after you actually get paid! I got a monkey that more people would pay to go see than you!" They would go on and on, playing the dozens and messing with each other big time, just to see who would get the biggest laugh from the rest of us.

In this relaxed setting, K-Doe's boasting amused his peers, but in serious business circles, his overblown self-image hurt his career. Pro football player Roosevelt "Rosey" Grier attempted to counsel K-Doe. "In 1961 I was playing with the New York Giants . . . but sometimes I would go out on tour with some of the R&B bands. I would sing and host the show, although I didn't have any records of my own out until later on in the '60s; I was out there because I had a name as a professional athlete. On some of these shows, in the spring of '61, the lineup was Ernie K-Doe, the Coasters, Jerry Butler, and others. K-Doe was hot then with 'Mother-in-Law,' but the people running the tour told Ernie that the Coasters should close the show. Ernie told them, 'I have the number-one record in the world, and *I* should be closing!' Sometimes he did close. I remember one show in particular when the Coasters went on before Ernie. They did all of their big numbers and they tore the place up! Then Ernie came on. The crowd recognized 'Mother-in-Law' but that was it. He only had that one hit, and he couldn't touch where the Coasters had taken the crowd. . . . I tried to get Ernie to realize how powerful the Coasters were, with all their hits. But Ernie wanted what he wanted."

Grier, who is now a minister, assessed K-Doe from the perspective of his new profession, adding a cautionary note: "If you get a break in life, like a number-one record, the idea is to learn how and what to do with that opportunity. It can open a lot of doors, so treat it with the utmost dignity."

Singer Ben E. King, whose "Stand by Me" deposed "Mother-in-Law" from number one on the R&B charts, showed more sympathy and understanding toward K-Doe's attitude: "I played on some of those Henry Wynn shows with Ernie. I liked Ernie. If Ernie was egotistical, I think that we all had a bit of that going on. We all bragged about ourselves because we didn't have nobody to brag *for* us. We *needed* it, we needed strength to hold our own when we were on shows with people like Jackie Wilson, James Brown, Sam Cooke—we needed to at least feel equal to them . . . The guys from New Orleans, Ernie K-Doe and all the rest of them that I knew and loved—Lee Dorsey, Fats Domino, the cats in Sam Cooke's band like [drummer] Leo Morris—they had a goodness in the way that they treated each other. When you go out on the road and step out of the world that you're used to, then you really need to give each other strength. You're a cat from New Orleans coming up North, you're coming into different territory, and the people whose territory you're entering, they have their own ego and bragging situation too. You have to hold your own."

K-Doe also had to contend with the pressure of playing segregated venues, where his family was unwelcome. "Sometimes we weren't allowed to go see Ernie perform," K-Doe's cousin Jackie Williams said matter-of-factly, yet with obvious disappointment. "This was after 'Mother-in-Law.' He'd call and tell us and say, 'I'm playing at such and such a place in Baton Rouge, and I'll come by and see you'—because *we* couldn't go see *him*. It wasn't right, but that's just how it was then. The white people at those clubs loved Ernie and his music, but they didn't love *us*. Whether we could go or not, though, Ernie would always visit."

Sudden success meant K-Doe had much to learn, quickly, and Larry McKinley coached him in preparation for his biggest show yet: "Oh, K-Doe was excited when he got booked to play the Apollo! So I told him, 'Now look, K-Doe, you are going to New York, my friend, and I don't want you to go up there acting all country, because you are going to play the Apollo Theater! I gave him this whole spiel. He listened and he said, 'Larry, you mean I can't eat no bullets?' He meant red beans—we used to call them bullets. That just cracked me up. I said, 'K-Doe, you can eat all the bullets you want!'"

There are many tales, none verified, of K-Doe alienating the owners of the Apollo. Not due to any deficiency as a performer—accounts by his colleagues suggest that K-Doe's week-long engagement was well received: "I saw K-Doe play the Apollo not long after 'Mother-in-Law' hit number one," Allen Toussaint said fondly, "and I felt so proud of him!" The problem, according to Art Neville, was that K-Doe again demanded top billing: "When I first met K-Doe, he was a very laid-back, nice dude; he wasn't into the ego thing yet. But when he got into singing then he got into that in a big way. And when he had his first hit, he got *two* Cadillacs. He drove one himself, and he got someone else to drive

ERNIE KADOE, popular recording star, receives a trophy from MORRIS F. X. JEFF, special assistant, New Orleans Recreation Department, for his contributions to Sports Kadoe, a basketball enthusiast, is a member of the Ernie Kadoe team and is recognized as a sharp shooter. His team won the popular summer basketball tournament which is sponsored annually by NORD.

THREE MAKE A TRIO - Show business is great business is these smiles on two of New Orleans top recording stars mean anything. Ernie K-Doe, left and Irma Thomas, both beam infectiously as they held the rewards of hard work and some play. Their trophy and award are gifts of the city's businessmen and the city's radio men. Sandwiched between them is popular Gus Lewis of WYLD radio.

the other. They'd pull up in front of the Dew Drop with those two cars and he would turn some heads. Then I heard that he was at the Apollo, on the bill with cats who had a *bunch* of big hits. But even with that, K-Doe thought that Ernie K-Doe should be headlining the show. So K-Doe said he wasn't going on if he couldn't go on as the headliner. And Frank Schiffman, who ran the place, supposedly told him, 'OK, you won't go on at all,' and after that Schiffman put a block on K-Doe."

The hit-making artists who appeared at the Apollo from August 18 through 24, 1961, included Dee Clark ("Raindrops"); Shep and the Limelites ("Daddy's Home"); Carla Thomas ("Gee Whiz"); and fellow New Orleanian Clarence "Frogman" Henry ("But I Do"). Even among all these leading lights, Art Neville said, "K-Doe thought that *Ernie K-Doe* should be the star. And that screwed K-Doe for ever playing the Apollo again. I doubt K-Doe really realized what he was saying and what it would do. You know, my mother used to tell me a story about a guy who was walking somewhere, just kicking things along in the dust, and next thing he knew he had kicked a *skull*. And that skull looked up and told him, 'It was my *mouth* that got me here!'"

Porgy Jones summarized the situation: "Now, can you imagine that you're the senior person at the Apollo and this country fool with one record is gonna tell you what the hell to do?" K-Doe did have a certain point; "Mother-in-Law" *was* a bigger hit than the other songs mentioned above. But it was also the only K-Doe song that had ever been heard beyond the Gulf South. If these tales indeed are true, K-Doe's self-absorbed stance was certainly ill advised, although not out of character. The Apollo's only verifiable comment on K-Doe was limited to a private notation in their files: "Just fair but has possibility."

"Mother-in-Law" earned Ernie K-Doe a considerable amount of money. Just how much is difficult to specify, however. Joe Banashak stated in several interviews that sales exceeded a million dollars. If so, the Recording Industry Association of America (RIAA), an impartial and independent trade organization, would have designated "Mother-in-Law" a Gold Record. A copy of the 45, with its black playing surface painted gold, would have been set in a fancy frame. This trophy would then have been presented to the artist and/or record company with great ceremony. Banashak asserted that such an event took place. But, he complained, the RIAA gave the award to Lew Chudd of Imperial; Chudd in turn presented it to a Los Angeles–based DJ in gratitude for helping break the record in California. Banashak took this as a profound insult to himself, K-Doe, and all the New Orleans DJs whose support had been equally critical. Even worse, Banashak claimed, a photo of the presentation appeared in *Billboard*. All of this may well have happened, but no evidence has been found.

If "Mother-in-Law" had actually sold a million copies, K-Doe would have netted around thirty thousand dollars in proceeds. In 1961 the prevailing artists' royalty rate came to slightly under three cents per record. (Artists' royalties were typically set at 3 percent of 90 percent of a record's list price. List price was usually set at ninety-eight cents. The use

LEFT
AD FOR K-DOE'S PERFORMANCE AT THE APOLLO THEATER
New York Amsterdam News
August 19, 1961

TOP RIGHT
K-DOE THE "SHARP SHOOTER"
Louisiana Weekly
September 1, 1962
Courtesy Bruce Raeburn

BOTTOM RIGHT
K-DOE, GUS LEWIS, AND IRMA THOMAS
Louisiana Weekly
March 16, 1963
Courtesy John Wirt

of such fractional increments as opposed to whole numbers could not have helped artists keep track of their money.) If K-Doe had also written "Mother-in-Law," he would have received another penny for each record sold; if he had owned the publishing as well, an additional penny per record. Songwriters and publishers split these "mechanical royalties" evenly, and the prevailing rate in 1961 was two cents.

Then, just as now, the key to making money in the music business was through the ownership of intellectual property. Cover versions of "Mother-in-Law" never brought K-Doe anything, although Allen Toussaint is justly recompensed as the writer. K-Doe earned royalties from sales of his rendition only. Looking back, he felt dissatisfied. "I did not make a lot of money from 'Mother-in-Law,'" he told filmmaker Stevenson J. Palfi; "Everybody made money but Ernie K-Doe."

K-Doe spent his earnings recklessly despite entreaties from colleagues such as singer and pianist Carol Fran. Fran, from Lafayette, Louisiana, was already a veteran of the Gulf Coast circuit and knew that hit records—such as her own poignant "Emmitt Lee" of 1957—had only so much staying power. "You know what K-Doe's problem was?" Fran sighed:

> He was a little fellow who had never had nothing and then when he got a few dollars, immediately it went right to his head. When he finally bought his first Cadillac, he called me. I was in Thibodaux, Louisiana. There was a wonderful nightclub there, the Sugar Bowl, Hosea Hill's place. Hosea took care of all the musicians, put them up and fed them, just like Frank Painia did at the Dew Drop. Lots of us worked both places. So K-Doe called the Sugar Bowl, long-distance, and he asked to speak with either Hosea Hill or me. We was both there, so we both had a chance to talk to him. K-Doe said, "You can't guess what I got!" Sitting backstage, right there, Hosea Hill said, "Yeah, yeah, I know what you got—a white Cadillac." K-Doe said, "How you know that, Hosea?" Hosea just rolled his eyes and say, "'Cause that's what they all get—a white Cadillac." Oh, K-Doe bragged about his white Cadillac!
>
> K-Doe and I were very, very good friends. He was a good guy, a nice-looking guy, a good-hearted guy underneath all that talk. I told him, "K-Doe, you ain't never gonna have nothing." He said, "Why you say that, girl?" I said, "Because you gonna give it all away." He said, "You think so?" I said, "I think so." He said, "Well, maybe so. I just like to treat my boys good, I want to share it." I said, "Well, there's such a thing as oversharing." And he said, "Well, Fran, maybe you're right."

Largesse certainly seemed to characterize K-Doe's relationship with his basketball teammate James "Tip" Williams. Williams remembered this generosity extending to all the guys on the team:

> K-Doe sponsored the team, paid for everything, and at one time there was six or seven cats on the team ridin' around in Cadillacs. I don't know was K-Doe renting them cars or what, but he gave all his money away. I told them cats on the team, "Man, y'all wouldn't hit a lick at a snake and you got brand new Cadillacs!" Years later, when K-Doe was down-and-out, sleeping under the Claiborne bridge, I told 'em, "Y'all some cold dudes, man, good as that man was to you; now y'all are on your feet, you need to chip in and go help him out."
>
> K-Doe was not no outstanding basketball player or nothing, but he knew the game. He could hurt you, make six, seven, eight shots in a row, and shoot from way out. He was already making music then, making records. It was unusual for a well-known cat like him to hang out and play ball; he was about the only musician that I know that did it. He had a team in the Y league, the YMCA on Dryades Street, the one for black people—this was in segregation. A lot of people don't understand what it was like back then, to live in the '50s and '60s. It wasn't nothin' nice for black people, man. There was a lot of hateful shit that went on—oh, man, come on, a lot of Jim Crow shit. There was a lot of places where me and K-Doe and them weren't allowed to play ball. But K-Doe was a good guy, I'll tell the world that, he'd help anybody. Me and K-Doe was good friends—but then K-Doe was friends with just about everybody.

K-Doe's benevolence quickly brought him a reputation as a soft touch. Poorly educated and with limited reading skills, he lacked many of the essential tools for managing his finances. And with money pouring in, amid the rush of success, very few twenty-five-year-olds would feel a need to mind the store. Larry McKinley observed all of these potentially harmful forces at work, which were especially evident on a night at the Dew Drop Inn when Sam Cooke was in town:

> Sam liked scotch. I liked vodka. We were sitting there having a drink and talking, and K-Doe comes in. This is when I got an indication of where his money was going. A woman came over and she sits down in the booth with us and K-Doe says, "Hey, baby," kind of flirtatious, and she said, "Aw, K-Doe, I just don't feel like it. I got too many problems. I need a hundred dollars." K-Doe got up and left, and then he came right back, slapped that hundred on the table, and said, "K-Doe don't let you down!" He didn't hit on her, he just helped her out. He didn't pull his wallet out in front of everybody, he went to the bathroom or wherever, came back and just gave her the money. Just like he used to do for the guys who played basketball with him. He bought them all uniforms and he would take them out to eat and drink, pick up the tab.
>
> K-Doe really was a warm-hearted guy, but this kind of stuff with his money made me sad, because at that time he wasn't drinking. But still, somehow, he

> would spend it all. I think he was giving a lot of his money to women. I had a power of attorney when I had his bank account set up, and at one time he had pretty good money deposited, for those days. In 1961 he had over twenty-five thousand dollars. And that meant he had at least that much again, or more, that he earned on the road from his personal appearances. But he would come to me and say, "Hey, Larry, man, write me out a check for three hundred dollars! Write me out a check for five hundred dollars!" Eventually, I gave him his check stubs and I said, "Here, maybe one day you may want to tell your grandkids how you blew twenty-five thousand dollars." So later on, when his records stopped selling, that's when he started drinking, I guess because of the frustration.

K-Doe's frustration was surely heightened by the fact that creditors were hounding him with increasing intensity and legal action. By the mid-'60s his name was more likely to appear in the paper's court records and in legal notices than in the entertainment section.

CHAPTER 10: *I Can't Tell Ya!*

Ernie K-Doe didn't see the wolf at his door in 1962 when he recorded the little-known song "Loving You." But the lines he sang foretold a bleak future. "People talk about me, they all scandalizin' my name, / They even sayin' that one day I'm gonna go insane." Yet life was good in the immediate wake of K-Doe's number-one hit. His next Minit release after "Mother-in-Law," in midsummer 1961, was the bouncy original "Te Ta Te Ta Ta," a song in celebration of sex. As K-Doe explained the chorus: "I can*not* sing a 'hickory, dickory, dock' song. Every song that I have sung in life, or will sing, come out my own private life. Like in 'Te Ta Te Ta Ta,' when I sing, 'Te ta te ta ta, every time she cha cha cha'—what I mean is, if you read between the lines, when me and my woman make love, that's what she make me say: 'Te ta te ta ta!'" *Billboard* praised the song in its "Singles Programming and Buying Guide": "The 'Mother-in-Law' winner has another chart item in his latest disk. The cute novelty, which paraphrases his chick's vocabulary, has strong and infectious rhythm."

While this unabashedly orgasmic tale of "his chick's vocabulary" may have come from K-Doe's private life, it was also alleged to have come straight from Sam Cooke's song "Everybody Loves to Cha Cha Cha." A copyright infringement lawsuit was threatened, despite there being only slim resemblance between the two songs. The words "cha cha cha" appear in both, but that phrase was ubiquitous in contemporary pop-music culture. Minit Records and its publishing arm, Minit Music, could easily have withstood this challenge, but curiously they settled out of court, giving up half their ownership of the song's music-publishing rights. Significantly, Cooke was never credited for any creative input, and K-Doe remains credited as the song's sole writer. The "Te Ta Te Ta Ta" contretemps

(FROM LEFT) K-DOE, SAM COOKE, AND LARRY MCKINLEY
Louisiana Weekly
1962
Staff photo by Hychew
Courtesy Larry McKinley

did not stop Cooke and K-Doe from continuing to perform together. Sadly, however, the old adage "Sue me—I need the publicity" proved untrue in this case: "Te Ta Te Ta Ta" failed to ascend either the pop or R&B charts, though it does remain a favorite in New Orleans.

In the fall of 1961, Minit followed up on this libidinous little ditty with the brilliant "A Certain Girl." Driven by Toussaint's insistent, percussive piano, K-Doe sings, "There's a certain girl I've been in love with a long, long time." Then a female backup chorus asks, "What's her name?" and K-Doe evasively replies, "I can't tell ya!" Immediately following K-Doe's coy reply, Benny Spellman ominously drones, "NO-O-O!," seeming to squelch any further prying questions and implore listeners to please give K-Doe and his girl some privacy. (Today New Orleanians still evade excessively nosy questions by singing K-Doe's catchy line, "I can't tell ya!" in the exact same inflection as the song.)

"A Certain Girl" features an eloquent, compact sax solo by Nat Perrilliat, one of the few session players Toussaint allowed to improvise. Toussaint recalled, "I didn't put a lot of solos on those Minit records, and if I did, I kept them short. I used to think of a record as if it were a live performance, and I didn't want my lead singer to be standing up on the stage doing nothing while somebody else played a solo. If there was a solo, I usually wrote it out. I wrote out every part for all my sessions back then, the drum parts, everything—except for when it was Nat playing. He was so locked in, and I loved what he did so well. Once Nat was in my midst, I didn't leave home without him."

"A Certain Girl" resembles "Mother-in-Law" in terms of its tune, tempo, and the use of Benny Spellman's deep voice—"NO-O-O!" But the song clicks on its own saucy merits, and Spellman couldn't claim extra credit this time—it was K-Doe who sang the hook, "I can't tell ya!" What's more, Toussaint said, "By the time I wrote 'A Certain Girl,' I didn't hear it with Danny White's voice anymore. I had locked into writing specifically for K-Doe." Toussaint continues to feature "A Certain Girl" in his live shows, including his collaborations with Elvis Costello. Costello was not the first British artist to perform the song; in 1963 "A Certain Girl" was covered by the Paramounts, a forerunner of Procol Harum, and then again the next year by Wayne Fontana and the Mindbenders. "We often played 'A Certain Girl' and 'Mother-in-Law' on our gigs," Fontana said. "And maybe we played some other Ernie K-Doe songs—but we never really knew whose songs they were. If we liked something, we did it."

Most significantly, the Yardbirds cut "A Certain Girl" in 1964 as the B side of their first single, the long-forgotten "I Wish You Would." The B side took off on the UK pop charts thanks in large part to Eric Clapton's searing guitar solo, which presaged his work with Cream two years later. Some four decades later, the Yardbirds' drummer, Jim McCarty, remained impressed by the longevity of his band's version of "A Certain Girl": "When our new lineup played in Glasgow a couple of years ago, everyone was yelling for it!"

K-Doe paired "A Certain Girl" with the swaggering good-riddance song "I Cried My Last Tear," still popular in New Orleans. Its traditional call-and-response dialogue between

K-Doe's voice and Wendell Eugene's trombone was praised as "interesting and unusual." Eugene's bent-note, elided phrasing harks back half a century to the "tailgate" sound, as played, for example, by Fred Robinson on Louis Armstrong's transcendent "West End Blues" in 1928.

Still, for most listeners, it was all about "A Certain Girl." Singer Carol Fran found the song fraught with personal significance: "K-Doe had a crush on two women in New Orleans, even though he was married, and when he sang that song 'A Certain Girl,' that certain girl was *me*! K-Doe made me miss many a show back then. He'd say, 'C'mon, Fran, be with me,' and he was so nice; he'd say, 'Aw, you don't need that gig, that ain't no money, I got more money than that.' And I'd say, 'Well, how I'm gonna get there?'—to wherever it was—and he'd say, 'Oh, I'm going to buy you a ticket, don't worry about it, let's go to the airport, come on!'" I would do it, but I told K-Doe, 'Man, you're gonna make your wife meet me out here in the street!' I meant his first wife, Shirley, not Antoinette. Hosea Hill knew that I was having an affair with K-Doe. Oh, those were the good old days; I had my flings! Me and Sam Cooke, back when he was singing gospel with the Soul Stirrers! Clifton Chenier, the king of zydeco! You know I'm from Lafayette, Louisiana, and I grew up speaking French. I loved the limelight! And I loved that K-Doe was talking about *me* on 'A Certain Girl'!"

For New Orleans writer and educator Kalamu ya Salaam, "A Certain Girl" represented "the joyful noise that blessed the springtime of my budding adulthood." Salaam reminisced about K-Doe on his blog, *Breath of Life*:

> 1961. . . It was near the end of 9th grade. . . . That spring, Ernie K-Doe was a major source of my youth's soundtrack.
>
> Most people outside New Orleans who know of this man, know only the song "Mother-in-Law" but for me it was "Certain Girl," "Hello My Lover," and "T'ain't It the Truth." . . . Almost all of K-Doe's songs had a sub-text of hearty humor. As a teenager I loved those two and three minute social relationship epics.
>
> K-Doe was one truly eccentric New Orleans character, and let me tell you, you've got to be really, really way out to be considered way out in New Orleans. New Orleans is the home of African American idiosyncrasy. Hell, my home town is a veritable "character" factory. . . .
>
> Anyway, this particular day I was remembering, our ninth grade class was having a spring picnic. I was on the swings with Sandra. . . . We were screaming and laughing. Just kicking it, literally. . . . Across the street somebody's front door or window was wide open, the music was pouring out (as was usually the case all over New Orleans). It was Ernie K-Doe. I was laughing then and still to this day every time I hear K-Doe crooning about a "Certain Girl," I have to smile. . . .

If I had to pick one musician to represent New Orleans music, all of the greats such as Louis Armstrong, Jelly Roll Morton, Allen Toussaint, Dr. John and so many others notwithstanding, I'd have to go with Ernie K-Doe.

CHAPTER 11: *K-Doe Was a Teacher*

K-Doe's glory year, 1961, climaxed in December in a tour of Jamaica with fellow pop and R&B stars the Shirelles, Big Maybelle, and Little Anthony (who performed without his well-known group, the Imperials). Everyone in this traveling troupe was backed by the New Orleans bandleader Joe Jones, then popular for his 1960 hit "You Talk Too Much." This song title would prove prophetic when Jones became a musicians' manager and a lawyer of sorts—loved in some circles, loathed in others—with a prodigious capacity for litigation. K-Doe thought very highly of Jones, who years later would help him recover thousands of dollars' worth of unpaid royalties.

For the Jamaican tour, Jones's band included Harold Battiste on sax, Fats Domino's brother-in-law Reggie Hall on piano, and a young drummer named Leo Morris. Morris, who went on to jazz prominence under the Muslim name "Idris Muhammad," recalled that "people in Jamaica knew K-Doe's music because he had a number-one record! And because of that, sometimes it was hard to get K-Doe off the stage." Not that Jamaican audiences were in any rush to see K-Doe leave. The *Daily Gleaner* newspaper in Kingston went wild about "the most popular live-entertainment package yet to hit Jamaica," a show that bulged "at its entertainment seams." Extensive advance coverage and multiple reviews emphasized the show's participatory nature: "A highlight is provided by a finale in which all the artistes do the twist" . . . "A cash prize will be offered to any male members of the audience who can 'out-twist' Big Maybelle." . . . "Ernie K-Doe, whose 'Mother-in-Law' was on the lips of the average radio listener a short time ago, spent some time with the audience—and now two persons have a cuff-link each."

Or did they? As Walter "Wolfman" Washington revealed, "When K-Doe started playing music, his mama had to hide her jewelry because he'd take her earrings and make them into cuff links! Then he'd go out and people would look at his cuffs and say, 'K-Doe, man, that ain't no cuff link—*that's an earring*!" And K-Doe would take knives and forks and bend them up to make jewelry and rings. He was very creative." Washington's own career was just taking off when K-Doe reached the top. For the most part, Wolfman viewed his cousin as a wise elder, although with some reservations:

> K-Doe was seven years older than me, and he was the oldest of our whole crowd of children. There was about ten of us, and I really looked up to him. Basically, K-Doe was a teacher; he tried to teach cats different things—both in music and in life. See, when you are a musician, after a certain amount of time, if you

TOP
K-DOE (SECOND FROM RIGHT) ON TOUR IN JAMAICA WITH "AMERICA'S TOP RHYTHM & BLUES ARTISTS"
Daily Gleaner
December 5, 1961

BOTTOM LEFT
(FROM LEFT) JOE JONES, BIG MAYBELLE, AND K-DOE IN JAMAICA
Daily Gleaner
December 7, 1961

BOTTOM RIGHT
AD FOR THE SHOW AT THE CARIB THEATRE, KINGSTON
Daily Gleaner
November 30, 1961

BOX PLAN OPENS TOMORROW FOR ALL SHOWS!

The BIGGEST Show OF 1961

★ SO BIG IT BULGES AT ITS ENTERTAINMENT SEAMS!

The Record-Breaking Show Of The Year With AMERICA'S TOP RHYTHM & BLUES ARTISTS:

★ BIG MAYBELLE (Queen Of The Blues)
★ THE SHIRELLES (Three Times On America's "TOP TEN")
★ ERNIE K-DOE (Twice On The "TOP TEN" with "The Truth" & "Mother-In-Law")
★ JOE JONES (With His Big Hit "YOU TALK TOO MUCH")
★ LITTLE ANTONY (Of The Imperials)
PLUS
★ THE JOE JONES BAND
Featuring the new dance craze — "The Crazy Twist"

LISTEN TONIGHT 6.30 OVER R.J.R. TO "THE BIGGEST SHOW OF 1961"

Opening CORAL THEATRE
TUESDAY, Dec. 5
5.30, 7.30 & 9.15 p.m.
BOX PLAN AT WOOLWORTH'S

Playing TUDOR THEATRE
WEDNESDAY, Dec. 6
7.00 & 9.00 p.m.
BOX PLAN AT JOSEPH'S SUPERMARKET

CARIB THEATRE
Big Smash Opening On:
● FRIDAY, Dec. 8th 4.30, 7.00 & 9.00
● SATURDAY, Dec. 9th 4.30, 7.00 & 9.00
BOX PLAN AT ISSA'S OF KING STREET

> spend time with other musicians, the right ones, you can learn a lot about music. And you can learn about yourself, learn how to understand yourself. I learned a lot about life through music, just by being quiet, paying attention, watching.
>
> Now, I'll show you how that comes around. With my drummer, Wilbert Arnold, we called him Junkyard Dog; I put Wilbert through some *changes*. I'd take Wilbert and we'd walk—we'd both have taps on our shoes—and we'd walk to see how timing sounded. I'd walk a certain way and have him walk that way too, with a certain pressure in our feet. And that's how I taught Wilbert about *time*—how to play *on* time, play *around* time, play *with* time, play *without time*—that's what made Wilbert such a great drummer. And the complexity that I taught to Wilbert, I learned that from Ernie K-Doe.
>
> K-Doe would sit down with me and show me different songs, and how to think about singing a melody—how not to sing *with* it but instead how to try to sing *against* it, like how to stretch notes, sing over the beat instead of singing right on the beat. And that's the only way I know how to sing now. That might not make sense to someone who doesn't play or sing—but musicians know exactly what I mean.

Washington went on to describe a rite of passage that had started at the Tiajuana, when K-Doe set aside his guitar to focus on singing: "Now, when 'Mother-in-Law' took off, K-Doe really started traveling, and that's when he gave me his guitar. After a while I fooled around and learnt how to play it. K-Doe heard me, and he hired me. At that time K-Doe had a guitar player in his band, a dude called Chili Pot Red, but Chili Pot got sick. There was a cat named Beaver who was the bass player, and a cat called Peter Rooster; he was the drummer. So when Chili split, that's when K-Doe asked me did I want to play with him. I said, 'Man, I don't know nothin' about playing no guitar,' but K-Doe showed me the songs. This band I was in that backed up K-Doe was called the Matadors. Chili Pot Red came back later and played sometimes. I didn't really go on the road with K-Doe, not far like to the Apollo Theater, like I did with Lee Dorsey. With K-Doe I mostly played the Chitlin' Circuit, around here—Thibodaux, Houma, Slidell, Port Allen. Most of our gigs was in Port Allen, right across the river from Baton Rouge. We played the White Eagle, and Byrd's Satellite."

The renowned writer Ernest J. Gaines was born in Pointe Coupee Parish, where he set many of his fictional works. Gaines knew the Kador family and admired K-Doe's music. In his memoir *Mozart and Leadbelly*, Gaines described some vivid moments at the White Eagle: "Baton Rouge was a dry town on Sundays; so I . . . would go across the Mississippi River into Port Allen, into the White Eagle bar. The White Eagle was a rough place, and there were always fights . . . One novel, *Of Love and Dust*, and a short story, 'Three Men,' came out of my experience at the White Eagle." The White Eagle presented national-level blues artists such as Bobby Bland and regional favorites such as Bobby Rush, a Jackson,

THE MATADORS: (FROM LEFT) CHILI POT RED, PETER ROOSTER, K-DOE, AND BEAVER
ca. 1962
Courtesy Antoinette K-Doe

Mississippi–based R&B singer, comedian, and raconteur. Rush remembered meeting Ernie K-Doe at the White Eagle and other local bars as early as 1957:

> I met him through Buddy Guy, before Buddy moved to Chicago. K-Doe was just an open kind of person, and he would joke about "You know, I been messed over by my mother-in-law"; he would joke about that and have you laughin' so much that, in a conversation, he would take it where *he* wanted it to go. He was one of the cleverest kind of people like that. If you asked Ernie, "How old are you?" he'd say, "Well, how old are *you*?" You might answer, "I'm twenty," and he'd say, "Twenty? That's my age too!" In other words, he would lead you around the world, he was so keen to lead you to what *he* wanted you to know about him. I thought he was a genius at that, and he left it with me today that when people interview me, we talk about the things *I* want to talk about. I have a unique way of doing that in interviews—because of K-Doe. K-Doe never made anyone feel bad about the answers he gave them, you follow me? Ernie never went down like a bad guy when he didn't answer the way *you* wanted, because he did it in a charming way. . . .
>
> Those are the things that I remember about K-Doe, because, oh, would he make you laugh! And even way back, at the White Eagle, K-Doe had all the moves, all the clothes, he had *the shit*, man! He was like Liberace, you follow me? K-Doe was an en-ter-*tain*-er! He had some big records, but he didn't make his name as a singer, a record maker, a songwriter—he went out as an *entertainer*, like Sammy Davis Jr.!

The White Eagle had a deservedly rough reputation, but Walter "Wolfman" Washington had no reservations about playing in Port Allen's other major venue, Byrd's Satellite:

> You talk about fun! Lightnin' Slim, Slim Harpo and his guitar player Rudy Richard, Howlin' Wolf, Little Willie John—I met all of those cats playing at Byrd's Satellite. I played there a lot. With K-Doe it was just bass, guitar, and drums: me, Peter Rooster, and Beaver. No keyboard player, no horns—just three-piece—but you'd swear to God it was a big band up there. And K-Doe would dance and do his splits, all those tricks with the mic stand, all that stuff he had learned from Joe Tex.
>
> With K-Doe it would be an hour-and-a-half or a two-hour show, doing his songs, Jessie Hill's songs, Fats Domino's songs. Plus K-Doe had songs that he never recorded but we would sit down and play them. Sometimes we'd get onstage and just make up songs. What was K-Doe like to work with? Oh boy . . . ahhhhhhh . . . *rough* sometimes . . . he wasn't crazy, but there was just a certain style of music that he wanted to be played, and that's the way you

had to play it. He was demanding. You had to really like him and really like the kind of music he was playing in order to get along with K-Doe. And if you didn't like his music, well. . . .

Did he have a big ego? Man, did he have a big ego! Oh boy, tell me about it! *Je*-sus Christ! In K-Doe's mind, nobody could beat him! He'd challenge anybody; he was always talking that shit, yes indeed, and *loud*, he'd get loud in a minute. He could be really fun, he'd keep you laughing, but many times he would piss people off, make them mad. But mad was about as far as it would go, because K-Doe would fight in a minute too! He'd tell you, "Come on, let's go," any time of day or night—just like his mama! But K-Doe was a good person. He'd pay a cat before he'd pay himself.

CHAPTER 12: *Down from the Mountain*

Pay became an increasingly serious issue as K-Doe's record sales tapered off dramatically. The quality of his music had not diminished in the least. K-Doe's recordings with Allen Toussaint through May 1963 continued to showcase an artist and producer in synergistic peak form. Their collaborations—released on Minit and then on another Banashak-owned label, Instant—epitomized the best elements of New Orleans R&B—soulful exuberance, deceptively simple finesse, and rhythms that were forceful yet never stiff. Critical acclaim remained strong too. *Billboard* gave "A Certain Girl" its maximum rating of four stars, praising the "strong sales potential" of the "showmanly chanting by K-Doe on catchy r. & r. ditty with infectious rhythm" and noting the record's burgeoning popularity in Baltimore and Washington, DC. Even so, "A Certain Girl" did not climb past the lower reaches of the Hot 100 and R&B charts. Several songs got similarly positive press but also stalled out. Others simply didn't chart at all. Many intangible variables could have contributed to this arbitrary, fickle outcome.

"Easier Said than Done," for instance, shines as an introspective gem, perfect for slow dancing—yet it went nowhere. Ditto for "Beating Like a Tom-Tom" a plaintive, understated ballad that Allen Toussaint cited as one of his "very favorite songs. . . . K-Doe wrote that himself and I just loved it. After it came out, Harold Battiste told me that he really liked the little semiclassical cadence I had put in the arrangement there, and I remember those words sticking with me forever." The flip side of "Beating Like a Tom-Tom," "I Got to Find Somebody," went to the other extreme: a wild, wailing workout, one of K-Doe's very best—if least-known—recordings. "An interesting ditty," noted *Billboard*, "in medium tempo with strong gospel and blues touches. K-Doe works with a chorus in chant and response style. Solid beat here and kids should like."

At a time when hit records routinely spawned contrived sequels, a rowdy clone of "Mother-in-Law" entitled "Get Out of My House" redeemed itself from follow-up tedium with clever lyrics by K-Doe, Toussaint, and Joe Tex: "I know I said that you and old Satan were both just about the same, / But I'll take it back and never say it again, 'cause you make the Devil shamed!" To perfect the copycat effect, Benny Spellman even started the song by singing the title phrase, "Get out of my house," with the identical tone and tempo that he'd used to kick off "Mother-in-Law."

Occasional retreads aside—and they are common in the record business—Toussaint and K-Doe continued to experiment with adventurous new settings. K-Doe's plea for his woman to "Come On Home," for instance, replaced the sparse, pianocentric accompaniment of so many Minit sessions with a reverberating swirl of tom-tom flourishes and dominant backup vocals. But these dramatic touches—reflecting the pervasive influence of Motown and presaging Phil Spector's "wall of sound" productions—dampened neither K-Doe's irrepressible informality nor his steadfast self-absorption. Following the lines "The sun is going down, it's getting so cloudy now, / The wind is a-blowin,' I hear my baby calling," an unidentified female voice shouts out, "K-Doe!" Before long, K-Doe stopped getting others to herald him in song. Instead, he took the next logical step and just started hollering "K-DOE!" himself—perhaps in part because his colleagues had grown tired of doing so. "*I* am *not* that voice calling out 'K-Doe!' on 'Come On Home,'" Irma Thomas stated firmly. "No, that definitely wasn't me. It would be one of the other ladies who Allen used on everyone's sessions back then. Although I did sing backup on 'Te Ta Te Ta Ta.'"

Inevitably—given the hectic release schedule at Minit and the constant pressure for new product—some K-Doe-Toussaint collaborations fell flat. Several of them celebrated ephemeral fads, and some hinted at other artists' hits. The flip side of "Come On Home," for instance, was "Popeye Joe," one of many Popeye-dance-craze songs to emerge from New Orleans in 1962. The local popularity of this dance, loosely based on the swaggering moves of the brawny cartoon character Popeye the Sailor Man, eclipsed the national popularity of the Twist. Huey Smith and Eddie Bo also recorded Popeye songs. The craze prompted Chubby Checker—the Philadelphian who had recorded the hit version of "The Twist"—to come up with "Popeye the Hitchhiker," referencing two dance steps in one song title. Eddie Bo's "Check Mr. Popeye"—with the classic line "You better check that spinach, 'cause Olive's in the danger zone"—remains popular in New Orleans, while other Popeye songs are largely forgotten. K-Doe's version now sounds especially dated, in stark contrast to the majority of his records.

The Motown-tinged "Pennies Worth of Happiness" (aka "Penny's Worth of Happiness") likewise falters and has not aged gracefully. It does stand out, however, as the only Ernie K-Doe record with a flute solo. Its flip side, "I'm the Boss," a litany of complaints about household chores, seems to spring thematically from the Coasters' 1958 hit "Yakety Yak." But K-Doe gave all these songs full-strength performances, as he did with the weak lyrics of "Hey Hey Hey" and "Love You the Best." *Billboard* loved this 1962 release, awarding it four stars and describing "Hey Hey Hey" in extreme music-biz jargon: "Exuberant reading by warbler on feelingful rockaballad with solid bluesy tempo." It was popular enough that its title phrase, both the words and their cadence, may have been lifted by Mick Jagger and Keith Richards—serious collectors of R&B records—for the refrain of the Rolling Stones' 1965 hit "Satisfaction": "Hey, hey, hey—that's what I say!"

In another reflection of the arbitrary decisions made by record companies, some of K-Doe's best Minit songs did not appear as singles. They were relegated instead to low-profile usage as filler on the Minit album *Mother-in-Law*, K-Doe's first LP, released in 1962. This material includes "Hurry Up and Know It," a second-line romp in the spirit of "Make You Love Me," and the gospel-inflected "Waiting at the Station." The latter, one of the most intense songs that K-Doe ever recorded, bears the strong stylistic stamp of his hero, Archie Brownlee. After an introductory piano chord from Toussaint, K-Doe comes in, stretching the word "I" into an eight-syllable moan. Then, after a dramatic pause, he completes the opening verse just as the band comes in: ". . . thought I heard train whistle blowing, thought I heard the fireman ring the bell." References to trains—and steam locomotives in particular—had been prominent in such genres as blues, country, and gospel music for generations by the time K-Doe recorded this number. Train-song lyrics typically dwell on themes of escape, abandonment, or taking the wrong path in life. But K-Doe explored the joyful theme of reunion: "My lover . . . will be waiting at the station for me."

Like many albums by hit makers during this era, the *Mother-in-Law* LP was thrown together by Minit with little thought beyond cashing in, again, on the title track. The liner notes were impressive, however, in terms of absurd hype and egregious use of alliteration: "When the young New Orleans belter of burnished blues turns his talents to a tantalizing tune, he embellishes it with an effervescence and an ethereal effect that, indeed, makes him a spokesman for all singers. . . . He manages to caress the age-old yearning blues with a subtle spiritual feel and mold it into the framework of a gentle rock 'n' roll beat to produce a hauntingly beautiful tonal composition that transcends the limitations of a popular song by soaring into the realm of a classic vocal masterpiece." Sadly, these notes did not include the author's byline. The anonymous scribe certainly deserves an appreciative "What *he* said."

Minit obviously felt happy with Ernie K-Doe, but such flowery sentiments didn't extend to the label's rather rapidly deteriorating relationship with Imperial Records. Initially thrilled that such a big company would distribute, market, and promote Minit's records, Joe Banashak came to feel that Imperial's president, Lew Chudd, was ignoring Minit's new releases and perhaps even sabotaging them with passive-aggressive inactivity. As Banashak told music historian Jeff Hannusch, "Chudd presented such a sweet-sounding deal . . . [but] didn't fulfill any of his promises. . . . Looking back on the situation today, I realize Lew Chudd was jealous of our success. At the time Imperial was cold, Fats [Domino] wasn't selling and neither was Ricky [Nelson]. . . . I think [Chudd] wanted to be the only one guy that was successful and making money. He really enjoyed controlling other people's destinies."

LP 0002
MINIT RECORDS
ERNIE K-DOE
MOTHER-IN-LAW

Based on his sense that Chudd was dropping the ball, Banashak started a second record label, Instant, in 1961. It had no affiliation at all with Imperial. Instant's very first release, Chris Kenner's "I Like It Like That," reached number two on the Hot 100, causing further strain between Banashak and Chudd. "When Lew Chudd found out about the record," Banashak told Hannusch, "he called me and said, 'Hey, what's going on?' He was just shocked. I told him, 'Hey, you aren't doing what you promised to do, so I'm gonna try to do something on my own.'" During the next two years, their relationship continued to sour.

Despite tensions at Minit and his own slumping sales, K-Doe closed out 1962 with a great milestone in his personal mythology. On December 30 he performed at the New Orleans Municipal Auditorium in the Big Battle of Blues: James "I've Got Money" Brown vs. Ernie K-Doe. Most of K-Doe's boasts made generalized statements about his greatness. But among all that rampant, vague hyperbole, this concert achieved specific gravity as "the night I beat James Brown onstage!"

"It was the biggest battle of my life," K-Doe told Jeff Hannusch. "Larry McKinley was the announcer, and Larry called me out first. It was a dressing thing. New Orleans against Macon, Georgia [Brown was, in fact, from Augusta], and I sure wasn't gonna let New Orleans down. I had a royal-blue smoking jacket on, but underneath that? Nobody knew. Then James Brown came out in a brown suit, white shirt, brown polka-dot tie. But while Larry was talking, everybody went to screaming! You see, when I pulled off that smoking jacket, guess what? Everything else I had on was ice blue! And on 'Certain Girl' I changed suits nine times! I had a clothes rack and a valet backstage. Every time I'd get to a certain part in the song, I'd just run straight around to the side, change my suit, and come back on the other side!"

As the old adage goes, "I told you a million times not to exaggerate"; let us remember that the Emperor was not under oath. As a *Village Voice* reader observed in a 2006 letter to the editor, "New Orleans has been dining out on its old stories since Ernie K-Doe's mother-in-law was in pigtails." K-Doe surely ate many a free plate of "bullets" by recounting the tale of his perceived epic victory, replete with ample embellishments. One could hardly expect objectivity from a man who would be Emperor, especially regarding his faceoff with a man known as Soul Brother Number One, soon to be lauded as the Godfather of Soul. But some impartial observers shared K-Doe's assessment of the evening. "It was incredible!" said Jimmy Moliere, a fleet-fingered guitarist who played for years with Fats Domino. As Moliere told Domino's biographer Rick Coleman and researcher-producer Jerry Brock, "I hate to say it, but James Brown couldn't hold a candle to Ernie K-Doe! K-Doe came out there and started doin' things with that microphone and all that stuff. He'd tip it all the way down to the floor, and then before it would hit the ground, he'd turn around and do a split and catch it. And, aw, man, he could dance!"

MOTHER-IN-LAW LP
Courtesy Billy Delle

Other witnesses of equal stature, including Art Neville, felt that K-Doe had clearly lost to Brown: "K-Doe always wanted to outdo James Brown, so K-Doe got Larry McKinley to book a show at the Municipal Auditorium with him and James. K-Doe went on first, and he *got* the audience, K-Doe had *got 'em*—but then he wouldn't stop. They had to use the Bo Peep hook to get him offstage! And James Brown was watching him the whole time; James just stood there looking at him. Then James came out, the band hit one pop, James did his one-leg move all around the stage, and that was *it*! K-Doe always said he beat James Brown at the Municipal Auditorium, but he didn't beat James Brown—I was there." Art's brother Charles, also in attendance that night, said, "K-Doe said he had beaten James Brown. But the talk of the town was that James had put something on K-Doe's *ass*!"

"Now when K-Doe was on that show with James Brown," Irving Banister elaborated, "we tried to get him to hire Danny White's band. But no, K-Doe's gonna use that little three-piece group with Peter Rooster. And K-Doe's on the radio, WYLD, talkin' about how he's gonna beat James Brown, blah blah blah. But he didn't have but three pieces, and then James Brown came out with his big band and they were smokin'!" Deacon John agreed that K-Doe's paltry band held him back: "I saw that battle of the blues at the Municipal, and James Brown *clobbered* K-Doe, man! K-Doe was a great showman, but he didn't have the band to back him up. No piano player, no horns, no backup singers—how you gonna reproduce songs like 'Mother-in-Law' without horns and a piano? But K-Doe was hardheaded like that. I worked with him a lot at that time, or should I say that he often sang with my band, the Ivories. I was big in the high-school and college market that Minit aimed at with its artists. Deacon John and the Ivories was the top prom band in the city then, and a lot of artists would come sing on my gigs—K-Doe, Irma Thomas, Benny Spellman, Aaron Neville, Lee Dorsey, all of Allen Toussaint's artists. I would get their music together and make sure my band could play it just like on their records. But K-Doe wanted to speed everything up, sing it way up-tempo. Plus he was trying to impress people as a ballad singer, doing songs like 'Danny Boy' the way that Jackie Wilson had sung it. And K-Doe was a good ballad singer, but he didn't have anything close to Jackie Wilson's range. We'd have to lower the key so that K-Doe could make it. K-Doe was a megalomaniac, though, and you just had to go along with him."

But megalomania, confidence, willpower alone could not stop a slew of larger forces that would quickly come into play. As K-Doe's record sales dwindled, so did his drawing power, and his performance fees began to dip. Dawning just two days after the Municipal Auditorium concert, 1963 would prove to be a bad year for Ernie K-Doe, Minit Records, and the New Orleans music scene in general. Allen Toussaint joined the army. Lew Chudd sold Imperial—including its by-then wholly owned subsidiary Minit—to Liberty Records. Liberty thus acquired a treasure trove of master recordings and publishing rights, but it did not opt to keep Minit going as an active company releasing new material. "I didn't leave Minit," K-Doe pointed out; "Minit left me." Liberty eventually resurrected Minit in 1966, but that incarnation, based in Los Angeles, had no connection with Joe Banashak and only limited dealings with New Orleans musicians. Every now and then, an old Toussaint production

AD FOR THE EPIC NEW ORLEANS CONCERT WHERE K-DOE "BEAT JAMES BROWN ONSTAGE"
Louisiana Weekly
December 22, 1962

Sun. Dec. 30
Tickets At: Bynum's Drug Store I. L.A. Drug Store
Dooky Chase Riverside Bar, 1406 So. Rampart St.
MUNICIPAL AUD.
ST. ANN STREET - 8:30 P. M. TILL ?
Advance Tickets $2.00 - - At Door $2.50
BIG BATTLE OF BLUES
JAMES "I'VE GOT MONEY" BROWN
VS
ERNIE K-DOE
"GET OUT OF MY HOUSE"
THE MATADORS
JOHNNY & BELL
TAMMY MONTGOMERY
THE BROWN IES
JOE JONES AND HIS
BIG 10 PIECE BAND

would be reissued—such as "Te Ta Te Ta Ta," in 1968. For the most part, though, the new Minit focused instead on the likes of Bobby Womack and Ike and Tina Turner.

Compounding the problems of 1963, a dispute with Local 496 of the musicians' union drastically reduced recording activity at Cosimo Matassa's studio. (With segregation still extant, although soon to end, the Local 496 represented African Americans only, while white musicians belonged to Local 174. The two merged in 1968.) The leaders of the 496 forbade rank-and-file members to record with nonunion musicians. Those caught doing so—union officials often stopped by studios unannounced—were fined and made to pay up. Eventually the union blacklisted Matassa altogether. (Veneration of the gifted engineer, and appreciation of his cultural contributions, would not enter public consciousness for another dozen years.) "The union looked on the recording people as the enemy," Matassa told music historian Jonathan Foose; Earl King informed Foose's fellow historian Tad Jones, "They [the black union] was nothing but crooks and swindlers . . . It's one of the primary reasons that New Orleans [music] crumbled. They made it difficult to record in New Orleans, and the major companies got tired of this and went elsewhere."

This blow to the recording scene sent many musicians into exile in Los Angeles, with Harold Battiste in the vanguard. Sadly, this exodus coincided with the decimation of live-performance opportunities in New Orleans. An ambitious new district attorney named Jim Garrison, elected in 1961—he would eventually garner global attention through his failed prosecution of an alleged plot to assassinate President John F. Kennedy—sought to enhance his reputation by harassing nightclubs with accusations of gambling and prostitution. These venues gave many local musicians steady, long-term employment in house bands, which offered security comparable to that of working the night shift at a factory. Mac Rebennack described the situation to his amanuensis, Jack Rummel:

> In 1962 or 1963, Jim Garrison, the New Orleans district attorney, got a political hair up his ass about the so-called corruption that existed in New Orleans. What was ironic about this action was Jim Garrison was backed when he ran for DA by a lot of the club owners, who threw together a considerable amount of cash to help in his campaign. I used to see Garrison around Stalebread Charlie's and Mickie's whorehouse and at other places too. I thought he must have been cool—and then all of a sudden, when he got in office, out of the middle of nowhere, he turns Mr. Jive-Ass Morality.
>
> The first sign on the wall was when he began setting up sting operations. Next, Garrison came in and started padlocking everything. . . . And Garrison didn't just hit a few joints; he went after them all. One night during a gig I went outside for a break and looked down the street, and half the doors up and down the street were padlocked. . . . This spasm of righteousness had its cost. . . . Unfortunately for the musicians, live gigs and vice went hand in hand, and with all the joints being closed, suddenly jobs began to get tougher to find.

> A few years after Garrison started his work, the whole guts of New Orleans had been ripped out. As a result, guys I had been working with, fine musicians, had scattered all over the place, to New York, Chicago, Memphis, and L.A.

By the end of 1963 these local problems began to be compounded by the nationwide effect of the British Invasion. This unprecedented pop-culture phenomenon escalated dramatically following the Beatles' performances on television's *Ed Sullivan Show*, on three successive Sunday nights in February 1964. As the hirsute young Liverpudlians rocketed up the charts, many long-established American artists began plummeting. This was ironic: the Beatles, the Rolling Stones, and their colleagues idolized the musicians whose careers they unintentionally torpedoed. American songwriters such as Allen Toussaint benefited from the numerous British renditions of R&B tunes. But musicians such as Ernie K-Doe—who had little or no songwriting income and depended solely on record sales and performance fees—suddenly found themselves devalued.

The British passion for American R&B—and the urge to replicate it—played a crucial role in the evolution of early-'60s rock in the UK. Virtually all the leading groups that would ultimately gain fame with original material started out as cover bands. Working long hours at venues similar to those on Bourbon Street in New Orleans, they primarily played songs by stateside R&B, blues, and rockabilly artists. The original renditions of these numbers could be hard to find, as few were released in England; if sold as imports they were very expensive. But tenacious devotees tracked these records down. Giorgio Gomelsky, who managed and produced the Yardbirds, was one such determined treasure-hunter-*cum*-music-detective: "I had a friend (Tony Palmer I think his name was) who worked for EMI, our UK record company. His job was to consider the UK release of songs on US 'regional' labels. Which, however, rarely happened. But he had boxes and boxes of 45 singles he got from the US in his office, and we regularly showed up there and raided them, looking for stage repertoire, if nothing else. Remember, most of those 'race' singles were not available in the UK." ("Race records," a marketing euphemism for music made by black artists for black audiences, was coined in the 1920s. Anachronistic by the '60s, it has long since faded from usage.) Gomelsky continued, "Listening to these records was a way of keeping up with what was going on across the pond. We were blues and R&B fans and collectors, specialists, for whom *all* the American artists were important!" As a result of one his "raids," Gomelsky heard "A Certain Girl" and presented the song to the Yardbirds, a top-tier band at the time. The group took to it, "performing 'A Certain Girl' on their shows both before and after recording it," and, as Gomelsky added with pride, "I sang that bass part, 'NO-O-O!'"

Many other prominent British musicians were New Orleans devotees too, and admirers of K-Doe in particular. Eric Burdon of the Animals—the British Invasion's most convincing blues singer—recalled that Ernie K-Doe was "well known in the UK, oh yeah! I finally got to meet him years later when I had a drink at his Mother-in-Law Lounge. He didn't say much. Didn't have to. The Animals played some New Orleans numbers, such as Jessie

Hill's 'Ooh Poo Pah Doo,' although we didn't do any K-Doe songs. But I do remember Mickie Most, our producer, taking K-Doe's 'Mother-in-Law' to Herman's Hermits."

As squeaky-clean teen heartthrobs, Herman's Hermits wisely avoided the awkward vocal mimicry that marred so many British bands' homages to African American music. Instead of ludicrously striving to sound black, the teen band crafted a light, melodic version of "Mother-in-Law" in the country-rooted harmony style of the Everly Brothers, the Kentucky-based duo who profoundly influenced the Beatles. "We performed 'Mother-in-Law' onstage right from the very early Herman's Hermits days," said Peter Noone, aka Herman, "and we played it for years, starting about two weeks after I first bought the record. Loads of British bands played 'A Certain Girl,' which is why we didn't, although I liked the other versions, especially Wayne Fontana's. Most great R&B records were covered in the UK by white 'greasy boys,' but there was a section of the public who bought *only* the original American artist's recording." Noone continued, "In those days it was necessary to be unique. The idea of a fifteen-year-old boy singing about his mother-in-law became a mainstay of the whole tongue-in-cheek aspect of Herman's Hermits. . . . I had no idea that calling a mother-in-law Satan was a bad thing, and I was so young that I probably didn't think that it could offend anyone. . . . I never thought about 'Mother-in-Law' as a New Orleans record. It was and always is just music for us. We never categorized—that is the American disease."

Ultimately it was a multifaceted business malaise that laid up the New Orleans music scene in 1963. Joe Banashak forged ahead with Instant Records nevertheless, steadily releasing new records until 1970. The label featured K-Doe on just two singles, produced by Allen Toussaint before he enlisted in the army. "Sufferin' So," cowritten by Joe Tex and K-Doe, provided a spelling lesson of sorts, with its key words of wisdom enunciated letter by letter: "M-O-N-E-Y without L-O-V-E ain't a T-H-I-N-G." The flip side of this 1963 release, "Baby, Since I Met You," was cheery but forgettable. In contrast, K-Doe's last Instant release, 1964's "Reaping What I Sow," was glum and self-critical, with a hauntingly understated delivery. Its flip side, "Talking Out of My Head," was gloomier still, and seemed to predict K-Doe's future days as a derelict:

> Getting drunk, talk out of my head;
> Cleaned out, wished I was dead.
> Can't eat, losin' sleep;
> My clothes don't fit me since you're not wit' me.
> Curse my boss, job I lost,
> Out on the street, no shoes on feet;
> I'm sorry to bore you with my trouble;
> I'm doing nothing but making it double,
> So please accept my apology,
> I'm sufferin' from a bad case of lonely-ology.

In a telling sign of the times, *Billboard* gave K-Doe's song a mere two-line reference, while the next page featured a large, splashy ad for the British pop duo Chad and Jeremy, whose label, World Artists, boasted that the two were "as English as a cup of tea." With American pop music thus beleaguered, and the New Orleans scene in particularly bad shape, it was time for Ernie K-Doe to make a move.

CHAPTER 13: *The Emperor and the Duke*

Although Ernie K-Doe was deeply affected by the problems plaguing New Orleans musicians, he did not join the growing number of hometown expatriates in Los Angeles. By 1964 he had been married for eight years and had two young sons, Ernest Jr. and Gerald. Twin boys, Keith and Kevin, would follow two years later. And—according to his own unverified boasts—K-Doe had sired numerous other children around town. The number he usually bragged of was twenty-seven, a figure that bassist Arthur Vigne actually considered low. Vigne played with K-Doe in "little pick-up bands, around 1953, '54. Back then we'd pay him two dollars to sing." With a dated reference to a once-popular patent medicine, Carter's Little Liver Pills, he asserted that "K-Doe had more women than Carter had little pills in a jar! The women *loved* K-Doe, and K-Doe had outside kids that he didn't even know about."

Even without paternal responsibilities, official or otherwise, it's unlikely that K-Doe would ever have moved away. Many people who are Crescent City–born and –bred find it extremely difficult to live anywhere else. The depth of their hometown attachment, which surprises non–New Orleanians, exceeds typical expressions of family bonds, civic pride, and sense of place. K-Doe continued to tough it out in New Orleans, where his problems multiplied and his marriage faltered. R&B singer Tony Owens summarized K-Doe's predicament: "K-Doe was a man who had a big hit record that was very popular all over the country. People knew him and respected him, including all entertainers from everywhere. He had a good bit of money, a couple of new Cadillacs, fancy clothes, and diamond rings. He also had about fifty thousand bucks," Owens asserted, "which was a lot of money at the time. I don't know who was taking care of his business then, by the mid-'60s, but I know that K-Doe had people who were supposed to be handling his affairs who obviously had not taken care of things like taxes. The IRS seized K-Doe's assets; he woke up one morning and he didn't have *anything*. His accounts were frozen; he had fifty grand but he couldn't touch it. That was a hard blow." K-Doe is not known to have mentioned tax troubles in public, but others have corroborated the gist of Owens's recollection.

Trumpeter Porgy Jones commented that "K-Doe could not handle the downfall of his marriage. K-Doe had money. He lived in Sugar Hill—that's part of Gentilly, near Dillard University. For that time it was considered a nice area, it was *the* area for a successful

N6204C

black man. K-Doe had a nice house, nice furniture, three cars, but he ended up sleeping under the Claiborne Avenue bridge. K-Doe's first wife, Shirley, was aloof, kind of distant. She'd come on the set sometimes, but she didn't seem tight with K-Doe like the way some people are tight with each other. I think that after the bread went, K-Doe's first wife, Shirley, went. He had written songs about her, literally singing her praises. But she wanted that certain lifestyle. Then the money was gone and K-Doe couldn't catch up. And as soon as he showed her something raggedy, she kicked him in the ass. At least that's how I saw it."

Ernest Kador Jr. painted quite a different picture, describing a lifelong bond between his parents: "Growing up, I wasn't deprived of anything that I needed and only a very few things that I wanted. My dad would bring home suitcases of money when he would come off the road. We had a beautiful house [at 1934] Abundance Street, two Cadillacs in the driveway, and a big old yard with a swing set. Although during a lot of that time I was basically being kept by my aunt and my Grandmother Lucy, because my mom and dad would fly here, fly there, come home, and then take off again. They was living large. So my aunt and my grandmother pretty much raised me up until the point when things started to slow down for my father. For some reason, later on in life, my mother and my father separated, but they always were still together. He would come over, he would eat, sleep, shower, they had a relationship and a bond that never broke. It was like they were still married as far as we knew."

At the same time, K-Doe maintained several relationships with other women. Doris Watson recalled that "K-Doe and I dated for years and years. . . . My mama was crazy about K-Doe and wanted me to marry him, and I wish now that I had. . . . I always believed in K-Doe. I always had faith in K-Doe. He was a good person; he treated me nice. . . . He took me to the dog races in Pensacola. He let me drive his Cadillac. His wife, Shirley, knew about me, but I never had no words with her, or his other girlfriend, Marie—they respected me and I respected them. When K-Doe fell on hard times in later years, I never did scorn him or make fun of him. He was living on the street and he had gotten kind of raggedy. He would come by, take a bath, eat, and relax. He had a perm then, and I would fix his hair for him."

This web of concurrent relationships had to be hard to juggle, and it came with the ever-present risk of violence spawned by jealousy. But K-Doe managed it adroitly, for the most part. His sincere kindness and deep generosity had long endeared him to many people, from his basketball teammates to his love interests. In the case of his romantic relationships, this genuine altruism may have helped mitigate K-Doe's flagrant philandering. Unlike most people in such a position, K-Doe did not burn all his bridges. By staying in the good graces of some of his exes and maintaining a connection with his wife—their separation notwithstanding—K-Doe created a canny survival strategy. He was committed to music for life, with no thoughts of working a day job, and during tough times he usually had multiple sources of comfort and shelter. It is not unusual for male musicians

TOP LEFT AND RIGHT
K-DOE AND HIS FIRST WIFE, SHIRLEY
early 1960s
BOTTOM
K-DOE, SHIRLEY, AND "LITTLE ERNEST"
December 22, 1962
All photos courtesy Ernest Kador Jr.

to convince several women to support them simultaneously—common enough, in fact, that some refer to the practice as "checking my traps." K-Doe's relationships, however, were not quite so one-sided, due to his own tendency to nurture.

K-Doe's flexible situation was generally accepted in his multiple domestic circles, but it also caused some understandable confusion. "I can honestly say," K-Doe's son Ernest Jr. reflected, "that I never heard my mother and father argue. I never knew why they split up. I've heard some stories from my mother's side, I've heard some stories from my father's side, and neither one of them were negative stories, just that it was time. My father was pretty much a ladies' man. He was good looking, my mother was good looking, and they pretty much had the world at their feet for a long time. They were very, very much in love. My mother had my brother Gerald after they had separated, and then she had the twins, Keith and Kevin. My mom and dad were separated in a way, but yet they were still seeing each other, and she still had those kids by him. They didn't actually get a divorce until right before he married Antoinette. It's a lot that can be read into things, but I'd rather not speculate because I really don't know."

But it was no matter of speculation that K-Doe's money was rapidly dwindling, from his suitcases and his bank account. In 1965 K-Doe went to jail twice for falling behind on child support. In both instances he was arrested in midsong, first while singing at a club called Say When, then at the Honey Hush Lounge. In the first case, Judge Frederick S. Ellis sentenced K-Doe to ten days in Orleans Parish Prison: "I remember," said the judge, now retired, "K-Doe coming to court wearing what had once been a beautiful bright-blue sport coat, but it was all frayed. He was clearly in contempt of court, and he couldn't come up with his arrearages, so I was legally bound to put him in jail. After the hearing, I told K-Doe's lawyer that it didn't have to be that way; if I was asked for a reduction in his alimony, I would give it to him, since K-Doe clearly couldn't afford his current payments. But K-Doe didn't follow up. I got the distinct feeling that he didn't want to accept or acknowledge being broke, even though it was obvious."

The *Times-Picayune* recounted this legal encounter with the headline ALIMONY BLUES SUNG FOR JUDGE. "Maybe you will learn," the newspaper quoted Ellis as telling K-Doe, "that you either have to obey a court order, or get the order changed." Only the merest passing reference—the terse clause "known for his song, 'Mother-in-Law'"—acknowledged K-Doe's musical accomplishments. The brief article identified K-Doe as a "young Negro entertainer." That New Orleans's paper of record would pay more attention to K-Doe's misdemeanor than it had to his huge career achievement of 1961 is not surprising; such minimal recognition and its implicit racism were typical for the time. As Cosimo Matassa told telejournalist Eric Paulsen: "Fats Domino made twenty million-selling records in a row, and the *Picayune* never heard about it? Now, if he'd gotten in a knife fight, that would have been on the front page."

Following his second arrest, K-Doe requested leniency. He explained that club owners were scared to book him for fear that he'd be busted while onstage—but without such bookings, he couldn't earn the money to pay alimony. Despite such impeccable logic, Judge Fred Cassibry sentenced K-Doe to thirty days in Orleans Parish Prison. Led away with his hands shackled, K-Doe wisecracked that the jailer had dressed him in "the wrong cuff links." His Jamaican fans surely would have agreed.

Fortunately no arrests interrupted K-Doe's performances at Tulane University. Michael Rothschild, the founder of Landslide Records in Atlanta, attended Tulane from 1961 to '65, and he booked K-Doe for frat parties. "I also hired him to play a big annual dance two years in a row," Rothschild said, "along with Irma Thomas and Benny Spellman. They played in a hotel ballroom that held a couple of thousand people. I hired one band to back all those singers—maybe it was Wardell Quezergue's Royal Dukes of Rhythm, because Allen Toussaint was in the army then. K-Doe was a very energetic performer, almost acrobatic. He did flips, splits, and all the classic microphone tricks. One time when Irma came on after K-Doe, no one could hear her sing a note because, with all his wild moves, K-Doe had unintentionally broken every mic we had."

Another Tulane alumnus who enjoyed K-Doe's music during this era was television host Jerry Springer. Springer recalled going to frat-house parties for ten straight nights during rush week in 1961, and hearing "Mother-in-Law" played many times at every event. In 1998 Springer—famous, by then, as a creator of tabloid TV—returned to New Orleans to attend the convention of the National Association of Television Programming Executives. As production executives in their own right—albeit with vague credentials—Ernie and Antoinette K-Doe attended the convention too. Who would dare tell this unstoppable couple—comparably extreme to some guests on Springer's show—that *any* event was off-limits? The *Times-Picayune*'s Lili LeGardeur reported that Springer "recognized K-Doe immediately from his days at Tulane and shook off his handlers, calling out, 'K-Doe, my man!' Springer remembers the encounter vividly. 'It was a thrill to meet him,' he said."

But thrill was not the dominant reaction to most K-Doe encounters in the mid-'60s. Hometown fans, in particular, became rather peevish when K-Doe showcased his new, post-Minit material instead of reprising his familiar hits. In 1964 K-Doe signed with the Houston-based Duke Records. K-Doe stated several times that Larry McKinley arranged the deal. McKinley recalled, in contrast, "I was no longer managing K-Doe at that time, and I'm not sure that he even had a manager then. I don't know how the Duke deal came about." (It's possible that Vic Despenza, who managed K-Doe and Irma Thomas at some point during the mid-'60s, put this deal together.) Before the Duke signing, K-Doe had approached Lloyd Price on his own, sans management, in hopes of signing with Price's label, Double L. "K-Doe used to run me crazy!" Price said. "He always wanted me to record him. I told him that I was trying to go straight to pop radio . . . [and his sound] would be a New Orleans record."

K-Doe was skeptical about doing business with Duke because the company's owner, Don D. Robey, had a reputation for dishonesty and violent intimidation. Little Richard told biographer Charles White about a business discussion that ended when Robey "jumped

on me, knocked me down, and kicked me in the stomach. . . . I had to have an operation." Such stories were common. Given K-Doe's limited options, however, Duke made a good match for an artist whose star had faded nationally but still gleamed along the Gulf Coast. Duke had emerged in the '50s as one of America's first successful black-owned and -operated labels. A major national player in blues, R&B, and gospel, Duke boasted a galaxy of secular stars that included Bobby Bland, Junior Parker, Gatemouth Brown, and Big Mama Thornton. The Mighty Clouds of Joy, the Dixie Hummingbirds, and the Sensational Nightingales topped its religious roster. Robey released this musical mixture on the Duke label and on the subsidiaries Peacock, Backbeat, and Sure-Shot. Ernie K-Doe was not the first New Orleans artist Robey had signed; in 1960 James Booker's instrumental "Gonzo" scored a significant hit on Peacock, which also released singles by both Billy Tate and Sugar Boy Crawford. Another New Orleanian who recorded for Duke per se was Edgar Blanchard, the leader of a popular band called the Gondoliers. And, for a time, Robey retained the respected pianist Edward Frank as his New Orleans Artist and Repertoire (A&R) man to seek out local talent.

Duke released ten K-Doe singles between 1964 and 1970. Stylistically diverse, the Duke material lacked the uniform feel of K-Doe's thirteen singles for Minit and Instant. This consistency had prevailed thanks to Allen Toussaint's comprehensive contributions as producer, principal songwriter, accompanist, and arranger. Cosimo Matassa's expert audio engineering added constancy as well. But Don Robey, not a musician himself, employed a variety of producers, arrangers, and accompanists. He did not have his own studio and booked his sessions at three different Houston facilities.

Most of K-Doe's Duke sessions were produced by the saxophonists Wilmer Shakesnider and Gilbert Caple. (There has been some confusion regarding the correct spelling of the latter's name, which also appears in print as Cople, Capel, Caples.) The two reedmen coproduced some sessions and worked separately on others. Shakesnider's résumé included the writing of sophisticated arrangements for jazz singer Ella Fitzgerald in New York, as well as Houston sessions accompanying the grittier likes of Gatemouth Brown and Clifton Chenier. Caple had made his mark in Memphis—where Duke Records had been founded—as a cowriter of such hits as the Mar-Keys' instrumental "Last Night." Robey acquired the label in 1952 and brought it to Houston, creating a merger with Peacock, which he had founded in 1949. Despite the move, Robey continued to maintain strong connections with the Memphis music community. K-Doe, ever the embellisher, claimed to have made some of his Duke records with the prominent Memphis producer Willie Mitchell. Duke's studio logs do not bear this out. But Mitchell did mastermind some important singles for Robey—such as O. V. Wright's "Eight Men and Four Women," on Backbeat—before striking it rich as Al Green's producer, for Hi Records, in the early '70s.

K-DOE PERFORMING AT ST. PAUL'S HIGH SCHOOL PROM, COVINGTON, LOUISIANA
The Conifer yearbook
1967
Courtesy Steve and Haydée Ellis

The diverse settings that Shakesnider and Caple picked for Ernie K-Doe included lush ballads, protofunk, a few bland pop songs, blues-infused R&B, and secular tunes with distinct gospel trappings. Accompaniment ran the gamut from sophisticated horn charts, elaborate vocal choruses, and swirling string sections to gritty small bands with a live-in-the-studio feel. K-Doe sang all this material with consistent strength and conviction, although most of it lacked the flair of his Minit songs. Several of his Duke songs lifted key phrases and hooks straight from other artists' hits. Although some of Toussaint's productions reflected obvious commercial influences, he never resorted to overt replication.

On K-Doe's first Duke single, Robey even tried to have K-Doe clone himself by cashing in on the lowdown legacy of his mother-in-law Lucy with "My Mother-in-Law (Is in My Hair Again)." Despite the obvious derivation—including a bass singer who intoned "mother-in-law" à la Benny Spellman—this remake sounds surprisingly fresh and vital, thanks to great singing, a hot band, and K-Doe's own witty lyrics:

> My mother-in-law is in my hair again! . . .
> She diggin' in the back yard a big hole;
> She say that she diggin' for a pot of gold.
> My mother-in-law is in my hair again!
> My mother-in-law, the woman works on my nerves every day!
> My mother-in-law, the woman works on my nerves—
> She even axed me about my pay!
> She say she believe in witchcraft;
> Stickin' pins in a doll, make me feel so bad!
> My mother-in-law is in my hair again!

K-Doe also makes topical reference to the then-heated space race with Russia, magnanimously nominating Lucy to serve as America's first astronaut: "My mother-in-law need to take a rocket to the moon, / If she leave right now it wouldn't be a minute too soon!" On the flip side, the mundane midtempo ballad "Looking into the Future," K-Doe's flubbed line evokes the rather painful image of his beloved as "the apple *in* my eye."

K-Doe's next Duke single, "Little Bit of Everything," released in 1965, delves into midtempo funk. This song had first been recorded as an instrumental by the veteran New Orleans saxophonist Herbert Hardesty, a longtime member of Fats Domino's band and a first-call session player at Cosimo Matassa's studio. K-Doe's version established a pattern for several of his ensuing Duke records: simplistic lyrics that listed the names of such popular dance steps as the Twist, the Swim, the Slop, the Dog, and the lesser-known Uncle Willie. K-Doe tagged each dance to a certain city—"In New York City, they doin' the Twist"—an obvious nod to James Brown's classic rendition of "Night Train." On similar numbers that followed—1966's "Dancin' Man" and "Gotta Pack My Bag" from '68—K-Doe would shout out the names of other steps: the Philly, the Pony, the Fly, the Boogaloo, and the Shang-a-lang. Curiously, he also mentioned the archaic Eagle Rock, which dates to the turn of the twentieth century and is typically associated with ragtime. But K-Doe may have been referring simply to a then-contemporary move rather than a dance all its own.The derivative approach of "Little Bit of Everything" extends to the borrowed phrase "Say yeah, yeah, yeah," sung with the same intonation as the hook on Marvin Gaye's 1962 hit "Stubborn Kind of Fellow." But it diverges in a lively call-and-response dialogue with the guitarist, whose insistent licks segue into a forceful, hard-edged solo egged on by K-Doe's shouts. Even as an occasional copycat, K-Doe stamped his strong personality on almost everything he recorded.

CHAPTER 14: *Later for Tomorrow*

When K-Doe's studio recordings didn't sell, Don Robey tried tapping into the lucrative market for audience fervor vérité. The success of the album *James Brown Live at the Apollo*, released in 1963, demonstrated the demand for such material. Brown had long implored King Records to release one of his famous live performances. Unable to convince the label's president, Syd Nathan, Brown produced and paid for the recording himself. His vision was vindicated when *Live at the Apollo* quickly won acclaim as a modern classic. Numerous live albums by other artists ensued, in R&B, rock, and country. So did raucous in-concert hit singles, such as Little Stevie Wonder's "Fingertips," recorded at Chicago's Regal Theater in 1963. Nineteen sixty-six saw K-Doe dive into this live format with "Please Don't Stop," backed with "Boomerang," recorded at a show at a Houston club creatively spelled "Pladium." (Presumably Duke recorded much more of this show, not just the two songs released, but the whereabouts of the tapes are unknown.) "Please Don't Stop" liberally borrowed its tune, tempo, and delivery from Gene Chandler's swoon-inducing and scream-laden "Rainbow," cut live at the Regal in '65. "Boomerang" celebrated—or at least attempted to spark a fad for—"a new dance that hit the nation, like a hurricane," as its lyrics proclaim. If any such trend ever resulted, however, it passed quickly. Neither of these live songs hit, so Robey tried studio sessions again. Duke's second K-Doe release of 1966 was "Little Marie," which paid gushing homage to one of K-Doe's several concurrent girlfriends: "I have a sweet little girl so very dear to me / . . . In case you want to know who I'm talking about, my little Marie."

"After K-Doe split with Shirley," Porgy Jones divulged, "he got with a chick named Marie, and he wrote a song about her. He wrote songs about all of his women." But Jones's use of the phrase "he wrote songs" brings to light a minor mystery. Eight of the twenty selections that K-Doe recorded for Duke, including "Little Marie," credit a songwriter named Marie Monley. More significantly, Monley's entire oeuvre consists of material recorded by Ernie K-Doe. Apparently she wrote for K-Doe and K-Doe only—or did she? Monley may have penned these songs herself, but it's also quite possible that K-Doe did so, in actuality, and then registered the songs in her name. This practice was fairly common at the time, either to get around exclusive songwriting agreements or to obscure income, among other reasons. Don Robey, for example, used the songwriting pseudonym Deadric Malone, a combination of his middle name and his first wife's maiden name. Rather than actually writing anything, though, Robey may just have bullied people into giving him lucrative cowriting credits. But Allen Toussaint—who quite definitely wrote his own songs—sometimes did this too, using the nom de plume Clarence Toussaint, his father's name, or Naomi Neville, his mother's maiden name.

Monley acknowledged, "Yes, I am 'Little Marie.' K-Doe and I started going together in 1961. I used to have all his paperwork from Duke Records, but it washed away in Katrina. We had a daughter together." Whatever the circumstances regarding authorship, Robey released "Little Marie" twice. The first incarnation was paired in 1966 with "Somebody Told Me." The second came out the following year as the flip side of "(It Will Have to Do) Until the Real Thing Comes Along." Written in the 1930s by Sammy Cahn and associates, this song was recorded by the likes of Andy Kirk and his Twelve Clouds of Joy, Billie Holiday, Fats Waller, Frank Sinatra, and—decades later—Rod Stewart, among many others. K-Doe's rendition marked for him a rare recorded foray into mainstream popular standards, although on the bandstand he often sang "(Won't You Come Home) Bill Bailey." With impressive versatility, K-Doe gives "Until the Real Thing Comes Along" a predominately suave, urbane treatment that compares favorably with its many celebrity interpretations. But he also interjects one brief, high-pitched laugh, in direct mimicry of the Walt Disney character Goofy. This jarring moment passes quickly, though, and his performance instantly resumes its debonair professionalism. K-Doe put a similarly subtle gloss on the ballads "How Sweet You Are" and "Don't Kill My Groove." The latter borrowed a fleeting but obvious hook from Jimmy Hughes's 1964 hit "Steal Away," repeating the line "I know it's late" with the identical cadence Hughes had used.

Convinced that another big hit awaited him, K-Doe sought to promote his Duke songs rather than rest on his Minit laurels. This understandable goal did not please New Orleans audiences, who wanted to hear the songs they knew and loved. Billy Delle, the knowledgeable host of *Records from the Crypt* on WWOZ, witnessed some of the clashes that resulted:

> In the early '60s, K-Doe could do no wrong. He was hittin' locally with one song after another: "Hello My Lover," "T'aint It the Truth," and "Come On Home." Besides "Mother-in-Law," of course. Those were all cut for Minit. Then, when he was getting ready to record for Duke, he told me, "You think you heard something from Ernie K-Doe before, wait 'til you hear what I'm going to do now!" He did "My Mother-in-Law (Is in My Hair Again)," and people said, "Oh, he's rehashing his hit, like Chubby Checker did with 'Let's Twist Again.'" But that was a good record, and so were some other Duke songs, like "Later for Tomorrow," a good soulful song. Same thing for "Dancin' Man."

FOLLOWING PAGES
K-DOE AND HIS FANS, THE WAREHOUSE, NEW ORLEANS
1974
Photo by Michael P. Smith
©The Historic New Orleans Collection, 2007.103.1356

> K-Doe wanted to perform his new stuff, naturally, but people in New Orleans didn't want to hear it! They'd start hollering, "Wanted, $10,000.00 Reward"! "Mother-in-Law"! And K-Doe would stand there, kind of sulking, and say, "I ain't gonna do it! I ain't gonna do it!" Then he'd say, "Now here's a song that I just had the pleasure of recording for Duke Records: 'Dancin' Man'!" He'd sing "Dancin' Man" and get a polite little round of applause, but as soon as it was over they'd start hollering for all his old stuff again—"Hello My Lover"! "A Certain Girl"!—and K-Doe would say, "I ain't gonna do it!" At first the people thought he was joking, but after a while they'd leave the club. So the club owners would tell K-Doe, "Either play your goddamn hits or hit the door!" And K-Doe would get mad, pack up, and go. . . .
>
> K-Doe would start pawing on women, and their dates didn't like that. You know how on his radio show, later, K-Doe would always say, "I'm gonna get me some tonight!"? Well, he worked on the law of averages—if you hit on a hundred women, one of them is bound to say yes! And he was drinking then, always. He was in this one place, one night, I forget where, but he showed up at two or three o'clock in the morning at a late-night jam session, and he said the wrong shit to someone. There were two or three big bruisers who were going to take care of him. I don't know how he got out of there. Snooks Eaglin told me, "Billy, I was on gigs where we had to flee for our lives because K-Doe was getting in trouble. We would pack up and leave without getting paid just to get away in one piece!"

Eaglin described a particularly harrowing night at a white club in a small town several hours' north of New Orleans: "One time we went to Columbia, Mississippi. K-Doe was on the show and the people asked him, said, 'K-Doe, we want to hear a little "Mother-in-Law."' K-Doe says, 'No, man, not now.' Them people said, '*What?* You mean to tell me you ain't gonna play no damn "Mother-in-Law"? Hit the road, man!' The white man who run the place said, 'Get the rope, Marv!' and then he come up and told me, 'Snooks, I know you, you a good person. You got a good band. But if this boy here don't play "Mother-in-Law," *we gonna hang him tonight*!' I said, 'Aw, shit!' and the man's saying, 'K-Doe, don't you look at our women, boy! I wanna hear "Mother-in-Law"!' Yassuh, boss! We raised up the roof, must have done 'Mother-in-Law' six times!"

For a man who had played the Apollo Theater on the heels of a number-one hit, such racism, disrespect, and diminished prestige were deeply humiliating. Still, some of K-Doe's labelmates had fond memories of cobillings with him during this era. Roy Head, the "blue-eyed soul" singer whose "Treat Her Right" rose to number two in 1965, said, "I worked the whole black circuit back then, all over the country. I was on some big shows with Ernie K-Doe: DJ conventions, stuff like that. Ernie K-Doe was the epitome of what a showman should be. He knew he had it, and he flaunted it. If you don't believe in yourself, who else is going to believe in you?"

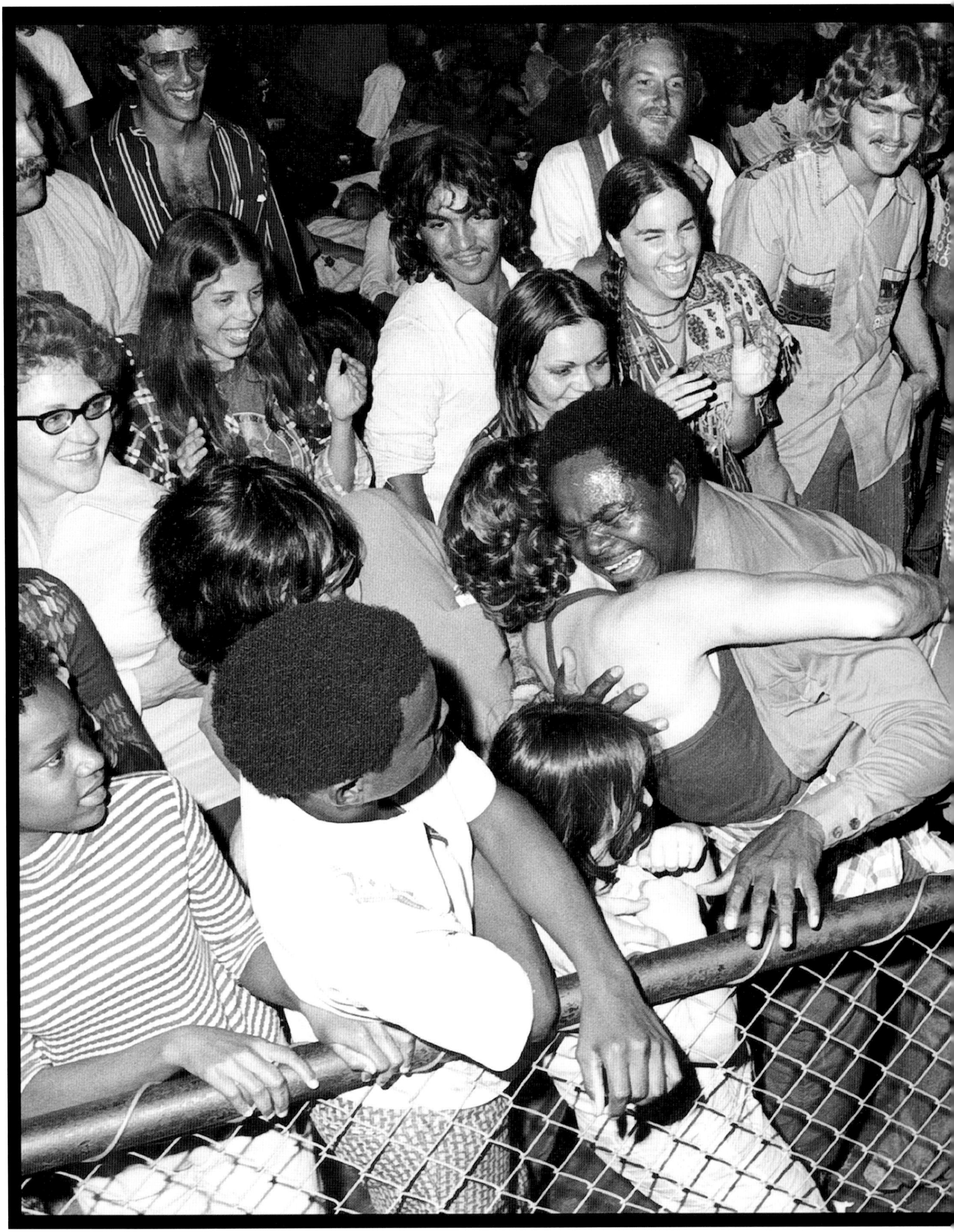

Fellow Houstonian Archie Bell—who with his band, the Drells, topped the charts with "Tighten Up" in 1968—also worked with K-Doe around this time, and he remembered Ernie's unfailing kindness: "Ernie would come to town a lot when he was with Duke. Me, I wouldn't have anything to do with Don Robey. But I was playing in the house band at a place called Club De Lisa, and we backed up everyone who came through. . . . People like Ernie, who were a little older and had big records, were our heroes! And Ernie was very down to earth. Not like some of those others who I would *not* work with, like James Brown or Wilson Pickett."

Such heroic regard of K-Doe was especially strong in New Orleans. The late Herman Ernest III, a masterful drummer and Dr. John's longtime bandleader, "played behind K-Doe when he had 'Boomerang,' around 1966. K-Doe was *the* cat. Me and K-Doe never had a bad chord. Working with K-Doe was a big deal to me, because I was seventeen years old then, and here's a guy who had a million-seller. He was a star—but *he* knew *my* name! That was *huge* for me!"

Although K-Doe touted mostly his Minit sides on his WWOZ show in the 1980s, he occasionally pushed the Duke material too. On one mid-'80s program, he spun "I'm Sorry," a 1969 release, as if it were brand-new. As the record ended, K-Doe started a self-reverential love fest with a female fan who had phoned in. Although she called from the small riverside town of Reserve, her demeanor, to the contrary, was absolutely bubbly.

[K-Doe:] This is Ernie K-Doe's new record called "I'm So Sorry!" The background singer is Joe Ligon of the Mighty Clouds of Joy. Some people have said I lost my voice. Listen to this record and see if I have lost my voice. . . . Where you callin' from BAY-BEE?

[Caller:] Reserve!

[K-Doe:] What y'all doin' in Reserve?

[Caller:] We partyin' hearty!

[K-Doe:] Baby, do you like the record *or do you like the record*?

[Caller:] I like it! You ain't lost nothin'!

[K-Doe:] I ain't did *what*?

[Caller:] You ain't lost nothin'!

[K-Doe:] I ain't lost nothin'?

[Caller:] *NOTH-thin'*!

[K-Doe:] You mean to tell me I'm still good?

[Caller:] *Still* good!

[K-Doe:] People say that I've lost my voice and all this other crap!

[Caller:] Oh, *no*, no way!

[K-Doe:] I'm gonna play my new record *again*! Hey, Reserve! Everybody stand up! Reserve, Louisiana, stand on up and say, "*How great thou are, Ernie K-Doe, with your bad self!*"

Bluster aside, "I'm Sorry" is a masterful record featuring K-Doe in full-throttle Archie Brownlee mode. An accomplished gospel quartet did indeed sing the hypnotic background vocals, but, despite K-Doe's assertion, that foursome was not led by Joe Ligon. "K-Doe claimed we sang on that record?" Ligon asked rhetorically after listening to "I'm Sorry": "Ain't that something? I'm gonna have to tell you the truth, now: I don't remember ever backing up Ernie K-Doe. I like K-Doe's singing on that record, but that is not the Mighty Clouds of Joy. We knew about Ernie K-Doe, though, because 'Mother-in-Law' was a big record, and we used to mess around and sing it. In private, that is—not on our shows, because we are gospel singers. But we knew very well who Ernie K-Doe was. And when we played New Orleans on gospel shows at the Municipal Auditorium, K-Doe would come hear us. K-Doe was a huge gospel music fan, just like Aaron Neville; Aaron used to come hear us too. K-Doe would always speak to us and tell us how he enjoyed our singing. He would tease us and say, 'I'm glad you're not in the R&B field, strong as you guys are,' stuff like that. Ernie K-Doe was a nice guy. Every time we saw him, he always had a big smile; he'd shake your hand, laugh and talk with you like he been knowin' you forever." With a preacher's consciousness and cadence, Ligon assessed "Mother-in-Law" as much more than a novelty song: "Ernie K-Doe made a record in a message kind of a way. Mother-in-laws play a great part in their daughters' marriages. A man has to get along with his mother-in-law whether he likes her or not. Ernie K-Doe showed men that they have to try to make the best of it—otherwise things are gonna be rough!"

Andre Williams, who produced "I'm Sorry," confirmed that Joe Ligon did not sing on it, but that "at least three of the other guys from the Mighty Clouds did. I asked them to do it because the song had such a spiritual feel and I thought they'd add the perfect type of background. Joe Ligon couldn't make it for some reason, so I sang his part. And, yes, that is a banjo that you hear on there; there aren't many banjos on R&B records. But I have always been the type of guy—'Give me something different.'"

Williams had come to Duke from Chess Records in 1969 to be Don Robey's new A&R man. He arrived in Houston with impressive credentials: successful records of his own, including the comedic recitations "Bacon Fat" and "The Greasy Chicken," and a cowriting credit on the Five Du-Tones' 1963 hit "Shake a Tail Feather." "Ernie K-Doe was due for a release," Williams said, "and I didn't want to miss the rotation, even though I had Bobby Bland in mind for 'I'm Sorry.' Bobby was on the road, so I had K-Doe sing it. But I did studio work with Bobby too; I produced his album *The Soul of a Man*."

Like K-Doe, Andre Williams experienced early success, hard times, substance abuse, and redemptive late-career resurgence. He understood K-Doe's battles with personal demons: "Ernie was famous to the world but not to himself. He never considered himself as a star; he never thought he had made it. He was never satisfied. Something was missing. He didn't get to the Bobby Bland status. He only had the one big hit with 'Mother-in-Law,' and he could never repeat it. . . . K-Doe was an extremely nice guy, you could say a spiritual guy—clean living and clean cut. So it was a surprise to me later when he got so low with the alcohol, because that just wasn't him. And Ernie wasn't necessarily the smartest guy in the world, but he had scruples. I was glad to see him bounce back finally."

K-Doe's last record for Duke, the ebullient "I'll Make Everything Be Alright," appeared in 1970. Its arrangement drew on both the previous decade—the rhythm pushed by raw '60s protofunk guitar chords—and the swirling horns and strings that would typify the decade ahead, in soul and disco. This cutting-edge accompaniment showed that K-Doe could easily adapt to new settings. But it did not sell. In fact, only two of K-Doe's ten Duke releases actually entered Billboard's R&B charts, and neither one—"Until the Real Thing Comes Along" nor "Later for Tomorrow," with its unusual yet compelling waltz rhythm—rose past number thirty-seven. This was far too low a position to keep any record company happy, since sales figures always trump musical quality. When "I'll Make Everything Be Alright" failed to fulfill its promising title—as predicted, perhaps, by the title of its bland flip side, "Wishing in Vain"—Don Robey decided to cut his losses. And thus, after ten shots at success, Duke gave the Emperor the royal heave-ho.

CHAPTER 15: *The God with Two Heads*

K-Doe responded to being dropped by Duke Records by quickly rekindling his working relationship with Allen Toussaint. He signed a contract with Sansu Records, a label that Toussaint had founded five years earlier with business partner Marshall Sehorn. In short order Sansu had a K-Doe album ready for the marketplace, and Sehorn made a deal for its release with a New York–based label, Janus Records. Somewhere in this process the album was mistakenly entitled *Ernie K. Doe*, as if "K" was Ernie's middle initial.

Released in 1971, *Ernie K. Doe* matched, and in some ways surpassed, the quality of previous Toussaint-K-Doe collaborations. It had the seamless feel of a fully realized, meticulously crafted new project. Such cohesion suggested that the album had been thoughtfully conceived all of a piece. In reality, *Ernie K. Doe* was a random compilation of songs recorded for various labels and production companies owned by Toussaint and Sehorn. When shown its cover forty years later, Toussaint's surprised comment was "I've never seen this before!" It had been Sehorn who assembled the album and found a willing taker. Even though Toussaint was quite familiar with the songs, he'd had no role in its patchwork configuration.

K-Doe clearly reveled in the strong songs and masterful arrangements Toussaint created for him. Both men were in their prime when the album was released, at age thirty-four and thirty-two, respectively, and the rapport from their Minit collaborations remained obvious. Yet both had changed, too, during the seven years since they'd last worked together. K-Doe now sang at a noticeably lower pitch than on his Minit sides, marking the

***ERNIE K. DOE* ALBUM**
1971
Photography by Joel Brodsky
Courtesy Billy Delle

ERNIE
K.
DOE

transition from his twenties to the cusp of middle age. Toussaint, while staying firmly grounded in R&B, now wrote, arranged, and produced with markedly more sophistication and complexity. The lead track on *Ernie K. Doe*, for instance, "Here Come the Girls," begins with a military parade beat that quickly segues into syncopated funk, with one of the most intricate horn charts of Toussaint's career to date. This blend of polyrhythm with sophisticated harmony epitomizes the Afro-Caribbean-European synthesis that so strongly characterizes New Orleans music. These same elements had converged in the evolution of New Orleans jazz in the late nineteenth century. But the complex syncopation of "Here Come the Girls" was also futuristic. It presaged, for instance, Toussaint's landmark arrangements for Dr. John on the hit single "Right Place, Wrong Time" in 1973, and then the brilliant album *Desitively Bonnaroo* in '74.

The second song, "Back Street Lover," also delves into New Orleans traditions, with a horn-section intro that evokes a jazz-funeral dirge. Then it leaps into swaggering second-line funk driven by percussive guitar chords. "A Place Where We Can Be Free," with an upbeat bass line similar to Otis Redding's "Can't Turn You Loose," maximizes the contrast between K-Doe's rough-edged lead singing and Toussaint's delicate, almost ethereal background vocals. (Lee Dorsey also recorded "A Place Where We Can Be Free," possibly using the very same instrumental track as K-Doe, but the Emperor's rendition is far more emotionally convincing.) The album's pace then slows with the wry tearjerker "Whoever's Thrillin' You Is Killin' Me"—a title that underscores Toussaint's skill at wordplay. (This same era found him writing a song for Lee Dorsey entitled "Who's Gonna Help Brother Get Further?") There is nary a dud among *Ernie K. Doe*'s six ensuing numbers, and expert sequencing makes them flow smoothly, with no abrupt transitions.

Janus Records took its name from a Roman god with two faces that look in opposite directions. Likewise, K-Doe shows two faces on his Janus album: serious and silly. He reveals his escalating eccentricity on a remake of Danny White's "Kiss Tomorrow Good-bye." Conventional renditions of this poignant midtempo song climax with the band laying out for a brief dramatic pause, followed by an a cappella reprise of the title phrase. But instead of simply singing, "So you can kiss . . . tomorrow . . . good-bye!" K-Doe fills this unaccompanied interlude with a seemingly endless array of smooching sounds, lip smacks, and sonic approximations of tonsil tickling. When the band finally comes back in—probably feeling like the ten-second interval lasted for hours—they have to cut K-Doe off in midslurp.

Supplementary saliva and all, vinyl copies of the *Ernie K. Doe* album are now valuable collectors' items, but the album did not sell much when it was first released. Two factors contributed to its commercial failure. The first problem was bad reviews. Reflecting a rigid purist mentality regarding American roots music—a common perspective in Europe—the respected British magazine *Blues Unlimited* complained that the "distinctive sound of the city just isn't here. . . . The whole thing is a lifeless bore." Other critics agreed, and still do today. More significantly, Janus Records had an improbably eclectic roster, which may have put great demands on the time and expertise of its promotional staff. This also may have meant that some records simply weren't promoted at all, a frequent complaint among recording artists. Artists signed to the label included the British nouveau skiffle band Mungo Jerry, of "In the Summertime" fame; the Anglo-Caribbean funk band Cymande; and the Canadian pop singer Ian Thomas, a Neil Young sound-alike best known for "Painted Ladies." Janus did not commission or produce all of its releases. Instead it often acquired finished albums from a wide variety of other parties, such as Marshall Sehorn's deal for *Ernie K. Doe*, and England's Pye Records' deal for Mungo Jerry. K-Doe was Janus's only New Orleans artist, and the company was probably clueless about how to promote the two K-Doe singles it released—"Here Come the Girls"/"A Long Way Back Home," in 1971, and "Lawdy Mama"/"Talkin' 'Bout this Woman," the following year. Still, Janus did have some history of working with erstwhile hit makers, including a late-career release by rockabilly pioneers Bill Haley and the Comets. Marshall Sehorn may have convinced the company that "Mother-in-Law" lightning could somehow strike twice.

Following the one-shot deal with Janus, K-Doe cut two singles for release by Sansu. The first one, released mid-decade, paired "Stoop Down"—a loose assemblage of risqué traditional blues verses heard in many other songs—with the ballad "You Got to Love Me." The lyrics to the latter strung together the names of K-Doe's favorite soap operas, based on his oft-mentioned love of "watching my stories":

> You not on the *Edge of Night*,
> And this ain't the *Guiding Light*
> This not the *Secret Storm*, baby,
> And you not playing on *As the World Turns*,
> But you got to love me, love me, love me, love me, baby!
>
> . . . Only have *One Life to Live*,
> Love you all the *Days of Our Lives*,
> If you get sick I'll take you to *General Hospital*, baby,
> And you really don't have to *Search for Tomorrow*—this why:
> But you got to love me, love me, love me, love me, baby!

A decade later, when spinning this record on the *Ernie K-Doe Show*, the Emperor would often break in on his own line about *General Hospital* to scream, "FOOL, YOU BETTER TAKE HER TO CHARITY!"

K-Doe regularly referenced soap operas on his radio show, inevitably connecting them to the biggest star in his firmament: Ernie K-Doe. "One thing I'm so glad to say is that I represent New Orleans. New Orleans is one of the best cities in the world. If you look at your television today, or you go to the movies, all they mention is New Orleans. The daytime stories—*The Edge of Night, The Guiding Light, The Secret Storm, As the World Turns, All*

the Days of My Life, General Hospital—they always mention New Orleans! New Orleans put a whole lot of cities on they feet. Until we meet again, you have been listening to the *Ernie K-Doe Show*, Mr. Ma-Naugahyde-Thuh himself, bar none and bow down to none, and God knows I'm great!" Some two decades later, the cast of *The Guiding Light* came to New Orleans on a post-Katrina relief tour. Their charitable sojourn included a visit to the Mother-in-Law Lounge. Much like Ernie, Antoinette K-Doe usually hid her more tender emotions behind a tough exterior. But when the soap opera entourage arrived, she unabashedly wept with joy.

The second Sansu single paired the generic funk of "Hotcha Mama" with a rare K-Do-evian interpretation of country music. K-Doe sounds quite comfortable and convincing on Conway Twitty's "(I Can't Believe) She Gives It All to Me." The choice of a country song, though atypical, was not really far-fetched. Twitty's soulful vocal phrasing was always stylistically compatible with R&B—in fact, one of his last recordings was a duet of "Rainy Night in Georgia" with Sam Moore of the '60s duo Sam and Dave. This cultural exchange went both ways, as K-Doe was known to unleash, on occasion, a mean version of Hank Williams's ode to Cajun culture, "Jambalaya (on the Bayou)." Ever the loyal Louisianian, K-Doe would sing this when sitting in with, say, zydeco accordionist Geno Delafose at New Orleans's MidCity Lanes, aka the Rock 'n' Bowl. (A similar guest appearance was planned with the Cajun-country band the Hackberry Ramblers, although a scheduling conflict kept it from fruition.)

The Emperor's familiarity with the Cajun-zydeco idiom came partly from his familial roots in Pointe Coupee Parish and his performances in the broader reaches of south Louisiana, where some people still speak Cajun or Creole French. Joe Citizen, a *frottoir* (rubboard) player in zydeco bands, recalled seeing "K-Doe perform at Bradford's White Eagle in Opelousas. K-Doe's music was highly liked around here. Bradford's would book musicians like K-Doe, Lazy Lester, Slim Harpo, Big Joe Turner, Bobby Bland, B. B. King, Fats Domino, and Earl King. The zydeco bands played out in the country in places like Lawtell. . . . I knew the Kador family. I worked construction with several of Ernie's relatives and we'd always talk in French. Living on a farm, way out in the country, we grew up on that French 'la-la' music and zydeco, but we loved blues and R&B too." R&B and zydeco have been closely related since the late 1940s, when Clifton Chenier started playing the latest R&B hits on his accordion while singing the lyrics in French. More recently, "Mother-in-Law" has been covered by zydeco artists such as Rockin' Dopsie Jr.

Only one other K-Doe single was released during the ten years he was signed to Sansu: "So Good to Me" / "Let Me Love You," which was licensed to the British label Island in 1975. Island rose to fame by helping bring Jamaican reggae to mainstream American audiences. The company also played a major role in the late-'60s British rock scene, signing such popular bands as Fairport Convention, Jethro Tull, and Free. But Island did not work extensively with R&B, and thus, like Janus, it was an unpromising match for Ernie K-Doe. Though K-Doe's performances were typically spirited, these two songs

K-DOE DOING MIC TRICKS, NEW ORLEANS
1971
Photo by Debbie Fleming Caffery

are quite routine—except for one classic couplet on "Let Me Love You": "I haven't been to Paris, just to see the Eiffel Tower, / But every time my woman spread her wings, this man got to love her for hours and hours!" The song is attributed to Marie Monley, but its actual authorship is obvious.

In a frustratingly familiar pattern, "Let Me Love You" didn't sell, and K-Doe left Sansu in a huff. "How can you be a popular performer," he asked Jeff Hannusch, quite reasonably, "when a record company won't put records out on you? . . . That killed me. I found out they were using me as a tax write-off. . . . Ernie K-Doe ain't no loser. I demanded my release when I found that out." In 1980, after five more years of inactivity, K-Doe and Sansu officially parted ways.

CHAPTER 16: *I Taught Him How to Play*

In 1972 the now-defunct New Orleans alternative weekly *Figaro* ran a feature on Ernie K-Doe written by Jon Newlin. Newlin, who went on to ensconce himself in the local literary pantheon with *Geopsychic Wonders of New Orleans*, evoked K-Doe's compelling persona with considerable flair of his own: "In conversation, K-Doe is remarkably articulate and ebullient, employing colorful metaphors and giving forth with a jive-Decameron unparalleled in my much-talked-to experience. . . . K-Doe sang an amazing number of songs in the two sets I heard—everything from 'A Certain Girl' to 'Moonlight in Vermont,' from 'Down by the Riverside' to [the Drifters'] 'There Goes My Baby.' It was almost a dizzying progression. . . . 'Only the strong survive,' says K-Doe, 'It's like a storm—if you're weak, you're beat. The ship has to drop the sails and ride the storm.'"

But what loomed on K-Doe's horizon was an antistorm, a lengthy lapse into limbo that would last throughout the 1970s. At thirty-six K-Doe had outlived the first blush of youthful acclaim but was still too young for elder-statesman gravitas. This unwanted relegation to the doldrums was interspersed with bursts in the limelight, after which K-Doe would quickly fade back into obscurity. On May 14, 1973, for example, K-Doe sang at an after-concert party for Led Zeppelin held at Cosimo Matassa's studio. Other performers included Allen Toussaint, Lee Dorsey, Earl King, Professor Longhair, Roosevelt Sykes, and the pianist Willie Tee (Wilson Turbinton), whose repertoire ranged from funk adaptations of Mardi Gras Indian chants to avant-garde jazz. A photo from the party shows K-Doe in animated conversation with Jimmy Page and Robert Plant, who hang onto the Emperor's every word. As a teenager, Plant had purchased a 45 of "Mother-in-Law" with money earned on his newspaper delivery route. He played it so often that his overwrought mother unplugged the family's gramophone.

"I was intoxicated by the sound of New Orleans," Plant told Keith Spera, music critic for the *Times-Picayune*, "by the way that a 12-bar blues would resolve, the way that the piano would have these little tags, which are classic New Orleans tags. I never guessed at

(FROM LEFT) JIMMY PAGE AND ROBERT PLANT OF LED ZEPPELIN WITH K-DOE
May 14, 1973
Photos by Sidney Smith

the age of 14 that by the time I was 21, I'd be actually raging around New Orleans, looking for clues. But that's how it turned out. . . . When I got here, I realized that the culture was just so radically different than anything else I could imagine in the whole of the United States. It was a different country, really. I was very impressed. I started reading up on it. I could feel something different here, something that was still alive, that hadn't been too Americanized and too messed with. Way beyond that, I found it exotic, frightening, a little bit intimidating. Mostly I felt quite ignorant. That didn't stop Led Zeppelin from having the greatest parties on Earth, with Earl King, Ernie K-Doe, Professor Longhair, the Meters . . . by the time we finished doing a gig here and taking a day off, most people would have to go into a rest home for a month to get over it."

Simply meeting such New Orleans legends would have made any evening memorable for Page, Plant, and company, who were all blues and R&B connoisseurs. But this particular night became indelibly etched in Led Zeppelin lore thanks to a salacious incident that occurred in the wee hours. Bassist John Paul Jones picked up a woman in a French Quarter bar and brought her back to his room. They fell asleep while smoking marijuana and set the bed ablaze. When the fire department arrived, the couple's state of dishabille revealed that Jones had actually snagged a transvestite, in the best Patsy Vidalia tradition. The other members of Led Zeppelin ribbed Jones, memorializing his bawdy blunder by recording a song entitled "Royal Orleans" in honor of the hotel where it happened. The song was released in 1975, to Jones's great displeasure. A consultation with Bobby Marchan would have saved him lots of trouble.

Ernie K-Doe rubbed shoulders again with the Brit-rock world when Paul McCartney visited New Orleans during the winter of 1975. The former Beatles bassist came to town to record the album *Venus and Mars* with his band Wings. McCartney hired Allen Toussaint to produce the project. In recent years Toussaint had expanded his scope beyond New Orleans music and musicians. Demand for his services increased significantly after he wrote arrangements for the Band's albums *Cahoots* and *Rock of Ages*, in 1971 and '72, respectively. The following year saw Toussaint and Marshall Sehorn open their new recording studio, Sea-Saint, in New Orleans's Gentilly neighborhood. There, in 1974, Toussaint produced the number-one hit "Lady Marmalade" for the R&B vocal trio LaBelle. "Allen is slow as all get out," Patti LaBelle recalled fondly; "slow and thorough. He took time to make sure that everything was perfect. I'm a fast-paced person and I can't sit around. But after Allen was finished, I realized that the wait was worth it."

A celebrity in such demand as Paul McCartney might well have sequestered himself to work undisturbed. But, as Toussaint commented, "When Paul was here he tried to connect with lots of people in the music community. He stayed for quite a while and he made his rounds. Paul was extremely generous. He pulled out all the stops and rolled the red carpet out for everyone." Sidney Smith, McCartney's official photographer during the six-week session, remembered that "people like Professor Longhair, Earl King, Benny Spellman, and Ernie K-Doe would come to the studio quite a bit. And McCartney welcomed them; it's not like they were hangers-on." As a group that started out playing rock and R&B cover songs, the Beatles were well versed in New Orleans material and particularly admired Fats Domino, Clarence "Frogman" Henry, and Larry Williams. They had picked Frogman Henry as the opening act for their first American tour and recorded Williams's original songs "Bad Boy," "Slow Down," and "Dizzy Miss Lizzy." This was quite a beneficent gesture for a group that wrote its own hit songs. Since Beatles albums sold extremely well, Williams earned a considerable amount of songwriting royalties.

Though McCartney made himself remarkably accessible to local musicians, he managed to keep the press at bay for most of his visit. Shortly before leaving town, however, he invited the local and national media to a party that he hosted on the riverboat *Voyageur*. "What we're doing now," McCartney told *Rolling Stone*, "is combining work, cutting an album, and doing the tourist bit. It gives you a sense of adventure. . . . We came here to see Professor Longhair." The party was described in some detail: "McCartney spent the muggy night out on the bayou with the cream of contemporary New Orleans music: Robert 'Barefootin'' Parker, Earl 'Trick Bag' King, Lee 'Workin' in the Coal Mine' Dorsey, Ernie 'Mother-in-Law' K-Doe . . . Clarence 'Frogman' Henry, Allen Toussaint, the Meters, a band called Chocolate Milk, and Paul's longed-for Professor Longhair. . . .

"During the more than five-hour cruise/party, the Meters and Chocolate Milk performed, but it was not long before McCartney and Wings joined the Meters and Ernie K-Doe in a rendition of 'I Want to Hold Your Hand' ('quite unlike the 1963 original,' one observer reported), followed by a tryst with 'Come Together' . . . and a wrapup soul medley as the ship steamed back to the Canal Street dock." K-Doe and McCartney were photographed singing together on the *Voyageur*; the shot, by Sidney Smith, appears in *The Rolling Stone Illustrated History of Rock and Roll*. According to Smith, McCartney also had the party filmed.

A month later, Ernie K-Doe was McCartney's guest at a second gala evening. This soiree, held in California, celebrated the completion of *Venus and Mars*, which McCartney had mixed in Los Angeles. *Rolling Stone* again deemed the event newsworthy, running this account: "Another day, another party: Linda and Paul McCartney gave a 'Leaving Los Angeles' party March 24th—in Long Beach, where the *Queen Mary* is docked. They were celebrating the completion (mixing) of their album, *Venus and Mars Are Alright Tonight*, begun in New Orleans in January. Guests included Bob and Sarah [*sic*] Dylan, George Harrison, Carole King, Joni Mitchell, Linda Ronstadt, Cher, Marvin Gaye, Harry Nilsson, Helen Reddy, David Cassidy, José Feliciano, John Mayall and members of Chicago, America, the Faces . . . Plus, of course, the usual quota of novelty guests: Rudy Vallee, Tony Curtis, Dean Martin and Karl Malden. Plus—of *course*—Tatum O'Neal. The McCartneys flew in a contingent from New Orleans as guests and entertainers: Ernie K-Doe, Allen Toussaint and Lee Dorsey, among others, partied; Professor Longhair and the Meters performed. The theme was the bayou and the food included gumbo pie, hurricane punch and a pea soup made from Linda's own recipe."

Professor Longhair's set was recorded and eventually released, by Harvest Records, as the album *Live on the Queen Mary.* As for Ernie K-Doe—never one to be starstruck by anybody but himself—there seemed to be some confusion as to just who had invited him. K-Doe always referred to the former Fab Four bassist as "Paul MacArthur." Then, with paternal, regal nonchalance, he would add, "That boy with the Beatles—I taught him how to play."

CHAPTER 17: *Mean Streets*

Times may have been tough, but Ernie K-Doe never dropped his game face. It became infinitely harder to maintain, though, in the wake of the horrendous tragedy that happened the day before the *Queen Mary* party in California. Back in New Orleans, a stray bullet hit K-Doe's nine-year-old son Kevin, killing him instantly. Presumably K-Doe could not be reached while traveling to Los Angeles and was not informed until after he had performed—it is hard to imagine that he could sing for McCartney while bearing the shock of such fresh, grim news. Ernest Kador Jr. recalled the calamity: "After my parents split up, we were living with my mother in the St. Thomas Housing Projects. My brother Kevin got killed there by accident, on March 23, 1975, because two gentlemen had a fight over a parking spot. They started shooting and Kevin got hit. Kevin was the youngest, him and his twin, my brother Keith. That was devastating. My mother tried to commit suicide several times, and my father was very angry. It took a lot of people to calm them down, because their child was gone, one of the babies of the family—and for him to be taken senselessly like that, over a parking spot. It was hard for my parents for a while; it was very hard for them."

Because of the frequency of such violent incidents in New Orleans, then as now, Kevin's death was simply lumped into a *Times-Picayune* article headlined 3 KILLED IN WEEKEND SHOOTING INCIDENTS. Several days later a news-analysis article pondered whether Kevin Kador and another child who had met the same fate on the same day were "killed by projects as much as bullets." There are no known public statements made by K-Doe, on air or otherwise, about his son's violent death. For a man who loved to talk at length on the radio—paying tribute to his parents, making general expressions of his love of children, and saying whatever else came to mind—this absence seems conspicuous. What's certain is that Kevin Kador's passing exacerbated K-Doe's drinking, which had already accelerated as his career began to falter.

With no new hit records and thus no national publicity, K-Doe found himself limited to a local performance circuit, in and around New Orleans, Baton Rouge, and Pointe Coupee Parish. He often used pickup bands, and his many varying accompanists included the Baton Rouge blues-harp blower Raful Neal and his guitar-playing son, Kenny. Kenny Neal recalled meeting K-Doe through his father when he was twelve or thirteen years old:

PARTY ABOARD THE RIVERBOAT *VOYAGEUR*
TOP LEFT
K-DOE WITH LEE DORSEY
TOP RIGHT
WITH PAUL MCCARTNEY
BOTTOM
WITH LINDA AND PAUL MCCARTNEY
March 24, 1975
Photos by Sidney Smith

K-Doe's brothers all lived in the same neighborhood, in Erwinville, across the river from Baton Rouge. His brothers Pete and June had played in my dad's band at one time, working joints like the White Eagle and Byrd's Satellite in Port Allen. There were K-Does, Kadors, all over this area, in Baton Rouge and West Baton Rouge Parish and on up into Pointe Coupee. I knew Ernie's daddy, too, Old Man K-Doe; he was a real gentle and kind guy, and a great singer and preacher too. He sang gospel.

Ernie's family was very proud of him for getting a hit record and being well known all over the globe. And that was exciting for all of us, not just his family, but all the people in the community. K-Doe always stayed tight with his family, and when he came around it was like the king coming into town. He'd have all of the flashy suits and a new car, and I've never seen so many diamond rings in my life! I was so impressed by the way he dressed when he came to the house to meet us—he made me realize that you *can* make a lot of money in this music business.

When I was in my dad's band I played a bunch of gigs with K-Doe, all out in the woods in south Louisiana. Juke joints. He used to have us way up in them bushes, but everywhere we played it was sold out. I would go to the gig with my dad, we'd get there early and sit in the car eating crackers and baloney sausage and sardines, waiting for K-Doe. My daddy would say, "We playin' with a big star tonight, we need lots of energy, we got to eat." We didn't always know if Ernie was going to show up or not that night; sometimes he was running late. And we didn't feel comfortable going inside before he got there because some of these places were white clubs, and we weren't sure we'd be welcome before we actually played. We'd be thinking, "Damn, how did K-Doe get *this* gig?" He would get gigs at places that my dad and I didn't even know existed, places that were really hard to find. I mean joints that were in the *sticks*.

Then K-Doe would show up, and we had to play all of his shit. Plus my dad would do some of his own songs, blues. That's two different styles—K-Doe could sing a down-home twelve-bar blues when he wanted to, but that wasn't his thing. His music had a lot more arrangements. He'd throw his show together real fast, but he always made it work. You should have seen him dance and move onstage with that mic; he would trip me out doing all those steps that James Brown and Joe Tex used to do. As a bandleader he was very demanding, but he gave it his all—he played a juke joint just like he was at Carnegie Hall. He was a nice cat to work with, he was down-home, and he paid good. He'd roll up them two twenties and a ten and stick them in my hand. Fifty bucks on a gig back in the early '70s was *a lot* of money, more than I expected.

K-Doe was starting to catch hell, as far as his career, when we were working with him. He could still pack the house at little clubs where everyone knew

K-DOE PERFORMING AT TIPITINA'S, NEW ORLEANS
1977
Photo by Michael P. Smith
©The Historic New Orleans Collection, 2007.103.1.651

him, but he was coming down off that international pedestal and I'm sure it hurt his pride. He was trying to hang onto his diamond rings and his cars. Eventually even those gigs played out, and he lost everything. I didn't hear from K-Doe no more for a long time, once things got bad for him. He would've ended up as just another wino on the street, or in the graveyard, if Antoinette hadn't saved him.

Kenny Neal's career took off in 1974 when he moved to Chicago to join Buddy Guy's band. K-Doe stayed put, kept scuffling, but still enjoyed occasional brushes with the big time. On July 16, 1978, he played an after-concert party in New Orleans for Bruce Springsteen's band, at a grubby backstreet venue called Acy's Pool Hall. It is not clear whether the Boss himself attended the show, but K-Doe was specifically chosen to entertain at the event, according to Robert Duncan, a writer on assignment for *Creem* magazine:

> By the time I arrived, the crew and band had decimated the Dixie beer, leaving only Miller and Pabst Blue Ribbon, and Ernie K. Doe and his pick-up band playing off in the corner have decimated the band and crew. Ernie K. Doe had his one and only hit record with 'Mother-in-Law' in the early 60's and until an intrepid advance scout from Springsteen['s] party unearthed him, had been living in relative obscurity like so many other greats of his era in New Orleans. As I walk in, Ernie K. Doe, dapper in a beige multivented suit over a dark open-neck silk shirt, every hair carefully pomaded into place, has run out of words to the song. But he doesn't want the folks to stop dancing, and is repeating "Well, all right" endlessly over the solid locomotive beat. When after a good five minutes Ernie K. Doe has run out of "Well, all right"s, he brings the music down and introduces the band—but not by name. "Let's have a hand for the man on the bass!" he shouts, and there's a round of applause. "Let's have a hand for the man on the drums!" and so on, until he gets to Clarence Clemons [Springsteen's longtime saxophonist], who is sitting in discreetly with his sax. I wonder. For all Ernie K. Doe knows, Clarence is just another guy who sauntered in off the street. Like I say, music is at least second nature to New Orleans. I listen carefully to his introductions. Without missing a beat, with not the slightest emphasis, Ernie K. Doe calls out, "Let's have a hand for the man on the tenor sax!" The locomotive beat continues. Ernie K. Doe falls silent (these party gigs get tired after a while) and then while the steady semi-drunk dance floor continues to bop, Ernie K. Doe goes through the introductions (one more time!) for want of something better. "Let's have another hand . . ." Clarence Clemons plays on discreetly, diligently, strictly "the man on the tenor sax" playing for the love of rock 'n' roll.

K-DOE PERFORMING AT THE NEW ORLEANS JAZZ AND HERITAGE FESTIVAL
1978
Photo by Matt Anderson

As the '70s rolled on, K-Doe continued to reinforce his increasingly spacey reputation. Reggie Scanlan, bass player for the New Orleans rock band the Radiators, described his own encounter with K-Doe at that time:

> I grew up here, and I heard Ernie K-Doe's records on the radio all the time. I figured that this was what everyone around the country listened to. Later I came to realize that it was only popular in New Orleans. And when I got to work with K-Doe I realized that he was a *nut*. Eddie Bo used to have a club on Broad Street near Esplanade, called Eddie Bo's El Grande lounge. This was around 1978, when the Radiators were just forming. Back then I was also working with Professor Longhair, and James Booker too. So through Booker I got a call that Eddie Bo needed a bass player for Sunday evenings.
>
> Some kind of way, this house band got hired to play somewhere with K-Doe. So we're on the gig, and K-Doe kept yelling, "Break it down!" like a lot of blues and R&B guys do, meaning, drop the volume down real low, for dynamics. So we break it down until we're playing at a whisper, but K-Doe keeps telling us to break it down. At that point we all stopped playing, including the drummer too, finally. K-Doe was singing completely by himself, but he still kept yelling, "Break it down, band! Y'all break it down!" Even though nobody was playing a note. He was *out there*. I had a day job back then, and I'd come crawling in at seven a.m. after playing all night. One of the guys I worked with knew K-Doe from his neighborhood. When I told him whom I'd been playing with, he just looked at me and said, "K-Doe? K-Doe ain't nothin' but a popcorn!"

But far worse epithets than "popcorn" would fly—along with bullets—as the decade neared its end. Back in 1966, K-Doe had embarked on a long-term romance with a woman named Jessie James. A dozen years into the relationship, James accompanied K-Doe to Tipitina's, a popular New Orleans club named for a Professor Longhair song. K-Doe was cobilled for the weekend of August 25 through 27, 1978, in an R&B revue with his old cohorts Jessie Hill, Irma Thomas, Johnny Adams, Jean Knight, Gerri Hall, and Oliver Morgan. Professor Longhair appeared too, as special guest on the Sunday matinee only.

"So it was late that Sunday night, Monday morning really, and we were standing by the stage," Jessie James said in a surprisingly calm tone, "And all at once this lady walked up. She looked at me and said to K-Doe, 'That's your first lady?' K-Doe said, 'Yeah, that's my first lady,' and the next we know she pulled out a gun and shot me in my leg! She was fittin' to shoot me again, in my chest, but K-Doe knocked her down. Then she got up and ran out. The bullet went into my thigh, and the doctors didn't want to take it out because they thought I might be paralyzed. They took it out four months later. Some people put out the story that K-Doe had got shot by a girlfriend named Jessie James, because I have a

LEFT
POSTER FROM THE TIPITINA'S CONCERT AT WHICH K-DOE'S GIRLFRIEND JESSIE JAMES WAS SHOT
1978
Courtesy Sonny Schneidau

TOP RIGHT
JAMES, WITH BANDAGED BULLET WOUND

BOTTOM RIGHT
GET-WELL CARD FROM K-DOE TO JAMES
1978
Courtesy Jessie James

JESSIE HILL
RHYTHM & BLUES REVUE
Jessie Hill
Johnny ADAMS
Irma THOMAS
Gerry HALL ☆ Jean KNIGHT ☆ Ernie K-DOE
☆ Oliver MORGAN ☆
TIPITINA'S
501 Napoleon cor. Tchoupitoulas - Ph. 899-9114
FRI. & SAT. AUG. 25 - 26
10 P.M. 'TIL ?
Admission $5.00 At Door
Sun. Matinee - AUG. 27 - 7 P. M.
with Guest Star: PROF. LONG HAIR

Get Well Soon
Hope that you'll keep improving
Till you feel as good as new
And that nothing but the best of health
Will be in store for you!
To My Baby Love
Ernie K-Doe

famous name like that other Jesse James [the bank robber]. See, before I was with K-Doe, I was married to a man with the last name James, but I was born Jessie *Davis*. So it did not go like that. I did not shoot K-Doe. K-Doe's other girlfriend shot *me*."

The shooter turned out to be Little Marie, the mystery songwriter Marie Monley from K-Doe's Duke Records days. Arriving by cab, she had told the driver to wait at the curb. Then she walked in, did the deed, hopped back in the cab, and sped off. Monley later turned herself in and eventually drew a three-year sentence at the Louisiana Correctional Institute for Women in St. Gabriel. "I had no idea Marie existed," Jessie James said, concluding her discussion of the turbulent event. "K-Doe never told me nothin' about no Marie, and I didn't know nothin' about her. I had never seen her. And when I asked him, he said he had left her and they wasn't together. I didn't get mad at K-Doe. But my family blamed him for me getting shot."

This was not K-Doe's only close encounter with New Orleans's sadly commonplace violence. On November 12, 1981, he sustained a "minor" knife wound in a barroom brawl. "He was trying to break up a fight," Jessie James said matter-of-factly, "and someone cut him. Not too bad, and it didn't scare him. You see, K-Doe would *fight*. When we was in the Watering Hole on London Avenue, men would come around me, and he'd say, 'You better back off of my lady before I peel your skull!' We went to Gentilly once, in some club off Chef Menteur Highway, and someone stole his battery. K-Doe told everyone, the whole place, 'Whoever took that battery, I'm going in to take me a drink. And when I come out, that battery better be back in my car—or I'm going to peel *everybody's* skull in here!' We sat down for a half an hour, and when we walked out, would you believe that battery was back in his car? Boy, we laughed about that! But K-Doe always said, 'Whichever way you want me to be—I can be a nice guy, or I can be a thug.' And that's just how it was."

CHAPTER 18: *Irene, Get the Smellin' Salts!*

Ernie K-Doe could be loud, verbose, and at times visibly unhinged. His colleagues knew this all too well, as did the loyal fans who came to see him perform. Those New Orleanians who did not enjoy K-Doe's eccentricity usually managed to tolerate him. But K-Doe could go too far, as he did at the funeral of Professor Longhair. Longhair (also known affectionately around town as Fess), passed away unexpectedly on January 30, 1980. He died on the brink of a major late-career resurgence. Filming was in progress for a documentary—Stevenson J. Palfi's *Piano Players Rarely Ever Play Together*—featuring Professor Longhair, Allen Toussaint, and the venerable Tuts Washington. In addition, his highly anticipated new album, *Crawfish Fiesta*, was being shipped from the pressing plant to record distributors when the sad news came.

Between Fess's career momentum and his stature as a hometown icon, his funeral sparked a media frenzy. Ernie K-Doe did have a long and sincere friendship with Professor

Longhair, so his death represented a significant personal loss. But, as a man with no visible career prospects, K-Doe also sought to work the well-connected crowd and possibly leave with a record deal. Jerry Wexler of Atlantic was known to be attending. Wexler had recorded Fess in 1953 and forged the R&B careers of Aretha Franklin and Wilson Pickett, among others, during the following decade. Bruce Iglauer of Alligator Records—the producer of *Crawfish Fiesta*—was also in K-Doe's ambitious sights.

K-Doe told Rick Coleman that "Miss Byrd asked me to speak over Professor Longhair at his wake and his funeral, and a whole lot of people, black and white, told me, 'Man, you missed your calling.'" But Iglauer remembered K-Doe's preaching quite differently: "Lots of musicians came up and did a song in memory of Fess. Toussaint did that lovely piece that was in *Piano Players*. Jerry Wexler and I were sitting close together at the front, and when K-Doe came up, we realized that K-Doe was auditioning for the two of us and basically refused to come down. Everyone was pretty irritated at his grandstanding and trying to use Fess's death as a launching pad." Jonathan Foose, an avid K-Doe admirer, agreed with regret, saying that K-Doe "went into a long and, I thought, out-of-place speech."

But if K-Doe was out of line at Fess's funeral, he fit right in on WWOZ. When he hit the airwaves in 1982, a whole new audience was exposed to his streams of consciousness. The station was founded in 1980 by Walter and Jerry Brock, two brothers with a love for community radio and south Louisiana music. The station gave them an outlet for both passions. One of the first popular DJs heard on WWOZ was Vern Dugas, aka the Duke of Paducah. Dugas borrowed this moniker from a country musician and comedian immensely popular in the 1930s, whose loopy refrain was "I'm goin' back to the wagon, boys, these shoes are killin' me!" But New Orleans's incarnation of the Duke of Paducah favored rhythm and blues rather than country. He and his cohost—his wife, BeBe—spun New Orleans R&B classics and interviewed many of the artists who had originally recorded them. "*Everybody* wanted to be on Duke's show," Jerry Brock said, "and we loved the idea of having musicians on—first as guests, and then as DJs too. Art Neville ended up hosting his own show, and then around '82 or '83 we gave K-Doe one." Brock continued, "[K-Doe] was drinking heavily at the time, but he could still maintain. He was always clean, never raggedy. More than once, though, I saw him chug a fifth of vodka before he came on the air—all those drinking jokes and drinking sound effects that he would make during the show—'glug, glug, glug, chug-a-lug!'—those were pretty close to the truth." (One of the most revealing such on-air remarks was "Hey kids, I got to get me a drink, that's the only way I can perform.") "But even with [the drinking] he still did a great job," Brock added. "K-Doe never really learned how to run the mixing board, though, so we'd get someone to engineer for him. And whoever it was would end up turning K-Doe's mic off at certain points because he never quit talking. If the engineer was astute and knew when to bring him back in, like timing it with a solo on a record or something, then it worked out great."

One of those engineers was Steve Armbruster, a cofounder of Tipitina's. WWOZ had set up its first studio just above Tip's. For a time, in fact, live broadcasts were presented by simply lowering a mic into the music room via a hole in the ceiling. "I worked the board for K-Doe's show for three or four months," Armbruster remembered fondly:

> K-Doe was not one of those people who was obsessive-compulsive or anal retentive about the condition of his record collection. He'd carry in a big stack, and half of 'em weren't in the covers or dust jackets. He'd rush in at the last minute and get started. He was friendly but sort of remote in a way, business-like. He was very focused on the show. And he did a good job—he played great R&B and blues records, not just his own material, and he was very entertaining. If he'd been drinking, it was never noticeable.
>
> The only problem was his shout-outs to his friends. That got imbalanced. K-Doe would get wound up, and he'd start hollering to all his people—like, "Hey, Mel-VIN!" or "Where y'at, Meatball? Hey MEATBALL! Call me up BAY-bee!" Sometimes he'd do that every ten seconds, or yell stock phrases like, "Is it good to you baby?" and get into a dialogue with the lyrics of whatever record was playing. I made an editorial decision that the listeners would like to hear at least a *little* music, and so I'd fade him in and out. He would just keep talking, and I don't think he never noticed. Another reason I'd do that is because all of a sudden, out the box, K-Doe would start *screaming*. The needles on those volume meters would peg out, all the way to the right and all the way into the red, and then he'd sound distorted.

Such flouting of conventional DJ protocol attracted the attention of *Billboard*, which ran a lengthy feature on the Crescent City's airwaves on September 4, 1982. It began, "The New Orleans radio market can be summed up in three words: 'Does Not Apply.' If it works throughout America, it won't in New Orleans. In 1964, at the height of Beatlemania, the Fab Four actually lost money playing in New Orleans. Things haven't changed much since. In fact, it's best to treat this city as a foreign country. To a great extent it looks, reacts, and sounds like one."

Struck by New Orleans's determined insularity, reporter Rollye Bornstein cited several cases in point, climaxing with K-Doe: "New Orleans is home to some of the finest musicians in America, including the infamous Ernie K. Doe of 'Mother-in-Law' fame, and believe it or not, Ernie has a weekly radio show—Thursday nights 7 to 8:30 on public radio WWOZ 90.7. I heard it. I still don't believe it. . . . By far the most unique feature of this market is its localism. Never have I heard so many local accents and local references."

"Many nights after K-Doe's show," Jerry Brock recalled fondly, "I would give him a ride home and we'd stop at little bars near the projects on Washington Avenue. I will never forget the impression I had going into these places, of people treating K-Doe like

PROFESSOR LONGHAIR'S FUNERAL
February 2, 1980

TOP LEFT
K-DOE AS PALLBEARER (WITH QUINT DAVIS, FAR LEFT)
Photo by Jim Scheurich

TOP RIGHT
K-DOE OVER THE COFFIN
Photo by James Macaluso

BOTTOM
K-DOE OVER THE COFFIN
Photo by Jim Scheurich

he was a king! They loved him! Everything was on the house for him and his guests, everybody was coming up to him to shake hands and talk, and it was like he was still in his heyday. The general public loved his radio show too. K-Doe got WWOZ more press and publicity than any other DJ we had. And soon I realized that tapes of his show were going all around the world."

One such hot item was a broadcast from the summer of 1985 that found K-Doe promoting an upcoming appearance at the Morrocco Room, a bar in the small town of Lacombe, Louisiana, that K-Doe operated briefly with his girlfriend Irene. K-Doe downplayed his usual self-promotion to focus on his costar, the extraordinary singer Johnny Adams. Also known as the Tan Canary, the late Adams's tone, range, and phrasing suggested a hybrid of Aaron Neville, Jackie Wilson, Lou Rawls, and Ella Fitzgerald. But, lacking management and music-industry connections, this world-class artist remained virtually unknown outside south Louisiana.

K-Doe launched into his justified hyperbole about Adams during the fade-out to Adams's song "From the Heart," the title track of his debut album for Rounder Records. "Yes, yes, yes, Johnny Adams . . . 'As long as you love me, from the heart,' yes, Johnny Adams! Johnny Adams! John-NEE! Oh my goodness! . . . Johnny Adams is back on the road. New Orleans's own! Have mercy, mercy, mercy, Morrocco Room, MERCY! . . . Slidell! Mandeville! Pearl River! What you gonna do, Covington, Louisiana? It's gonna be an invasion, a Johnny Adams invasion!"

Suddenly, K-Doe began to argue with himself: "Shut up! Don't you know Johnny Adams is singin'?" scolded K-Doe 2. Instead of fighting back, K-Doe 1 changed the subject, musing, erotically, "I wonder if some lady is gonna bless me with just a little bit before Johnny Adams get there, before Johnny Adams gets to the Morrocco Room in Lacombe, Louisiana. Is she gonna give me a half a pound, a quarter of a pound, or a whole pound? Whatever she give me, I'm gonna get me some Saturday night! Johnny! I got to hurry up and get it before you get there, 'cause them girls gonna kiss on poor Johnny Adams and love him to death! Boy, we gonna have a wonderful time!" K-Doe 1 raved on en route to introducing a host of new characters—animal and human, famous and obscure, even inanimate objects magically brought to life. "Oooh, Johnny, Johnny Adams, oh Johnny, we gonna have them coming out of the woodworks! They ain't gonna have no dogs! No cats! The birds is gonna stop singing because the singing canary's coming to town. Saturday night is gonna be a mess! The star of the show—Johnny Adams! That's right! The costar of the show, yours truly, Ernie K-Doe, along with Mr. Tony *Coo*-zan, the only live Indian that ever sung the blues in history! God knows Custer is turning over in his grave by now. Tony Cousin—you better know this, girls, he is a real Cherokee Indian, too! A real live Indian? Um-hmmm!"

K-Doe paused for a moment to comment on one of his own records, "T'aint It the Truth," which just happened to be playing in the background: "K-Doe, go on and sing that thing, go on and *sing that thing*! That Burn K-Doe Burn Band—you got to see 'em to believe 'em and hear 'em to understand 'em! The first time I ever had my own band in my life! It's all over, y'all out there—I ain't gonna play nowhere without my band and my whole entire show. And guess what, I got a eleven-year-old boy on my show too. He gonna start traveling with me within the next two weeks. Little Eric. Oh, you got to see, them girls just kiss on him and grown women want to bite on his cheek, that Little Eric is something else! K-Doe all over again, *ree*-carnation. And guess what, girls—he is a Charity Hospital baby!"

K-Doe then lapsed out of character, momentarily, to issue an FCC-mandated station ID: "This is WWOZ radio station, 90.7 on your radio dial!" Legalities thus completed, he spun one hundred eighty degrees into a rant that, even by K-Doevian standards, comprised a torrential stream of consciousness: "I want you to always remember, what you do today, you might have to answer for tomorrow. Here is a young man that's gonna walk up to the microphone Saturday night, um-hmmm, he's gonna walk up there just as good—and Jerry Brock, I hope he don't straighten them long legs out, and Laura she just laughs at everything, that child is so sweet, she laugh at everything, need her in the White House with Nixon, maybe he might laugh and give the poor people some more money! 'Cause that's what we need—we need money, we don't need talk talk—talk later, give me the money now! But when Cherokee, a real live Indian—girls, y'all got to come out and see this Indian, Tony Cousin—he gonna walk up to the microphone Saturday night in Lacombe, Louisiana, at the Club Morrocco, and he gonna make 'em fall down to his knees; when he pick up that guitar and drop down, he gonna say *these words*."

At this juncture K-Doe started playing Tony Cousin's rendition of the old blues classic "Trouble in Mind," but, as the record spun, he never stopped talking: "Yes, yes, yes, yes, yes, yes, it's gonna be a mess, y'all! Oooh, it's gonna be a mess! The woods and the trees is gonna start dancing by themselves! Oooh, at the Morrocco Room, Morrocco Room, Morrocco Room, MORROCCO! Say what? Tony Cousin, Mr. Tony Cousin, Cherokee, oooh what he gonna do, what he gonna do?"

When Cousin reached the verse—"I'm going down to the river, gonna get me a rocking chair"—K-Doe shouted, "Oooh, come on now, come on, come on, come on and rock me away from here!" Then, as the song ended, K-Doe launched into a loud, heavily rhythmic, wordless imitation of a Native American war chant, followed by "That's what got y'all killed! 'Cause they could hear you coming! That's why Custer tried to kill y'all!" Still chanting, K-Doe picked a new record, "Going Fishing," by the St. Louis blues artist David Dee, which includes such lines as "I believe my hook's still good!" Plunking down the needle on this double-entendre ditty, K-Doe shot off in several simultaneous directions, talking over the music:

[K-Doe 1:] Yeah, they heard y'all coming! [more Indian chanting]

[K-Doe 2:] Look-a here, fool, shut your mouth up! I'm going up to the fish hook and I'm gonna take my rod out, and I'm gonna sling it out, and catch it, and put the right bait on the end of that thing! Hee hee hee! And guess what, y'all got to see the fish hook to believe it! But that White House—I'm gonna tell you more about the White House! Washington, DC, think they got the only White House, they got to be crazy! 'Cause I'm fixin' to go fishin'! I'm gonna throw my rod out—OH, THAT ROD IS LONG!

[K-Doe 1:] That ain't none of your business, boy, I come to fish! I'm gonna get me some fishes at the fish hook tonight! Burn, K-Doe, burn!

Abruptly stopping the turntable in midsong, K-Doe 1 shouted, "I don't want to go fishin' no more!" and suddenly switched to Freddie Jackson's slow, sexy "Rock Me Tonight (For Old Times Sake)," repeatedly interjecting "Is it good to you?" and no small amount of heavy breathing. Then, in a flash, he came back to hyping the gig at the Morrocco Room: "We on a big show with Tony Cousin, better known as Cherokee. We on a show with 'Crazy' Rick Allen and the Burn K-Doe Burn Band. That band play so gooooood! Let me tell ya something, it make you want to go *crawdad holin' in the mornin'*! Oh Lord have mercy! But this fellow here is the star of the show—I'm just one of the costars! Oooh, Johnny Adams gonna shake up that part of town; I don't think the mayor, I don't think the head juror, I don't think nobody in the world gonna realize: they talkin' 'bout the storm called [Hurricane] Bob—Bob can't touch Johnny Adams! When Johnny Adams get through walking up onstage at the Morrocco Room in Lacombe, Louisiana, and sing these words, Johnny Adams gonna walk up onstage and when he sing this, them women just gonna turn over the tables and just pass out! I-RENE! IRENE, GET THE SMELLIN' SALTS! GET THE SMELLIN' SALTS, 'CAUSE THAT'S WHAT YOU GONNA NEED!"

The rest of the Burn K-Doe Burn Band did not share K-Doe's enthusiastic anticipation of this gig. Organist Rick Allen—a stylistically diverse veteran musician (who has long since dropped the nickname "Crazy")—described the Morrocco Room as "a really trashed-out dump of a place. It was a black club, what we would call a Creole club here in Lacombe. Ernie and his girlfriend Irene tried their best to clean it up, but it was still a dump. I don't think that anyone but Ernie K-Doe ever played the Morrocco Room. I had put a good band together for him, and after four or five gigs at the Morrocco we got to the better venues just as fast as we could."

But who could blame Ernie K-Doe—who, as Kenny Neal recalled, "played a juke joint just like he was at Carnegie Hall"—for his boundless enthusiasm about the music at the Morrocco Room and his broader fixation on his erstwhile fame? As Herman Ernest observed, "I know some people thought K-Doe was crazy. But you have to realize that when you get to be a big star at a young age, that puts a warp on your mind. Once a person has experienced that, it's hard to just go back to being a regular working cat and don't never talk about when you had a hit. You're gonna still try to live it; in fact, some cats flip out from that. But if they're still around, still doing gigs, and can still pull off their shit—I say more power to 'em!"

TOP LEFT
(FROM LEFT) HARRY CONNICK JR., K-DOE, AND WWOZ DJ VERN "THE DUKE OF PADUCAH" DUGAS, NEW ORLEANS JAZZ AND HERITAGE FESTIVAL
ca. 1982–83
Courtesy Jessie James

TOP RIGHT
BUSINESS CARD FOR ERNIE AND IRENE'S MORROCCO ROOM
ca. 1985
Courtesy Rick Allen

BOTTOM
A FEATURE ON K-DOE'S RIVAL JAZZ FEST
Times-Picayune
July 5, 1984
Staff photo by Kathy Anderson

PHONE 641-3746
OR 882-3512

ERNIE & IRENE'S
Morrocco Room

LACOMBE, LA.

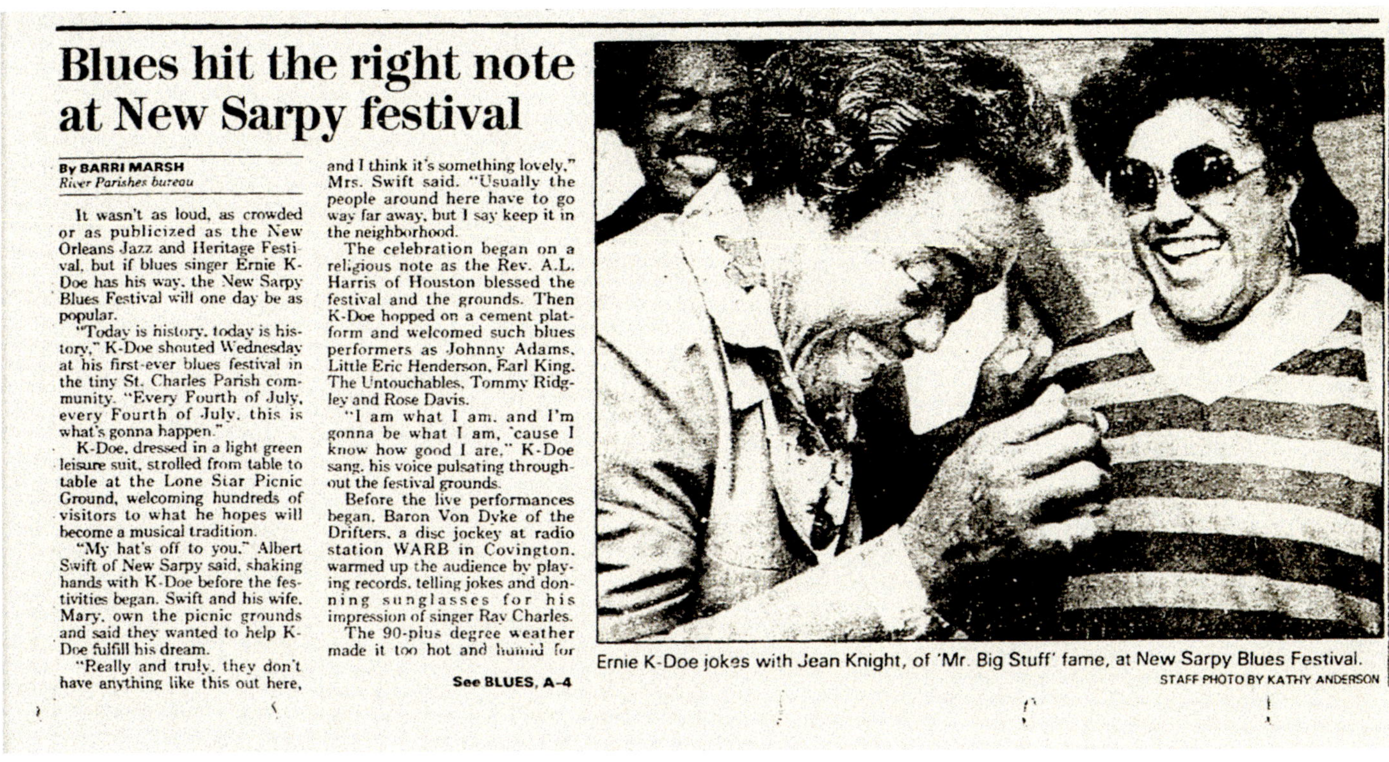

Blues hit the right note at New Sarpy festival

By BARRI MARSH
River Parishes bureau

It wasn't as loud, as crowded or as publicized as the New Orleans Jazz and Heritage Festival, but if blues singer Ernie K-Doe has his way, the New Sarpy Blues Festival will one day be as popular.

"Today is history, today is history," K-Doe shouted Wednesday at his first-ever blues festival in the tiny St. Charles Parish community. "Every Fourth of July, every Fourth of July, this is what's gonna happen."

K-Doe, dressed in a light green leisure suit, strolled from table to table at the Lone Star Picnic Ground, welcoming hundreds of visitors to what he hopes will become a musical tradition.

"My hat's off to you," Albert Swift of New Sarpy said, shaking hands with K-Doe before the festivities began. Swift and his wife, Mary, own the picnic grounds and said they wanted to help K-Doe fulfill his dream.

"Really and truly, they don't have anything like this out here, and I think it's something lovely," Mrs. Swift said. "Usually the people around here have to go way far away, but I say keep it in the neighborhood."

The celebration began on a religious note as the Rev. A.L. Harris of Houston blessed the festival and the grounds. Then K-Doe hopped on a cement platform and welcomed such blues performers as Johnny Adams, Little Eric Henderson, Earl King, The Untouchables, Tommy Ridgley and Rose Davis.

"I am what I am, and I'm gonna be what I am, 'cause I know how good I are," K-Doe sang, his voice pulsating throughout the festival grounds.

Before the live performances began, Baron Von Dyke of the Drifters, a disc jockey at radio station WARB in Covington, warmed up the audience by playing records, telling jokes and donning sunglasses for his impression of singer Ray Charles.

The 90-plus degree weather made it too hot and humid for

See BLUES, A-4

Ernie K-Doe jokes with Jean Knight, of 'Mr. Big Stuff' fame, at New Sarpy Blues Festival.
STAFF PHOTO BY KATHY ANDERSON

CHAPTER 19: *I'm Giving Away Diamonds!*

Perhaps the most highly sought recording of the *Ernie K-Doe Show* was made in late June 1984, when K-Doe announced that he was staging his own "jazz fest" to compete with the New Orleans Jazz and Heritage Festival. From then on, he told "everyone under the sound of [his] voice" that he would perform, instead, at his own Ernie K-Doe Mother-in-Law Blues Festival Picnic, in the small town of New Sarpy, just upriver from New Orleans. K-Doe had played the Jazz and Heritage Festival annually since 1973, the festival's fourth year, and he was featured on a live album recorded there in 1976. But he continually argued with festival producer Quint Davis regarding his pay. The mere mention of K-Doe's name elicited eye rolling at the festival office; several people would sing a two-line parody of "Mother-in-Law" that went "The worst person I know—Ernie K-Doe!" The accent was placed on the last syllable of his name to underscore the rhyme.

K-Doe boycotted the 1984 event because of this pay dispute, and because of a perceived slight in terms of scheduling. At the time, Jazz Fest had two components, one outdoors, one in-. The outdoor component made the festival famous—and has kept it in business since 1970, a remarkable achievement. Originally held in Armstrong Park, since 1972 the Jazz Fest has been held on the grassy infield of the Fair Grounds Race Course, a thirty-three-acre site. The festival also used to stage a series of evening concerts. (The latter segment was discontinued; now the entire festival takes place at the Fair Grounds as an outdoor, daylight event.) K-Doe objected to being scheduled for a daytime show. He found this al fresco venue demeaning. A man of his stature, he felt, should appear on evening concerts only—why not save the best for last? "I'm sick and tired of playing out in *the yard*!" K-Doe complained, even though many global headliners played there quite happily. No matter. Attempting to make his point, K-Doe staged his own event and promoted it relentlessly:

> Ernie K-Doe got one of the biggest shows that has ever happened in the state of Louisiana. Burn, K-Doe, burn, number one, Mr. Ma-Naugahyde himself, is giving the biggest festival that's ever been held in the state of Louisiana. I would like for all the Charity Hospital babies to come to New Sar-*pee* on the Fourth of July. I am the first black man in the state of Louisiana, with a period behind it, to give his own festival. Elvis Presley didn't do it, B. B. King haven't did it, Bobby Bland haven't did it, them people 'cross the seas haven't did it, named the Beatles, they haven't did it. But guess what? I'm a Charity Hospital baby, AND I DID IT! I DID IT!
>
> I'm giving away diamonds! You can take 'em to your jeweler or you can take 'em to my jeweler, BUT I'M GIVIN' AWAY DIAMONDS! DIAMONDS! AIN'T NOBODY DONE IT! Kool and the Gang, Zap, Gap, ain't nobody givin' 'em away,

the Commodores—ooooh I can just go on—Diana Ross, Sammy Davis Jr., Frank Sinatra, ain't nobody ever give diamonds away! I am the only one in the United States of America that's going to give away diamonds, and ain't ask you for a dime when I give it to you! You know, some people in the world has never had a diamond in they whole life, ain't never put they hands on a real diamond. You have a chance on the Fourth of July in New Sarpy. I'm not giving one or two or three or four or five or six, I done got happy and I'm givin' a *bunch* of 'em away! Some people say, "K-Doe, WHAT IS WRONG WITH THE BOY?" I say, "There ain't nothin' wrong with me—I just want to show the public HOW GREAT THOU ART!" On the Fourth of July, the mayor is coming down, and also my people tell me that the governor is gonna come because this is history—and I *love* to make history. And then October the nineteenth is Ernie K-Doe Mother-in-Law Day across the country.

In 1982 the US Congress did create a National Mother-in-Law Day, to be celebrated on the fourth Sunday of October—but K-Doe was not mentioned in the resolution.

K-Doe's rant then veered into a dialogue with himself:

[K-Doe 1:] But right now all I want to do is just spin records, and I'm gonna tell you more about the Fourth of July, hear?

[K-Doe 2:] Really?

[K-Doe 1:] Really! I am Burn, K-Doe, Burn! Number one, Mr. Ma-Naugahyde-Thuh himself, giving the biggest blues festival that's ever been held in the state of Louisiana. . . . But the most important thing, something that never happened in the state of Louisiana, that a black man give his own festival, and something that never happened in the United States of America with a period behind it—that an artist is still throwing away trinkets and cuff links! Elvis Presley didn't do it, he throwed away a few handkerchiefs and neck scarves and things; when the Beatles came here they didn't do none of this, you understand? Many, many more that you can name. Boy George, he don't throw away *nothin'*! Oooooh, on the Fourth of July it's gonna be a wonderful day, the Fourth of July is gonna be a *glorious* day! You dealing with the man this time and not the boy. . . . New Sar-*pee*! New Sar-*pee*! I am on my way! . . . [Y]ou gonna see things that you never saw before . . . I'm gonna be giving away big blue white diamonds—that's right—on the Fourth of July! Some people say, "Is he retarded?" or, "Has he gone crazy?" It's not none of that! I don't have the problem! *You* gonna have the problem if you don't be at the Lone Star Picnic Grounds on the Fourth of July for the Ernie Mother-in-Law K-Doe Blues Festival Picnic!

[K-Doe 2:] K-Doe, you gon' give away all them diamonds?

[K-Doe 1:] As fast as I can! The man above done blessed me and the people done stuck by me—why shouldn't I? . . . Burn, K-Doe, burn, with your bad self!

K-Doe suddenly turned contemplative, soft spoken: "it's a thing that happens to all great mens that reach that peak where things happen to them as they start digging into life. You know I sit down one day and I said, 'The world been good to me. I been all over the world twice and I enjoyed myself and I'm fittin' to go a third time.' But a rose that is pretty will wither away and die. You don't know *when* it's gonna happen, but you know it *will* happen." But the pensive moment quickly passed, and K-Doe raised the volume again: "The state troopers gonna ask them people, say, 'What is wrong with y'all tonight? What is wrong with y'all this morning?' And the people gonna tell them state troopers, say, 'Don't you know what's happening? You ought to pull your badge off, you ought to be in line with us, we goin' to New Sar-*pee* to the Lone Star Picnic Ground to see Ernie K-Doe. The man can dance, the man can perform!' And you see, on the Fourth of July, while I'm settin' history, every woman under the sound of my voice and every man under the sound of my voice, just come up and shake my hand, fellas, and every woman come up and give me a kiss, and you will get a chance to shake hands with all of my kids. I want all my kids to be there to see they father make history."

From this paternal sentiment, K-Doe's mercurial mind ricocheted from a passing thought of lust to shout-outs to his musical colleagues, a brief spell of messianic delusion, and, finally, to sincere reflection: "Sunday I *must* have me some! . . . The only one man I found that can go toe-to-toe with me—see, at one time it was five of us, but now it's only two of us left. When I speak about the Big Five it was Little Willie John, Joe Tex, Jackie Wilson, James Brown, and Ernie K-Doe. There's two of us left behind, that's Ernie K-Doe and James Brown! Once you go against us and you win, please believe me you will have a star in your crown!" The rockabilly pioneer Jerry Lee Lewis—a fellow Louisianan and equally shameless egomaniac—had a penchant for similar statements: "Y'know, son, there's only been four of us: Al Jolson, Jimmie Rodgers, Hank Williams, and Jerry Lee Lewis. That's your only four fucking stylists that ever lived."

"I learned my dancing by watching Sammy Davis Jr.," K-Doe raved on. "I learned how to act from the one and only Sidney Poitier. I learned how to have a heart and grab and take it and walk with it from Frank Sinatra. I learned from a young man who weighed only one hundred forty-five pounds, from the Five Blind Boys, Mister Archie Brownlee. I wouldn't say that the battalion is not good as the general that's in the front, but a battalion need the general to show them the way. *I am the way! Believe in me and follow me,* 'cause I can't keep that door open like I did in the early '60s as long as I did. . . . So we like for you to always listen to WWOZ where we play the best. . . . We be playing the records that everybody in the country like. It's just like a good pot of red beans and ham hocks or pigtails or whatever you want to say it—everybody want a piece of the pie, and if the pie is good, why not give them a piece? We making a little bitty station be bigger than what we are, because our American dream will come true! Twenty-two years I waited for this chance, and I did it my way! I did it everybody else's way before, and I failed, so if I go out now, let me go out smiling, my way. Thank y'all out there for sticking by Ernie K-Doe, *and I won't let you down*!"

CHAPTER 20: *No Officer of the Court*

The Ernie Mother-in-Law K-Doe Blues Festival Picnic got a nice front-page mention in the *Times-Picayune*: "It wasn't as loud, as crowded, or as publicized as the New Orleans Jazz and Heritage Festival, but if blues singer Ernie K-Doe has his way, the New Sarpy blues festival will one day be as popular." But only a few hundred people attended the event, and, not surprisingly, the career bounce K-Doe anticipated did not materialize.

As a public figure and a driven man who felt compelled, in Allen Toussaint's words, "to always be onstage, even when he was offstage," K-Doe rarely acknowledged any sense of doubt or defeat. For the most part he doggedly played the role of an undiminished star. This persona, which had a decidedly manic edge, often incorporated the upbeat facade of a clown. Conversations about K-Doe invariably cite his ability to keep people laughing. Even so, he would vent his frustrations on occasion: "Martin Luther King ain't the only one been to the mountaintop. I been there. It ain't sweet up there at the top. I'd rather be down in the valley." And, "A whole lot of people in the United States of America today is riding off of my money!" And, "I'd like to tell you all one thing that I found out for myself. I trusted some people. I fed them from my own pocket. I fed them with my own entertainment. I fed them because I had the talent! But you know what happened? My faith and my trust went just a little bit too far. I should have went back and checked up on them. But you see, *now*, some people say I'm hard to deal with—*yeah* . . . some people say I'm hard to get along with—*yeah* . . . But it ain't that! I done been to the mountaintop. I went to the mountaintop in nineteen and sixty-one! And I'm here to tell everyone under the sound of my voice: at the top is worser than at the bottom! People at the bottom can't do you no harm! But the ones at the top is trying to cut your throat, any kind of way, stab you in the back, whatever way they can do you. You know why? They think you crazy, they think you a fool because you tryin' to treat 'em nice. But one thing I'm gonna leave you with: he that believeth in me, yet so they will live. Burn, K-Doe, burn!"

K-Doe stewed for years about a perceived slight from Dick Clark, the music-business entrepreneur and host of *American Bandstand*. Clark never booked K-Doe, although many other artists with number-one records were summoned to lip-synch their hits on his nationally televised show. An appearance on *Bandstand* could spur even more sales and thus extend a song's tenure on the charts. Along with alleging racism, K-Doe claimed that Clark found "Mother-in-Law" offensive and controversial. In some renditions of this complaint, he even described a heated, face-to-face argument with Clark about the song's lyrics. This tale is extremely dubious but multiple retellings have firmly established it in K-Doe mythology.

The mere mention of Clark's name usually set K-Doe off. "I told that motherfucker, 'YOU BETTER PUT ME ON THE AIR!'" he shouted one night at the Mother-in-Law Lounge, just weeks before his death. In calmer moments K-Doe assessed the *American Bandstand* issue with reasoned detachment: "I'm going to put it in a nice, respectable way. Different people have different views of everything. If I was in Dick Clark's place at that particular time, some records I hear I would never play under no circumstances." But this comment, and the context in which it was made, did not apply to the music of 1961 so much as to 1990s rap and its four-letter words. K-Doe distanced himself from the use of foul language by explaining: "It's not what you say, it's how you say it—and whoever listenin' to it, it's the way *they* minds are goin'. You didn't say no obscene language or none of this. You get 'em right up to the point *and cut it off*!"

But even if "Mother-in-Law" had been filled with obscenities, K-Doe felt that Clark had no business being judgmental. "What I'm saying is this: to come [like I did] with a number-one record . . . but [Dick Clark thought], 'He's saying something I don't like'—it's not for an announcer or a narrator or a jock to say. What a jock is supposed to do with the record is *play it*! If the people like it, *play it*! If they don't like it, *pull it off*! . . . He thought that I was saying something bad, but all I was saying was the truth about mother-in-laws. Once you get married you will know what type of mother-in-law you have."

K-Doe then took a logical step, analyzing the racial politics of America in 1961 and the resulting impact on his career. K-Doe is not known to have actively supported the civil rights movement, in contrast to such committed colleagues as Sam Cooke. On a personal level, however, he embodied the sentiments expressed in James Brown's 1968 hit "Say It Loud—I'm Black and I'm Proud." K-Doe underscored his worldview by posting photos of African American icons, including Muhammad Ali and Martin Luther King Jr., on the walls of the Mother-in-Law Lounge. "Truthfully, I feel it in my heart—if I'm wrong you can have my apologies—but if I was a white boy at that particular time singing 'Mother-in-Law,' it would have been a tee-total disaster!" ("Disaster," in this case, meant an even bigger hit, and more attendant trappings of success.) "But I was a black boy coming out the heart of New Orleans. . . . If I was a white boy I'd have been in movies and everything, commercials, the whole bit." Joe Banashak of Minit agreed with K-Doe, grumbling that Clark would never play "Mother-in-Law," even though the TV host had to mention its title during the weekly countdown to number one.

The aging and ill Dick Clark was unavailable for comment. But Eddie Ray, a pioneering African American record executive and the national director of sales and promotion for Imperial Records when "Mother-in-Law" was released, summarily dismissed the story and its implications. "I don't think it was racism," said Ray. "I know Dick Clark very well. The thing is that 'Mother-in-Law' hit so quickly that we didn't need to do any national promotion tours. We got picks from stations all over, simultaneous airplay everywhere. I don't recall making an attempt to get K-Doe on *American Bandstand* because the record had broken open already. And we had already done well with a Minit record, Jessie Hill's 'Ooh Poo Pah Doo.'" In certain bleak moods, K-Doe felt profoundly cheated—by Clark, the record business, the legal system, the institution of marriage, and life in general. Accordingly, it seems unlikely that he would have been satisfied with Eddie Ray's explanation.

Once he was away from the public eye, K-Doe's manic side could swing one hundred eighty degrees into deepest despair. "K-Doe got *depressed*," Jessie James, with whom K-Doe was romantically involved for eighteen years, said sadly:

> Every time he used to go play, Internal Revenue was there to take his money, and K-Doe would get disgusted. He owed sixty-six thousand dollars in back taxes. He would tell me all the time, "Sometimes I want to know why the Lord keepin' me here." K-Doe was a guy that loved his music, but he got to where he didn't want to play his music no more. He was all depressed about the government taking everything away from him. He said there was bad bookkeeping and it wasn't on his account; he said he let people run his business and they run it all wrong. He always would tell me about it, losing his money, losing his house in Sugar Hill. Thinking about that is why he started going downhill. His dad would say, "When the boy had money I used to tell him to send some so I could buy real estate for him, but he wouldn't send a penny."
>
> See, when I met K-Doe in '66, he wasn't drinking bad. But through the years he would get more depressed. He'd just sit there, watch TV, sleep all day. He would feel sorry for himself; he even cursed the Lord because he didn't want to live. He never said anything about committing suicide, but he sure cursed the Lord, and I couldn't get that one. It was hard for me to be around that—that got next to me. One time when he was booked at the Jazz Fest he got rained out and he took it so hard, he took it personally. It was sad.

The situation continued to worsen, as James detailed: "Sometimes K-Doe got so depressed that he said he hated his music. He'd say, 'I don't even want to sing "Mother-in-Law."' When people booked him they wanted to hear his hits, but K-Doe would go there and act like James Brown or Little Richard, he would sing *their* songs but not *his*, be everybody but him*self*. Now, when I would be there with him on a show, he would do *his* show—so the people always wanted me to come, and they would send for me. Like Irma Thomas and her husband Emile, they used to book him. But if I was angry with K-Doe, then I wouldn't take him to the show. And if I didn't take him, then he might not go—he might miss it." Many venues essentially hired K-Doe to provide dinner music. He was

1982 or 83
K-DOE & wife

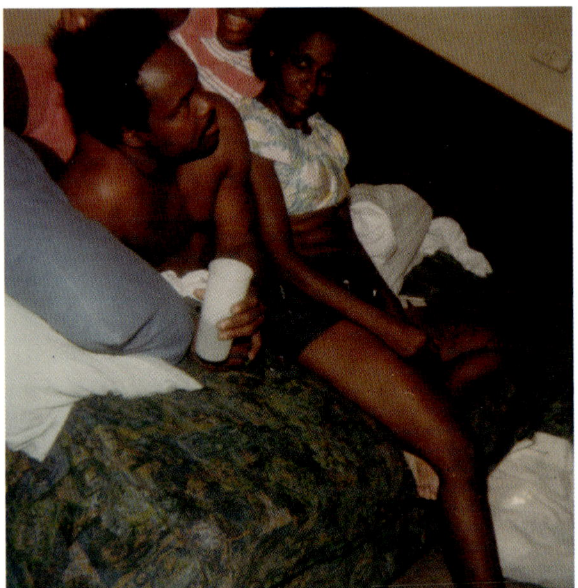

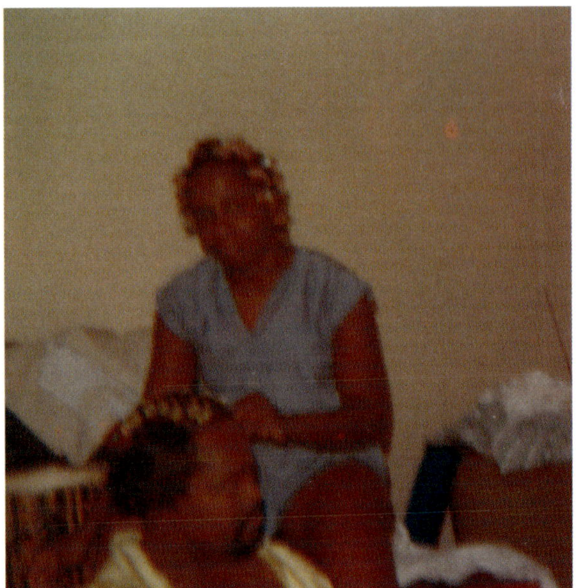

surely displeased when a 1983 newspaper ad touted the "$6.95 Luncheon Lobster" above K-Doe's name, and in bigger type.

As a responsible, hard-working woman, James could not tolerate K-Doe's unreliability. "He was driving me crazy with this," she said, "and finally we broke up, in 1984. By him not getting a steady job, I just decided that I had to move on with my life. I didn't mean a day job—I just wanted him to make his music gigs. And I would tell him, 'You can make a lot of money, a lot of people like you and your music.' Sometimes I got him to stop drinking, but then he'd go do a show out of town, and when he came back he'd be just as crazy. Whatever they did to him out of town I don't know, but he'd come back with no money, even though he had gotten paid good. K-Doe could not hold onto money. If he just would have settled down, we would have been alright. It was the drinking and the depression. He wouldn't go get any help. He always talked about he was a Charity Hospital baby, but he wouldn't go to Charity Hospital and tell them how depressed he was. He just wasn't getting it together. He wanted to get married, but I didn't think things were solid. I had been divorced and I just didn't want to get back into another marriage."

The depth of K-Doe's feelings for James can be gauged by a note, in his handwriting, on the back of a snapshot of him and James: "Ernie K-Doe + wife." This revealing inscription certainly belied K-Doe's brash statement, "I will never marry again! That's why I tell the whole world, if they waiting for Ernie K-Doe to get married again, I'll sing a song like when I used to sing in church: 'We shall meet on that beautiful shore'! Then I'll marry again 'cause I know they got [good women] there!"

James concluded, "Once I had decided, I had *decided*. It took me a long time to make up my mind before I felt I had to move on. I felt like I gave him every possible chance to straighten him up. I was the one who kept it all going. I had a day job, I was a foster parent, and then I had my own tailoring business; I had a shop. It was very hard to break up after eighteen years, and K-Doe took it *hard*; he was brokenhearted. He used to send his cousin Wolfman to talk to me, to try to get us back together, to take K-Doe back, but I wouldn't do it. I never regretted breaking up with K-Doe because I did everything I could and I gave him a lot of last chances."

Despite this domestic upheaval, 1984 saw K-Doe play one of his most high-profile and affirming shows in decades. New Orleans club owners had grown wary of taking chances with K-Doe. But few people outside New Orleans knew of his problems; out of town, K-Doe was still revered as an R&B luminary. Author, publicist, and promoter Bill Bentley—a music-industry veteran and longtime champion of New Orleans music—decided to bring K-Doe to Los Angeles. Bentley recalled:

> Late in 1983 I got the idea for doing a series of New Orleans shows at the Club Lingerie, in Hollywood. The series was called Friday Night in New Orleans. There was a huge group of New Orleans musicians in Los Angeles, centered around Harold Battiste, and we put together a house band called the New

TOP
K-DOE AND JESSIE JAMES AT THE FAIR GROUNDS RACE COURSE, NEW ORLEANS, AND K-DOE'S NOTATION ON THE BACK OF THE PHOTO
BOTTOM LEFT
JAMES AND K-DOE AT HOME
BOTTOM RIGHT
JAMES DOING K-DOE'S HAIR
ca. 1982–83
All photos courtesy Jessie James

Orleans Natives. We'd fly in a New Orleans artist, rehearse on Friday afternoon, and do the show that night. We kicked off the series with Lee Dorsey, then the next week was Johnny Adams.

To book K-Doe I had to go through Joe Jones, a guy from New Orleans who had moved to L.A. He'd had a big hit in the '60s with "You Talk Too Much." He acted as some artists' manager. We made a deal, and Joe wanted a deposit. He said, "Meet me on the corner of Hollywood and Vine with five hundred dollars in cash," which I did. Then, a week out from the show, I called Joe to check in, and he said he couldn't find K-Doe. This show was all set up, so I decided to go to New Orleans and bring K-Doe back with me.

I had an address on the contract, 2419 Derbigny Street, for K-Doe's aunt—Wolfman Washington's mother—but she had no idea where K-Doe was. Another act I'd been trying to book was King Floyd, and I couldn't find him either. But I had a number for King's brother, Cleon. Cleon Floyd said, "Man, I can find anybody for you, including dead people!" because he booked a band called the Living Dead Review, where the singer would jump out of a coffin and impersonate dead artists like Otis Redding. Cleon said, "I will call you back at midnight." He did, and he told me, "Meet K-Doe at the Colt 38, on Basin Street in Tremé, and make sure you bring the other five hundred."

When I got to the Colt 38, there was only one customer in there, and that customer was wearing a cowboy hat and a cowboy jacket with long fringes. I walked up and said, "Hi, Ernie K-Doe?" and he whispered, "Watch what you say—I'm working undercover!" Then he pulled out a badge and said, "I transport prisoners from Orleans Parish Prison to the courthouse. Prisoners aren't always happy about being prisoners and going to court. And, one day, prisoners get out!" Then he said, "OK, here's how it's gonna be, we will take the 6:30 a.m. flight and get to L.A. at 10:30 a.m. and check into the motel. That way when I leave to fly home the next afternoon, I will have had my full twenty-four hours in the room. Because some places make you leave before you've been there a full twenty-four hours. I have to have the room for a complete twenty-four-hour period!" And here K-Doe wasn't even going to be paying for it, but I said, "Whatever you want."

A few hours later we drove to the airport in a big Cadillac. K-Doe pulls out his badge at the ticket counter and whispers, "I am an officer of the court, and I have to board this flight." And the guy looks at him, says, "You ain't no officer of the court, YOU'RE MR. MOTHER-IN-LAW!" *Everybody* at the airport knew him. . . . K-Doe did not look healthy. His face was puffy, he drank the whole time, and I never saw him eat the whole trip. During the first set he was dragging. Then he did one of his splits and he could not get up. Jerry Jumonville had to help him.

K-DOE'S FORTY-FIFTH BIRTHDAY PARTY, WINNIE'S LOUNGE, NEW ORLEANS (JESSIE HILL ON TAMBOURINES)
1981
Photo by Michael P. Smith
©The Historic New Orleans Collection, 2007.0103.1.1017

MUZIK
& EVERY SAT

"I really don't remember doing that," Jumonville said. "But then, to me, it was no big deal to play with Ernie K-Doe. Those singers come up onstage, you don't really talk to them, you play their songs exactly like on their record, and then they split. He was just another singer. And I had already played with K-Doe, and *everyone*—Professor Longhair, Prince La La, you name them—in the '60s in New Orleans."

"I didn't think K-Doe would be able to finish," Bill Bentley concluded. "In fact, I thought he was having a heart attack. But for the next set, he got his second wind. He was on fire, doing all the mic tricks, getting the band all fired up. And that night Ernie K-Doe was as good as any performer I have ever seen!" This well-publicized performance put K-Doe's name back on the music-business grapevine, adding to the momentum created by his WWOZ show.

The 'OZ broadcasts attracted an ever-growing group of global admirers, many of whom avidly traded tapes of the show. One notable fan was the eclectic pianist and songwriter Bruce Hornsby. "To me," Hornsby said, "Ernie K-Doe was a good solid singer, but there were a thousand and one of them. What was special was the hilarious persona that he affected as a DJ. 'Mother-in-Law' was just a springboard, a tiny kernel of achievement, that allowed K-Doe to be a star twenty-some years after his big hit. I wouldn't say he *re*-invented himself; he really invented his K-Doe persona in the '80s and went from there. None of us would have been interested in K-Doe without the radio show. It's all about showbiz, creating an image, and taking that extra nutty step."

As a part-time member of the Grateful Dead during the early '90s, Hornsby "used to phone prank Jerry Garcia all the time. Garcia was a walking encyclopedia of American music, and he already knew about Ernie K-Doe and the tapes of K-Doe's show. So I didn't turn him on to those, but I did use them to fuck with him." The tapes Hornsby referred to were part of an underground genre of mailed tapes known as "bus tapes" and "way-out takes." By contemporary, internet standards, it is hard to imagine that sending cassette tapes by snail mail could create a buzz—the practice certainly lacks the broad, immediate access of a viral video. Yet K-Doe's WWOZ tapes made a huge splash in certain music circles. Hornsby continued: "Impersonating K-Doe was one of the few times that I really got Jerry. I called one time and said, 'Jerry Garcia, it's Ernie K-Doe, K-dash-D-O-E on 90.7, WWOZ, whatcha got to say to the Crescent City?' And he was like, 'Oh, hi, Ernie, well, I'd just like to say Merry Christmas to everyone in New Orleans!' And I said, 'Grateful Dead don't play "Mother-in-Law," Garcia; when the Grateful Dead gonna play "Mother-in-Law"?' And he said, 'Well, we like "Mother-in-Law," Ernie,' and I said, 'How about the Grateful Dead and Ernie K-Doe on a show? It's a bad combo, Garcia! When the Grateful Dead gonna play Crescent City, Garcia?' And Jerry said, 'Well, man, I really feel bad about that. We want to play New Orleans again, but we had a little problem there one time.'" (The "little problem" was the band's 1970 drug bust on Bourbon Street, mentioned in their song "Truckin'.") Hornsby "kept Jerry on the phone, winding him up, giving him shit like that, and asking him, 'Why aren't you showing me any respect, Garcia?' Finally

I couldn't take it anymore and I said, 'Hey, Jerry, it's me—Bruce!' He said, 'You weasel!' and he cracked up."

But Ernie K-Doe did not crack up the new owners of WWOZ, the New Orleans Jazz and Heritage Foundation, which took over the station in 1987. His show was canceled shortly thereafter. Former owner Jerry Brock was disappointed to see this happen. "The Foundation did not want K-Doe on the air. They just felt that he did not represent what they wanted to represent. They thought he was too much black, too much shuck and jive. . . . The attitude of many people who were trying to affect 'OZ at that time—and some of these people I'm talking about were black—was that they wanted to hear music like Kenny G, they wanted a smooth-jazz format. I felt that K-Doe represented a great segment of the local community and the local community's music, and that's why we had him on. What K-Doe did was part of a tradition."

Though the details surrounding the termination are murky, K-Doe saw it coming and discussed it on the air: "Whatever way the wind blows is gonna be cool with me . . . everything got a draw line, and I know where to draw my draw line. . . . I love you for calling Ernie K-Doe. And all the people in the city of New Orleans, I want y'all to call me up now and wish me luck, whether I stay on this station or whether I go to another radio station or whether you never see me on another radio station, in life, or hear me. . . . God knows I love you to the bone. It's been a ball being with you almost five years, and I love you; yeah, I don't want to lose you." Then the phonograph needle dropped on "I Cried My Last Tear," the perfect backdrop for the topic at hand: "That's right, I have cried my last tear over you. I try to get along with you but you don't understand, so somethin' got to give. I believe in the old folks' saying, 'Dust your feet and then you can understand.' . . . I believe that who that believeth in me I believeth in them. If you don't believe in me, I might not be on this station, but I will be on another station. I would love it to be 'OZ because I started with 'OZ. I think we gonna come to an agreement before the night is over with, one way or another. I hate to sound so harsh, but . . ." Here K-Doe paused, committing the cardinal sin of radio: dead air. Palpable tension filled the lengthy silence. Finally he finished his sentence: ". . . maybe one day we'll work it out that everybody will understand everybody."

While wishing for this rapprochement, K-Doe resurfaced on Tulane University's WTUL, in 1990. (Back in 1973 he had played a benefit concert for the station alongside the stellar lineup of Earl King, the Meters, Chris Kenner, Benny Spellman, Robert Parker, Aaron Neville, and saxophonist Earl Turbinton.) K-Doe gushed with pride about coming back on the air. "The students have been coming to the other radio that I was on, WWOZ, and listening to me. But I never thought that they was making progress and telling the dean if I ever would leave that station that they would like to have me on Tulane University's station. . . . If I had to crawl I was going to make it! They gonna give me more days. I'm bringing up their ratings already! . . . It's good for me to be on the radio where people can listen to me, it remind me of when I was young, very young, when Joe Louis used to

K-DOE OUTSIDE WWOZ'S ARMSTRONG PARK STUDIO
early 1990s
Photo by Harold F. Baquet

have fights on the radio; if it come on eight o'clock everybody would be home by quarter to seven to listen to it!"

K-Doe returned to WWOZ when the New Orleans Jazz and Heritage Foundation hired new staff in 1992. He did not host his own show this second time around. Instead he played the dual role of an honored guest and elder statesman. His impassioned pitches during fund drives included some raucous jam sessions and amicably competitive trash talk with Eddie Bo and Snooks Eaglin. His appearances on Billy Delle's *Records from the Crypt* left listeners smiling for days. "I was unaware," said general manager David Freedman, "that K-Doe was unwelcome at some former stage of management at WWOZ. If that is what happened, if his style was considered too rough-edged, it certainly was a loss. For me one of the marks of K-Doe's genius was how creatively he used language. When I became GM in 1992, it wasn't even a conscious decision on my part whether to put him on our airwaves. K-Doe, as every other musician from our world, was always welcome at the station—he, perhaps, more than most. And, following the time-honored industry tradition of endless and shameless self-promotion, K-Doe was right up there with the best when it came to turning the knob on our open-door policy." More than a decade after K-Doe's death, WWOZ continues to air choice excerpts from his old shows.

CHAPTER 21: *Hitting Bottom*

A happy reunion between K-Doe and WWOZ could not have seemed possible when he was dismissed in 1987. He took it hard, and not just as a blow to his huge ego. K-Doe had also enjoyed spotlighting such old friends as Johnny Adams and Tony Cousin, and giving initial exposure to protégés, including Little Eric. Before 'OZ had webcasting capability, its signal could not be heard very far beyond New Orleans. But this did nothing to diminish K-Doe's fifty-thousand-watt, clear-channel enthusiasm. "WWOZ is the station for New Orleans!" K-Doe proclaimed with pride. "We play New Orleans talent. If you got a hit record, you don't have to wait two or three weeks before it be put on the radio. Bring it up here, and we'll put it in the record stack! The charity start at home, and then it's spread abroad . . . the reason why it start at home: you feed your children first, and then, if you have anything left, you do like they used to do in the country. You put it in a big old skillet pot and you take it 'cross the street." K-Doe also felt that working musicians who sought airplay themselves were uniquely qualified to be DJs, "Because they know what an artist feel like. And if you never been an artist, you would never know."

K-Doe mentioned his dismissal from WWOZ in a 1989 interview with *People* magazine. The article, by Patricia Freeman and Michael Small, recounted the efforts of Joey Dee, best known for the 1962 hit "Peppermint Twist," to help his fallen colleagues. In 1987 Dee had created the Foundation for the Love of Rock 'n' Roll. He planned to build a retirement community, provide health insurance, and the like. The interview was set up to further this goal. Ernie K-Doe's was one of the seven sad cases profiled in the *People* article, alongside the likes of Thurston "Little Bitty Pretty One" Harris, James "Pookie" Hudson of the doo-wop group the Spaniels, and the impassioned singer Dee Clark. (Clark had been on the bill—and at his peak, with his hit "Raindrops"—when K-Doe debuted at the Apollo Theater in 1961.) As Freeman and Small reported:

> Sitting still as a statue in a blue polyester three-piece suit, Ernie K-Doe shows the ravages of a 17-year affair with the bottle. His half-closed, bloodshot eyes stare aimlessly; his slurred sentences trail off, to be completed by his manager, Milton Batiste.
>
> Three years ago, Batiste found K-Doe wandering drunk in New Orleans and decided to help. It hasn't been easy. When Batiste got him bookings in jazz and soul festivals, K-Doe sometimes stood up and rambled incoherently. "I told him," says Batiste, "you are not Jesse Jackson. The people don't want to hear you preach. They want to hear you sing.'"
>
> That's what K-Doe, 53, did so well in the early '60s with exuberant rhythm-and-blues hits like "Mother-in-Law" and "T'ain't It the Truth." Though he had perfected his voice as a teenager with the Flamingoes, he was hindered by his eighth-grade education. He changed his last name from Kador to K-Doe—because he liked the way it looked—and went solo in 1955. "There was a whole lot of people who did me wrong and rubbed me wrong," he says. "Everybody else was ridin' around in a Mercedes-Benz and a Rolls-Royce, and Ernie K-Doe was ridin' around in nothin'."
>
> K-Doe never learned to do anything but sing. Earning no royalties, he has scraped by for the last 15 years on just a few hundred dollars a month in performance fees. Still, he hasn't given up hope. Divorced many years ago and living with a female friend in downtown New Orleans, he has cut back a bit on his drinking, with Batiste's help. Until recently he had a weekly music show on a local public radio station. "They loved me.... Even the little children would call me up. I had fans." As for his singing, he says, "I don't want to sound like I'm braggin', but right now I'm at my peak. Just turn me loose and let me go."

Despite K-Doe's rough condition, he could still sing at full strength when sober. Recognizing this fact—and motivated by a blend of concern, loyalty, and entrepreneurial spirit—Milton Batiste began recording K-Doe in 1986. Batiste's first release, appearing on cassette only, was entitled *Chiterling [sic] Circuit Society Featuring Ernie K-Doe and Guitar Slim, Jr.* "Chiterling Circuit Society" served both as the album's title and as the name of the label on which it was released, one of several owned by Batiste. Guitar Slim Jr. (Rodney Armstrong), whose father attained iconic status in 1954 with "The Things

MILTON BATISTE AND K-DOE ONSTAGE AT THE NEW ORLEANS JAZZ AND HERITAGE FESTIVAL
1987
Photo by Syndey Byrd

that I Used to Do," reprised that hit on this album, giving it a new twist with a call-and-response dialogue between his guitar and Batiste's trumpet.

Other than this one Armstrong performance, the uneven album is focused on K-Doe. The hands-down highlight (and one of the very best New Orleans R&B songs of the '80s) is "Jump into Your Love." It features K-Doe's reinvented nursery rhymes in its lyrics, along with a Hendrix-style guitar solo by Wilson Victorian, aka June Victory. Victory also helped craft the song's fiery, catchy arrangement. (As the leader of an all-star aggregation of Mardi Gras Indians called the Bayou Renegades, Victory made some fine recordings of his own during this era for Syla Records, another Batiste-owned label.) "'Jump into Your Love' had already been recorded," Victory said, "and K-Doe told me he wanted to sing something over the track, in a James Brown bag. I told him, 'OK, come up with some lyrics,' and when I heard what he had, I said, 'You *know* you crazy!' And K-Doe nailed it on the first take." Guitarist Ernie Vincent, of "Dap Walk" fame, played on the song too.

Chiterling Circuit Society also showcased K-Doe sharing aural space with a shamelessly cheesy synthesizer on "Do You Want Some?" As the title suggests, the lyrics celebrate the theme of feeling frisky. A similar mid-'80s feel with ad-libbed vocals prevails on another track, "Father-in-Law, the Devil's Son-in-Law." This strange spin-off of "Mother-in-Law" consists of a lone, continual funk riff that borrows liberally from "Rise," a 1979 hit by trumpeter Herb Alpert. While a backup singer with a Spellman-esque bass voice endlessly chants the title phrase, K-Doe recites a series of thematically vague, rhythmically clunky, and ill-rhyming lines: "Mother-in-law was always on my case, / Worryin' my mind each and every day. / I thought mother-in-law was the kind, / I found out later father-in-law was always on my time / . . . He tried to turn my lady against me, / But what the fool didn't know, / She loved only me."

But K-Doe delivers these weak lines with his customary enthusiasm and presumption of profundity, lending charm to the half-baked, unoriginal song. The second half of its title was especially derivative, in that a 1930s blues artist named William Bunch had enjoyed great success under the moniker "Peetie Wheatstraw, the Devil's Son-in-Law." This sobriquet was also used by comedian Rudy Ray Moore for characters in x-rated "toasts," recitations, and as the title of a 1997 blaxploitation film.

Milton Batiste chose his DuBat label to showcase K-Doe's next album—a live set released in 1988 that resurrected some of K-Doe's '60s hits with accompaniment by the Blue Eyed Soul Revue. Thanks to a typo, it came out emblazoned with the title *Ernie K-Dor.* Though well respected as a thoroughly professional musician, Batiste did not take the same pains with his graphic designs, which reflect a homemade sensibility and at times suggest folk art. Basic data on his album covers, such as names, release dates, and songwriting and publishing credits, do not always appear accurately—or at all. Misspellings occur, sometimes with multiple variations. Many small record labels—in genres including blues, Cajun, zydeco, and country—present a similar do-it-yourself look, and some record collectors see such imperfect covers as an indicator of great music within.

K-DOE'S LATE-CAREER CD RELEASES
Courtesy Ben Sandmel

Despite its sloppy cover, the music on *Ernie K-Dor* is tight and professional throughout. But there are certainly some loose moments on Batiste's next album by the Emperor—*I'm Cocky but I'm Good Just Standin' on Top of de' World,* released on CD by DuBat in the mid-1990s. The loosest is a live rendition of "Georgia on My Mind." In the first line K-Doe—quite possibly drunk—pronounces the southern state at hand as "JOR-jer," setting the tone for a lyric-butchering rendition so bad it almost attains brilliance. Batiste would have done better keeping this song shelved. But *I'm Cocky* also reprises several strong songs from *Chiterling Circuit Society*, most notably the red-hot "Jump into Your Love." Batiste's scattershot approach to K-Doe's albums mirrored that of Joe Banashak at Minit a quarter century before. Both favored the quick release of randomly assembled material over cohesively conceived projects.

Unfortunately, Batiste did not resemble Banashak in terms of the latter's methodical marketing, distribution, and promotion. The DuBat CDs were hard to find in New Orleans record stores and essentially unavailable out of town. Nor did Batiste aggressively seek airplay, except on WWOZ, where it was already a given. For the most part, Batiste sold CDs—including his own recordings with the Olympia Brass Band and his other group the Magnificent Sevenths—at shows. Sales were especially brisk on his frequent trips to Europe, where he played a circuit of annual summer festivals. (Batiste took K-Doe along for the Emperor's one and only European performance, at the 1988 North Sea Jazz Festival, in the Hague.) Astutely, Batiste also licensed his recordings to other labels and to film production companies. Substantial money can be made in soundtrack licensing deals, and all owners of small record labels hope to hit this jackpot one day.

So Batiste enjoyed a major achievement when "Jump into Your Love" was picked up by HBO for use in *Doublecrossed* in 1991. This true-story film made expressly for cable television stars Dennis Hopper as Barry Seal, a drug dealer turned DEA informant. The real-life Seal hailed from Baton Rouge and was gunned down there by a Colombian cartel, so much of the film is set in south Louisiana. K-Doe lip-synched his song in a nightclub scene that features Hopper dancing with costar Adrienne Barbeau. Batiste, Ernie Vincent, and the Magnificent Sevenths back him up. K-Doe's powerful on-screen cameo lasts less than a minute, but as usual he approached it with maximum commitment.

Despite his brief encounter with Hollywood, K-Doe was nowhere near his peak, as he had tried to convince *People* magazine. During the 1980s he often slept under the Claiborne Avenue overpass, near the future site of the Mother-in-Law Lounge. Opportunity still knocked sporadically during this rough patch, and K-Doe could still rise to the occasion and meet it—but not with any consistency. "The thing about K-Doe that was so amazing to me," said Kenneth "Afro" Williams, "was that when K-Doe would come on a gig, we wondered what we were gonna get, if he'd be drunk or sober. Either way he'd always be talking about, 'I can sing in any key!' and he would always tell the band to play in E flat—E flat was our running joke for years! But sometimes this dude had magic—sometimes K-Doe could be skunk-down *tore up* and walk out onstage and fire the whole place up! Come out singing 'Burn, K-Doe, burn!' and just take it over! I'd be playing, watching him, mesmerized, thinking, 'How this dude do this?' Then the show would end and he'd walk off the stage and be tore up again."

Afro Williams, who often performed with K-Doe, produced K-Doe's album *Fever!*, released in 1995 on DuBat. Williams had gained considerable studio experience and a commercial sensibility as a member of Chocolate Milk, one of New Orleans's preeminent R&B-funk bands of the 1970s and early '80s. After recording for a major label, RCA, Williams found Batiste's equipment somewhat lacking. But he coaxed good results from it just the same. "Milton had [already recorded] some keyboard and drum machine tracks," Williams explained. "And he said, 'I want you to take these and come up with something, get K-Doe to sing over them. We're going to do a new CD on K-Doe.' Me and the other cats used to call Milton's place Sunshine Studios. It was a building in back of his house, with a leaky roof. If it rained you couldn't record. The acoustics could be a little weird too. But Milton knew how to cut a corner."

Fever! features the requisite R&B standards, including its title track—made famous by both Little Willie John and Peggy Lee—and Sam and Dave's "When Something Is Wrong with My Baby." But Williams also picked atypical numbers, such as reggae adaptations of the Jimmy Reed blues classics "Honest I Do" and "Baby What You Want Me to Do": "We were looking for a modern edge," Williams explained. Though K-Doe mastered this new setting with his usual confidence and verve, the album suffered some from overuse of his Disney-esque Goofy laugh. Nevertheless, K-Doe's power impressed Williams: "You might think that K-Doe could sing, but people don't know that K-Doe could *really sing*. He was absolutely on the top level of New Orleans singers. We'd give him the lyrics and he'd say, 'When I go in there, Junior, you just turn it on and let me get it!' Most of the songs on that album are first takes. I didn't expect him to be that good in the studio; usually you have to get lots of takes because the singer has to get used to the material. K-Doe had the ability to come in, take a quick look at stuff he didn't know, and feel it right away. He blew me away. I remember sitting behind the board recording K-Doe, thinking, 'Why this man didn't make it? This shit is unbelievable!'"

Although *Fever!* does not include a standout number à la "Jump into Your Love," Williams "had high hopes when we did the CD. K-Doe was getting healthier, and I thought this would be his comeback and my breakout. One problem was that K-Doe would do a good job recording the new songs when the lyrics were in front of him, but he didn't memorize them. Since he never really learned them, we couldn't play them live." At this time K-Doe was wildly inconsistent: he might be on, but he might be shaky, even with a program of old, familiar material. In 1991 he brought down the house at a New Orleans Jazz and Heritage Festival evening concert, as opposed to a daytime, "in the yard" performance, which K-Doe found so insulting. But then, in 1994, the Jazz Fest booked him to join in an all-star evening concert called the Dew Drop Inn Revisited. The stellar lineup also featured his Crescent City cohorts Johnny Adams, Tommy

Ridgley, Bobby Marchan, and conductor-arranger-producer Wardell Quezergue, aka the Creole Beethoven. Special out-of-town guests graced the bill as well: the suave crooner Charles Brown ("Please Come Home for Christmas"), Ruth Brown ("Mama, He Treats Your Daughter Mean"), and jazz-blues shouter Jimmy Witherspoon, known for his renditions of "Mean Old Frisco" and "Ain't Nobody's Business If I Do."

The Dew Drop Inn Revisited offered K-Doe a return to the halcyon days of his biggest hits—and a rare chance to start over. Disastrously, he showed up late, "skunk-down tore up," and apparently wearing someone else's clothes. Holding tight to the waistband of trousers that were three times too big, K-Doe immediately harangued the audience to "Stand up!"—then "Bow down on your knees to Ernie K-Doe!" After less than one torturous minute, the concert's producers yanked K-Doe offstage with Art Neville's proverbial Bo Peep hook.

Such debacles made K-Doe's family and friends increasingly concerned about his deteriorating condition. "When K-Doe was drinking," Walter "Wolfman" Washington said, "we tried to talk with him, tried to get him to straighten his life out, but K-Doe had a mind of his own. If something really bothered him he would just go off on his own. He wouldn't open up; he was a private person about his private life. But he was definitely going through a period where he really couldn't get a handle on things." Lloyd Price "kept up with Ernie, and when I heard he was doing a lot of drinking, I talked with him about that. Because I saw what had happened to James Booker, who was an excellent musician! Ernie would say, 'Oh, yeah, OK, Lloyd, OK, man,' but he wasn't really listening."

Drummer Charles Connor, who had played with K-Doe at the Tiajuana before joining Little Richard's band, was horrified to hear about his colleague's condition. "[K-Doe] carried himself like a star. He looked great. He would wear silk suits, sharkskin suits, and really keep his process [hairdo] up. So it was shocking to hear later that he was living on the street." K-Doe's childhood friend Ken Jones remembered a similar reaction from R&B star Bobby Bland: "One night I was backstage at the Municipal Auditorium talking to Bobby Bland and his guitarist Wayne Bennett. And K-Doe came along, wearing one of those $9.98 suits and drinking out of a pint bottle. Wayne Bennett shook his head and said, 'What's the matter with that cat? He's got so much talent.' And Bobby Bland said, 'Is that the same cat who used to be around the Dew Drop? Oh man, he's become an alcoholic.'"

"But a lot of the cats I played with fell on hard times," Charles Connor reflected. "The racism in New Orleans was so bad then—and when you were getting treated well in New York or L.A., then it would break your heart to come back to that. Some of those cats killed themselves, not by committing suicide but by using drugs. And Ernie K-Doe, I guess, did it with alcohol. Two of Fats Domino's guitar players, Roy Montrell and Walter Nelson—everyone called him Papoose—they both overdosed. And so did Nat Perrilliat. Nat was my good friend, and he was such a great sax player."

Jean Knight (of "Mr. Big Stuff" fame) took a sharp breath at the memory of "K-Doe just sitting on the curb under Claiborne. It was heartbreaking to see him like that. I would always stop and holler and talk to him, sure did. He didn't want you to know just how bad he was doing, but you could tell it just by looking at him. He wasn't dressed so great. He would talk about the old days, not about the present and what was going on then. This was when him and Jessie James had broke up."

Despite their breakup a decade earlier, James did not cut K-Doe out of her life: "I used to go check on him. He would be down and he would beg me to take him back, he acted kind of helpless sometimes. He had really hit the skids; he was living on the street. It upset me; it really did. And I don't know why but I just kept going to see about him. I never would stop seeing about him. We definitely stayed close friends. He was a lovable person. I always missed K-Doe after we broke up; K-Doe was a person you don't forget. I used to meet him and go have a drink with him, but he then didn't ever want me to leave. He was a lonely person in some ways. He had a lady on Dumaine Street, and she drank a lot too; I would go see them and sometimes they would be so drunk that when I left I would cry. I hated to see him like that."

The Dew Drop Inn Revisited show was not K-Doe's only blown opportunity at this time. Frankie Ford, who parlayed his hit "Sea Cruise" into a long-term career, attempted to add K-Doe to a booking roster of fellow New Orleans R&B artists. Ford recounted:

> At one point [around 1990], my manager Ken Keene and I were handling the Dixie Cups, and Jean Knight, and we told Ernie [K-Doe] and Milton Batiste, "We would like to talk with you about putting you on tour. But first the people want to see you, to make sure you've straightened up. So we will start you with a thousand a night plus air and hotel. If it works out, the money will keep going up. We want you and Milton to get an attorney of your choice to collect your money so that you can save some of it." And K-Doe said, "Nobody is going to collect Ernie K-Doe's money except Ernie K-Doe!" So I said, "OK, this conversation is over." We were at my house, and Milton just shook his head. He said, "K-Doe, look at this beautiful place! These people are doing something right to live like this—and think about how *you* live." And K-Doe said, "Oh yeah? Well all this ain't nothin' but crap!" So I said, "Maybe that grand piano and everything is nothing but crap, but it happens to be *my* crap!"
>
> K-Doe isn't the only musician who's had these problems. It happens; people don't take care of business, don't watch their money. See, I saved mine; my father always had me put some of that money in the bank. Al Hirt used to say, "One night Fats Domino came in my club, bought a drink, put a thousand dollar bill on the bar—and Frankie Ford reached in his pocket and gave Fats his change!"
>
> K-Doe had so much talent and he just blew it. He was his worst enemy. At Jellyroll's in the Quarter, where Al Hirt used to play a lot, I was working upstairs with the big band and K-Doe was working downstairs with Bobby Lonero. K-Doe

would be onstage with a pint in his back pocket because the club wouldn't serve him. On the break we could see him through the window on Saint Louis Street, drinking out of that bottle. I was so embarrassed for him.

Saxophonist Amadee Castenell "played some of those gigs at Jellyroll's, and I felt bad for K-Doe; I felt like they were using him. He would always say that he was going back in the studio, and he wanted me to be with him, like Maceo [Parker] with James Brown. I would try to boost his confidence—not that he needed it. And he'd always call out songs in E flat and then start singing in a different key." Bobby Lonero, a singer, guitarist, and skilled Louis Prima impersonator, saw how badly these drunken evenings could end: "One night I was heading home from Jellyroll's. It was around four in the morning. I was driving down Claiborne and there's K-Doe. He couldn't afford a car at the time, so he would ride to work on a bicycle. And he was sitting on his bike, leaned up against a phone pole, passed out. He was in terrible shape, and that's not even the worst."

"You know," Frankie Ford observed:

> We all go through some hard times. In 1958 I was working at the Woodmen of the World Hall on Almonaster Avenue. Mac Rebennack was in my band, and "Sea Cruise" had just come out. Johnny Rivers was playing during the intermission, and he was counting on selling some records just to get pocket money, but he didn't sell anything. And Johnny said, "Frankie, I don't have seven cents to get back to the French Quarter on the bus; can you give me a ride?" I said, "Sure." So I understand. But it's a question of attitude. In the early '90s me, Frogman Henry, K-Doe, and Oliver Morgan were all on Angela Hill's TV show on WWL. This was about the same time that I'd asked K-Doe if he wanted me to book him. We were backstage getting ready to go on, and Frogman and Oliver told K-Doe, "We're here to talk about music, so don't bring up all that crap about why you didn't get your due." Because at that point, K-Doe was full of hate and bitterness.
>
> So there we were on TV and K-Doe looked like hell—he was wearing mismatched shoes—and he said, "The only reason that Frankie Ford succeeded is because he's white, and Dick Clark wouldn't book me because I'm black." I said, "Er-*nee* . . . what about Sam Cooke? What about Jackie Wilson? Dick Clark had them on his show all the time!" And I was offended. Because I had gone on the road with Huey Smith and the Clowns back in the days of segregation. When we were driving through Mississippi, I had to duck down and hide. I'd stay in black hotels with the band when they weren't welcome at white places.

Yet even during these difficult times, K-Doe didn't lose his generosity. A man named Cotton attested to this fact, recalling K-Doe's attendance at his wedding. In some communities in south Louisiana, black and white alike, it is traditional for wedding guests to honor the happy couple by pinning money on their clothes, particularly on the bride's veil. (At this writing, anything less than a twenty is considered chintzy.) "K-Doe came to our wedding," Cotton said, "and after the ceremony K-Doe comes up to me and my new wife and he says, 'Congratulations to the new Mister and Missus Cotton! I'm so happy for you.' Then he says, 'Look here, I ain't got no money right now, but I want you to have this'—and instead of cash, K-Doe pinned us up with food stamps!"

CHAPTER 22: *Like God Removing a Devil from His Body*

By the early 1990s, some three decades after "Mother-in-Law" topped the charts, Ernie K-Doe had burned almost all his bridges, personal and professional. Few people besides Milton Batiste still stood by him. "Nobody but Milton would fool with K-Doe at that time," producer Afro Williams attested. "Milton wanted to be the Berry Gordy of New Orleans, and he'd help people when no one else would. But eventually him and K-Doe fell out." That rift developed in direct proportion to Antoinette's ascendancy in K-Doe's life. Antoinette had seen K-Doe perform decades before she met him personally. "What first attracted me to Ernie K-Doe was his music. I used to go see him perform at Lincoln Beach when I was a teenager. Of course then I never dreamed that I'd marry him. Earl King would be on those shows, Irma Thomas, and Lee Dorsey, my first cousin on my father's side; my maiden name is Dorsey. But K-Doe would usually close the show. And we'd stay 'til the end to see him, me and my cousins, so we'd miss the last Hayne Boulevard bus and get home late. That meant trouble . . . but it was worth it."

Years passed before Antoinette would see K-Doe again. Her parents, Warren and Leola, moved from the Lower Ninth Ward, in Orleans Parish, to Plaquemines Parish, downriver from the city. There the Dorseys lived in semirural fashion, providing much of their own food by gardening, hunting, and fishing. And there Antoinette married a man with the surname Fox. In some interviews she stated that she bore no children of her own. In other narratives she became pregnant but was never blessed by giving birth. Another version made reference to living offspring. Whatever the case, Antoinette consistently claimed to have raised twenty-seven foster children—some out in the country, some after she moved back to New Orleans. Upon her return to the city, Antoinette met Ernie K-Doe, she estimated, around 1970.

"I was tending bar at a little club," Antoinette said, "and K-Doe came in. There were about twenty-five people in line ahead of him, and he ordered a Jack Daniels and Coke. Everybody was clapping his back and getting him to sign autographs, and he said, 'I want a Jack Daniels and Coke!' I said, 'Young man, you're going to have to wait like everyone else.' He said, 'I'm Ernie K-Doe,' and I said, 'I don't care; you're going to have to wait!' After that, I didn't see him again 'til the late '80s. I was managing another bar. He would come in and the customers would call him, 'K-Doe!' Some would call him Ernie, but I never put the name and the face together because something like twenty years had passed. Finally I asked him, 'Are you *the* Ernie K-Doe?' and he said, 'Yes—I just wanted to see how long it was going to take you to recognize me.' I think he was flirting with me."

K-Doe was indeed flirting. Guitarist Ernie Vincent observed the blossoming rapport between the two: "I used to play at a place called the First Stop, at Pauger and Marais, in the Seventh Ward. Antoinette tended bar there. At that time her last name was Fox. K-Doe used to come in and sit in with my band. Gradually he and Antoinette sparked up. I guess this was around 1989. I went to work at the First Stop one Sunday night and there was a sign saying HOME OF ERNIE K-DOE, and people are saying, 'Yeah, Ernie's running with Antoinette!' I said, 'Oh, no, not *this* Ernie!' They thought it was *me*. What's a trip is that I had just recorded a song on K-Doe called 'Night Fox'—how ironic is that? It came out on Fordom, the label that put out 'Dap Walk.'"

Antoinette had no illusions about K-Doe's precarious condition. "People ask me," she reflected, "why would I get involved with someone who had so many serious problems. The answer is that I had three miscarriages, and I raised twenty-seven foster children. Part of the time in New Orleans and part of the time out in the country, in Plaquemines Parish. So my heart has always been with people who took a downslide—I figured there was always a reason for them doing that. . . . I knew he needed a friend, and I was that friend. I helped him. If you can't help a man when he's down, don't help him when he's up."

At first their relationship was platonic, and the two did not marry until 1996. Initially Antoinette served as "K-Doe's banker, and clothes designer." She was "wearing many hats for this man, at first just as his *friend*. I had to get him to trust me because he had been very badly damaged by people abusing his career. That is no excuse for his drinking, because with that he abused himself. And his drinking just helped other people abuse him even more. But when Ernie stopped drinking it was like God removing a devil from his body. And I give K-Doe a lot of credit, because here we was, living above a bar, being in a bar every day, but he stayed sober. I'm not saying it was easy for either of us. It's painful being married to a man who's an alcoholic, and I have some scars inside from that. But once he stopped drinking *he was the best husband in the world*."

Several people stated that K-Doe never stopped drinking completely. "People always said that K-Doe was clean," Jessie James scoffed, "but he never got clean." "That O'Doul's bottle of his," Afro Williams pointed out, "well, it wasn't always filled with O'Doul's." "Antoinette was in denial," said Ken Jones, who knew K-Doe as a teenager and managed the Mother-in-Law Lounge when it first opened, in 1995. "K-Doe still drank. It was rough working for them. Business and friendship are two different things. I ordered the liquor, did inventory, tried to get the place going. But that jealousy took over between Ernie and Antoinette and myself. People used to come in there looking for *me*, because of my personality, and because I knew people who worked at City Hall who would come by for a drink

ERNIE AND ANTOINETTE AT THE OPENING OF THE MOTHER-IN-LAW LOUNGE
May 5, 1995
Photo by Rick Olivier

Ernie-K-Doe
Mother-In-Law
L.A.

K-DOE PERFORMING AT THE OPENING OF THE MOTHER-IN-LAW LOUNGE
May 5, 1995
Photo by Rick Olivier

after work. Ernie and Antoinette didn't like that; they got jealous and said that I was stealing from them. But there really wasn't anything to steal because they wasn't really making any money. After they got crazy on me, I never would work for them anymore, although I would still go see them. They fought with each other too; they'd scream and throw chairs at each other. One of their fights is how Antoinette got her finger cut off."

Doc Mancina and Louis "the Nooge" Nugent, two rabid K-Doe fans (and well-known characters in their own right), saw Antoinette just hours after this accidental amputation, which took place in the late 1990s, a few years after the couple married. Mancina reported:

> Me and Louis Nugent had started making K-Doe merchandise for Ernie and Antoinette—T-shirts and pillows and stuff. We were going to make a delivery, and I called the lounge around 5 p.m. to tell the K-Does that we'd be there in about an hour. When Antoinette answered the phone I heard a bunch of yelling and screaming—a marital spat. She dropped the phone receiver and for a couple of minutes it was nothing but four-letter words. Then I heard a major scream by Antoinette, and the line went dead. Eventually me and the Nooge showed up, around midnight. Everything was calm; Antoinette was there, but no K-Doe. We asked where he was, and she said, "K-Doe's upset and he's out drinking; I don't know where the hell he is." I noticed a big white bandage on Antoinette's finger and asked what happened. She said, "Well, me and K-Doe got into a big fight earlier this evening. He slammed the iron security gate on my finger when he stormed out, and cut off the top of my finger. I screamed at him to find it and ice it down. He was looking everywhere, but he couldn't think straight. I told K-Doe to keep looking while I took a cab to Charity Hospital. He said, "When I find your finger I'll take the Claiborne bus and meet you there." At Charity the doctors asked me for the top of my finger, and when I didn't have it they just sewed me up at the midbone. K-Doe finally showed up at Charity about two hours later, berserk; he'd had a few to drink, he was very upset, he had never found the finger, and once he saw that they'd already sewed me up, he left—and I haven't heard from him since." Then, real nonchalant, Antoinette says, "Hey, you guys want another drink?" And that was that. We left at 2 a.m. with Antoinette in good spirits, like this was no big deal. She had lost half of her finger and come right back to work.

In 1995 a laudatory article entitled "Comeback Kid," by *Times-Picayune* writer Reginald Owens, noted that K-Doe's "days of alcohol abuse may be behind him, but he still drinks socially. He nursed a short whiskey while giving an interview." By strict twelve-step standards, of course, nursing a short whiskey does not qualify as recovery. But if Antoinette did not wean K-Doe from the bottle altogether, she certainly ended his notorious days of drunken performances and missed shows. "I had to bring K-Doe back around," Antoinette said, "and make him believe in himself. Once I did that everything was smooth sailing, and he was very easy to work with. Of course, when I went out to book him, people didn't want to take a chance on him because he had a reputation for not showing up. He had damaged his career so badly. One person I went to was John Blancher, of the Rock 'n' Bowl, MidCity Lanes. It's a nightclub and a bowling alley all in one. John had said that he would never let K-Doe play for him again, because K-Doe had burned him so bad."

"Boy, did K-Doe burn me bad," Blancher affirmed:

> In 1990 Porgy Jones brought [K-Doe] to the Rock 'n' Bowl as a special guest on his show. That first gig went fairly well. I do remember K-Doe asking if he could get some bowling shoes and join two women who already had a lane. K-Doe was a big fan of bowling and considered himself, of course, as being rather proficient; he told me had learned to bowl when he worked as a pinsetter when he was a teenager. But the second gig was disastrous because again K-Doe wanted to bowl—with only minutes to spare before the show. I pointed out how close we were to starting time. He assured me that he'd be up in a few minutes. Half an hour later, after much urging, he finally got onstage. Right out the gate, he started singing "Mother-in-Law," but then midway through the song he excused himself to go to the bathroom. The band kept playing, and fifteen minutes later there was still no K-Doe.
>
> We had a pretty good crowd in the house, and I kept wondering what was taking him so long. One of my customers came up and asked if K-Doe was finished for the night. I told him, "Oh no, he's in the bathroom, he'll be right back"—but then this guy said that he'd just seen K-Doe leave in a cab! Porgy Jones's band kept playing, but with no vocalist, and there were some very unhappy people in the house. The cover charge that night was three dollars, and I returned anyone's money that requested it. Back then the bands would play until 2 a.m., and we still had a handful of people at 1:30 when suddenly K-Doe comes popping up the stairs, jumps onstage, and starts singing. He did two songs, the band wrapped up for the night, and then he came to me wanting to get paid. Of course I blew a gasket. I paid Porgy Jones; the deal was that I would pay K-Doe separately. I told K-Doe how chickenshit he was and how embarrassed I was with his actions, but he insisted. So I gave him his money—but I also told him to *never* walk into my place again, and that he was a washed-up asshole. I meant it. And at that point, he definitely was—until Antoinette stepped into his life.

Antoinette worked hard to get K-Doe back in Blancher's good graces, telling him several years later, "'Look, don't take a chance on K-Doe, take a chance on *me*. Let *me* present *you* the new Ernie K-Doe!' And I told K-Doe, 'Right now, it's not about you—it's

Budweiser

about *me* and what *I* can do for you.' At first K-Doe didn't understand. He said, 'Well, it's my talent!' and I said, 'Yes, but you are wasting *my* time if you don't try to help me.' And then he understood, and he did try to help." Antoinette's approach worked well: K-Doe emerged as a beloved regular at the Rock 'n' Bowl, a reliable performer and reliably good draw. Many of his R&B buddies often performed there too, including Johnny Adams, Snooks Eaglin, and Eddie Bo.

Straightening up, fortunately, did not dampen K-Doe's outrageous self-absorption. December 1998 brought the announcement that henceforth he would be known as the Emperor of the World. No official ceremony or press release marked K-Doe's assumption of this imaginary throne. It might well have passed unnoticed—just more K-Doe shenanigans—if not for columnist Chris Rose. Rose spread the word to his *Times-Picayune* readers with the headline THE ARTIST FORMERLY KNOWN AS ERNIE K-DOE. "Who would know what currents flow inside the mind of Ernie K-Doe," Rose mused, concluding, "If there is another town like this in the world, take me there." From then on, "Emperor" and "K-Doe" became synonymous in New Orleans.

Once coronated, K-Doe displayed his perpetual sense of celebrity at the debut signing party for this writer's first book, *Zydeco!*, a collaboration with photographer Rick Olivier. The bash was held at a highbrow French Quarter photo gallery on April 22, 1999. R&B musicians Earl Palmer, Carol Fran, and Clarence Hollimon graced the party with their presence. So did the enigmatic rocker Alex Chilton. Live, accordion-driven dance music by Nathan and the Zydeco Cha-Chas set the house rocking. But the already high energy level escalated dramatically when Ernie and Antoinette double-parked their gaudily lettered Mother-in-Law van out front and made a grand, head-turning entrance—much to the gallery owner's consternation. Glamorously attired in matching outfits and big hairdos, the couple worked the room for a few minutes, the center of attention. *Times-Picayune* photographer Steven Forster had them pose for the Living section's "Big Easy Partying Shots." And then K-Doe sat down at the authors' table and began signing copies of the book, blithely unconcerned that his connection with it was absolutely nil. In rapt recognition of a surreal moment, no one attempted to stop him. To the contrary, he was cheered on.

Another exquisitely oblivious moment occurred in December 2000, when K-Doe met filmmaker Ken Burns. New Orleans figures prominently in Burns's ten-part series *Jazz*, and he'd spent time in the city conducting research and shooting interviews. With PBS's national debut broadcast of *Jazz* just weeks away, Burns returned to town to generate prelaunch publicity. He also agreed to be the guest of honor, and the celebrity draw, at a benefit for the nonprofit New Orleans Musicians' Clinic. Appropriately, this event took the form of a New Orleans music extravaganza, held at the palatial Garden District house of Johann Bultman, one of the clinic's cofounders. Bultman's house offered ample space for several simultaneous live performances of jazz and R&B, augmented by wandering groups of Mardi Gras Indians.

K-DOE AT NEW ORLEANS ROCK 'N' BOWL / MIDCITY LANES

TOP LEFT
BOWLING

TOP RIGHT
WITH OWNER JOHN BLANCHER

BOTTOM
PERFORMING

February 1991
Photos by Paula Burch-Celentano

The Bultmans invited many of the city's cultural icons, including the K-Does. The regal couple arrived while Burns was surrounded by a throng of devotees. But when word spread that Ernie and Antoinette had made their grand entrance, the room emptied out completely. After chatting with the fans who had made this mass exodus to greet him, K-Doe eventually wandered into the double parlor, where Burns now stood alone, looking rather perplexed. K-Doe had never heard of Burns, but, ever the amiable extrovert, he sensed the guest of honor's discomfort and sought to ease it. K-Doe introduced himself and then asked the youthful-looking filmmaker where he was from. "New Hampshire," replied Burns, who then proceeded to explain in detail who he was and why he was there. Burns told K-Doe about his two previous acclaimed series, *The Civil War* and *Baseball*, and reinforced his bona fides by mentioning that *Jazz* would start airing on PBS on January 8, 2001. For K-Doe, the only significant point conveyed was that Burns did not hail from New Orleans. No wonder he looked upset. The Emperor listened sympathetically. Then, with sincere, reassuring kindness, he told the multiple-Emmy winner, "Don't worry about it, son. That ain't nothin' to be ashamed of."

By now such behavior was almost routine for K-Doe, whose life had seemingly become a continuous performance-art piece. K-Doe functioned in a world all his own, where he even had his own language. He eschewed established dictionaries in favor of *Webber's*, a fanciful compendium of his own invention. He dwelled on such arcane verbiage as "Ma-Naugahyde-Thuh." But the real *Webster's* encompasses the spirit of such thinking in its definition of "surrealism": "the workings of the unconscious mind as manifested in dreams: it is characterized by an irrational, fantastic arrangement of material." Ernie K-Doe didn't subscribe to the uppercase Surrealism of Salvador Dalí and others, but "irrational, fantastic arrangements of material" were clearly his métier. In this regard, K-Doe personified a distinctive gene within the Big Easy's cultural DNA, as S. Frederick Starr discusses in *New Orleans Unmasqued*, his astute study of Crescent City caprice: "Scholars claim that Surrealism was invented by the French poet André Breton in 1924. Surrealists shocked good burghers by announcing that the real is unreal, that the world as we see it is nonsense, and that only what we feel intuitively really exists." (Ernie K-Doe once summarized this same postulate by stating, "What's cold is *hot*.") "Now Breton was clever," Starr continues, "but he should not be given all the posies, for New Orleans has been turning its whole population into surrealists for a century. They do not think of themselves as surrealists, and some may invite you to step outside if you call them that. Nonetheless, you may be sure they are convinced believers in the doctrine. . . . New Orleanians, it seems, perceive naturally what French intellects toiled to explain by writing books that are largely forgotten today. Mr. Breton could have saved himself a lot of time by visiting the Crescent City, and he would have had a good time besides." Starr goes on to cite specifics, including Mardi Gras, "a city-wide indulgence in pure fantasy." Ernie K-Doe had avidly indulged in Mardi Gras—expressing both pure fantasy and fierce cultural pride—when he masked Indian with the Young Sons of Geronimo. Decades later he invented and disseminated his own fantastic language. And then, after dying—when most mere mortals hang it all up for good—K-Doe had embarked on his posthumous career in statuary form, thanks to the equally surreal Antoinette.

But surrealism is just one interpretation of Ernie K-Doe's worldview. Willie Birch, a painter whose nationally exhibited work depicts New Orleans's African American neighborhoods, assessed the Emperor with both the enthusiasm of an insider and the overview of a professional artist:

> I grew up in K-Doe's neighborhood, in the Magnolia Projects, right across the street from the Dew Drop Inn. You couldn't grow up in that area without knowing lots of musicians—Earl King, Allen Toussaint, Esquerita, Bobby Marchan, Huey Smith, Patsy Vidalia. And Ernie K-Doe. I remember after K-Doe hit it big with "Mother-in-Law," he sponsored a basketball team that used to play at the YMCA and in Shakespeare Park. But after a while, because of the shenanigans that would go on . . . fighting . . . and K-Doe would be drunk, raising hell, my thought towards K-Doe was I don't have to *be around* you to celebrate and appreciate and respect you, which I certainly did. So I would give K-Doe space and admire him from afar. . . .
>
> K-Doe is part of the New Orleans vernacular culture that is so rich. To the rest of the world that New Orleans vernacular may seem like a fantasy, but to us this is real. It's not just carnival, Mardi Gras—it's how we live every day. Like Ellis Marsalis and the artist John Scott said, "In New Orleans, culture bubbles up from the ground." The difference between here and other places is—well, for example, take jazz in New York. It's intellectual and cerebral, music that you sit down and listen to. But New Orleans is about shaking your booty, and if a musician comes here to play and doesn't have that, we just look at him like he's crazy. And remember that, in New York, it was cats like Charlie Parker and Dizzy Gillespie who helped allow the music to become self-expressive and have freeness—but those cats weren't *from* New York. . . . it took cats from *outside* New York to make the New York scene. Which is definitely not the case with New Orleans.
>
> So, how this all relates to Ernie K-Doe is that he was someone who not only said, "I'm king for a day," but then he went and *lived* it *every* day. And when K-Doe would shout, "I'm a Charity Hospital baby," he was signifying! Just like when the Mardi Gras Indians sing and shout, "I won't bow down!" That's a big part of the beauty of New Orleans . . . And it's all part of the traditions that we came here with from Africa.

FOLLOWING PAGES
ERNIE AND ANTOINETTE IN A TREMÉ NEIGHBORHOOD PARADE
2000
Photo by Syndey Byrd

Those African traditions include music, dance, speech, foodways, and funerary customs, among many other practices. Such African cultural retentions run deep

in New Orleans, partly due to the relative racial tolerance of the city's French and Spanish colonial regimes. America's British colonies, predominately settled by Protestants, brutally suppressed the culture of their enslaved African population. But in the majority-Catholic confines of New Orleans and environs, slaves were allowed to assemble on Sundays for drumming, dancing, singing, and playing African instruments, such as the forerunner of the banjo. This limited and controlled expression, it was thought, could serve as an emotional safety valve, which would reduce the chances of a slave rebellion. A successful revolt in Haiti at the turn of the nineteenth century heightened such fears. It was pure self-interest that prompted the comparatively permissive policies of the French and Spanish—not kindness nor any beneficent interest in cultural conservation. But conservation resulted just the same, especially in terms of music. The best known of these weekly slave gatherings took place in New Orleans's Congo Square, on the present-day site of the Municipal Auditorium. After the Louisiana Purchase, New Orleans was governed by the nascent United States, but the Congo Square gatherings continued.

"K-Doe also fits in as a visual icon," Birch went on, "and his flamboyance goes back to the African concept of dress—you don't submerge yourself in a crowd, you draw attention to yourself! Flair is very much a part of New Orleans. In New Orleans your worth is not based on how much money you got but on how much respect you get. It's a warrior culture where the men are like peacocks, and K-Doe was a peacock for sure. K-Doe is totally coming out of the tradition of the trickster. He's a *gede* from Haitian voodoo culture. A *gede* will seduce you, a *gede* will get you in trouble."

In voodoo, a *gede* is a powerful spirit, or *loa*, a guardian of crossroads who possesses great charm, sexual potency, and, at times, a dangerous, contrary edge. In African American folktales, trickster figures—exemplified, for instance, by Br'er Rabbit—neutralize authority figures by outsmarting them. The wily tactics that imbued trickster tales often served as a primer for survival in the harsh realities of slavery and, later, segregation. These survival tactics include the tradition of verbal dexterity, which K-Doe drew upon and personalized. Birch expanded on this notion:

> Like *gede*, K-Doe had a childlike quality. He was very playful. And when you're a child you do not always recognize danger. K-Doe is the perfect person to be totally engaged with—he's all our fantasies—and I'm sure that's why, when I was fifteen, I was following K-Doe too. But then there comes a point when you realize, this may not be good for your health, young man! The beauty of it is that there are hundreds of *gedes* here in New Orleans. Each one is his own person, and so Ernie K-Doe is one in a long history of what this city represents in terms of African retentions. In the context of New Orleans, K-Doe is totally normal, just like he would be in Haiti, or Bahia, or Cuba. But if you put K-Doe somewhere else, he ain't normal at all.

K-DOE PERFORMING IN NEW ORLEANS
1989
Photo by Syndey Byrd

Was K-Doe a surrealist? Certainly not in terms of André Breton. Our thing in New Orleans is not surreal, just like Haitian art isn't surreal. What our thing in New Orleans does instead is take into account, consciously or unconsciously, all of those African deities that come out of Yoruba. . . . K-Doe was an icon to me but at the same time a little went a long way. Now, in the African tradition, as long as I call your name, you're alive. So obviously this brother is still here, and he's going to be here for a while.

As for the statue of K-Doe, I believe that things which start off as something good can also, over time, become an albatross. One has to be very careful about how they maintain a certain sense of respect and reverence, because it doesn't take much to tip it over to where it becomes a caricature. . . . K-Doe is pure right now. We'll see how history treats him.

CHAPTER 23: *Ernie K-Doe, James Brown, and Ernie K-Doe*

By 1998 Ernie K-Doe had bounced back further than most of his friends and fans would ever have thought possible. His regular Sunday-night performances at the Mother-in-Law Lounge attracted local regulars and musical pilgrims from around the world. He delighted loyal fans at other nightclubs, at annual events such as Jazz Fest, and at numerous benefits and charitable functions. One night, at the Aquarium of the Americas, K-Doe sang in front of the two-story shark tank. The swirl of predatory fish put a new spin on his performance of "A Certain Girl." Whenever an attractive woman walked by, K-Doe would strut behind her, a shark chasing its prey, while winking at the audience. If another "certain girl" walked by in the opposite direction, K-Doe would whirl around and follow her too.

Booking K-Doe—considered a high-risk proposition just a few years before—became a routine matter, free from concerns of a no-show or a disaster. His apparent redemption did not convince everyone that K-Doe had been saved from the brink and made whole. "No," said Jessie James, K-Doe's longtime girlfriend, "I was not relieved when he got with Antoinette. Because he never really wanted to be there with her. He still would call me and ask me to come get him and take him away. He would get mad because I wouldn't do it. Antoinette had got the grip on him. I never thought she was good for him. I think he was just pushed into marrying her and being in that barroom. And she should have kept an eye on him better than what she did when he was sick." James dismissed the notion—an article of faith in the New Orleans music community—that Antoinette had saved K-Doe from the gutter. "Antoinette got all the praises but she didn't do nothing to help K-Doe. People said Antoinette was a saint, but she wasn't a saint—she just used K-Doe to make a name for herself. She started putting all them Little Richard wigs and stuff on him. I don't think he liked that too much, but he didn't have no choice but to dress crazy. And that *was* crazy! She made him look like a cartoon, like a clown! Now look at these pictures of K-Doe here in a regular suit and a tie—that's how he liked to dress. I don't think he was ever happy there."

K-Doe clearly seemed happy when Antoinette shepherded him to New York for the Rhythm and Blues Foundation's annual awards banquet, held at a swanky Midtown hotel on February 26, 1998. She watched with pride as he received a Pioneer Award, which came with a fifteen-thousand-dollar honorarium. K-Doe's selection for this honor was advocated by singer Mable John, best known for the 1966 hit "Your Good Thing (Is about to End)" and for her longtime leadership of Ray Charles's female backup singers, the Raeletts. John reported that she and K-Doe were old friends from "back in the early '60s. He was on a tour with me and my brother, Little Willie John. K-Doe always had that southern hospitality and love, and he was a hard worker. We all were; we had to be. We would do thirty one-nighters in a row."

This grueling lifestyle, with its risk of substance abuse, along with the vast underpayment of artists' royalties, inspired the creation of the Rhythm and Blues Foundation in 1987. Its stated mission is "the historical and cultural preservation of Rhythm and Blues music and recognition of participants in its community." Some critics have decried such efforts as insufficient. This has not deterred strong support by musicians, including respected elders such as Mable John. "I was instrumental in K-Doe getting that award from the R&B Foundation," John stated. "I entered K-Doe's name as a person who was deserving because he'd been around a long time. He'd done a lot of good work, he'd had hit records, he'd paid his dues, so he was a prime candidate. At that time I had not been in touch with K-Doe recently. I was just trying to remember all of the artists whom I'd worked with over the years . . . [who] people would not even remember or know about, and who therefore might miss out."

Fellow awardees at the 1998 event included Bobby Byrd (James Brown's longtime sidekick), Gladys Knight and the Pips, Tyrone Davis, Faye Adams, the O' Jays, saxophonist David "Fathead" Newman, Kim Weston, the doo-wop groups the Five Satins and the Harptones, the histrionic "Screamin'" Jay Hawkins, and Atlantic Records cofounder Herb Abramson. Each musician was scheduled to perform one signature number accompanied by an all-star house band featuring guitarist Ry Cooder and, from James Brown's band, saxophonist Maceo Parker and trombonist Fred Wesley. The proceedings had already grown rather wild after Hawkins—a man just as wild as K-Doe—literally set the piano on fire during a frenzied rendition of his signature hit, "I Put a Spell on You." But K-Doe turned the heat up far higher without using one drop of lighter fluid.

Taking the stage as if shot from a cannon, K-Doe launched into a supercharged rendition of "Mother-in-Law." By the second verse, he urged the band members to their feet. They complied. As the song ended, K-Doe shouted, "How about a standing ovation—FOR ME!" Amidst roaring applause, presenters Phoebe Snow and Branford Marsalis tried to escort K-Doe to the podium for his acceptance speech, but K-Doe launched into an

unauthorized encore and brought down the house again. Decorum was briefly reestablished, until K-Doe began his acceptance speech: "There have only been five great singers of rhythm and blues—Ernie K-Doe, James Brown, and Ernie K-Doe!" Sensing that he was primed for an endless, anarchic monologue—as a New Orleanian, Marsalis certainly knew of K-Doe's propensities—the presenters gently led K-Doe to the wings.

"People were amused, not annoyed," Jerry Butler recalled, cracking up all over again. "I was sitting with Gerald and Eddie Levert [of the O'Jays], and they were just rolling in their chairs. They kept yelling, 'Bring him back! We want K-Doe!' Stevie Wonder was in hysterics, too." Eddie Levert added: "To see how much K-Doe loved what he was doing, to the point where they had to drag him off the stage—that was super! It was a testament to his enthusiasm. That will stick with me the whole of my career."

"Ernie was acting just like the old Ernie I'd known way back," Mable John said with affection. "He had a message, and he still had to tell it. I told him, 'You haven't changed your outfit, you haven't changed your act, and that's exactly why I wanted you to be here!' See, my thing is that everybody needs to be themselves. Whatever and however they made it in life, they made it being *themselves*, not somebody else. If you won't allow me to be myself, then you should call the person that you want me to be like, and get *them* instead!" The only naysayer was a reporter who complained about K-Doe "overstaying his welcome like the proverbial mother-in-law."

When K-Doe was finally offstage, Smokey Robinson, the evening's suave emcee, returned to the podium—but was too convulsed with laughter to continue. Robinson had the giggles for a full five minutes before he could gather himself and resume his official duties. Throughout the rest of the evening, calls from the audience rang out, urging K-Doe to return. Quite simply, he stole the show. A bemused buzz about him began to resonate once again in music-business circles.

K-Doe assessed the banner evening in the matter-of-fact tone of one who has merely received his due: "Everybody was there—Jerry Butler, Smokey Robinson, who all you can name—to see if I could still do it. Those that thought I couldn't, they made a mistake—they made a *big* mistake. The band playin' behind me was James Brown's band, and Bobby Byrd just fell out; he told the band, 'Y'all are gonna see something,' and Fred Wesley said, 'I am ready to *play*!' They went to playin' and I made them close up their books. And then I said, 'Y'all are sittin' down, y'all stand up, *don't nobody sit down on Ernie K-Doe!* STAND UP, 'cause we gonna do it the Ernie K-Doe way! And when we got through that evening, everybody was standing, and everybody was singing, 'Burn, K-Doe, burn!' I'd like to tell everyone to keep on sayin' your prayers and stickin' by me. I did it in the early '60s and I'm coming back. And just like a prizefighter, I'm not gonna duck anyone, I tell 'em, 'Don't push and shove; I *will* get to you. Don't be shamed, just stand in line and get your punishment while you can!'"

ERNIE AND ANTOINETTE EN ROUTE TO THE RHYTHM AND BLUES FOUNDATION'S ANNUAL PIONEER AWARDS
1998
Courtesy Antoinette K-Doe

K-Doe followed up his triumph in Gotham with a wildly received set at the 1998 New Orleans Jazz and Heritage Festival. As he had done back in 1984—the year he held his own event in New Sarpy—K-Doe boycotted the 1997 Jazz Fest. A pay dispute contributed to this situation, as did other business issues. The '97 performance had been contracted through Milton Batiste, who was generally regarded around town as K-Doe's agent and manager. But Antoinette informed the festival, just ten days out, that Batiste had no authority to book her husband. For K-Doe to appear, she demanded, the deal would have to be renegotiated through her, and at a significantly higher price. "I just can't do this anymore," Batiste said in response, more with weariness than anger; "I am through working with K-Doe."

K-Doe reinforced his demand for a raise on a local television newscast, demanding that festival producer Quint Davis come to the Mother-in-Law Lounge with a briefcase containing five hundred thousand dollars in small-denomination bills. Davis refused, of course, both sides stood firm, and the '97 festival came and went sans Emperor. Though annoyed, Davis put the incident in perspective:

> Over the years, K-Doe gave Jazz Fest some of our most-extreme-possible moments. The alpha and omega of Ernie-ness and festival-ness. He did some amazing performances on our night shows. Those were high points of my respect for Ernie. Then fast-forward to his perception that the night shows were the *only* place for a legitimate artist to play. For a while Ernie decided that playing the fair in the daytime was beneath him. Never mind all the major artists who played there. And '97 was not the only time he called a press conference. During one of the years of our worst rain, way back, the grounds were all flooded. There was thick mud, and we were out there hanging on by the skin of our teeth. And—I'll never forget this—one of the TV stations came out to the Fair Grounds, supposedly to do a story about me, the festival, and the impact of the weather. But all they really wanted to ask about was why Ernie K-Doe wasn't playing. I'm thinking, "The whole festival site almost got destroyed by a storm, and all you want to talk about is K-Doe?" I couldn't believe it! But K-Doe was such a powerful, important, transcendent personality. When you think of the New Orleans music landscape of incredible greater-than-life characters: James Booker, Earl King, Professor Longhair, Snooks Eaglin—people that in every way were unique personalities, unique talents, and just really surrealistic characters—I think Ernie K-Doe has to pretty much lead that parade.

Negotiations for '98 went smoothly, however, and K-Doe turned in a strong set accompanied by the Blue Eyed Soul Revue. Afterward he came to the festival's oral-history venue, the Allison Miner Music Heritage Stage, for an onstage interview. There K-Doe unleashed a non sequitur of mystical proportions. Apropos of nothing, he announced: "Last night, my wife and I were sitting on the side of the bed, eating peanut butter and jelly. Not because we *have* to, but because we *want* to!" A long, pregnant pause followed as people tried to grasp what K-Doe was talking about. Even serious K-Doe-philes—and there were many in the audience—reacted to this gem with amazement.

K-Doe's Jazz Fest performance and interview especially thrilled the Mandeville Free Thinkers Society, a loosely formed club led by Doc Mancina and Louis Nugent. The Free Thinkers offered the public a "Fantasy Bus Ride" to the '98 Jazz Fest, with special guest hosts Ernie and Antoinette. En route the bus stopped at Charity Hospital, where K-Doe yet again recounted the story of his birth. *Times-Picayune* writer Angus Lind came along for the ride, noting that "strange, mysterious and bizarre things go on during the Jazz Fest that don't show up on the stages," and quoting Nugent on the Free Thinkers' raison d'être: "We are people who want to think about stuff that society doesn't want us to think about. We will not fall victim to the societal trapper's way of life. We cure things by showing you how to free think. When you do this, all of a sudden you lose your type-A personality, the sinking ship syndrome, work-a-holism, pre-mature adulthood, acute intimacy issues, or whatever societal malady you've been afflicted with . . . When you're with us, you can touch, feel and breathe the breath of these luminaries. It's kinda like a petting zoo on a bus."

Fantasy Bus riders were also treated to the company of J. Monque'D. A skilled blues singer and harmonica player, Monque'D (pronounced MUNK-uh-DEE) stands alongside the Emperor as one of the more outré characters in New Orleans's musical demimonde. Monque'D and K-Doe shared several significant traits. Admirably, both were sincere and tireless boosters of local music, although their passion worked many people's last single nerve. Both were immersed in the historical minutiae of R&B and blues: with almost encyclopedic accuracy, both could tell you exactly who played on such-and-such a New Orleans record in, say, 1954. But both lost all objectivity when discussing themselves, often veering into wild embellishment if not totally baseless fiction.

Sometimes Monque'D claimed to be black—specifically, the light-skinned love child of Slim Harpo—and a victim of racism. In other tales he was white, set upon by discriminatory black people. Neither version explained the outburst "I'd have been a big star years ago if only I was born Jewish like Stevie Ray Vaughan!" These rants and contradictions made him eminently suitable for cobilling with the K-Does on the Fantasy Bus. So did the titles of some J. Monque'D albums. *Butter Churnin' Man*, for example, exploited the double-entendre potential of this laborious dairy process and its repetitive hand motions.

As a fly on the wall among this exotic elite, Angus Lind closed out his article on a contemplative note: "When the day finally drew to a close and 'Big Tweezers' Nugent could reflect on what had taken place, he said this: 'It was kinda like an alien abduction, where you got picked up and jostled around for about 12 hours then dropped off. You didn't quite believe all that happened.' But this time—it did." Three years later, just after K-Doe died, Nugent looked back again on the Jazz Fest adventure. Ernie K-Doe, he told

K-DOE BACKSTAGE AT THE NEW ORLEANS JAZZ AND HERITAGE FESTIVAL, WEARING HIS "I'M COCKY BUT I'M GOOD!" BOXER SHORTS
1998
Photo by Syndey Byrd

Lind, "was the only real magnetism we had left in terms of characters. We got Dr. John, sure, but Dr. John ain't gonna let the Mandeville Free Thinkers Society pick him up in a bus and drive him around with a bunch of drunks. Ernie would and did."

CHAPTER 24: *Mr. K-Doe Goes to Washington*

In July 1999 folklorist and radio host Nick Spitzer brought K-Doe to Washington, DC, to perform in an Independence Day concert. The show also featured such diverse and seminal figures as Latin percussionist Tito Puente, bluegrass banjoist Ralph Stanley, gospel singer Shirley Caesar, and blues-country-rockabilly guitarist Bill Kirchen. Held at the Sylvan Theater, at the foot of the Washington Monument, the show was broadcast live on NPR. Spitzer hired Eddie Bo and his band to back up K-Doe, who did not carry full-time accompanists at the time. But the Emperor did bring his own duo of dancing backup singers—Antoinette and Tee-Eva Perry, collectively known as the Paradise Ladies. Perry was already well known around New Orleans as an actress and the owner of a popular praline shop. (In later years, after K-Doe's death, the Paradise Ladies became a threesome with the addition of Geannie Thomas, who helped Antoinette run the lounge.)

While waiting in the airport for the flight to Washington, K-Doe reminisced, with some embellishments, about his previous performances in the capital city: "I used to play in Washington back in the '60s, at the sweet old Howard Theater. I was on a big show there with Del Shannon, Chuck Jackson, Smokey Robinson and the Miracles, and a young lady called Baby Face Washington. I played at the White House several times when John F. Kennedy was president," K-Doe claimed, "but I never got to meet him. This time I'm going back under President Bill Clinton. What would I say to President Clinton if I got to meet him? 'Come on up on this stage and blow your tenor saxophone!' Am I nervous about playing in front of such a big crowd?" K-Doe asked rhetorically. "Let's just put it like this: I am ready for them, and I hope they are ready for me. I haven't missed yet. There is a first time for everything, but I don't believe that this will be it. And I'm glad that I had the pleasure of making a record that will stand the test of time, because people gonna have a mother-in-law until the end of the world. There is plenty of competition for me now, because the young generation has heard about Ernie K-Doe, and now they are going to get a chance to see Ernie K-Doe, and they will find out that their parents was telling them the truth."

K-Doe was feeling enthusiastic about his brand-new album, *The Best of Ernie K-Doe*. This title implied an anthology of K-Doe's old hits. In truth, the New Orleans–based Mardi Gras label released an assemblage of K-Doe's late-career remakes, previously issued on DuBat and licensed from Milton Batiste. These performances were nowhere near as good as the early-'60s Minit sides. But the misleading title did not faze K-Doe, who was long accustomed to record-company shenanigans. Nor was he surprised when, shortly before the DC trip, the New Orleans music magazine *OffBeat* dispensed with conventional journalistic protocol by having the Emperor review his own album. Bunny Matthews, a prominent New Orleans cartoonist and a pioneering chronicler of the city's R&B scene, wrote a preface for K-Doe's critique: "In honor of Independence Day, we felt it would be appropriate to grant Ernie K-Doe the independence to review his own latest release. No other individual, born at Charity Hospital or not, could possibly fathom the innate genius of Mr. K-Doe with anywhere near his facility or resonance. On the Fourth of July, the Emperor of the World, appropriately costumed as Uncle Sam, will perform in Washington, D.C. This concert will be heard throughout the nation, from sea to shining sea, on National Public Radio and locally via the airwaves of WWOZ. Hail to the Chief, Mrs. K-Doe, and his Mother-in-Law!" Never one to engage in false modesty, K-Doe began his self-assessment with "Hopefully I'm right this time, and I have been right so far, but I think I have 12 solid hits." He concluded, "You see, this CD is like a puzzle. To put a puzzle together you need the right pieces. Each of my songs is a different piece to that puzzle, but they all fit together."

Waiting at the New Orleans airport for his flight, K-Doe discussed his new release: "I got a new album that's a gas. Warren Hildebrand put it out on Mardi Gras Records. And I got a song on there called 'You Done Did It, Baby.' It goes, 'You done did it, baby, you made my love come down.'" (This song also includes the line "The way you make love, baby, the King of Sweden ought to give you a Nobel Prize!") "It's the first blues song that I ever recorded; the others were all different styles, but this is my first real blues on record. And in this record, the lady that I'm singing to, I call her 'Booty.' You see, every woman in the world carry a booty, and she thinks that her cargo is the best in the world. I'm relying on all the ladies in the world to let this be their national anthem. When I holler, 'Oh, booty! Good booty! Welfare booty! Every kind of booty!' then all the ladies gonna stand up and holler, 'I got one!' and then the lady across the hallway, she gonna holler, 'I got one too!' All the ladies is proud of what they're carrying around. It's a ladies' theme song. I want the ladies to feel proud about themselves. And I want them looking forward to me making my comeback."

A crowd gathered during this soliloquy—a large group of Boy Scouts in full uniform, on a field trip to the nation's capital. They clearly sensed the presence of greatness, but they were far too young to recognize the celebrity whom destiny had booked on their flight. No matter. Ernie K-Doe, resplendent in an orange suit and shoes, did not disappoint them. As the scouts waited patiently in line, he graciously signed autographs for them all and posed for snapshots.

Upon arrival in DC the musicians and their entourage were whisked straight to the stage for a rehearsal. A deli tray awaited the hungry travelers, but the caterer obviously was not from New Orleans. "What the hell is this?" several musicians asked with revulsion. They rummaged through to the lower layers of piled food, muttering imprecations and searching in vain for red beans and rice with hot sausage, shrimp po'boys on French

K-DOE AND THE PARADISE LADIES (ANTOINETTE AND TEE-EVA PERRY) PERFORMING AT THE SYLVAN THEATER, WASHINGTON, DC
July 4, 1999
Photo by Ben Sandmel

bread. The portobello-mushroom-and-roasted-pepper sandwiches remained uneaten. So did the bowls of couscous and tabbouleh.

The next morning, the concert's headliners gathered in the hotel lobby. All were leaders in their respective genres, but one excelled in terms of sartorial splendor. En route to the theater, Ernie K-Doe sported a blinding cobalt-blue suit. Upon arrival, he wandered into the musicians' hospitality tent and encountered the members of Shirley Caesar's band. Like the Boy Scouts in the airport, these gospel players knew that K-Doe was a celebrity, yet they couldn't ID him.

"Aren't you a famous singer?" one of Caesar's musicians asked.

K-Doe replied, after a lengthy pause, "Yes, I am." Then he stood in silence, letting the full profundity of this fact sink in.

"Well, who are you?" his inquisitor continued.

"Let's just put it like this," K-Doe intoned. "There ain't but two songs that will stand the test of time, until the end of the world. One of them is 'The Star Spangled Banner.' The other one is 'Mother-in-Law.'"

After more dramatic silence, K-Doe turned and strode to his trailer. Following lengthy preparations, he emerged with the Paradise Ladies, Antoinette and Tee-Eva Perry, all three in full patriotic regalia: Uncle Sam costumes done up in red, white, and blue, complete with oversize stovepipe hats—designed and handmade by Antoinette. When his wife addressed him as Uncle Sam, K-Doe responded, "Y'all behave, or I'm gonna start signing them dollar bills on the left!" Like many K-Doe-isms, this sounded quite deep—but upon reflection no one had a clue what it meant.

K-Doe and Eddie Bo were relaxed and nonchalant about the upcoming show, but the Paradise Ladies radiated excitement. "From a little girl," Tee-Eva gushed, "this has always been my American dream, to be an entertainer, singer, and dancer. . . . I'm so proud that Antoinette and Ernie chose me to perform with them. It's the Fourth of July, and here I am in Washington, DC!" "I thank God that Ernie is finally getting the recognition that he deserves," Antoinette reflected. "I thank God that he's living to see it. God has been a healing process for the two of us. I respect Ernie because he respects ladies, and he never tries to clip a lady's wings in business. That says a lot about him, especially for a man from his generation—they don't like to see a lady fill a man's shoes. But he respects me as a bar owner, and he supports me and Tee-Eva 100 percent. I love performing with him, and sewing our costumes gives me an outlet for different sides of my personality and my creativity. The main thing to understand is that I'm married to the man, not the legend. The legend belongs to the people. I know him as the legend but I love him as the man behind the legend. As long as you can separate those two things then you can handle it. I respect his career, and he respects mine. When I'm busy at my sewing machine, the legend leaves me alone."

K-Doe went on to do a great show, as did all the performers on the bill. The audience and the stage crew were all clearly under K-Doe's spell, with one notable exception—the understandably confused interpreter on the far right of the stage who attempted to sign such slogans as "Burn, K-Doe, burn!" for the hearing impaired. After the show, exhausted but exultant, K-Doe assessed his own segment of the concert: "It went good, man, very nice! I enjoyed myself! You got over sixty thousand people out there. That shows you I still have drawing power. That makes me feel good, a Charity Hospital baby from New Orleans dressed up like Uncle Sam on the Fourth of July in Washington, DC! And it proves my point too. Let's just put it like this: There ain't but two songs that will stand the test of time . . ."

CHAPTER 25: *Theme People and a Father Image*

After returning home from the July Fourth concert as heroes, the K-Does enjoyed a dramatic increase in business at the Mother-in-Law Lounge. Ernie loved to meet and greet the public, and it was he who usually opened the door to give visitors a warm, hospitable welcome. This was just as true on mundane weeknights, when visitors might find Ernie and Antoinette watching TV in their slippers, as on busy weekends or special occasions such as New Year's Eve. A bash to usher in the new millennium was thrown at the lounge by Michael Burke, a frequent visitor to New Orleans. Burke is emblematic of the many people who come to New Orleans—for a Jazz Fest weekend, perhaps, or for Mardi Gras—and instantly fall in love with the city. New Orleans amazes with its exotic ambience, subtropical beauty, and soulful local culture—especially its culinary and musical traditions. Repeated praise of these attributes has made them a cliché, but justifiably so. Equally significant, although less touted by the tourism industry, is the city's intangibly liberating feel, the absence of pressure to conform. In 1989 Michael Burke worked as lighting technician on the Coen brothers' film *Miller's Crossing*. "Coming from New York to shoot that movie in New Orleans," Burke said, "I was captivated by the city in every way. It was inexpensive, accessible, loose, and filled with characters. That's why New Orleans is the closest thing to heaven on earth. That's why I spend two or three months there every year." Burke explained the impetus for his party:

> In the fall of '99 everybody was going crazy about Y2K. But most places were charging exorbitant covers to celebrate it, to see if all the computers would fail and the world would stop. I thought it would be great to have something for those folks that didn't want to get ripped off. And an idea popped into my head: Ernie *K*-Doe and Y2*K*. I went down to the Mother-in-Law Lounge and talked to Antoinette. She beamed and said, "That is just too precious—I don't know why I didn't think of that!" The party was great. I sent out an invitation to "Celebrate the birth of Ernie-2K-Doe" as "Emperor of the New Millennium." Ernie and Rico Watts played a couple of sets, and people came and went while

CELEBRATE the BIRTH of

ERNIE -2K- DOE

EMPEROR of the NEXT MILLENNIUM

at

THE CENTER of the UNIVERSE

THE "MOTHER-IN-LAW" LOUNGE

NEW YEAR'S EVE 9 PM

1500 N. CLAIBORNE • NOLA • 504-947-1078

making their rounds around town. The preacher who had married Ernie and Antoinette came down, blessed the bar and all the customers, and then he started collecting donations. In other words, he shook everybody down for his church. . . . It was a classic case of the Mother-in-Law Lounge as a real comfort zone. My parents came down from New Jersey, and they finally understood my love of New Orleans and why I spend so much time here. Whoever I bring to the Mother-in-Law Lounge always walks out smiling, with the feeling, "My God, this place is really special!" And anyone who doesn't get it just tends not to be a friend of mine—they bounce off instead of targeting home.

K-Doe spent the first months of Y2K preparing for a tribute to himself, organized by a gaggle of youthful rock bands. At first glance, Ernie K-Doe might have seemed an unlikely inspiration for the cadre of rock musicians whom he collectively called "the children." Most of these tattooed and tongue-pierced acolytes were half the Emperor's age, and many of them felt utterly starstruck. Such awe, combined with culture shock, caused some tension and strained communication. Maria Berg, guitarist for the Rubber Maids, took it upon herself to serve as an intermediary. "Not a single one of the bands would practice with Ernie if I wasn't there," Berg related, "because they were afraid of him, afraid to even speak to him personally." Sometimes K-Doe's arcane language exacerbated their reticence. During rehearsals K-Doe grew dissatisfied with one band's rendition of his classic material and allegedly offered this lone sentence of instruction: "If I wanted my red beans runny, I'd have put more water in 'em!" This cryptic metaphor, which none of the children understood, only confused and rattled them even more. But, Berg said:

I always felt comfortable, from the minute I first walked into the lounge. I liked the coziness of the place, and then when K-Doe started singing along to his own records through the taxi dispatcher's mic, it was instant love. So I was glad to speak for everyone. I treated K-Doe like I treated my grandfather. I respected K-Doe so much, and I felt like I got so much out of knowing him. We became very close, and the communication was very important. We would have this conversation: he'd say, "The boy child hasn't been born that will replace Ernie K-Doe," and I'd say, "But, K-Doe, what if it's *me*?" The idea was not to be gender specific. We had that conversation a lot, and he would love it, absolutely adore it, when I would banter with him. That's what we did all the time, and that's why I was the communicator for the bands.

But I also had the feeling, like everybody else on the show, of "Why would K-Doe want to work with *us*?" He was such a legend, with such an ego; why in the world would he be interested? I think it was because he was smart, aware, and he realized that we young people—the bands, our followers, our scene—were one of the biggest parts of his clientele. We would be in the club when no one else was.

TOP
INVITATION TO THE ERNIE-2K-DOE CELEBRATION
1999
Courtesy Michael Burke

BOTTOM
K-DOE PERFORMING AT THE CELEBRATION
December 31, 1999
Photo by Syndey Byrd

> The program was all K-Doe songs, for every band. And K-Doe just thought that we should know all his material automatically. He assumed we did, and he didn't want to practice as much as we thought we needed to. He would get really frustrated because he wanted us to find "the pocket," get in the pocket. K-Doe's big complaint was that we didn't have his groove, and he needed that. He would try really hard to teach us, but we didn't know what "putting it in the pocket" meant, and what it means is more of a feel, anyway, rather than anything specific. He was very determined that we should do exactly what he said, but at the same time he couldn't always explain exactly what he meant. A couple of times he screamed at people. Not often, but that was why I had to be there every moment, because if a band needed something from K-Doe, they didn't know how to ask him. So they'd tell me, "Maria, would you please ask Mr. K-Doe if he would please do whatever." And sometimes K-Doe got very cranky and short tempered, but you have to remember he was practicing every single day with a different band of twenty-year-olds.

K-Doe abjectly craved glamour and glory while many of his young protégés rejected fame as crass. But even with such ostensibly different attitudes toward success and conformity, K-Doe and the children shared a distinct sense of estrangement from mainstream society. K-Doe had opted out of being "a regular working cat," as drummer Herman Ernest put it, in order to doggedly pursue his dream of more hit records. Many of the children—some forty years younger than K-Doe—shunned conventionality simply out of youthful rebellion. Despite converging from opposite directions, their bond was strong, as Antoinette analyzed:

> K-Doe picked up that young audience because when we opened the Mother-in-Law Lounge, a lot of the punk-rock kids would come in and hang out. Nobody would give these kids a chance. They had on the black clothes, the earrings, the dyed hair, et cetera, et cetera. A lot of them was a long ways from home and down on they luck. K-Doe, knowing he had been down on his own luck at one time, like them, he took these kids to his heart. He taught them his music, and he tried to teach them to turn their habits around with the drinking. . . . Bein' that K-Doe was a big artist, these kids were surprised that he took time with them. He taught them his music, and they taught him their music. He taught them how to play their music backwards and get a whole new sound. And he would come to their gigs, at these little rock holes, as we call them in New Orleans, and he would get up there and perform with them. They were able to combine their punk-rock music and K-Doe's music. And so that grew into a world of new fans for K-Doe. Those kids wanted to repay me and K-Doe for what we had done for them. We were like a mother and father to them away

> from home. We told them, "Once you get successful we're not going to have to go through secretaries to see you, because we've been like your black mama and daddy!"

Lefty Parker, the bassist for Fireball Rocket, said he "heard Antoinette say this so often that black customers in the lounge would sometimes whisper, 'K-Doe had *white* children?'"

Antoinette concluded, "So what the children did to pay him back was hold that tribute to him with the five different bands. Each band had to perform six K-Doe songs. The lounge was so full that the crowd spilled out onto Claiborne. That was a beautiful time in K-Doe's life. For K-Doe, these young white kids were like his own kids; they made him so proud, and he was a father image for them. None of the kids realized what they did, but they replaced something in K-Doe's heart that he was missing then: having his own kids around him. His real children didn't come to his shows or take an interest in his music."

Ernest Kador Jr. politely dismissed this notion: "I didn't go to my father's shows at the lounge because I am not the type to drink or smoke. But I *would* go the lounge early in the morning and have a conversation with my father, drink coffee. Or I'd pick him up and we'd go for rides and talk. He was a wonderful man, he was good to me and my brothers, and we were very close. I saw him perform when I was a kid; he would sneak me in the side door at the Dew Drop, things like that. But in later years, no, I didn't see him perform. But that is just because I am not a nightlife person."

How gratifying for K-Doe, then, that young nightlife people were eager to absorb the musical knowledge that he felt impelled to impart: "What you need to know about Ernie K-Doe," he stated shortly after the tribute show, "is that I got some cockiness I can lend to someone else. You only as strong as you want to be. With those bands, the children, I took two weeks of rehearsal with them and I showed them the Ernie K-Doe way. One thing I liked about them, they kind of remind me of myself. I never said 'No,' I never said the words 'I can't.' You never know what you can do until you try it, so try it and then you will know. Now, as a band, you play as a unit. If one man starts going wrong, everybody play that note wrong along with him, and then it's right—it is *right*!" (This observation echoed a quote from the late zydeco accordionist Boozoo Chavis, a man who amply matched K-Doe in terms of feisty opinionation: "If it's wrong, *do it wrong, with me*! If I'm wrong, *you wrong too*!") K-Doe continued, "The bands have been listening to what I tell them, 'cause I done been there. I know I'm not gonna live forever, and some people don't realize that there ain't but one Ernie K-Doe in the world. By me knowin' so much and being so qualified, why not take y'all under my wing and teach y'all? And I'm having fun as well y'all having fun!" ("Fun?" Tim Smith, guitarist for Fireball Rocket, exclaimed during rehearsals for the tribute. "Fun? I haven't slept for two weeks!")

Lefty Parker identified strongly with K-Doe's unorthodox technique as an instructor: "K-Doe has taught us about intuition: he puts the feel in it; he makes it breathe. And his do-it-yourself way of pulling things off is similar to the way I grew up as a punk-rock-noise musician." Uncharacteristically, K-Doe felt that he, too, was learning: "I don't never stop studying, just like a lawyer, a doctor, a judge. Because every day something new is coming up. But if you just sit down and pay attention, and listen, it will all come out in the washer. I ain't talking about in the wringer; I mean in the washer. When it gets to the washer, it's supposed to be a finished product. That's where all the damage is done, is in the washer."

A Night to Honor Ernie K-Doe was covered for *OffBeat* by Bunny Matthews. A frequently tough and acerbic critic, Matthews loved this show:

> One of the lessons I learned from K-Doe was [that] humility is for losers and Buddhists. . . . On the evening of March 25, 2000, K-Doe and a contingent of young associates—the Rubber Maids, the McGillicuddys, Egg Yolk Jubilee, Fireball Rocket, and Quintron—staged a concert at the Mother-in-Law Lounge that will forever be etched into my cerebrum as a transcendental experience. The place—about the size of the average bedroom—was crammed to nearly ten times its capacity. The temperature was very, very hot. The patrons were my age, my elders and kids the same age as my kids. Whites and blacks. Ex-hippies and ex-punks. R&B fanatics and B&D fetishists. Bettie Page look-alikes and victims of bad tattoo artists. We were all drenched in sweat, gasping for oxygen, loving every second. And K-Doe *ruled*!
>
> Sometimes, K-Doe looked like the most feeble old man. Then the minute his hand touched a microphone, K-Doe was a cocky teenager, exploding like an H-bomb and radiating his musical power through every mortal soul in the vicinity. Pablo Picasso created masterpieces when he was 90 and K-Doe was creating his own flamboyant masterpieces, as well as inspiring a whole new generation of music lovers, until the very end.

"I think the show was really successful," Maria Berg stated, "and it really changed Ernie and Antoinette's lives. It changed the lives of everyone involved. But," Berg added, "sometimes I regretted doing it because I became responsible for it, and then afterwards in a way I felt responsible for Ernie. K-Doe just came to life after that; he was asked to do shows constantly, we were asked to do shows with him often, like at the Rock 'n' Bowl. And he was doing shows at the lounge all the time too; the lounge was hopping. It was like, once you played that show, you were tied to Ernie for the rest of your life, and you couldn't do anything else. It was almost like I'd created an amazing monster. I felt like I didn't have a chance to explore other options; it was like, all Ernie, all the Time."

Ernie and Antoinette also maintained a very close relationship with tribute participants Mr. Quintron and Miss Pussycat. He is an organist, composer, singer, inventor

TOP
PERFORMERS IN THE TRIBUTE TO ERNIE K-DOE
March 25, 2000
Photo by Scott Saltzman

BOTTOM
***TIMES-PICAYUNE* FEATURE ON THE TRIBUTE**
May 5, 2000
Staff photo by David Grunfeld

JAZZFEST 2000

K-DOE BURNS ANEW

After overcoming a sidetracked career, rhythm and blues star approaches work with renewed fervor and ego intact

By Keith Spera
Music writer

Ernie K-Doe may or may not be the "emperor of the universe," as he often proclaims, but for one night in March he was the undisputed king of North Claiborne Avenue.

Some 300 of his subjects, many of them young, tattooed hipsters decked out in their finest thrift store chic, overwhelmed the two rooms of the Ernie K-Doe Mother-In-Law Lounge and spilled into the street for "Ernie K-Doe Tribute Night." Five of the city's underground rock bands — the Rubber Maids, Egg Yolk Jubilee, Fireball Rockett, the MacGillicuddys and Mr. Quintron — backed the New Orleans rhythm and blues legend on a program

See **ERNIE K-DOE,** *A-12*

ERNIE K-DOE W/ BLUE EYED SOUL REVUE
4:10-5:10, Fox 8/ Sprint PCS Stage

'I'm coming back as a singer, and I'm going to sing more harder now, because we got a new generation that mother, father, sister and brother done told the young ones about Ernie K-Doe, and I want to live up to the standards,' says K-Doe, center, with his wife, Antoinette, left, and backup singer Tee Eva Perry.

STAFF PHOTO BY DAVID GRUNFELD

CARDINA
DIES AT

of musical instruments, and pioneering creator of the electronica-punk-funk fusion known as swamp-tech. She is an accomplished puppeteer, animator, performance artist, composer, and filmmaker. Their multimedia duet performances—such as an infomercial for Quintron's patented creation, the Drum Buddy—often included performances by K-Doe and the Paradise Ladies. Despite a growing, global touring schedule, the duo stayed in town in 2010 when the New Orleans Museum of Art mounted the thirteen-week performance-art exhibition *Parallel Universe: Quintron and Miss Pussycat Live at City Park.*

Antoinette described the two couples' relationship to *OffBeat* writer Aimée Toledano: "We would always visit—they call it the Spellcastle [Quintron and Pussycat's nightclub, the Spellcaster Lodge]—we would visit their parties over there. A lot of the older musicians and older people our age would say, 'We noticin' y'all always at the Spellcastle, y'all always over there by what they call the punk rock and the chains and the wild gangs, and drinkin' the whiskey out the douche bag . . .' They were a different type of music and different type of fans than Ernie usually has, but they were human beings and they reach out, and we enjoy being with them because they understood that we are senior citizens and we understood they were a younger generation. What really kept us so connected is because they are character people and so are Ernie and I. They are theme people and we are theme people."

For Quintron, the connection was both practical and spiritual. His description of it reflects the influence of K-Doe's convoluted cadences: "K-Doe inspired me musically because he came closer than anyone to taking church out of church but still making it church, if that makes any sense. Lots of R&B singers come from church; they have that style and that feeling and sing that way. But K-Doe took church away from church and into a bar, and then turned it *back* into church." K-Doe actually proposed this when he told John Sinclair, "Every Sunday, we gonna have church in the Ernie K-Doe Mother-in-Law Lounge. And we gonna have different preachers."

"K-Doe was such an exotic, bizarre, ethereal person," Quintron said with obvious admiration. "In his mind he really was on a higher plane. We *do* have something in common with K-Doe musically; that's why people in our scene were drawn to him, absolutely! And that common thing is that he was totally chaotic and he did not give a fuck about failing onstage. To him there was no failure onstage; he held stuff up with energy and emotion and screaming and shouting and turning disaster into glorious, successful, beautiful music. It's exactly what I do and what I have to do; it's how me and my friends make music. It was K-Doe's music that made us gather around him—the way that K-Doe would perform. He was as punk as anyone," Quintron added, pointing out a perhaps surprising parallel. "And *I*, me personally, I was not any kind of leader in making young white kids appreciate K-Doe, as some people have said—his appeal was obvious to everyone. At first you might think there was this crazy person up on that stage, but if you observed him then you'd see how K-Doe brought it back around. And then when you'd talk to him you'd see he wasn't crazy

ERNIE AND ANTOINETTE WITH MISS PUSSYCAT (IN BERET), QUINTRON (WITH KEYBOARD), AND FRIENDS
July 2000
Photo by Rick Olivier

at all, he was just different and very committed to his vision of music, the way it's made and the way it's performed. He was an outsider from way back."

"Ernie had a huge impact on my life" Lefty Parker said with reverence. "He used to say, 'If everyone hits the wrong note at the same time, it's the right note.' That didn't really make sense in a musical way, but it was his self-assuredness that made sense. He once called me a musician, which I had never claimed to be, and I told him, 'Oh, not me. I'm a guy who straps a guitar on my body to make noise.' And he grabbed my arm and said, 'You played with Ernie K-Doe; you *are* a musician!' I've agreed ever since."

Besides the white rockers who participated in the tribute, K-Doe also enjoyed high respect from youthful black musicians working in various genres. Soul singer, songwriter, and producer Tondrae Kemp, whose originals include "Reason Season Liftetime" and "Still Searching," praised K-Doe as "the closest thing New Orleans ever had to James Brown. My uncle owned a bar, and I remember K-Doe's music from when I was coming up. When K-Doe came on the jukebox people would jump up and shout, 'That's my jam!'" Kemp has made some recordings (yet to be released) making beats with samples of K-Doe's rants from WWOZ. "My man was pure narcissistic grandeur," Kemp said, smiling, "with steam and skills to back it up. One phrase from K-Doe's shows stands out to me as his calling card and long-lasting motto: 'You ain't got to love me, you ain't got to like me . . . but *one thang*—I STAND MY GROUND!' That is classic!" K-Doe likewise earned admiration from young rappers such as "Josephine Johnny" Watson, who admired K-Doe personally and professionally. (Despite New Orleans's penchant for androgyny, the moniker "Josephine" refers to the Uptown street where Watson was raised.) Though rap often tends toward deafening bass lines and minimal melody, Josephine Johnny's recordings set the bass at a milder level and explore an atypically wide and melodic range of textures and harmonies. Watson met K-Doe when he was nine years old:

> He was dating my mom. She was crazy about him. She knew all his songs, and she was in my ear with his music. Did my mom listen to K-Doe's music around the house? Oh yes, yes, yes, yes, yes! She played it a lot, and she'd even sing his songs by herself when his music wasn't playing. K-Doe is the one who started calling me Josephine Johnny. He was constantly putting that through my head, and I ran with it. But I didn't know who K-Doe was at the time, how big he was. I knew that he sang, but he was just a regular person in our house. K-Doe was pretty close to us, close, close.
>
> When I got a little older I saw K-Doe singing the "Mother-in-Law" song in a club. I saw the vibe in there, I looked at all them people, and I thought, "Oh, y'all *love* K-Doe, huh?" and I got it then. K-Doe knew I was really into music because I always liked to sing and hum and rap and beat on things. He really gave me some advice, and he would try to get me straight in the music business and encourage me to do what was best with my life. He knew I had potential.

> He influenced me because I saw and heard who he was. You know what? I just might do a remix of "Mother-in-Law"! It would be terrific! It would be easy for me, just by me being so versatile. And just like K-Doe had his "Mother-in-Law," I got my "Workin wit Sumthing." That's about a girl who's fine, she's pretty, she got a sharp look—she workin' with something!

A young lady with such a sharp look would surely qualify as "A Certain Girl."

CHAPTER 26: *Even the Most Anarchic Madness Can Yield an Elegant Method*

Shortly after A Night to Honor Ernie K-Doe, a less glorious but equally storied event unfolded at the Mother-in-Law Lounge: the confrontation with Neil Strauss and Ebet Roberts of the *New York Times*. Even the K-Does' strongest admirers were embarrassed and annoyed by their actions and subsequent attitude. Both Ernie and Antoinette refused to acknowledge that there was anything wrong, or even extreme, in imprisoning a reporter and photographer and then calling the cops on them. The K-Does would not budge on insisting that, thanks to their vigilance, a vague but pernicious conspiracy had been stopped. The closest they came to contrition was Antoinette's statement absolving Strauss of guilt by blaming everything on photographer Roberts. "Neil's a nice guy," Antoinette conceded, "but he was led astray by that evil Jezebel, that woman with the camera. Oh, yes he was. I'm a woman, and I *know* what women are like."

Columnist Chris Rose wrote about the incident in the *Times-Picayune* and interviewed all the principal characters. "Them slick-ass people from New York, Chicago, Detroit," K-Doe raved, "they've been coming 'round here making millions of dollars off Ernie K-Doe and his music for years, but I'll tell you what: they run against the wrong black man this time. . . . I been lettin' it go all my life. They treated me like I was a joke, but I tell you this: I AM SOMEBODY in the music world and you should treat me like a cat on a hot tin roof. You should tread lightly around Ernie K-Doe." K-Doe seemed especially miffed that he had granted Strauss an interview in his private sanctuary before the ruckus started. As he told Rose in an aggrieved tone, "I don't let just anyone in my van."

The K-Does' indignation elicited little sympathy. Incredulity and disappointment prevailed. So did envy. Many fellow musicians felt that the K-Does' bad behavior had been lavishly rewarded with favorable national publicity. The *Times* would likely have charged them at least fifty thousand dollars to purchase an ad the size of Strauss's article with Roberts's accompanying photo. To land on one's feet after such reckless behavior could happen only, as Dr. John put it, to "some other kind of man."

Neil Strauss's comments to Chris Rose were far more measured and tactful than K-Doe's: "It was the strangest disregard for journalistic protocol I have ever experienced.

I once had someone hang up on me during an interview and, until now, that's the worst thing that's ever happened to me on the job. I had never been detained while working on a story." In the article itself, Strauss had expressed similar amazement:

> For six years Ernie K-Doe's Mother-in-Law Lounge, a corner bar opened by this 60's rhythm-and-blues singer, has been a perfect embodiment of New Orleans unpredictability: every visit to Mr. K-Doe's shrine to himself is an adventure. But nothing in my experience interviewing musicians or spending time at the Mother-in-Law Lounge could have prepared me for what happened there this month. . . . During his last number, the racial unity song ["White Boy / Black Boy"] he stopped singing and looked directly at me. "I was good to you, wasn't I?"
>
> "You sure were, K-Doe."
>
> "Then why are you trying to record my show?"
>
> I looked down at my lap: the recorder I had used to tape our conversation was sitting there, though, of course, it hadn't been turned on since the interview. Suddenly, the music stopped and Mrs. K-Doe came roaring from behind the bar, demanding that the tape be handed over. . . . I wasn't going to relinquish the tape especially since it included other interviews I had conducted in New Orleans. "Lock the door!" she barked at a man who was either a heavy-set regular or a security guard. . . . As an R-and-B singer coming up in the 50's and 60's, [K-Doe] was no doubt cheated out of his fair share from his music, which may help explain why they thought I was trying to make a bootleg of the show to sell for personal profit at some sort of K-Doe black market swap meet.
>
> In addition the K-Does had been extremely exhausted and busy the weeks of Jazz Fest, with Mrs. K-Doe staying up all night to make costumes and cook for her husband's concerts, parties and interviews. After an hour of surreal negotiations outside the club with two police officers (which included a search of the photographer's bag for more K-Doe bootleg tapes), Mrs. K-Doe calmed down, and no arrests were made. "I'm sorry this misunderstanding happened," I told her and pointed out to her that the article I intended to write would let more people know about Mr. K-Doe and their bar.
>
> She barked back: "This man is a legend. He doesn't need any publicity."
>
> Well, he's going to get it anyway, and don't let this tale discourage you from dropping in. Take it from someone who will probably never be allowed to enter the Mother-in-Law Lounge again, my visits to New Orleans won't be the same without it.

Three years later, Antoinette forgave Strauss completely, and he returned to the city in 2003 to write a *Times* article about the K-Doe statue: "All Dolled Up in His Lounge and Shrine."

The Strauss affair was certainly the most dramatic reprimand of a lounge patron, but it wasn't the first. Several years earlier, two women started dancing together during one of K-Doe's Sunday-night performances, incurring his instant wrath. "Uh-uh, baby, get you a *man*," he said sternly, midsong, summarily ordering them off the floor. Then K-Doe told the audience, "They might go for that shit on Bourbon Street—but *not here in my club*!" Leaving in a huff, one of the women shouted, "FUCK ERNIE K-DOE!" on her way out the door. Same-sex dancing was not the only bee in K-Doe's bonnet. Dave Pirner, singer-songwriter with the band Soul Asylum, recalled going "to the Mother-in-Law one night to hear K-Doe sing with Egg Yolk Jubilee. They came out of the gate just kicking ass—it was one of those special moments that makes you know why you spend your whole life in music. Then all of a sudden Antoinette walks up and speaks to Ernie, Ernie stops the band, looks at a guy in the audience who's wearing a tank top, and says, 'This ain't no juke joint, this ain't no cathouse, this is Ernie K-Doe's Mother-in-Law Lounge, and you're gonna dress the way we want you to dress!' Apparently Antoinette was not into the sleeveless look. K-Doe throws the guy out, gives the band a four-count, and they go back into the song right where they'd stopped. I had never seen a lead singer bounce somebody out of his club in midsong without missing a beat. The guy came back later wearing a long-sleeved shirt."

During the summer of 2000, following the *Times* contretemps, K-Doe reaffirmed his bond with "the children" by recording two thematically linked new songs that he had taken to singing on every show. "Children of the World" and "White Boy / Black Boy" were K-Doe's first compositions since 1986's "Jump into Your Love." This fourteen-year dry spell corresponded with his roughest years, marked by depression and alcoholism—and with two CDs of cover songs during that time, K-Doe had little need for new material. Even at peak form, though, K-Doe placed secondary importance on tunesmithing. He is credited with contributing to a total of forty-six songs over the span of forty-eight years. "K-Doe wasn't real prolific, back in the day," Allen Toussaint commented, "and maybe that was better for me, because I might have not written so much for him. But K-Doe was definitely a talented songwriter."

Both new K-Doe numbers made sociopolitical commentary in typically cryptic fashion. "Children of the World" reiterated James Brown's 1960s admonitions, à la "Don't Be a Dropout," for kids to stay in school. But K-Doe took this plea several steps further by announcing how he would reinforce it: "I'm gonna talk to the pope, the president, and the mayor!" As if increasing volume might demonstrate his qualifications to confer with such leaders, the chorus of "Children of the World" consisted of ever-louder shouts of "K-Doe! *K-Doe*! K-DOE!" "White Boy / Black Boy" suggested a gritty version of Paul McCartney and Stevie Wonder's "Ebony and Ivory": "White boy! Play that black boy's music! / Black boy! Play that white boy's music! / It sound so good, it sound so good, when you play it together . . . / We belong together, and we sure 'nough need each other. / You for me, and me for you."

K-Doe recorded both songs live at the Mother-in-Law Lounge. Quintron produced and engineered the session, eliciting a remarkably rich and professional sound from the low-tech environs. The Blue Eyed Soul Revue accompanied K-Doe expertly, as always. Rico Watts sang background vocals. At sixty-four years old, K-Doe's voice had grown quite rough and ragged. Watts's suave Elvis Presley–isms provided the perfect contrasting balance, like a cool, palate-cleansing sorbet between the courses of a spicy meal. Antoinette had a two-song CD manufactured, and, seeking a deal, she sent copies around to dozens of record companies and producers.

No recording contract materialized from this mass mailing, but the CD indirectly propelled K-Doe onto the silver screen. Director Michael Almereyda, a prolific documentarian and feature filmmaker, used both songs in a cyber-detective film entitled *Happy Here and Now*, starring David Arquette, Ally Sheedy, Shalom Harlow, and Clarence Williams III. Almereyda also cast Ernie and Antoinette in the movie. Their scenes, which included live performance segments, were shot at the Mother-in-Law Lounge during the fall of 2000. Though the story and most of its lead characters were entirely fictional, the K-Does played themselves. K-Doe, of course, announced to anyone who would listen that he was the film's star.

Reviewing the film, David Ng of the *Village Voice* stated, "*Happy Here and Now* takes Michael Almereyda's usual reality-blurring, video-mediated experimentation to new what-the-fuck levels, which is a good thing for the most part. Souls transmigrate, identities recombine, and conflicts solve themselves, though the central mystery . . . remains ambiguous. 'If there was a point, there wouldn't be a story,' says [one character]. Almereyda adheres to the phrase's screwy logic with grace, humor, and the confidence that even the most anarchic madness can yield an elegant method." This last clause would have made a perfect slogan for Ernie K-Doe's business card.

One short snippet of dialogue from the film encapsulates Almereyda's dual depiction of New Orleans: "You heard of the French Quarter? Well, this ain't it!" Stephen Whitty of the *Newark Star-Ledger* expanded on this idea, noting, "Movies usually show us the world as it is, or at least as we'd like it to be. But sometimes, almost accidentally, they show us the world as it was. . . . *Happy Here and Now* is set in the neighborhoods of New Orleans that never made the postcards. Twisted bohemian streets that end in juke joints and oyster shacks. Desolate neighborhoods where squatters turn the corner and disappear into deserted mansions." Significant parts of this cinematic landscape changed during Hurricane Katrina, so, while fictional, *Happy Here and Now* doubles as a documentary.

Almereyda did not know Ernie K-Doe well. He did not spend much time with him before or after the film shoot. Nevertheless, his comments on K-Doe reflect a simpatico, intuitive connection between the two. Almereyda explained why he cast K-Doe in the film:

> Visiting New Orleans, I'd been a casual listener of WWOZ, so I'd heard and liked K-Doe's music. Then I happened to be at the House of Blues for a benefit

ERNIE AND ANTOINETTE, BACKED BY THE BLUE EYED SOUL REVUE, PERFORMING "CHILDREN OF THE WORLD" IN THE FILM *HAPPY HERE AND NOW*
December 2000
Photo by Aimée Toledano

for John Sinclair after his house burned down. A variety of performers had paraded across the stage, and then Sinclair matter-of-factly introduced K-Doe as the Emperor of the Universe. Ernie appeared in a yellow suit with gold appliqués, accompanied by his wife in a matching outfit. "This is my wife, Antoinette," K-Doe said. "She's the best I can do. And the best I want to do!"

K-Doe was fierce, joyful, and a bit deranged. The only equivalent in my experience was the avant-garde jazz musician Sun Ra. K-Doe carried that same kind of conviction, conveying the sense that he was a mythic being visiting the planet, and that his chosen and primary mode of expression was bound up with singing and performing onstage. To me, K-Doe embodied a particular New Orleans spirit—I could call it life-affirming, and generous, but it was also tied up with a quintessential New Orleans quality of brazen self-display. Anyhow, I tried, on our threadbare budget, to reproduce that introductory thrill. I asked Ernie to repeat the lines about Antoinette being the best he could do, the best he *wanted* to do. For some reason he tripped over the lines repeatedly, as if they didn't make sense, as if someone else had written them, and they didn't make it into the finished movie.

I'd taken note of other things he said onstage and off-, wrote them into the script, and I assumed he'd have no trouble recognizing and repeating them. But it turned out that almost all of these lines were strange to him—he tripped himself up trying to memorize his own patter. We did take after take. He wasn't well—although nobody but Antoinette knew how unwell he was—and we spent a long morning slogging through dialogue that sounded increasingly absurd. You can see where we're cutting around him. I was determined to get K-Doe saying one particular thing: "I have never had a flop record in my life, because I write from reality." For me this was a key to K-Doe's sense of himself, and it related to what the movie was about, the idea of embracing life rather than hiding from it. Plus the idea that we reflect and construct a private reality along the way. As you may recall, this line was followed by a slightly more outlandish assertion: "When I wake up in the morning, I wake up with a hit record." As if his career was an extended dream.

Part of K-Doe's charm was the transparently intense effort he projected to maintain his own shtick. From my first impression, I sensed that this persona was derived from James Brown, plain and simple, but then over time, clearly, K-Doe had stepped off that particular curb and floated into another realm. A surreal superhero aspect went into effect—he had the cape and the galactic name. And then there were the low-end marketing tie-ins: T-shirts and bumper stickers, and, as I recall, K-Doe peanut brickle and wine. In other words, I never lost sight of an element of desperation and pain. He was a star and wanted to be recognized as such, but you couldn't altogether smother an awareness of the

ON THE SET OF THE FILM
HAPPY HERE AND NOW
TOP
A STYLIST PREPARING K-DOE FOR A SCENE
BOTTOM
K-DOE IN CHARACTER
December 2000
Photos by Aimée Toledano

SUPA STAR
K-
DO

mortal creature who had enjoyed some early success but who had fallen hard and was still, perhaps forever, finding his way back. And despite or within all this mannerist style—the wig, the suits, the vampire fingernails—it's important to insist that he was an artist.

CHAPTER 27: *King for a Day*

It was nearly Christmas 2000 by the time Michael Almereyda's crew finished filming *Happy Here and Now* at the Mother-in-Law Lounge. Antoinette jumped right from the shoot into planning a flurry of activities for the holidays and the coming year. The lounge had become *the* funky-but-chic place for a wide variety of affairs, including a fiftieth birthday party for Nick Spitzer, host of public radio's popular show *American Routes*. Many musicians attended the festive event; in the best New Orleans tradition, the line between guest and performer quickly blurred. Oliver "Who Shot the La La" Morgan engaged in a long and lively conversation with writer and radio commentator Andrei Codrescu, for instance, before sitting in with K-Doe and Rico Watts. Though K-Doe clearly enjoyed playing the role of genial host, he fumbled when recognizing the evening's honoree. "Let's have a big round of applause," the Emperor proclaimed, "for our good friend, Dr. Nick *Spencer*!" But at least K-Doe knew who Spitzer was—moments later he was approached by a woman wearing sunglasses despite the lounge's dim lighting. Buttonholing the birthday boy, she removed her shades, pointed to her left eye, and asked the "doctor," "Now what am I supposed to do about this sty?"

Spitzer's relaxed, informal party had required only minimal planning. The really big event on the horizon—the party that called for months of preparation—was K-Doe's impending reign as the king of a Mardi Gras parade. Such processions and their attendant festivities are set up by organizations known as krewes. Most krewes take themselves very seriously, throwing postparade masqued balls that center on faux-royal pageantry, rooted in part in New Orleans's French heritage. Well-heeled, high-society citizens can easily spend thousands of dollars per year to participate. But K-Doe would lead Krewe du Vieux, an outfit famed for its irreverent counterculture aesthetic, biting political satire, and unbridled sexuality. This last aspect includes a propensity for festooning its parade floats with giant papier-mâché phalluses, which mainstream krewes would never dream of displaying. Krewe du Vieux further stands apart because its parade rolls more than two weeks before Mardi Gras Day, heralding the start of the carnival season. The accessible scale of this parade is likewise unique: Krewe du Vieux features comparatively small floats drawn by mules, which can navigate the narrow streets of its route through Faubourg Marigny and the French Quarter. The parades of Rex, Bacchus, and other more conventional krewes employ towering two-story tableaux pulled by tractors, which belch noxious diesel fumes. The crowds that come to these parades are also significantly

K-DOE AS KING OF KREWE DU VIEUX
February 10, 2001
Photo by Syndey Byrd

larger. For safety's sake, their routes are restricted to the city's broader boulevards, such as Canal Street and St. Charles Avenue.

There is an important element of commonality, however, in that all Mardi Gras parades are headed up by "royalty" whose reign lasts for much of the year. In some cases—such as that of Rex, who is officially toasted by the mayor of New Orleans on Mardi Gras Day—the reign constitutes the attainment of peak social stature, and it is trumpeted as such by the mainstream media. Krewe du Vieux receives relatively little prime-time coverage compared to Rex, Comus, Endymion, and the rest. The krewe spreads the word, instead, via a newsletter entitled *Le Monde de Merde*. The proud headline announcing K-Doe's reign read KREWE DU VIEUX EXPLORES 2001: A SPACE FALLACY—ERNIE K-DOE TO FIRE UP FRENCH QUARTER PARADE. A detailed description followed:

> Ever since crawling out of that first primordial gumbo, humankind has lusted for the stars. From asstronomy to asstrology, from poetry to science friction, the greatest (and sickest) minds of our species have pondered the secrets of the universe and the possibilities of zero gravity sex.
>
> This burning desire will reach its climax on Saturday, February 10, as Krewe du Vieux launches this year's parade, "2001: A Space Fallacy" . . . Reigning over this spaced oddysey will be the Emperor of the Universe himself, King Ernie K-Doe, accompanied by his wife, Queen Antoinette, and Grand Duchess Tee-Eva. As a major star in the New Orleans galaxy, King K-Doe certainly has the right stuff to take Krewe du Vieux to the final frontier.
>
> As the Krewe's space cadets, space cowboys, space invaders, darth vaders, darth naders, pregnant chads, black holes, star whores, astronaughties and other heavenly bodies boldly go where no krewe has gone before, missionary control advises . . . drink mass quantities of rocket fuel and watch Uranus.
>
> The Krewe du Vieux's seventeen sub-krewes will present their own phallic, fallacious, salacious, spacious, specious, ass-tronomical, anatomical, comical, cosmic, cosmopolitan, and conflicting interpretations of this theme.

It was no small honor for K-Doe to ride as the king of a Mardi Gras parade. When segregation still ruled, no krewe would have thus feted a black man—even one with a national hit record—except the African American Krewe of Zulu, founded in 1909. Zulu's most famous king was Louis Armstrong, in 1949. The city's strict racial restrictions had in part influenced him to pursue his career away from New Orleans. But as Armstrong told *Time* magazine: "There's a thing I've dreamed of all my life, and I'll be damned if it don't look like it's about to come true—to be King of the Zulu Parade. After that, I'll be ready to die." Racial controversy has often surrounded the Zulu parade. Its members have donned blackface since the krewe's inception. Mardi Gras historian James Gill

TOP
ERNIE AND ANTOINETTE ONSTAGE AT JAZZ FEST
BOTTOM
BACKSTAGE WITH QUINT DAVIS (K-DOE'S COUSIN ADRIANNA CADOR, RIGHT)
May 6, 2001
Photos by Tabitha Haggerty

BURN
K-DOE
BURN!

described this ironic display as "lampooning the white man's racial stereotypes." But some observers—from out of town and within the city—have long found such masking repugnant and demeaning, "a warped picture of the Negro painted by segregationists." In 1961, K-Doe's banner year, the *Louisiana Weekly* urged Zulu to cancel its "farcical, disgraceful spectacle."

But no such controversy diverted attention from K-Doe's reign. He felt thrilled to be king of Krewe du Vieux. He beamed continually throughout the parade because, as he had told *Le Monde de Merde*, "I'm gonna be up where all those other kings were, with a queen of my own. There have been kings, queens, duchesses, but we're gonna give all the others a run for their money. If anyone thinks they can outdo the Krewe du Vieux royalty, take my advice and stay home. Rex and the others are gonna to have to catch up; we're gonna leave them breathless." Antoinette found the honor deeply touching: "K-Doe was a guy who traveled national and international, and had a number-one hit, but Krewe du Vieux made him happy in his own hometown. That says a lot, and also that they chose me to be his queen. . . . It took me three months to make his clothes, and they had to be just perfect because he was going to be the *king*. . . . I love Krewe du Vieux for making him king."

At the 2001 Jazz Fest, K-Doe pointedly informed the crowd, "I might be old, but I ain't cold yet!" He proceeded to prove his point with a strong performance. During fest season he also played two successful shows, with Egg Yolk Jubilee and with Fireball Rocket. Then, on May 12, the state of Louisiana honored his lifetime achievement at the Governor's Arts Awards ceremony in Baton Rouge. Decked out in a suit of shocking pink, K-Doe gave a rather gray-flannel acceptance speech devoid of flash and egotism, urging kids to stay in school.

During the next six weeks K-Doe held court at the Mother-in-Law Lounge while awaiting responses from Antoinette's latest mailing of "White Boy / Black Boy" CDs. His mood was upbeat and expectant—a major record label would surely license the songs, he predicted—but he also appeared to be increasingly tired. In reply to expressions of concern, Antoinette claimed that Ernie had the flu.

Performing always energized him, however, and on June 10 K-Doe rose to the occasion for what would prove to be his last public show. The event, held at Tipitina's, honored a cause near and dear to his heart—Charity Hospital. Joining K-Doe and Blue Eyed Soul on the bill were Aaron Neville; New Orleans's trumpet-playing coroner, Dr. Frank Minyard; the masterful singers Leigh Harris, also known as Little Queenie, and John Boutté; the self-described "alternative dixieland-omni-pop" artist Chandler Travis; and Red Priest, a respected veteran blues and rock guitarist. Priest recalled the evening as "one of the best shows I ever saw K-Doe do. I knew K-Doe in and out, because I worked with him a lot, and so I had definitely seen him at his worst. Plus, Blue Eyed sounded great behind him. They were very reverent towards his material and they had it down really good. So many times when I had played with K-Doe the band was just

BACKSTAGE AT K-DOE'S FINAL SHOW, A BENEFIT FOR CHARITY HOSPITAL, TIPITINA'S, NEW ORLEANS

TOP
ERNIE AND ANTOINETTE

BOTTOM
(FROM LEFT) K-DOE, AARON NEVILLE, ADRIANNA CADOR, AND ANTOINETTE

June 10, 2001
Photos by Tabitha Haggerty

thrown together—he'd call out a song, and call out the key, and everyone would go in six different directions. K-Doe looked terrific too. He looked like the Emperor, like he was feeling good. He didn't look puny at all, no signs of impending doom. He still had that total-commitment attitude of 'This gig right here and now is the greatest gig of all time.' K-Doe always kept that lofty vision in his head, no matter where he was. I talked with him that night, paid my respects; he was talking shit and holding court, shaking hands and kissing babies. . . . it was one of those great nights, and K-Doe was on his game. It was a good way for him to go out."

K-Doe died, less than a month later, on July 5. Antoinette had booked four dates for him in July, most notably a July Fourth–related event called From the Twilight's Last Gleaming to the Dawn's Early Light, at Trinity Episcopal Church in New Orleans. The Emperor would have joined "more than a hundred musicians, singers, dancers and actors in a 10-hour marathon concert of all-American music" and performed, as billed, "in full Uncle Sam regalia." Following that extravaganza, another show with some of "the children" had been arranged. K-Doe was also slated to appear at a benefit for singer-songwriter Coco Robicheaux in New Orleans. And Jean Knight and Frankie Ford were looking forward to working with him in Baton Rouge. But toward the end of June, K-Doe's fatigue deteriorated into torpor. Antoinette led him forth one last time from his castle, the Mother-in-Law Lounge, and checked him in to his storied birthplace, Charity Hospital. There, Keith Spera reported in the *Times-Picayune*, "he was mostly unresponsive . . . but would perk up when she played his music on a portable stereo."

"As far as I know," Lefty Parker recalled, "me and Tim [Smith] and Lauren Dinkler from Fireball Rocket were the last people to see K-Doe alive, aside from Antoinette. We had a gig scheduled for that week with him, and Antoinette wanted us to go to the hospital. We saw him lying in bed with the wig kind of cockeyed on his head, and Antoinette kept playing his new songs really loud. At some point we were rushed out and we sat downstairs in the lobby for three or four hours until we heard." K-Doe had slipped into a coma and died. It was a testament to his and Antoinette's optimistic courage that no one knew he had been seriously ill.

Charity Hospital spokesman Jerry Romig announced K-Doe's passing and praised him for helping the hospital at the benefit show just weeks before his death: "In typical fashion of Ernie K-Doe, he appeared at no cost to us, he gave of his time. He was a very generous guy." K-Doe's years of drinking had led to cirrhosis of the liver, which weakened but did not kill him. Antoinette, eager to publicize the distinction that he had not died from drinking per se, requested an autopsy. It stated, "The single most important diagnosis related to the immediate cause of death was squamous cell carcinoma (cancer) of the gastro-esophageal junction." During the months that followed, one of the many new missions Antoinette took on was informing "the children" about the risk and symptoms of esophageal cancer.

K-DOE PERFORMING AT THE CHARITY HOSPITAL BENEFIT
June 10, 2001
Photo by Tabitha Haggerty

CHAPTER 28: *K-Doe Would Be So Satisfied*

K-Doe's wake and funeral were held July 12 and 13 at Gallier Hall, an antebellum Greek Revival edifice on St. Charles Avenue that once served as New Orleans's city hall. Mayor Marc Morial made the city-owned facility available to Antoinette at no charge, and Jackie Harris of the city's Music and Entertainment Commission coordinated all the details. Morial felt keenly aware of the moment's cultural and political significance. "If they could lay out [the Confederate general] P. G. T. Beauregard here," Morial asked rhetorically during a speech at the visitation, "why not Ernie K-Doe?" (Funeral services for Confederate president Jefferson Davis had also taken place there.) Only one other musician—the jazz guitarist, banjo player, and raconteur-historian Danny Barker—had been honored with a state funeral at Gallier Hall. Looking back, Morial—who became the president of the National Urban League in 2003—commented, "That might have been seen as sacrilege in some circles. But I thought that having K-Doe's funeral at Gallier Hall was an appropriate way to accentuate New Orleans culture, and the fact that it created a little bit of controversy was not a bad thing." Although he was only three years old when "Mother-in-Law" hit number one, Morial had great regard for K-Doe and his music:

> Ernie and Antoinette really helped connect people with a whole generation of musicians who should not be forgotten. And K-Doe was a quintessential New Orleanian. The biggest sin in New Orleans is to be boring—you can do a lot of things, but don't be dull. Ernie never was. . . . Another important point is that a lot of artists of that era, such as Ernie K-Doe, started out being very confined because of segregation. But as they gained recognition in the white community, they became ambassadors for black culture. They provided entertainment with humor and purpose and social commentary all wrapped together. . . . K-Doe disappeared from the scene for quite some time, and he reemerged around the time that I became mayor, in 1994. When I took office I really wanted to make a substantial contribution to helping rebuild, and highlight the artistic contributions of New Orleans—with a lot of emphasis on music, which is such a big part of the New Orleans brand. . . . In the '90s there was a renaissance in the city, and there was a new interest in musicians of Ernie's generation and a desire to reconnect with them, even though they were seen as being old. People wanted to know about the Ernies and the older jazz musicians. . . . One personal reason this interests me is that my family is related to the great jazz trombonist Kid Ory. So I had Ernie perform at events and activities, and he was wonderful! I love a showman, and people like K-Doe represented the New Orleans brand in everything that they said and did, what they sang about, in their nicknames, their costumes, how they brought so many elements together

TOP
K-DOE'S WAKE, GALLIER HALL
BOTTOM LEFT
ANTOINETTE WITH HER GRANDDAUGHTER
July 12, 2001
Photos by Tabitha Haggerty

BOTTOM RIGHT
IRMA THOMAS AND MAYOR MARC MORIAL
July 12, 2001
Photo by Syndey Byrd

BELL
abc
abc NEWS

to make a distinctive style of music. New Orleans has this incredible culture and musical tradition that comes up from the ground, and I think this is something that the city should aggressively promote.

Politicians figured prominently at K-Doe's send-off, drawn like moths to the incandescent media blaze. City councilmen Eddie Sapir and Troy Carter attended, as did then state representative Jackie Clarkson. As a city councilwoman, she had long been an ardent supporter of Ernie, Antoinette, and the Mother-in-Law Lounge. The visitation, held on the evening of Thursday, July 12, began with an invocation by Reverend Zebadee Bridges Sr., a leader in the religious community and a civil rights movement veteran. Irma Thomas followed with an a cappella gospel number. Mayor Morial addressed the overflow crowd while aspiring power players jockeyed for position on the pulpit. "I'm just waiting for [K-Doe] to jump up and dance. . . . We love you. We love you, buddy. . . . We're not going to forget you." As mourners filed past the casket, Walter "Wolfman" Washington bent over, repeatedly kissed K-Doe's corpse, and then fell to his knees, sobbing inconsolably.

After the big-voiced blues woman Marva Wright sang the gospel number "Somewhere Around God's Throne," a tribute by K-Doe's R&B peers began, in precisely the manner that he would have wanted. The Blue Eyed Soul Revue started it off, soon joined by Oliver Morgan on "Who Shot the La La." Reggie Hall, who had toured Jamaica with K-Doe forty years earlier, sat down at the piano and played "Mother-in-Law," quickly prompting a spirited sing-along. Al Johnson belted out his perennial Mardi Gras anthem "Carnival Time"; its celebratory theme was aptly bittersweet under the out-of-season circumstances.

Barbara George, a surprise guest given her long absence from the music scene, reprised her 1962 hit "I Know" and enjoyed a poignant reunion with her old AFO colleague Harold Battiste. Wolfman Washington assembled his band, the Roadmasters, for a rowdy romp on Jessie Hill's "Ooh Poo Pah Doo." By then many who filed past the casket were secondlining rather than walking slowly with reverence. One particularly exuberant mourner tippled liberally from a half-gallon bottle of bourbon and hospitably offered swigs to others. Photographer and champion of New Orleans music Pat Jolly reported an instance at the other behavioral extreme: "There was one stunned moment of silence in the midst of dancing, clapping and yelling, when a lady, surely not a native, turned around and was heard to say, 'Isn't it terrible . . . why he's not even in the ground yet and everyone is yelling Burn K-Doe Burn.'"

Pianist Davell Crawford—whose grandfather Sugar Boy had memorialized Mardi Gras Indian lore on "Jock-A-Mo"—sang the Ray Charles hit "Drown in My Own Tears," interspersed with a repeated question directed at K-Doe's corpse: "Why did you have to leave us?" Jean Knight unleashed her 1971 chart topper "Mr. Big Stuff," an appropriate number to honor a decedent with such swaggering self-esteem. Then Knight jumped into her 1985

TOP LEFT
WALTER "WOLFMAN" WASHINGTON PERFORMS AT K-DOE'S WAKE
July 12, 2001
Photo by Syndey Byrd

TOP RIGHT
ALLEN TOUSSAINT AT K-DOE'S FUNERAL
July 13, 2001
Photo by Tabitha Haggerty

BOTTOM
THE EMPEROR LIES IN STATE
Photo by Syndey Byrd

hit, a cover version of Rockin' Sidney's zydeco novelty number "Don't Mess with My Toot Toot." Coco Robicheaux honored K-Doe by singing "A Certain Girl."

The shifting lineup also included drummers Willie Cole and Kerry Brown; guitarists Jimmy Ballero, Detroit Brooks, and Bobby LaCour; keyboardists David Batiste and Quintron; and multi-instrumentalist Bruce "Sunpie" Barnes. As the visitation wound down, J. Monque'D delivered a dissertation on K-Doe's history as a Mardi Gras Indian, then sang the anthemic "Big Chief," bringing the crowd to its feet yet again. Solemnity returned as Allen Toussaint got everyone's rapt attention with a solo version of "Just a Closer Walk with Thee." After another rendition of this dirge, sung by Marva Wright, J. Monque'D, and others, the crowd dispersed for the evening. In Europe a New Orleans R&B concert with this lineup would have been a big-ticket item—and would certainly have earned high approval from K-Doe as "a *mess*!"

The grand spectacle of the visitation had all the trappings of a fashion show. Pat Jolly wrote a review worthy of Oscar-night coverage: "Ernie looked magnificent. Since K-Doe is the reigning 2001 King of the Krewe du Vieux, he was decked out in his white tuxedo lined with sparkling silver braided trim. Under the artistic eye of the Empress Antoinette, Ernie's royal sash gently rested near his left shoulder as his royal glistening crown adorned his long tussled [*sic*] black hair. The Empress complimented [*sic*] her Emperor by wearing a striking two piece white suit with matching sash and crown. She proudly wore the Queen sash presented to her by the Krewe du Vieux and the golden bagel around her neck presented by the Krewe du Jieux. While the Emperor's shoes were white trimmed with silver, the Empress wore solid white pumps. You may remember that Antoinette and Ernie were the first in New Orleans to design funeral clothing and casket decoration for fellow musician Jessie Hill's funeral. They recently donated those matching black and gold 'Mourning Suits' to the Louisiana State Museum."

Antoinette had designed three such matching suits: one for her, one for Ernie, and one for Jessie Hill's corpse. At this writing, a rather macabre photo of this trio is posted on a K-Doe tribute website, along with an anonymous, faux-academic photo caption claiming, "In the years since [the K-Does'] appearance at Hill's funeral, scholars have searched in vain for a historical precedent for the funeral practice of dressing to match the deceased. It turns out that even as far back as Ancient Egypt, dressing like the dead is unprecedented. Once again, the name K-Doe has made history." To date, no thanatologists, Egyptologists, or scholars of any other stripe have stepped forward to refute this assertion.

The next morning—Friday the thirteenth, July 2001—Gallier Hall opened up at 8 a.m. for the funeral and was soon declared filled to capacity. Some mourners sported scanty, risqué costumes worthy of Krewe du Vieux. As a lover and creator of costumes, Antoinette had announced that any attire would be appropriate for the wake and funeral. Reverend James Landrum began the funeral service after several hours of visitation. Sherman Washington, leader of the Zion Harmonizers and an old friend of K-Doe's, came to the podium to offer prayers and a song. The latter inspired Reverend Landrum to dance with sanctified rapture, eliciting cheers from many segments of the diverse congregation. "Deacon" John Moore commanded rapt attention with "Many Rivers to Cross," a secular song of transition by the reggae artist Jimmy Cliff. Moore prefaced the song by noting that "K-Doe would be so satisfied seeing all of you people come out here to bow down to him."

Philip Baptiste of the Zulu Social Aid and Pleasure Club regaled the crowd with anecdotes from K-Doe's life, including stories of his legendary generosity. Allen Toussaint reminisced about recording with K-Doe and then played a medley of their collaborative hits. Pausing for a moment, Toussaint said, "You can feel how thick the spirit is in this place." That spirit inspired K-Doe's nephew Charles Johnson to jump up from his chair and burst into a rendition of "Take My Hand, Precious Lord." Johnson's intensity would have made K-Doe and Archie Brownlee proud. During the final viewing, the Zulu Gospel Ensemble sang a medley including "This Little Light of Mine," "Jesus on the Mainline," "Leaning on the Everlasting Arms," and "I Am a Soldier." Then the coffin was closed, and Zulu attendants ushered it out onto St. Charles Avenue.

In the brutal midday July heat, a crowd of mourners estimated at five thousand followed K-Doe's casket on a long trek through downtown New Orleans. City officials had cordoned off streets and provided ample police supervision. In keeping with the hallowed tradition of jazz funerals, the bereft throng followed behind a succession of brass bands. The assemblage at K-Doe's funeral included some of the city's best groups, both traditional and modern. The Little Stooges, the Little Rascals Brass Band, Troy "Trombone Shorty" Andrews, and the Young Tuxedo Brass Band—led by trumpeter and cornetist Gregg Stafford—all played in tribute to the Emperor. K-Doe's coffin, plainly visible inside a glass-walled, horse-drawn hearse, was escorted by three grand marshals and followed by members of the Young Men Olympian Junior Benevolent Association. All were dressed in black suits and white gloves, and all took slow, rhythmic, stylized steps in unison.

The parade filed through the Central Business District, picking up numerous participants on the streets, while people in office buildings waved from on high. Skirting the French Quarter, the procession arrived at St. Louis Cemetery #2, a venerable graveyard where many of the weathered inscriptions are written in French. There, another unprecedented act of homage took place, as K-Doe was welcomed into the ancestral vault of a white family. The idea had evolved a few days earlier, in a conversation between Antoinette and her old friend Anna Ross Twichell, a regular at the Mother-in-Law Lounge. Ernie had left no burial instructions, Antoinette confided, and she had no plan herself, nor substantial resources with which to implement one. Anna Ross's daughter Heather Twichell told Antoinette that Ernie would be welcome in the tomb, which held six generations of their family. "It's always been our understanding," she told Lili LeGardeur of the *Times-Picayune*, "that any of our friends who didn't have a place to go could be buried in our tomb. . . . it's not a difficult thing to give. And," the twenty-two-year-old

FOLLOWING PAGES
A CROWD GATHERS OUTSIDE GALLIER HALL FOR K-DOE'S FUNERAL PROCESSION AND SECOND LINE TO ST. LOUIS CEMETERY #2
July 13, 2001
Photo by Tabitha Haggerty

concluded, "I'm not getting in there anytime soon." Despite the Twichells' kindness, burial space did prove a difficult thing to give. St. Louis Cemetery #2 is controlled by the Archdiocese of New Orleans, which needed to see the deed to the tomb to approve an interment. Anna Ross could not find the document, and some "legal dancing" followed before permission was finally granted. On the morning of the funeral, the paper turned up in her lingerie drawer.

After K-Doe was entombed—or "cut loose," in jazz-funeral parlance—the next phase of the tradition unfolded: the brass bands abandoned their slow dirges and went up-tempo. The second-liners burst into spirited strutting to the strains of "Didn't He Ramble." Some crawled on all fours in the frenzied move known as popping gators. Others went so far as dancing atop St. Louis Cemetery's narrow, crumbling brick walls, enacting a historic preservationist's worst nightmare. The multitude left the cemetery and headed downriver on Claiborne Avenue, converging on the Mother-in-Law Lounge for the repast, as such postfuneral gatherings are known in New Orleans. Very few mourners could actually enter the club, which held barely a hundred people, and the celebration soon spilled onto the street. "I Cried My Last Tear" T-shirts were for sale. Handbills distributed to the crowd announced that Ernie K-Doe was now the Emperor of the Afterlife, and in short order the website www.k-doe.com proclaimed, "The Emperor is dead. Long live the Emperor."

Some two months after the service, Antoinette reinforced this notion by unveiling the K-Doe statue. "It was hard at first," she reflected, "losing K-Doe. I felt like my world had crumbled. But I was there with K-Doe when he passed, and I made a promise to him that I would keep his legacy alive. And to keep that promise I had to be very successful with it. My kids didn't understand what I wanted to do; they thought I should come live with them and raise my grandkids, and I said, 'No, no, no, no, no.' Then Jason Poirier said, 'It's too soon for Mr. K-Doe to die. I will make a bust of him for you.' I said, 'Well, make a whole statue.' Jason did, and it was so much of an image of K-Doe that I knew I was given a second chance. And I promoted the statue, kept on with that, and now the statue have taken off in a world of its own—it is a legend too. So I feel that I'm very, very grateful to have known the original legend, and now I also have a statue. Getting a second chance gives you the strength to carry on. . . . And if God gives you a second chance, don't let the Devil in to make you give up."

In response to those who found the statue creepy and macabre or who bluntly questioned Antoinette's sanity, she declared (and rationalized), "Of course *I* know that K-Doe is deceased. But the *fans* don't consider it a statue; to them it's Ernie K-Doe. I want people to remember K-Doe as a legend; I want his music and legacy to live on. It's hard for the fans to know him the way I did; he was only my husband but he was their *legend*. So I can't tell them how to mourn."

ANTOINETTE AT K-DOE'S GRAVE, ST. LOUIS CEMETERY #2
July 13, 2001
Photo by Tabitha Haggerty

Several months after the funeral, a eulogy of sorts ran in Chris Rose's column in the *Times-Picayune*: "I must begin with a confession. When Ernie K-Doe died this July, after the surprise and sadness wore off, I felt a personal if somewhat discomfiting pang of despair: I wondered: What about me? . . . Simply put, he was great copy . . . right up there with . . . [fellow Louisianan] Britney Spears." Then, in February 2002, Antoinette's mother, Leola Clark, passed away. She, too, was buried in the Twichell family tomb. Rose attended the funeral and wrote a column picking up where his previous K-Doe piece left off: "It was a Friday, a week ago, and I was in St. Louis Cemetery #2, standing next to Ernie K-Doe's tomb in a small crowd—maybe twenty people—while the remains of the R&B warrior's mother-in-law were being laid to rest beneath his body. It was a moment not quite funny, not quite sad. As always with anything involving K-Doe, dead or alive, you can never really tell whom the joke is on. . . . Why is it I always end up at his tomb, his lounge, spinning inside the vortex of Ernie K-Doe and writing stories about him that, for all I know, conjure a collective shrug from readers? Why did I always answer K-Doe's calls when he was alive and what the hell am I doing following his pranks now that he's dead? . . . This was Ernie K-Doe's world. We just happen to be in the audience. That's what it's like to live in New Orleans." Rose concluded by referencing the film shot in part at the Mother-in-Law Lounge just eighteen months before: "Happy Here and Now, indeed."

CHAPTER 29: *Blessed Like You with Tonsils Gold*

When my mother died," Antoinette remembered, "the winter after K-Doe passed, I felt like the world had fell on me." Tears streamed down her face, although her resolute voice never cracked. "But whatever *I* did to keep their legacy going, the fans taken it to another level for me. So I knew I was on the right track." This sense of certitude received validation during Mardi Gras 2002—the first carnival after K-Doe's death—when the statue rode as a king in the Krewe du Vieux parade. It did not reign as monarch of the entire procession this time but as ruler of the Krewe of Mama Roux, a subkrewe of Krewe du Vieux that takes its name from the title of a song by Dr. John.

For its annual theme Mama Roux 2002 chose "Ernie K-Doe for Mayor—Keep the Jive Alive!" Everyone in the krewe dressed as K-Doe. Some insisted that their costumes should include blackface à la the Krewe of Zulu. Whites have been parading with Zulu since the mid-1960s, and do so in blackface alongside their black compadres. Antoinette strongly supported the idea. "Why can't the white boy be a black boy for a day?" she asked, referencing K-Doe's final recording, "White Boy/Black Boy." "The magic of Mardi Gras," she told Orissa Arend of the *Louisiana Weekly*, "is that any of us can be something entirely different just for a day. After that we can come back."

Mardi Gras is indeed about being entirely different for a day, and the role reversals enacted often involve sexual and racial identity. On occasion, virulent prejudices are exploited on this day of no boundaries, and ugly biases are expressed in the guise of harmless fun. Such attitudes will not disappear on Ash Wednesday. Many visitors have felt profoundly shocked, for instance, to see members of Zulu satirically sporting blackface makeup suggestive of minstrel-show caricatures. Mama Roux's membership was all white in 2002, and, as Orend noted, "prominent members of this Krewe that raises political incorrectness to a high art form drew the line at blackface." One reveler expressed a desire to "'be outrageous and confront a century-old taboo,' but only if he could completely wash it all off before venturing away from the parade or out of his group. He [saw] the face paint as a 'startling and essentially liberating statement.'" The majority of Mama Roux members wanted no part of blackface, however, and their decision prevailed. According to Vivian Cahn, the captain of Mama Roux, a higher power guided this conversation: "Ernie continues to instruct from the Great Beyond." Antoinette, the sole participant who did not sport a K-Doe costume, went instead as Elvis Presley, with pale makeup. "I myself," she told Vivian Cahn, "am going as three things I'm not: a man, white, and dead."

Ensuing Mardi Gras events saw the statue and Antoinette featured in diverse settings. The statue paraded as the lone male amid a troupe of women known as the Camel Toe Lady Steppers, who march every year in the all-female Krewe of Muses parade. Muses honored Antoinette as its queen in 2009. A dance troupe composed of "20- to 30-something ladies" who have gained "celebrity on their flamboyant city's parade circuit," the Steppers maintain close ties with such fellow distaff troupes as the Pussy Footers and the Bearded Oysters. Ersatz Antoinettes were also out and about: at one particularly decadent Mardi Gras ball, a woman dressed as Marie Antoinette K-Doe "had a picture of some pastry on her panties," according to her escort, music photographer Dylan James Stansbury, "and she kept lifting her dress and yelling, 'Let them eat cake!'" Stansbury dressed for the event as Ernie K-Doe, and "brought some flash paper, so that I could literally be 'Burn, K-Doe, burn,' but I accidentally set myself on fire. I woke up the next day with second-degree burns on my hands. Thank goodness I was wasted, so I really didn't feel it 'til the next morning. The worst thing is that we didn't even make it to the costume contest finals." In Antoinette's eyes, Ernie K-Doe's memory was honored by such lascivious celebrations, not degraded.

The statue's growing popularity reached a critical mass with the 2004 debut of the play *Burn K-Doe Burn! A Romantic Comedy from Another Dimension*. Penned by playwright and actor Rob Florence and directed by John Grimsley, *Burn K-Doe Burn!* featured Harold Evans in the title role, with Adella Gauthier as Antoinette, and, somewhat strangely, the real Antoinette playing the role of her mother, Leola Clark. Others in the cast included Tee-Eva Perry and Geannie Thomas, who appeared in multiple capacities. Witty and quite wild at times, with dance segments that added the ambience of a musical, the play traced K-Doe's career in both linear and skewed fashion. Florence's script explored K-Doe's highs and lows, from his early success to his rival music festival in New Sarpy to the Neil Strauss incident. It also included fanciful encounters with space aliens, the pope, and Martin Luther King Jr. Florence peppered his script with numerous local-culture references but kept the tone consistently inclusive and accessible.

David Cuthbert, *Times-Picayune* theater critic, enthusiastically stated that the play "not only defies criticism, I am quite sure it is impervious to it. Rob Florence's two-act homage is described as a 'romantic comedy from another dimension' and it certainly is that, but the description doesn't go far enough. It is myth, folklore and legend, set to a rhythm and blues beat. It distills the essence of Ernie K-Doe's grandiose public personage and patois . . . Like its subject, 'Burn K-Doe Burn' is a good time show." In the gay-community magazine *Ambush*, Brian Sands praised the play's "absurdist, slapdash, wonderful glory," with slight reservation: "While Rob Florence's script aspires to the epic, it doesn't fully overcome the 'And then this happened and then that happened' style endemic to biographical tales. . . . Yet . . . Florence aptly gives us a sense of K-Doe's ego-fueled nature."

Perhaps the most striking commentary on *Burn K-Doe Burn!* appeared on the blog of musician Chandler Harris, writing under the nom de plume Thurston Kelp: "I saw a play . . . in New Orleans . . . that was at least in part a biography of both Ernies (man and mannequin), in which Antoinette starred as her own mother, Ernie's 'Mother-in-law' of legend. About midway through the play, the mother-in-law, well portrayed by Antoinette until this point, morphed somehow into an older woman, who obviously had never been in a play before and didn't know any of the lines; still, she gamely soldiered on, supplying a few muted words of some kind whenever one of the other actors seemed to be asking her a question. After the scene had gone on for four or five minutes, she wandered off, and the next time we saw the character, it was again played by Antoinette. . . . consumed by curiosity, I asked Antoinette why her character had changed in midstream. She replied matter-of-factly that she had received a call on her cell phone, and one of her friends had filled in for her while she was taking the call."

Playwright Rob Florence explained his play's elliptical, illogical plot and his decision to include space aliens in the script: "I didn't think a straightforward, literal approach was right for K-Doe, particularly in theater where the top priority is to entertain. The beauty of the K-Doe story is that he does have this classic narrative that you find in the Ray Charles or Johnny Cash movies, or in so many episodes of VH1 *Behind the Music*. Like them, K-Doe was an artist who started from humble beginnings, soared high, crashed low, then rose again. But sticking to just that story with K-Doe would have been too mundane. To answer the question of how K-Doe became the Emperor of the Universe, I used the character of an alien from outer space who offers K-Doe the title of emperor if he undergoes and passes a series of tests. It made the story like the journey of a mythological hero, including a scene where the statue comes to life. Antoinette came up with a lot of out-the-box ideas, like serving free gumbo during the intermission and having costumed characters in the audience to encourage interaction. Audience members would get up and dance with these characters during party scenes." Florence explained these choices in theatrical terminology: "Involving the audience in this way is known as breaking down the fourth wall. It's risky, sometimes disastrous, but I think it paid off here.

TOP LEFT
K-DOE "CAMPAIGN" BUTTON
Courtesy Ben Sandmel

TOP RIGHT
K-DOE WITH PLAYWRIGHT ROB FLORENCE
February 9, 1991
Photo by Paula Burch-Celentano

RIGHT
FLYER FOR *BURN K-DOE BURN! A ROMANTIC COMEDY FROM ANOTHER DIMENSION*
2004
Courtesy Ben Sandmel

Allen Toussaint came to see it—there is a character who plays him, in the scene where K-Doe records 'Mother-in-Law'—and Allen loved it."

Drama was not the only literary form used to memorialize the late Emperor. In 2003 a series of poems entitled "K-Doe Codas," by Brett Evans, appeared in the anthology *Another South: Experimental Writing in the South*, published by the University of Alabama Press. In his introduction, editor Bill Lavender stated, "For too long the South has been considered, even by some fairly literate folk, to be an experimentalist's backwater . . . By 'experimental' I mean poetry that pushes at a boundary, that attempts to cover new ground." In the preface, poet Hank Lazer—coeditor of the University of Alabama's Modern and Contemporary Poetics Series—writes of "a movement beyond habitual modes of coherence"—a K-Doevian concept if ever there was one, worthy of embossment on the Emperor's business card.

It is easy to picture K-Doe responding to Brett Evans's poetry with a beatnik rapture à la Dean Moriarty in Jack Kerouac's novel *On the Road*—or, at a minimum, with a heartfelt "What *he* said!" Evans explained that his rapture for K-Doe evolved when he returned to New Orleans in 1999 after living in New York and Philadelphia for four years:

> My future wife and I really only hung out with a few people, so once we found the Mother-in-Law Lounge, we were there probably three out of the four Sundays in a month—we thought of it as night church. It was a place to fit in and hang out with folks from at least three generations. And to me the lounge represented the most distilled version of a New Orleans-ness I had so long been away from. On the East Coast, when people would ask me who my influences were, I would list the poet forebears, and then add, 'and New Orleans music,' meaning especially people like K-Doe and James Booker. Aside from the music which had that distinctive New Orleans feel, these guys practically made their own language. Things that barely made literal sense were of course completely genius if you could just hang on for the ride.
>
> . . . In K-Doe's case, I had been hearing the mysterious phrase "The Manaugahide The" repeated by some of his admirers for years . . . poetry strives to recreate a feeling without explaining it, which is what I was going for in the "K-Doe Codas." There's really not much to MISinterpret, since there's scant intellectual content to them—other than just the idea of "coda" being an afterthought (hopefully a BIT poignant) after the verse, or in this case, the song proper. . . . I can truly say that I never had a bad time in all the many times I went to the lounge; I never even had an OKAY time: it was money in the bank. K-Doe just had a way of pushing the joy around the room, whether you thought you were ready for it or not.

Brett Evans (*excerpts from* "K-Doe Codas")

$

K-Doe save me!

in Merkinland it seems to be all/nothing
moneywise

either starving oughtist or starved for time
and sunlight

I who was not blessed like you
with tonsils gold

bit like Ponchatoula straw
berries are dipped

in chocolate nor a fit zip
llauren hutten gap in

a Bunny suit   God I could huff
some Bunny moneycash!

empty wallet or soul the choices
I run with
. . .

$

til the butter cuts him down

a purple stone now

on the 22nd day

of the 2nd month God

makered K DOE

the manaugahyde the.

        policy against making the word
        more spreadable dress him as the Mardi
        Gras Vitamin judicious to the night-
        timers a real crown on his head and like
        Antoinette too matchless
. . .

$

        kcs for e k doe

                in the pre
                cinct of crepe
                myrtles every

                time I open
                my mouth a train
                whistle blows

Beyond such direct tributes, K-Doe continued posthumously to push joy and infiltrate public consciousness in more oblique ways. In 2004 a controversy erupted regarding the Louisiana Superdome, a major local landmark and the home of New Orleans's professional football team, the Saints. A proposal sought to honor the Louisiana governor who had supported funding the stadium project by renaming the building the John McKeithen Louisiana Superdome. Objections were raised that bestowing this accolade gratis would preclude selling the naming rights to a corporate sponsor—preemptively squandering a domeload of money. In a letter to the editor of the *Times-Picayune,* a concerned citizen named Geoff Worden suggested a solution worthy of King Solomon: "Now that Superdome officials have temporarily shelved efforts to sell the naming rights, maybe they'll consider the option that would generate news coverage all over the country, generate positive cash flow, promote New Orleans, honor a local legend and not limit their ability to sell the rights in the future . . . What about renaming the Superdome the 'K-Dome'? I for one would be willing to send a donation for that cause," Worden offered. "Perhaps a portrait of the Charity Hospital baby himself on top of the Dome for all to see? . . . Announce that this is a short time arrangement (one year for example) so it will not discourage potential naming rights sales. This story would amuse and entertain potential visitors from around the country, reminding them that New Orleans does indeed march to the beat of a different drummer. Burn K-Doe Burn!"

A precedent of sorts for this proposal existed, since New Orleans's airport had recently been rechristened Louis Armstrong International. Cyril Neville made similar suggestions in an interview with *OffBeat* writer David H. Jones: "Yeah, I think of Satchmo, the great Louis Armstrong, Irma Thomas, Ernie K-Doe, Eddie Bo . . . It's people like that who have contributed so much to this place that there should be an Irma Thomas-ville, an Ernie K-Doe Land, here in their own hometown." A year later, the Superdome would indeed generate news coverage—horrifically so, when thousands of people were stranded there after Hurricane Katrina.

CHAPTER 30: *Katrina, You Bitch!*

When Ernie K-Doe died, in 2001, few people imagined that his widow could keep the Mother-in-Law Lounge going without its star attraction. But Antoinette was never one to shrink from a challenge. She had, after all, taken it on herself to save K-Doe and revive his moribund career. Combining steely persistence and nurturing, maternal hospitality, Antoinette not only kept the lounge open but saw it thrive. Business was generally brisk, and a diverse lot of musicians enjoyed playing there. Regular performers ranged from favorites among Ernie and Antoinette's "children," such as Quintron and Miss Pussycat, to R&B stalwarts, including singers Al "Carnival Time" Johnson and Tommy Singleton and guitarists Ernie Vincent, Irving Banister, and Rockie Charles. Rico Watts continued to appear regularly on keyboard, and Allen Toussaint came by for special events. Cyril Neville ensconced himself for several months, leaving all his equipment set up. Even the famously reclusive Fats Domino would leave his Lower Ninth Ward bailiwick to stop in for an occasional afternoon beer. Prominently displayed, the K-Doe statue reminded all who entered of the lounge's raison d'être. On slow nights Antoinette would leave her station behind the bar, repair to the sofa, and watch TV. Customers were welcome to join her. The lounge was literally her living room, where everyone was made to feel at home.

This unlikely, happy second act proceeded until the summer of 2005, when Hurricane Katrina approached New Orleans. As the storm closed in on August 28, Antoinette refused all entreaties to evacuate. Instead she spent a week holed up in her apartment above the lounge. With her gun close at hand, Antoinette zealously guarded the artifacts she'd dragged upstairs to escape the water that seeped in the front door and eventually rose five feet. "I put the statue in the closet," she recalled, "just in case the National Guard might think it was a looter and start shooting. I run a tavern here, so I had enough food and water to last me for weeks. The power went out, and it was damn hot. Lots of thugs was running the streets and looting. But they didn't bother me because they all know me from the neighborhood, and I show them respect—they are people too."

During those seven days Antoinette's legions of friends and fans were terribly worried, especially when news footage showed the tops of both her limos barely above water, parked beside the half-submerged lounge. The scene was not identified, but lounge regulars recognized it immediately. "I absolutely need her to contact me asap," Quintron announced in an e-mail to everyone in his address book, "she is my mother." After turning down several offers of rescue from people whose credentials she did not trust—"Did you think I was going to go to the Superdome and get raped?" she asked rhetorically, worried by a prevalent rumor of sexual assaults at the stadium—Antoinette finally got in a boat staffed by the National Guard. Eventually she was flown to Georgia, where her arrival as a celebrity evacuee sparked front-page coverage in the *Macon Telegraph*. In a phone interview broadcast on the New Orleans radio station WWL-AM870, Antoinette said she would return to New Orleans, clean up, and start over, not for herself but for the music community. She said that's why the Lord put her here. She would reopen the Mother-in-Law Lounge as soon as she could, and throw one hell of a party.

After leaving Georgia, Antoinette sojourned at the home of beach-music DJ Savannah Rose, in Lincolnton, North Carolina. There she purchased a hearse to replace her drowned limos and drove back to New Orleans. "[The hearse] was inside my budget," she explained with pragmatic nonchalance to John Harris of the British newspaper the *Guardian*, "and it's something nobody wants to steal. Besides, I can carry Ernie's statue in it!" Once home, Antoinette immediately went to work, first gutting most of the sodden lounge by herself. Her sole complaint concerned the day "they gave me thirty-seven

ERNIE-K-DOE

dollars' worth of food stamps to last me a whole month. Laura Bush spends more than thirty-seven dollars on one goddamn pair of drawers!"

In late November 2005 Antoinette was interviewed by Dr. Sara Le Menestrel, a Parisian cultural anthropologist conducting posthurricane research in Louisiana. Asked why she didn't evacuate, Antoinette replied:

> I'm one of those stubborn ones. I wouldn't leave because I was in the storm [Hurricane] Betsy forty years ago in the Lower Ninth Ward, and I survived it . . . it's the water I didn't survive. . . . Sometimes I feel like K-Doe. You remember K-Doe used to always say, "I'm going to do it my way"? . . . When people say you can't do something, that's the exact time to do it, and this is the wrong time to abandon New Orleans. . . . What would K-Doe say? K-Doe would say, "I'm not leaving New Orleans." . . . So, why should I leave? You know, his remains is here, and so is my mom's. So I have all the reasons to stay . . . because if I leave I would feel mighty bad coming back two or three years from now. . . . K-Doe wouldn't have done it. Him and Fats Domino are two people who never wanted to leave New Orleans.
>
> I feel like I'm blessed because I still have my apartment over the lounge, even though I don't have the lights on now. . . . I don't have hot water, but I'm sixty-two years old and I wasn't born with hot water. . . . We had no running water inside. We had outdoor toilets and we had kerosene lamps. . . . I'm from the old school. I know how to survive. And then I'm a Girl Scout. I'm a Girl Scout from high school, I mean, elementary school all the way through high school. So I can survive. . . . If I survived the marriage of Ernie K-Doe, then I can survive anything.

From this straightforward narrative Antoinette took the interview in a paranormal direction—perhaps shedding light on her decision to commission the statue:

> As long as K-Doe's been deceased, I've never *seen* him, but I can *smell* him. When I'm in trouble or the wrong person is around me, it's a certain scent and I can smell him. . . . A couple of weeks ago I was taking a bath, just sitting in the tub, just meditating, and he came to me. Not as a ghost or a long white gown. I mean he had a blue and silver suit. Actually I *seen* him, and he says to me, he said, "You're gonna be OK." He said, "But what you got to do is feed the people. You have to feed the people." . . . My cell phone rung . . . and Denise called, one of my friends. . . . She said . . . "I want you to do something and you need to do it." And I said, "What's that?" She said, "You need to cook some red beans and feed people." I said, "Denise, did you talk to K-Doe?" . . . I cooked fifty pounds of red beans two weeks ago and fed the people outside.

THE MOTHER-IN-LAW LOUNGE FLOODED AFTER HURRICANE KATRINA
September 8, 2005
Photo by Josh Levin

> Anybody that came up to eat. Anybody. You could be a Red Cross worker, you could be a FEMA person, anybody that can stop to eat. . . . it was wonderful. . . . And it was amazing that K-Doe came to me and told me, and that girl called me. Oh yeah, he never left my side, him nor my mother. That's where I get my strength. . . . And what made this building so unique to me now is because it's named after Ernie K-Doe. K-Doe and I got married here. Yes, we did, and the mother-in-law [Antoinette's mother, Leola] stayed here with us. And my mom died six months after him; my mom died here. . . . You don't throw that away. If you do, you crazy.

Ever enterprising, and impatient with the limits of her own labor, Antoinette soon cultivated a relationship with an Atlanta-based philanthropy, the HandsOn Network. A well-publicized visit from HandsOn's spokesperson, the contemporary R&B star Usher, inspired a cadre of well-scrubbed young volunteers from around the nation to complete the renovation of the Mother-in-Law Lounge. Local organizations Sweet Home New Orleans, the Tipitina's Foundation, and the New Orleans Musicians' Clinic/Hurricane Relief Fund offered financial assistance as well. "I never could have done it without them," Antoinette stated with deep gratitude. But many people felt sure that she could have finished the job herself with willpower alone. Efficiently refurbished with no loss of its original ambience, the Mother-in-Law Lounge reopened on the hurricane's first anniversary, August 29, 2006. As part of the festivities, "Katrina, you bitch" was buried in effigy. Just as "them Duke boys of Hazzard" failed to hold Ernie down in life, not even a disaster of biblical proportions could suppress Antoinette and the posthumous K-Doe juggernaut.

But this milestone hardly ended Antoinette's involvement in hurricane relief. The lounge quickly emerged as an important hub for community outreach. Antoinette spent hours helping people—especially the elderly and illiterate—tackle the paperwork required to rebuild their houses and lives. To the many who felt overwhelmed, Antoinette also offered encouragement and, when needed, tough love. "This is the place where you get a little psychiatry work," she told *Blender* magazine's Mike Errico. And Antoinette continued to cook, providing free food for all who were hungry. Visitors to the lounge could always count on free red beans and rice.

CHAPTER 31: *We Put the "Fun" in "Funeral"*

Just two months before the lounge's reopening, Antoinette graced the cover of the June 2006 issue of *OffBeat*. More precisely, Antoinette and the statue graced the cover; they were seated at Galatoire's—New Orleans's leading old-line, high-society restaurant—with an attentive waiter by their side. Back in 1961, when the real-life K-Doe had his number-one hit, Galatoire's would never have let him in to dine. Segregation included a firm color line at upscale restaurants, as vividly described firsthand in

THE MOTHER-IN-LAW LOUNGE UNDER RENOVATION AFTER HURRICANE KATRINA

TOP
THE STATUE, ANTOINETTE, AND USHER

BOTTOM
THE STATUE STANDS GUARD

2006
Courtesy HandsOn, New Orleans

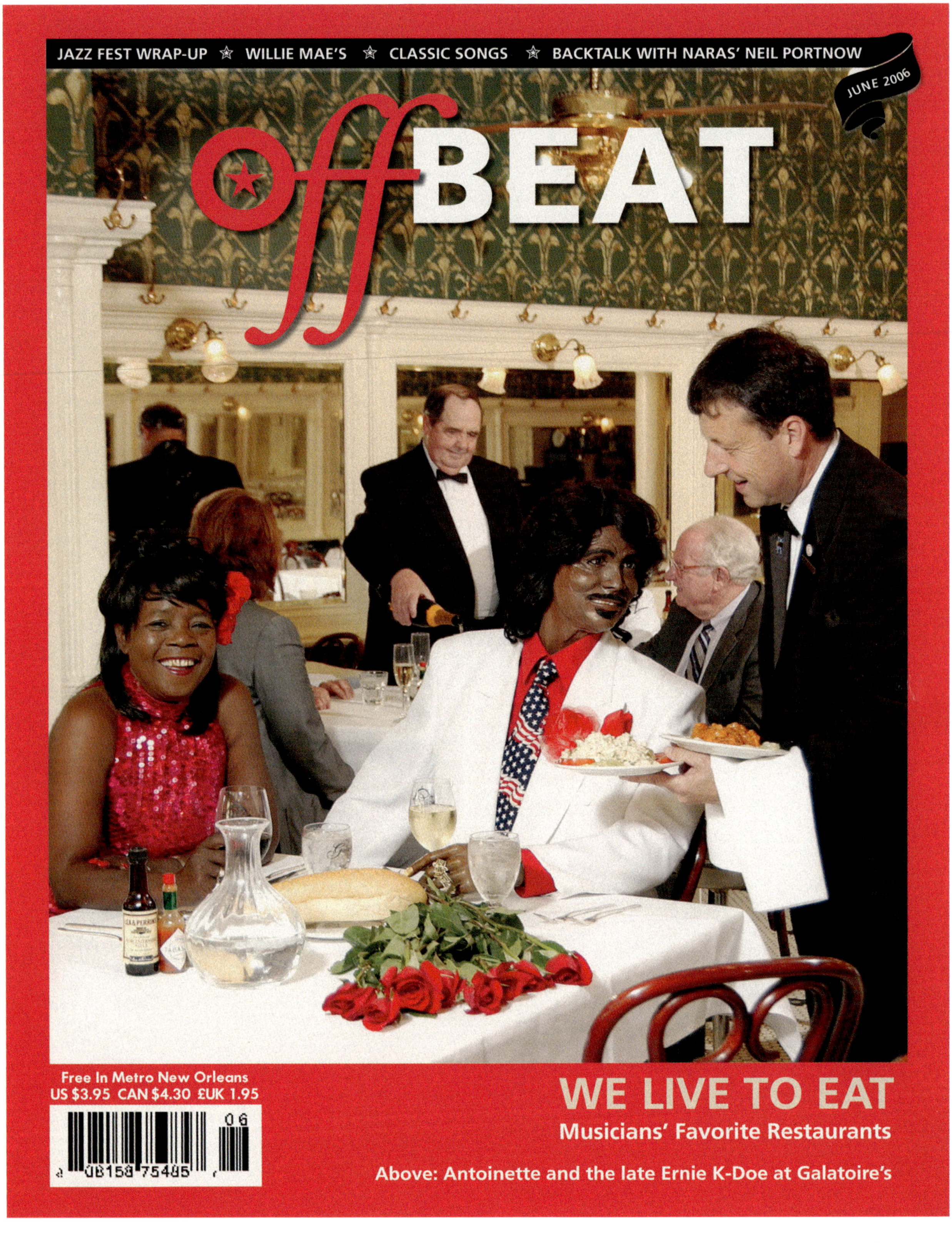
JAZZ FEST WRAP-UP ✯ WILLIE MAE'S ✯ CLASSIC SONGS ✯ BACKTALK WITH NARAS' NEIL PORTNOW
JUNE 2006
OffBEAT
Free In Metro New Orleans
US $3.95 CAN $4.30 £UK 1.95
WE LIVE TO EAT
Musicians' Favorite Restaurants
Above: Antoinette and the late Ernie K-Doe at Galatoire's

John Howard Griffin's *Black Like Me*. But the plaster K-Doe had been invited to this exclusive eatery before, for the birthday of a woman named Valerie Cahill. That milestone inspired *OffBeat* editor Alex Rawls and publisher Jan Ramsey to set up a professional photo shoot of Antoinette and the statue, at table.

Ramsey, a native New Orleanian, recalled growing up "with K-Doe's music, and we covered him [in the magazine] a lot when he was alive. We had already done a food issue, back before Katrina, with Kermit Ruffins on the cover. . . . I thought I'd combine the two and do it at someplace really nice. Since Antoinette had venerated K-Doe and dressed him in kingly robes, Galatoire's seemed appropriate. All the staff were very receptive, and everyone who was there just totally got into it—it really worked. I thought, 'Oh my God, it looks like he's alive!' even though we had to take one arm out of the socket so that the statue looked natural sitting at the table. I didn't want to shoot this cover in a way that was cheesy or tactless, or that would make Antoinette look foolish, because I respected Antoinette so much. And she had a real good time; she was laughing and cutting up." The statue, by all reports, was a very cheap date.

After gracing the cover of *OffBeat*, faux K-Doe's next high-profile appearance in print came in Chris Rose's January 7, 2007, *Times-Picayune* column. Under the headline HIZZONER RAY NAGIN REMAINS A MAN OF MYSTERY, Rose pondered the mayor's curiously low profile at a time when post-Katrina New Orleans sorely needed firm leadership. He quoted a reader who had written, "We really don't have a mayor [but] just a dress-up doll propped up for funding and sympathy spewing a bunch of unpredictable commentary. [He's] kind of like the wax K-Doe statue that Antoinette . . . takes out to events, only not as amusing."

But tragedy touched K-Doe's legacy too. On the cusp of 2007, New Orleans was rocked by the murders of two admired community members: brass-band drummer and music teacher Dinerral Shavers and, a week later, filmmaker Helen Hill. Hill's bereaved husband, Paul Gailiunas, wrote a guest editorial in the *Times-Picayune* decrying the city's rising murder rate, in which he noted his late wife's love of New Orleans, especially "bringing visitors to the Mother-in-Law Lounge." Antoinette made the lounge available to Hill's friends for a postmemorial parade gathering, announced on a flyer: "On February 24, 2007 (the Saturday after Mardi Gras), we're having a jazz-funeral style second-line for Helen Hill. . . . The Panorama Jazz Band and the Jazz Vipers will lead us down Cleveland to Jeff Davis, then on to Orleans, down to Claiborne and then right to the Ernie K-Doe Mother-in-Law Lounge. . . . Helen loved pigs and chickens. Dressing up as either or something else entirely is encouraged. When we get to the Mother-in-Law Lounge, there will be a tea party, with more bands and an open mic. It promises to be a great celebration of Helen's life, as only New Orleans can provide. After all, we're the city that put fun in funeral."

COVER OF *OFFBEAT* FEATURING ANTOINETTE AND THE STATUE AT GALATOIRE'S RESTAURANT
June 2006
Photo by Romney

TV host Tavis Smiley and scholar Cornel West visited the lounge in the early weeks of 2007, where they shot an informal interview with Antoinette to introduce a segment about her for the PBS series *Right to Return: New Home Movies from the Lower 9th Ward*. ("Lower Ninth Ward" is an inaccurate descriptor for the lounge's location; it actually lies on the fringe of the Tremé neighborhood, or in Tremé proper by some definitions, in the Seventh Ward. But after Katrina "Lower Ninth Ward" emerged as a term with national-media resonance, and its broad-brush symbolic usage became commonplace.) *Right to Return* aired in late May 2007 on Smiley's eponymous nightly program on PBS. Filmmaker Jonathan Demme's piece about Antoinette and her recovery efforts presupposes the audience's familiarity with both her Katrina experience and Ernie K-Doe's musical career. The absence of background information may have baffled viewers outside New Orleans, but the piece was affecting. The most poignant moment came when Smiley said to Antoinette, "It's important to you, obviously, to keep the legacy of Ernie K-Doe alive. I get the sense that you live for that." "I live, eat, and breathe it," she replied. "His legacy's too big to sweep it under the bed somewhere."

Antoinette appreciated the attention and television coverage, but the biggest K-Doe news of 2007 was the dramatic reemergence of "Here Come the Girls." This tour-de-force collaboration by Toussaint and K-Doe had sunk without a trace after its 1971 release. Then, thirty-six years later, the British retail chain Boots (comparable to Walgreens in America) plucked it from obscurity for use in its annual Christmas commercial. In the UK, holiday TV ads entail effort and expense similar to that of Superbowl commercials in the States, and they generate a parallel level of interest. The ad, directed by filmmaker Jonathan King, features hundreds of women getting ready for an office Christmas party with an array of Boots beauty products. Their makeup, hair, and fancy clothes in place, the "girls" confidently march en masse to the yuletide gathering while K-Doe lustily sings "Lookin' so good it's a doggone shame that they couldn't all be mine!" The clever ad appealed to viewers. As a result, the British label Soul Jazz, which licensed the song to Boots, released "Here Come the Girls" as a single. The song entered the British pop charts in December 2007 and stayed there for several weeks.

The commercial went on to win several advertising-industry awards, piquing the interest of the business press. Writing in the *Independent*, Claire Beale of the trade magazine *Campaign* gushed: "And joy, a Christmas ad without a jingle bell soundtrack: the song is 'Here Come the Girls', Ernie K-Doe's soul jazz track. . . . The giddy optimism of it all makes you want to take up arms (hair tongs, blusher brushes) and join them." Impressed enough with the ad to discuss it twice, the *Independent* also ran a piece by media critic Peter York. Following the headline BOOTS PUTS THE SEX BACK INTO SEXISM WITH A CRACKLING CHRISTMAS TALE, York declared, "Boots' new minute-long Christmas cosmetics commercial really celebrates women, and must have been directed by someone who likes them a lot. Its theme? The lengths women go to and the enthusiasm they put into making things nice—better-looking and more fun. . . . As the joyous work starts there's a marching drumbeat, then a nice old soul-y riff that develops into the utterly wonderful 'Here Come the Girls' by the late Ernie K-Doe. (It's from 1970 and I'm amazed I didn't know it because it's glorious.) 'Tis the Season to be Gorgeous, it says on-screen . . . This commercial is in direct line of descent from 'Nine to Five' and all sorts of celebratory commercial feminism."

Celebratory feminism certainly ensued the next summer, when the popular British girl group the Sugababes released a cover version of "Here Come the Girls." Their bubblegum-meets-hip-hop rendition reached number three on the British pop charts, prompting a *Times of London* reference to the song as "a soon-to-be ubiquitous party anthem." The group dropped some of Allen Toussaint's lyrics and replaced them with updated lines, including "I'm filled with sexuality; with or without a man I feel complete." As the writer of "Short Dress," K-Doe would have loved these sentiments (though he'd have flipped if they led to same-sex dancing). Another of the Sugababes' added lines, "All independent women know, we got the guts to run the show," could well have been written about Antoinette. Thrilled by the ad and the Sugababes' reprise of K-Doe's song, Antoinette threw a "Here Come the Girls" party at the Rock 'n' Bowl in the summer of 2008. All women sporting fancy evening dress were admitted at no charge.

As the 2008 presidential election approached, Antoinette made the lounge available to local volunteers for the Obama campaign. (A reader of the *Times-Picayune* dismissed John McCain with the comment "The Ernie K-Doe statue looks more lifelike.") Antoinette bought a gigantic TV and held debate parties that doubled as voter-registration drives. The huge screen and contagious political fervor—plus the ever-present free food—drew claustrophobia-level crowds. The overflow spilled into the lounge's side yard, where Antoinette had created a folk-art installation. One of its most distinctive features was a series of toilets painted in bright DayGlo colors and used as planters. "You see that?" she asked one afternoon after the election, pointing at a commode full of verdant flora. "At one time Ernie K-Doe was as bad off as what you usually see in one of those things. But I made him bloom again! That's what I do," she added, in a rare self-congratulatory mood. "I make things bloom again." Soon the side yard also featured a tiki bar, replete with a thatched roof, and a bandstand. All-weather tables and chairs offered seating for dozens, providing a welcome alternative to the lounge's main drawback—air thick with cigarette smoke. While this outdoor extension greatly increased the lounge's capacity, it also somehow intensified the intimate, casual atmosphere, the sense of its being a private home. Al fresco evening events by candlelight created a garden-party ambience.

It was in this yard, on Monday, February 23, 2009, that Antoinette hosted a Lundi Gras gathering of Mardi Gras Indians from various tribes. In their honor, she wore a wig with pigtail braids, suggesting a Native American princess. Though resplendent in their full-feathered costumes, the Indians faced some literally stiff competition, because the K-Doe statue had been moved outside, where it towered over the crowd on its tabletop perch. Dressed in one of K-Doe's especially ornate suits, it emanated the totemic gravitas of an Easter Island monolith. Antoinette was still buzzing from her honorary reign, the previous week, as the queen of the Camel Toe Lady Steppers in the all-female Muses parade. She also gushed with anticipation about parading on Mardi Gras Day with the Baby Dolls—a group of grown women who dress in frilly infant's wear and matching bonnets. Antoinette had recently revived this century-old (and long-dormant) carnival custom, drawing many eager new recruits and adding yet another gust to her one-woman cultural whirlwind.

Time seemed suspended on that festive, sunny afternoon amid a convergence of all the soulful elements—whimsy, fun, funk, kindness—that made the Mother-in-Law Lounge so unique and so emblematic of New Orleans. The assembled multitude included the whole spectrum of the lounge's clientele: young and old, black and white, sober and silly. Many were already dressed for Mardi Gras Day, in outfits of every conceivable design. In addition to beaded Indian suits, grown men sported spiked medieval jester hats while boho boys pranced in tutus, tank tops, and willfully bad wigs, their hairy chests emblazoned with glitter and body paint. Tattooed twenty-something women shimmied in dominatrix suits made of stiff leather resembling Naugahyde. Revelers of indeterminate gender swathed themselves from head to toe in Spanish moss, revealing no facial features except the narrowest of eye slits. There was a palpable sense of a moment to be savored, along with an implicit fervent wish that the good times would roll indefinitely. As K-Doe often told his radio listeners, "I hope you live forever and that I will never die!" The scent of home cooking—gumbo, barbecue, Antoinette's red beans and rice—filled the air, as did joyful seasonal music blaring from inside the lounge and from passing cars: "New Suit" and "Handa Wanda" by Bo Dollis and the Wild Magnolias; "Big Chief" and "Mardi Gras in New Orleans" by Professor Longhair; the Meters' "Hey Pocky A-way" and "They All Axed for You"; "Second Line," by Stop, Inc., with its refrain of rhythmic accents that all New Orleanians know by heart; "Carnival Time" by Al Johnson. Not to mention a year-round favorite titled "Mother-in-Law." Many in attendance planned to stay up all night and greet Mardi Gras Day at dawn.

But Antoinette K-Doe would not be among them. At three o'clock in the morning of February 24, she dropped dead in the Mother-in-Law Lounge of a sudden, massive heart attack. Curiously, she'd also had a heart attack on Mardi Gras Day 2008. She had tried ever since to cut back on her innumerable projects, her long hours of sewing costumes and cooking and tending bar and helping people with their posthurricane paperwork. But Antoinette's low gear resembled most people's overdrive, and her steady diet of coffee and cigarettes did not help. Her body just gave out.

By midmorning, word began to spread around town. Geannie Thomas, who had become second in command at the lounge, conferred with Antoinette's son-in-law, Gary Hughes. They decided to keep the lounge open all day, per Antoinette's undoubted wishes. Even so, the revelry inside was muted. Full-blown pandemonium did ensue across the street, however, in the broad median that separates the up- and downriver lanes on Claiborne Avenue. Indians came and went, with rival tribes occasionally staging mock battles as

TOP
THE NEW PARADISE LADIES: (FROM LEFT) GEANNIE THOMAS, TEE-EVA PERRY, AND ANTOINETTE
May 3, 2007
Photo by Erika Goldring

BOTTOM
ANTOINETTE AND THE STATUE OUTSIDE THE MOTHER-IN-LAW LOUNGE, ONE DAY BEFORE HER DEATH
February 23, 2009
Photo by David Peltier

their spy boys faced off in fierce, primal pantomime. Brass bands—formally organized outfits and ragtag aggregations alike—funneled in from side streets. Their music merged with the Indians' chants and drumming and with the bass-heavy hip-hop that poured from huge speakers powered by noisy portable generators, all of it swirling, surging, echoing under the concrete ceiling of the I-10 overpass some fifty feet above.

Just when the fever pitch seemed to peak, a fabulous Fellini-esque car arrived—an erstwhile Cadillac stripped of all body panels down to the frame, festooned with gobs of beads and trinkets and a splattered paint job worthy of Jackson Pollock. The driver and passenger, middle-aged black men dressed in drag à la Bobby Marchan yet also sporting scraggly beards, repeatedly circled the block in front of the Mother-in-Law Lounge. They held large dolls high in the air, pointing at random men and shouting, "You the daddy! *You* the daddy! *YOU THE DADDY*!" Every so often this pair of antic mummers would underscore their accusations of paternity by turning on a piercing police siren and driving up on the sidewalk straight toward the accused, as if to make an arrest, stopping within inches of committing vehicular assault.

This uninsurable jalopy—a neighborhood favorite for one day every year—rolled along at five miles an hour, leaving drivers of more mundane vehicles stuck in gridlock. Carnival celebrants spilled into the street, chugging beer and dancing in complete oblivion to the concept of right-of-way. It was pointless for stranded motorists to beep their horns. Every ten minutes or so, a gap in the crowd would briefly open up, allowing a few cars to creep through. No police were present to regulate traffic on this major artery. The best that immobilized drivers could do was try to honk in harmony with one of the ubiquitous brass bands. Cars even stopped on the interstate overpass, disgorging Carnival-costumed passengers who jumped out to watch the action below. This ecstatic anarchy prevailed until dark, and under normal circumstances it would have continued until the wee hours inside the lounge too. But Antoinette's family shooed everyone out at five o'clock sharp. They had a funeral to plan.

Antoinette's was not the only impending send-off in the New Orleans music community. K-Doe's old cohort Snooks Eaglin had died the previous Wednesday, but his service was delayed more than a week after his death, presumably because no brass bands were available to play his funeral during the busy Mardi Gras weekend. Accordingly, Eaglin's service took place on the Friday after Carnival Day, on February 27. In a move that surprised (and offended) some, it was held in the cavernous confines of a downtown nightclub, the Howlin' Wolf. Allen Toussaint, Jazz Fest producer Quint Davis, and John Blancher of the Rock 'n' Bowl each gave eulogies that were eloquent in quite different ways. Blancher suggested that if the notoriously feisty Eaglin were asked to play in heaven, he would doubtless demand his money up front. Toussaint recalled his teen days as Eaglin's bandmate in the Flamingos. (Flamingos' drummer James Jackson added the tale of a memorable drunken night when he gave the wheel to the relatively sober but blind Eaglin—but then felt alarmed because he drove too fast.) Quint Davis fondly reminisced about a trip to Woodstock, New York, with Eaglin and Professor Longhair, where the hypersensitive Snooks complained of being kept awake by the overwhelming silence of falling snow.

Many of Eaglin's colleagues performed gospel numbers at the service, including Deacon John, Irma Thomas, Clarence "Frogman" Henry, zydeco-soul singer Rockin' Dopsie Jr., and clarinetist Dr. Michael White. Then Eaglin's coffin was wheeled out of the Howlin' Wolf, followed by the Hot 8 Brass Band and the senior division of the Young Men Olympian Junior Benevolent Association. Behind them, in turn, streamed a second line of Eaglin's diverse fans. After second-lining for a few blocks, most of them proceeded straight to the Mother-in-Law Lounge for Antoinette's visitation.

A long line of mourners waited patiently in line to see Antoinette laid out in a sparkling silver outfit with a matching tiara. Her left hand clasped a scepter, which some interpreted as a magic wand. This childlike costume accentuated the youthfully enthusiastic side of Antoinette's personality, which coexisted with her vigilant street smarts, fierce loyalty, and at times formidable temper. Just as on the day before her death, the side yard was packed with the whole spectrum of Antoinette's admirers. None wore costumes this time, but many dressed formally, as if for church. Allen Toussaint arrived, greeting the public with his usual grace and strolling around shooting video with a small hand-held camera. He and Antoinette had always maintained a cordial relationship. During a Jazz Fest tribute to K-Doe in 2002, an audience member asked Toussaint what advice he would give to an aspiring young musician. His unhesitating recommendation—"I'd tell them to hit on Antoinette"—underscored Toussaint's respect for all she had done to resurrect K-Doe and his career.

Antoinette's funeral did not take place where Ernie's had, at Gallier Hall—as she presumably would have wanted—but rather at a neighborhood church, St. James Methodist, in Tremé. It was much too small for the occasion. By the time the service started, a huge overflow crowd stood outside, despite threatening weather. Jackie Clarkson addressed the crowd, as did Ernest Collins, an emissary of Mayor Ray Nagin. Then Geannie Thomas spoke. Unaccustomed to such public prominence and deep in the throes of emotion, Thomas's few words were hushed yet heartfelt. Charmaine Neville (the daughter of Neville brother Charles and a popular singer in her own right) sang several gospel numbers that quickly elicited a lively call-and-response dialogue with the congregation. Jo "Cool" Davis did the same, as did Frogman Henry. Deacon John sang "Many Rivers to Cross," as he had at Ernie's funeral. Porgy Jones serenaded the casket with a soulful flügelhorn improvisation.

Where Snooks Eaglin's second line had been orderly, a chaotic and raucous spirit overtook Antoinette's. Its ranks continually swelled as people joined in along the route. Once again traffic on Claiborne Avenue ground to a halt as brass bands, Mardi Gras Indians, mourners, and second-liners filled the street. They strutted and swaggered behind Antoinette's casket, which rode inside the same glass-walled hearse that had carried Ernie. A separate mule-drawn carriage transported the statue, which had been placed in a sitting posture and was supervised by an attendant. The parade climaxed upon arrival at the

FOLLOWING PAGES
ANTOINETTE'S FUNERAL PROCESSION AND SECOND LINE
LEFT
THE HEARSE ON CLAIBORNE AVENUE
RIGHT
(FROM LEFT) JENNIFER JONES, TEE-EVA PERRY, AND CHARMAINE NEVILLE
February 27, 2009
Photos by Erika Goldring

Mother-in-Law Lounge, when Antoinette's coffin was pulled from the hearse and lifted high in the air three times in tribute. There was no burial ceremony because a procedural problem with New Orleans's archdiocese prevented her immediate interment in the Twichells' tomb with Ernie. A few weeks later, however, she was quietly laid to rest alongside her husband.

From the lounge Antoinette's mourners proceeded to the Rock 'n' Bowl for the repast. The club was packed, seeming to take in all who had attended the funeral, both inside the church and out. Despite the long, steep steps that led to the second-story joint (which moved later in 2009 to a new, ground-floor location), Frogman Henry managed to get himself and his walker upstairs so that he could sing Antoinette's praises for the second time that day. A steady stream of other musicians performed, echoing Frogman's devotion: Eddie Bo, Mac Rebennack, Irma Thomas, J. Monque'D. A jolly mood prevailed, as Antoinette would certainly have wanted, especially since the Rock 'n' Bowl was one of her favorite venues. Still, the cumulative effect of the week's intense emotions left many in the crowd feeling drained. As people left they found that the temperature had suddenly plummeted, turning a hot, humid morning into a blustery winter afternoon. In that big chill, under a damp, leaden sky, it felt for the moment that all of New Orleans's joy had been lowered into a grave.

CHAPTER 32: *And Now We Will See*

Although Ernie and Antoinette are gone, their conceptual empire remains intact. It lives on in cyberspace. It survives in the real world, too, in the continued interaction of the diverse people who worked, played music, and hung out at the lounge. Much like the populace of the post-Katrina diaspora, this tightly knit crowd is determined to stay connected and keep celebrating the K-Does' legacy.

Such resolve is essential now that the Mother-in-Law Lounge is gone. It shut down in December 2010, some nineteen months after Antoinette's death. At this writing, all that remains of its splendor are the murals on the outside walls. The interior has been gutted, and no statue stands guard. A new nightclub venture, operated by jazz trumpeter Kermit Ruffins, was slated to occupy the space in early in 2011. Its grand opening has yet to occur.

When Antoinette died, most lounge regulars considered Geannie Thomas the logical person to carry her torch. Thomas had helped Antoinette behind the bar for eight years. She knew the bar business in general and all of Antoinette's practices in particular. She had a good rapport with the customers and a public profile as a member of the Paradise Ladies. She knew exactly how to slide the statue in and out of Antoinette's hearse, utilizing the casket rollers. But Betty Fox, Antoinette's daughter, wanted to take the reins. Betty had relocated to Memphis after Katrina. She saw running the lounge as a way to start over in New Orleans and, in her grief, to maintain a connection with her mother and Ernie. Betty moved back to New Orleans and moved in above the lounge. Within weeks she was cooking red beans and rice—"I hope they taste as a good as my mom's," she said often—and attempting to emulate Antoinette in umpteen other ways.

Betty Fox tried hard, but, as she was the first to acknowledge, "The only person who could run Ernie K-Doe's Mother-in-Law Lounge was Antoinette K-Doe." Just like when Antoinette was living, business was erratic, ranging from nights when the house was jam packed and liquor sales were great, to nights when the club was completely empty. Few people, if any, understood exactly how Antoinette had ever made a secure living from the lounge, especially since she gave away so much food. But whatever it was, that unknown factor did not kick in for Betty. By the spring of 2010, she had fallen behind on the rent. A car had careened off Claiborne Avenue, missed the protective row of bathtubs, and hit the front door, rendering it useless. The dimly lit side door, which opened to the garden, was hard to see from the street. The lounge often looked closed when it was actually open. Betty feared she would have to shut it down for good.

The music community reacted with horror. "It's going to be like losing oxygen," blues guitarist John T. Lewis observed. After sixteen years of operation, the Mother-in-Law Lounge had attained the stature of a crucially important resource, a multicultural crossroad, and a living shrine. Well-connected people attempted to reinvent it as a museum run by its own registered nonprofit organization, or to have the building designated a historic landmark. The fact that Antoinette had only rented the property complicated their plans. Despite genuine effort and considerable dialogue, nothing materialized. During the summer and fall of 2010, announcements of imminent closure prompted benefit shows that drew big crowds. These profitable nights kept the lounge open for another month or so. But when the fundraiser money dissipated, another dire announcement would follow, and the cycle would continue. Out-of-town journalists came to New Orleans to document several last hurrahs, none of which had real finality. At one such event, Betty tried to explain her state of stress and bewilderment to radio documentarians Barry Yeoman and Richard Ziglar: "When my mother passed away, it took a lot out of me emotionally." Referring to Ernie and Antoinette, Betty added, "It's hard to follow in the footsteps of two people like that."

This ongoing string of near-closures created a false sense of security that the lounge would not in fact close. A benefactor of some sort would surely appear, just like after Katrina. But when Betty held a huge yard sale on December 3 and 4, 2010—and customers walked off carrying hangers full of K-Doe's stage outfits—everyone knew she was serious. The following Sunday, December 12, marked the last night of live music at the Mother-in-Law Lounge. Pianist Armand St. Martin and guitarist John T. Lewis put the evening together. After they played, Ernie Vincent and Guitar Lightnin' Lee each did long, separate sets, the latter demonstrating the Lower Ninth Ward blues style that he'd learned from "Boogie" Bill Webb. Sidemen came and went at random, some taking a proffered instrument in midsong without missing a beat. The love and communal feeling that filled the room recalled the buoyant mood of Lundi Gras 2009, the day before Antoinette died.

After the last song of a raucous evening, musicians and patrons would usually hang out at the Mother-in-Law until all hours; New Orleans has no mandated last call. Endless backslapping, bonhomie, and loud trash talking had long enlivened such gatherings. But this night fizzled quickly, with a note of sad incredulity. Shaking their heads in disbelief, everyone left at the shockingly early hour of 1:30 a.m. But it was not until the inside of the building was gutted, in February 2011, that the reality of the lounge's demise finally sank in.

At this writing, Betty Fox has the statue of Ernie K-Doe in her possession. She has announced plans to open a new Mother-in-Law Lounge, in another location. But even if this never happens—even if the statue crumbles and New Orleans is engulfed by a hurricane that dwarfs Katrina—the legacies of Ernie and Antoinette K-Doe will keep shining brightly. The year 2011, for one ephemeral example, saw both the reprisal of Rob Florence's play *Burn K-Doe Burn!* and depictions of the lounge and statue on HBO's acclaimed New Orleans–based drama, *Treme*.

Ernie and Antoinette's story springs from roots in a specific place and moment, from a solid foundation of musical accomplishment and a slippery slope of human foible. But their story is also based on some timeless, bedrock beliefs: the indomitability of the human spirit; the ultimate vindication of rugged individualism; the eternal possibility of redemption; the conviction that all things are attainable with faith and motivation; and, last but not least, the essential therapeutic quality of silliness. As Oscar Wilde—a man who presumably would have respected K-Doe, and vice versa—succinctly stated, "Seriousness is the only refuge of the shallow." When first-time visitors to the lounge immediately proclaimed "There's a lot of love in this place," they recognized the huge spirit that issued from its small yet vast confines. This spirit connects a community that extends around the world. Its members who do not live in New Orleans can be found looking long and lovingly in the city's direction.

Just as Ernie K-Doe had felt thrilled by the success of his song "Mother-in-Law," he and Antoinette would surely delight in the accolades that fill their absence. According to African tradition, such adoration keeps them figuratively alive. "People thought I was finished," K-Doe often said, "but them what *say* they are gone don't always *be* gone. No, indeed," the Emperor would elaborate, with his usual abstruse sagacity. "Let's just put it like this: sometimes when they fight a forest fire out in the woods, they have to start *another* fire as a diversion. And so now we will see which fire burns the longest."

ANTOINETTE'S DAUGHTER BETTY ANN FOX OUTSIDE THE MOTHER-IN-LAW LOUNGE
December 4, 2010
Photo by Dean M. Shapiro

ERNIE K-DOE'S
MOTHER-IN-LAW
LOUNGE
ORLEANS
FROM THE STORM" BOB DYLAN

love YOU BEST!!
"AFTER I'M GONE, THERE WILL BE NO OTHER"

AUTHOR'S NOTE

I have edited some of the interviews conducted for this book for the purposes of narrative clarity and concision. Great care has been taken to respect and preserve the precise meaning of all original statements, with no changes in nuance.

Quotes from Ernie K-Doe's radio show, which flourished on WWOZ from circa 1982 to 1987, are cited in the notes with "undated recording." They are taken from cassette recordings I acquired in the 1990s and CDs that were given to me after Hurricane Katrina. Very few recordings came marked with broadcast dates. Copies of these recordings will be available to researchers at The Historic New Orleans Collection's Williams Research Center.

THE MOTHER-IN-LAW LOUNGE
March 5, 2009
Photo by Melissa Carrier

NOTES

CHAPTER 1

1 *I don't need your little paper*] Neil Strauss, conversation with author, May 2000.

2 *All you got to do*] *Ernie K-Doe Show*, WWOZ New Orleans, undated recording. Popularly known and regularly referred to as the *Ernie K-Doe Show*, the program, which aired for several years in the 1980s, did not have a formal title. References to the show in these endnotes cite a collection of undated recordings housed in the Williams Research Center of The Historic New Orleans Collection.

3 *The worst person I know*] "Mother-in-Law," lyrics by Allen Toussaint, published by EMI UNART, used by permission.

has made a big showing] Laurie Henshaw, "The MM Pop Shop," *Melody Maker*, Apr. 22, 1961, 6; information courtesy of David Nathan, archivist, National Jazz Archive, Loughton, England.

a cute comedy number] Mike Hellicar, "New to the Charts," *New Musical Express*, May 4, 1961, 4; information courtesy Gordon Thompson, Bill Millar, and John Broven.

4 *Give up all hope of peace*] Juvenal, *Satires*, 6.231.

I bought my mother-in-law a chair] Geoff Tibballs, *The Mammoth Book of Zingers, Quips, and One-Liners* (New York: Carroll & Graf, 2004), 198.

5 *ideas about hateful maternal relatives*] B. Lee Cooper, "Women's Studies and Popular Music Stereotypes," *Popular Music and Society* 23, no. 4 (1999): 31–43.

My first wife's mother's name] Ernie K-Doe, onstage interview with author (Allison Miner Music Heritage Stage, New Orleans Jazz and Heritage Festival, New Orleans, May 3, 1998).

Have you ever found a love] *Ernie K-Doe Show*, WWOZ New Orleans, undated recording.

I had a mother-in-law at one time] Ibid.

My father exaggerated] Ernest Kador Jr., interview with author, New Orleans, Nov. 7, 2009.

6 *I do not mess with no drugs*] *Ernie K-Doe Show*, WWOZ New Orleans, undated recording.

Louis Armstrong, Fats Domino, and Ernie K-Doe] Ibid.

Doctor O. J.] Ibid.

7 *Prayer to Ernie*] ButterBean, "Prayer to Ernie!," *HI-COOL*, www.hi-coolblogspot.com (accessed Feb. 6, 2007).

a divine manifestation] Jason Poirier, correspondence with author, Mar. 7, 2009.

What's cold is hot] *Ernie K-Doe Show*, WWOZ New Orleans, undated recording.

CHAPTER 2

12 *I never judged him by conventional standards*] Lafcadio Hearn, *Favorites and Other Fancies*, ed. Charles Woodward Hutson (Boston: Houghton Mifflin, 1919), 18.

Whoever think they can beat me] *Ernie K-Doe Show*, WWOZ New Orleans, undated recording.

I'm leading the people of New Orleans] Ibid.

a seamstress by trade] Antoinette K-Doe, interview with author, July 4, 1999.

15 *Some folks said I had lost my voice*] WWOZ New Orleans, Mar. 1998.

K-Doe would sew] Walter "Wolfman" Washington, interview with author, May 19, 2004.

19 *Wear those short dresses*] "Short Dress," lyrics by Ernest Kador Jr. aka Ernie K-Doe.

CHAPTER 3

20 *When I have to grab him*] Chris Rose, "K-Doe Incarnate," *Times-Picayune* (New Orleans), Oct. 20, 2001.

I'm just working poor Ernie to death!] Antoinette K-Doe, conversation with author, Mourning Glory Ball, New Orleans, Sept. 28, 2002.

I first became aware of K-Doe] Steven Forster, interview with author, Jan. 2006.

CHAPTER 4

23 *You been listening*] *Ernie K-Doe Show*, WWOZ New Orleans, undated recording.

If I was born somewhere else] WTUL New Orleans, 1990. K-Doe's session at WTUL was filmed by Stevenson J. Palfi; audio recording courtesy Mary Katherine Aldin.

On the second month] *Ernie K-Doe Show*, WWOZ New Orleans, undated recording.

Some people ask me] Ibid.

Daddy shot me] Ibid.

And I'm glad] Ibid.

24 *Some black people in New Orleans*] "Deacon" John Moore, interview with author, Mar. 2007.

Ernie K-Doe was definitely not] Cyril Neville, conversation with author, Feb. 19, 2007.

K-Doe was like Muhammad Ali] Harold Battiste, interview with author, June 2007.

25 *I am the greatest*] George Lois, ed., *Ali Rap: Muhammad Ali, the First Heavyweight Champion of Rap* (New York: ESPB Books, 2006), 52–53.

I'm here, and I'm back!] *Ernie K-Doe Show*, WWOZ New Orleans, undated recording.

26 *The woman got the hyde*] Ibid.

I'll play that record for you] Ibid.

I do not like the cursing] Ernie K-Doe, interview with Stevenson J. Palfi, 1990; audio recording courtesy Mary Katherine Aldin.

When I hit that stage] Ernie K-Doe, onstage interview with author, May 3, 1998.

27 *I remember one time*] *Ernie K-Doe Show*, WWOZ New Orleans, undated recording.

That was Geronimo] Ibid.

Play that git-tar, boy!] Ibid.

I want to know, is it good to you?] Ibid.

28 *That's what I say*] Ibid.

I wonder what Jack and Jill] Ibid.

Oh, that made dog look like a cat] Ibid.

Jack be nimble] "Jump into Your Love," lyrics by Ernie K-Doe and Milton Joseph Batiste, published by Olympia Music.

30 *Little Sally Walker*] For a discussion of this British play song, see John Bealle, "Notes to Song Tracks," *Bullfrog Jumped*, Alabama Folklife Association, http://www.alabamafolklife.org/content/history-behind-songs (accessed Sept. 22, 2011).

All you want to do] "Mustang Sally," lyrics by Bonny Rice (Sir Mack Rice), published by Fourteenth Hour Music and Springtime Music.

the number-one DJ] *Ernie K-Doe Show*, WWOZ New Orleans, undated recording.

CHAPTER 5

31 *a character based on*] For more on the origins of the character, see Lafcadio Hearn, *An American Miscellany* (New York: Dodd, Mead, 1924), 201–8, and Dr. John with Jack Rummel, *Under a Hoodoo Moon: The Life of Dr. John the Night Tripper* (New York: St. Martin's, 1994), 140–41.

I don't know how many] Mac Rebennack (Dr. John), interview with author, Jan. 7, 2002.

I was at K-Doe's gig] Ibid.

There was definitely some weird sides] Ibid.

33 *They're fixin' to put my picture*] Ernie K-Doe, conversation with author, Mother-in-Law Lounge, New Orleans, 1999.

K-Doe and his crazy act] Kenneth "Afro" Williams, interview with author, Oct. 23, 2010.

We were in some joint] Chuck Badie, interview with author, Sept. 9, 2007.

Some people thought K-Doe was obnoxious] Skip Alexander, interview with author, June 15, 2003.

34 *K-Doe and I appeared*] Irma Thomas, interview with author, Feb. 1, 2007.

All styles are Jelly Roll] Brian J. Wolle, "The Young Music of Yesterday: Early Jazz," *Perfect Sound Forever*, www.furious.com/perfect/earlyjazz.html (accessed Sept. 5, 2011).

personally originated jazz] Alan Lomax, *Mister Jelly Roll: The Fortunes of Jelly Roll Morton, New Orleans Creole and "Inventor of Jazz,"* 2nd ed. (Berkeley: University of California Press, 1973), 68.

epic self-praise] Lomax, *Mister Jelly Roll*, 28.

so big it bulges] *Daily Gleaner* (Kingston, Jamaica), Nov. 30, 1961.

K-Doe and my brother] Charles Neville, interview with author, Jan. 2007.

35 *they're doing it all over*] Ernie K-Doe, onstage commentary (New Orleans Jazz and Heritage Festival, New Orleans, May 3, 1998).

I'm just like a rabbit] Ernie K-Doe, interview with author, July 3, 1999.

CHAPTER 6

38 *It's a strange story*] Adrianna Cador, interview with author, Apr. 5, 2009.

So Ernest [Kador] Sr. was married] Ibid.

40 *Reverend Ernest Kador was my brother*] Mary Kador, interview with author, Aug. 14, 2010.

K-Doe didn't live with us] Eugene Kador, interview with author, Apr. 5, 2009.

41 *Lightnin' Slim was sort of like*] Wade Williams, interview with author, July 12, 2005.

Our Aunt Carrie] Jackie Williams, interview with author, June 25, 2011.

I practically lived there] Mary Kador interview.

Some people say] *Ernie K-Doe Show*, WWOZ New Orleans, undated recording.

42 *Everyone in the family was either in music*] Eugene Kador interview.

If you ever been] Ernie K-Doe, onstage interview with author, May 3, 1998.

I knew of Ernie K-Doe] James Parnell, interview with author, Summer 2007.

Parnell don't know] Jo Davis, interview with author, Summer 2007.

There used to be a church] Jeff Hannusch, *I Hear You Knockin': The Sound of New Orleans Rhythm and Blues* (Ville Platte, LA: Swallow, 1985), 333.

one time he tried to fly] Art Neville, interview with author, Dec. 2006.

44 *Archie started that scream*] Tony Heilbut, *The Gospel Sound: Good News and Bad Times* (1971; repr., New York: Limelight, 1992), 47.

When you hear me sing] *Ernie K-Doe Show*, WWOZ New Orleans, undated recording.

When I came out of church] Ernie K-Doe, interview with Rick Coleman, Jan. 23, 1982; courtesy Rick Coleman.

See, I was staying at] John Sinclair, "Back Talk: Ernie K-Doe," *OffBeat*, Feb. 1996, 84.

Izzicoo could outsing us all] Ernie K-Doe, interview with Rick Coleman, June 6, 1982; courtesy Rick Coleman.

Champ Clark inspired me] Ernie K-Doe, interview with Courtney Egan, Apr. 2000; courtesy Courtney Egan.

We used to have water] Ernie K-Doe interview with Coleman (Jan. 1982).

45 *back around 1948, 1950*] Skip Alexander interview.

When I first started] *Ernie K-Doe Show*, WWOZ New Orleans, undated recording.

Who do you think] Ibid.

46 *That's true*] Robert Parker, interview with author, Apr. 20, 2007.

48 *You can't talk about*] Jerry Butler, interview with author, Nov. 17, 2003.

In his autobiography Malcolm X] See the closing pages of chapter 3, "Homeboy," *The Autobiography of Malcolm X*, first published in 1965 by Grove Press.

Why does K-Doe keep talking] Overheard by the author (Rhythm and Blues Foundation Pioneer Awards, Sheraton Hotel, New York, Feb. 26, 1998).

CHAPTER 7

49 *K-Doe had a tendency*] Irving Banister, interview with author, Jan. 20, 2007.

Musicians would stand in line] Eddie Bo, interview with author, July 15, 2007.

They used to have talent shows] Earl King, interview with David Kunian, Oct. 17, 1997; courtesy David Kunian.

I led the house band] Eddie Bo interview.

50 *Pioneer*? That's a guy] Cosimo Matassa, interview with Todd Collins, May 4, 2007; http://www.toddcollinsmusci.com/cosimo-matassa-interview/ (accessed Sept. 22, 2010).

51 *lots of spirit here*] "Review of New R&B Records," *Billboard*, Sept. 4, 1954, 32.

an unusual gimmick] Ibid.

A lot of recording executives] Robert Parker interview.

52 *Kador sends this one through*] "Reviews of New R&B Records," *Billboard*, Dec. 3, 1955, 63.

K-Doe knew how to work] Mac Rebennack interview (2002).

I have never seen] Allen Toussaint, interview with author, Nov. 11, 2003.

53 *Ernest Kador, the handsome crooner*] "Stars Put On 'Big Show' for WMRY," *Louisiana Weekly*, Apr. 7, 1956.

The Dew Drop was] Bobby "Blue" Bland, interview with author, Nov. 25, 2006.

Ain't no tellin'] Eddie Bo interview.

if you were in the house band] Porgy Jones, interview with author, July 13, 2007.

Frank Painia took care] Bobby "Blue" Bland interview.

It was like a family] Jason Berry, Jonathan Foose, and Tad Jones, *Up from the Cradle of Jazz: New Orleans Music Since World War II*, new ed. (Lafayette: University of Louisiana at Lafayette Press, 2009), 61.

54 *If you needed to hire*] Porgy Jones interview.

One night I was playing] "Deacon" John Moore interview.

dancing with three tables] Jeff Hannusch, "The South's Swankiest Night Spot: The Legend of the Dew Drop Inn," www.stachmo.com/ikoiko/dewdropinn.html (accessed October 28, 2011).

when Patsy brought your ass on] Tabby Thomas, interview with author, Nov. 2, 2010.

and then somebody would tell] Irving Banister interview.

Little Richard gave me] Bobby Marchan, onstage interview with author (New Orleans Jazz and Heritage Festival, New Orleans, Apr. 30, 1998).

If you got a little girl] Bobby Marchan, onstage commentary (Theater of the Performing Arts, New Orleans, ca. 1993).

56 *Fuck it, we all grown!*] Ibid.

Bobby Marchan was flamboyant] "Deacon" John Moore interview.

there was a certain Dew Drop-ness] Mac Rebennack interview (2002).

CHAPTER 8

57 *I had an advantage*] Hannusch, *I Hear You Knockin'*, 143.

which beams at Negro audiences] *Billboard*, Oct. 21, 1950, 18.

probably the hottest jock] Hannusch, *I Hear You Knockin'*, 142.

McKinley played a crucial role] Ibid.

58 *They saw me as being able*] Giacomo Friedman, "Allen Toussaint: The Man behind All That Great New Orleans Music," *DISCoveries*, May 1990, 34.

Larry McKinley and I held auditions] Allen Toussaint interview (2003).

We put a 'K'] Bill Griggs, "Spotlight on New Orleans Featuring Ernie K-Doe," *Rockin' 50s* 33 (Dec. 1991): 10.

Kay-Dash-Dee-Oh-Eee] *Ernie K-Doe Show*, WWOZ New Orleans, undated recording.

The reason I did it] Joe Banashak, interview with Rick Coleman, May 1984; courtesy Rick Coleman.

59 *We had a group of guys*] Allen Toussaint interview (2003).

From the time I woke up] Friedman, "Allen Toussaint," 34.

We'd try one song] Allen Toussaint interview (2003).

At Minit we helped out] Ernie K-Doe interview with Palfi.

We were all like a big family] Aaron Neville, interview with author, Nov. 14, 2007.

61 *In an arrangement*] Berry, Foose, and Jones, *Up from the Cradle of Jazz*, 212.

Allen wrote out everything] John Boudreaux, interview with author, Oct. 24, 2008.

62 *I'm going to take me*] "Make You Love Me," lyrics by Ernest Kador, published by Minit Music/K Do Music; used by permission.

If you come back] "Hello My Lover," lyrics by Ernest Kador, published by EMI/UNART.

tells a story] Ernie K-Doe interview with Palfi.

63 *Wake up, goddamn it*] Snooks Eaglin, onstage commentary (Tyler's Beer Garden, New Orleans, 1986).

Don't play it pretty] Snooks Eaglin, onstage commentary (Rock 'n' Bowl, New Orleans, ca. 2007).

Trained as a young child] Rick Coleman, *Blue Monday: Fats Domino and the Lost Dawn of Rock 'n' Roll* (Cambridge, MA: Da Capo, 2006), 39.

K-Doe believed in himself] Dave Bartholomew, interview with author, Sept. 7, 2007.

I'm proud of Dave Bartholomew] Ernie K-Doe interview with Coleman.

64 *Restaurants: Please call*] *Louisiana Weekly*, July 30, 1960.

when they used to have] Cosimo Matassa, onstage commentary (Tribute to Ernie K-Doe, New Orleans Jazz and Heritage Festival, New Orleans, May 5, 2002). Clyde McPhatter was a major R&B artist of the 1950s and '60s, best known as the lead singer on such Drifters' hits as "Money Honey" and for his solo hits "A Lover's Question" and "Lover Please."

Working with K-Doe] Porgy Jones interview.

the wind and the trees] *Ernie K-Doe Show*, WWOZ New Orleans, undated recording.

CHAPTER 9

66 *There wouldn't be no Ernie K-Doe*] Geraldine Wyckoff, "Percussions: Musical Months," *Gambit Weekly*, July 28, 1998, 39.

During that time] Ernie K-Doe interview with Palfi.

It was odd] Steve Wildsmith, "Allen Toussaint on Songwriting and Inspiration," Apr. 8, 2010, wildsmith.blountblogs.com/2010/04/08/allen-toussaint-on-songwriting-and-inspiration/ (accessed Apr. 9, 2010).

She called me at home] Allen Toussaint, interview with Billy Delle, WWOZ, Dec. 1986; courtesy Rick Coleman.

I was in with a bunch of snakes] Ernie K-Doe, onstage interview with author, May 3, 1998.

Sometimes K-Doe would talk] Tony Owens, interview with author, Jan. 2007.

67 *Don't you never think*] Ernie K-Doe interview with Palfi.

The story that "Mother-in-Law"] Allen Toussaint interview (2003).

68 *No, I didn't think much*] Chuck Badie interview.

Guitar Slim . . .] Tony Scherman, *Backbeat: Earl Palmer's Story* (Washington, DC: Smithsonian Institution Press, 1999), 80.

69 *Lawrence Nelson*] Nelson's mysterious death prompted singer Oliver Morgan—who had previously recorded for AFO under the nickname "Nookie Boy"—to record the local R&B classic "Who Shot the La La?"

Melvin Lastie's cornet solo] Mac Rebennack (Dr. John), interview with author, July 1981.

vocal interjections of] Henshaw, "The MM Pop Shop," 6.

70 *a hen-pecked husband*] Hellicar, "New to the Charts," 4.

yelling and running] Walter "Wolfman" Washington interview.

Benny was kind of disappointed] Cosimo Matassa, "Tribute to Ernie K-Doe."

Benny and K-Doe started] "Deacon" John Moore interview.

72 *A promoter named Henry Wynn*] Jerry Butler interview.

In 1961 I was playing] Roosevelt Grier, interview with author, June 3, 2009.

73 *I played on some of those*] Ben E. King, interview with author, June 8, 2009.

Sometimes we weren't allowed] Jackie Williams interview.

Oh, K-Doe was excited] Larry McKinley, interview with author, May 15, 2003.

I saw K-Doe play the Apollo] Allen Toussaint, interview with author, Sept. 15, 2005.

When I first met K-Doe] Art Neville interview.

75 *K-Doe thought that* Ernie K-Doe] Ibid.

Now, can you imagine] Porgy Jones interview.

Just fair] Record book 1959–1962, Frank Schiffman Apollo Theatre Collection, 1935–1973, Archives Center, National Museum of American History, Washington, DC.

Banashak stated] See Hannusch, *I Hear You Knockin'*, 147. Banashak repeated the story of the snub in his May 1984 interview with Rick Coleman.

76 *I did not make a lot of money*] Ernie K-Doe interview with Palfi.

You know what K-Doe's problem was?] Carol Fran, interview with author, July 2003.

K-Doe sponsored the team] James "Tip" Williams, interview with author, Jan. 2010.

77 *Sam liked scotch*] Larry McKinley interview (2003).

CHAPTER 10

79 *I* cannot *sing*] Ernie K-Doe, onstage interview with author (Allison Miner Music Heritage Stage, New Orleans Jazz and Heritage Festival, May 4, 2000).

The "Mother-in-Law" winner] *Billboard*, May 29, 1961, 25.

80 *I didn't put a lot of solos*] Allen Toussaint interview (2003).

By the time I wrote] Ibid.

We often played] Wayne Fontana, correspondence with author, Nov. 5, 2009.

When our new lineup] Jim McCarty, correspondence with author, May 25, 2009.

interesting and unusual] Ted Plonas, "DISCussion," *Press-Telegram* (Long Beach, CA), Oct. 19, 1961.

81 *K-Doe had a crush*] Carol Fran interview.

the joyful noise] Kalamu ya Salaam, "Ernie K-Doe: 'Certain Girl,'" *Breath of Life*, June 9, 2008, http://www.kalamu.com/bol/ (accessed Sept. 8, 2011).

If I had to pick] Kalamu ya Salaam, "VARIOUS ARTISTS: 'Classic New Orleans Mixtape,'" *Breath of Life*, Jan. 26, 2009, http://www.kalamu.com/bol/ (accessed Sept. 8, 2011).

CHAPTER 11

82 *people in Jamaica knew*] Idris Muhammad, interview with author, March 12, 2008.

A highlight is provided] "'Biggest Show' Opens at Carib Today," *Daily Gleaner* (Kingston, Jamaica), Dec. 8, 1961.

Ernie K-Doe, whose "Mother-in-Law"] "Swinging Preview to the 'Biggest Show,'" *Daily Gleaner* (Kingston, Jamaica), Dec. 5, 1961.

When K-Doe started playing] Walter "Wolfman" Washington interview.

85 *Now, when "Mother-in-Law"*] Ibid.

Baton Rouge was a dry town] Ernest J. Gaines, *Mozart and Leadbelly* (New York: Knopf, 2005), 26–29.

86 *I met him through Buddy Guy*] Bobby Rush, interview with author, Oct. 9, 2007.

You talk about fun!] Walter "Wolfman" Washington interview.

CHAPTER 12

87 *strong sales potential*] "Reviews of New Singles," *Billboard*, Oct. 9, 1961, 34.

very favorite songs] Allen Toussaint interview (2003).

An interesting ditty] "Singles Reviews," *Billboard*, July 21, 1962, 21.

88 *I am* not *that voice*] Irma Thomas interview, Feb. 1, 2007.

Exuberant reading by warbler] "Singles Reviews," *Billboard*, Apr. 7, 1962, 71.

89 *When the young New Orleans belter*] liner notes, *Mother-in-Law,* Minit LP 0002, 1962.

Chudd presented] Hannusch, *I Hear You Knockin'*, 147.

91 *When Lew Chudd found out*] Ibid.

the night I beat James Brown] Ibid., 339.

New Orleans has been] Glenn Dixon, "Story of the Hurricane," *Village Voice*, Jan. 24, 2006, www.villagevoice.com/2006-01-24/pazzandjob/story-of-the-hurricane.html.

It was incredible!] Jimmy Moliere, interview with Rick Coleman and Jerry Brock, Apr. 17, 2004; courtesy Rick Coleman.

K-Doe always wanted to outdo] Art Neville interview.

92 *K-Doe said he had beaten*] Charles Neville interview.

Now when K-Doe was on that show] Irving Banister interview.

I saw that battle of the blues] "Deacon" John Moore interview.

I didn't leave Minit] Ernie K-Doe, interview with Rick Coleman, June 6, 1982; courtesy Rick Coleman.

94 *The union looked on*] Berry, Foose, and Jones, *Up from the Cradle of Jazz*, 146.

They [the black union] was nothing but] Ibid.

In 1962 or 1963] Dr. John with Jack Rummel, *Under a Hoodoo Moon*, 112–13.

95 *I had a friend*] Giorgio Gomelsky, correspondence with author, Dec. 10, 2008.

well known in the UK] Eric Burdon, correspondence with author, Oct. 24, 2008.

96 *We performed "Mother-in-Law"*] Peter Noone, correspondence with author, Aug. 12, 2006.

Getting drunk, talk out of my head] "Talking Out of My Head," lyrics by Naomi Neville (Allen Toussaint), published by SCREEN GEMS-EMI.

97 *as English as a cup of tea*] *Billboard*, Apr. 25, 1964, 24–25.

CHAPTER 13

97 *little pick-up bands*] Arthur Vigne, interview with author, July 22, 2010.

K-Doe was a man] Tony Owens interview.

K-Doe could not handle] Porgy Jones interview.

99 *Growing up, I wasn't deprived*] Ernest Kador Jr. interview.

K-Doe and I dated] Doris Watson, interview with author, July 2010.

100 *I can honestly say*] Ernest Kador Jr. interview.

In 1965 K-Doe went] *Times-Picayune* (New Orleans), May 5 and July 30, 1965.

I remember K-Doe] Frederick S. Ellis, interview with author, Dec. 26, 2008.

Maybe you will learn] "Alimony Blues Sung for Judge," *Times-Picayune* (New Orleans), May 5, 1965.

Fats Domino made] Cosimo Matassa, interview with Eric Paulsen, *Eyewitness News*, WWL-TV, Feb. 8, 2007.

101 *the wrong cuff links*] *Times-Picayune* (New Orleans), July 30, 1965.

I also hired him] Michael Rothschild, interview with author, Dec. 30, 2006.

going to frat-house parties] Jerry Springer, interview with author, Jan. 27, 2009.

recognized K-Doe immediately] Lili LeGardeur, "Young Harpist Gives K-Doe a Resting Place," *Times-Picayune* (New Orleans), July 19, 2001.

I was no longer managing] Larry McKinley, interview with author, Jan. 2010.

K-Doe used to run me crazy!] Lloyd Price, interview with author, Oct. 23, 2010.

jumped on me] Charles White, *The Life and Times of Little Richard* (1984; London: Omnibus, 2003), 37.

104 *My mother-in-law is*] "My Mother-in-Law (Is in My Hair Again)," lyrics by Ernest Kador Jr, published by Songs of Universal, BMI; used by permission.

K-Doe may have been referring] Robert Pruter, correspondence with author, June 3, 2010.

CHAPTER 14

105 *After K-Doe split*] Porgy Jones interview.

106 *Yes, I am "Little Marie"*] Marie Monley, interview with author, Feb. 2010.

In the early '60s, K-Doe] Billy Delle, interview with author, June 1, 2007.

107 *One time we went*] Snooks Eaglin, interview with author, Mar. 1989.

I worked the whole black circuit] Roy Head, interview with author, June 7, 2007.

110 *Ernie would come to town*] Archie Bell, interview with author, Feb. 5, 2010.

played behind K-Doe] Herman Ernest, interview with author, New Orleans, Nov. 5, 2007.

This is Ernie K-Doe's new record] *Ernie K-Doe Show*, WWOZ New Orleans, undated recording.

111 *K-Doe claimed we sang*] Joe Ligon, interview with author, Nov. 28, 2007.

at least three of the other guys] Andre Williams, interview with author, Jan. 25, 2010.

CHAPTER 15

112 *I've never seen this before!*] Allen Toussaint, interview with author, Apr. 18, 2011.

114 *distinctive sound of the city*] Mike Leadbitter, *Blues Unlimited* 87 (Dec. 1971): 24.

115 *You not on the* Edge of Night] "You Got to Love Me," lyrics by Ernie K-Doe, published by Martu Music, ASCAP.

FOOL, YOU BETTER] *Ernie K-Doe Show*, WWOZ New Orleans, undated recording.

One thing I'm so glad to say] Ibid.

117 *K-Doe perform at Bradford's*] Joe Citizen, interview with author, Jan. 10, 2010.

118 *How can you be*] Hannusch, *I Hear You Knockin'*, 34.

CHAPTER 16

118 *In conversation, K-Doe is*] Jon Newlin, "Ernie K-Doe: At 35, Rock's Grand Old Man," *Figaro*, July 8, 1972, 4.

On May 14, 1973] Keith Shadwick, *Led Zeppelin: The Story of a Band and Their Music, 1968–1980* (San Francisco: Backbeat, 2005), 200. See also Richard Cole with Richard Trubo, *Stairway to Heaven: Led Zeppelin Uncensored*, rev. ed. (1992; New York: HarperCollins, 2002), 207.

As a teenager, Plant had] "Dispatches: A Record that Changed My Life," *Uncut*, ca. 2004, 4.

I was intoxicated by] Keith Spera, "He Found His Thrill," *Times-Picayune* (New Orleans), May 5, 2007.

120 *a salacious incident*] Andrew Heritage, ed., *The Rough Guide to Led Zeppelin* (London: Rough Guides Ltd., 2007), 237.

Allen is slow as all get out] Patti LaBelle, interview with author, July 5, 2008.

When Paul was here] Allen Toussaint interview (2003).

people like Professor Longhair] Sidney Smith, interview with author, 2003.

121 *What we're doing now*] "Band on the Bayou," *Rolling Stone*, Mar. 27, 1975, 11.

McCartney also had the party] Sidney Smith interview.

Another day, another party] "Random Notes," *Rolling Stone*, May 8, 1975, 26.

CHAPTER 17

123 *After my parents split up*] Ernest Kador Jr. interview.

killed by projects] Richard E. Hart, "Killed by Projects as Much as Bullets?" *Times-Picayune* (New Orleans), Mar. 26, 1975.

124 *K-Doe's brothers all lived*] Kenny Neal, interview with author, Jan. 26, 2009.

127 *By the time I arrived*] Robert Duncan, "Lawdamercy, Springsteen Saves!: Testimony from the Howling Dog Choir (Or Tramps Like Us, Baby We're Born Again)," *Creem*, Oct. 1978, 64.

128 *I grew up here*] Reggie Scanlan, interview with author, Jan. 3, 2007.

So it was late that Sunday] Jessie James, interview with author, Nov. 2010.

CHAPTER 18

131 *Miss Byrd asked me*] Ernie K-Doe interview with Coleman (Jan. 1982).

Lots of musicians came up] Bruce Iglauer, correspondence with author, July 10, 2011.

went into a long] Jon Foose, correspondence with author, July 10, 2011.

The station gave them an outlet] Years later, Jerry Brock coproduced the Grammy-winning jazz album *Doc Cheatham & Nicholas Payton*.

I'm goin' back to the wagon] For more on Benjamin Francis "Whitey" Ford, the original "Duke," see Country Music Hall of Fame and Museum, "The Duke of Paducah," http://www.countrymusichalloffame.org/full-list-of-inductees/view/the-duke-of-paducah.

Everybody *wanted to be*] Jerry Brock, interview with author, July 27, 2007.

133 *I worked the board*] Steve Armbruster, interview with author, Feb. 18, 2007.

The New Orleans radio market] Rollye Bornstein, "New Orleans Market Profile," *Billboard*, Sept. 4, 1982, 22.

New Orleans is home] Bornstein, "New Orleans Market Profile," 26.

Many nights after K-Doe's show] Jerry Brock interview.

134 *a broadcast from the summer of 1985*] The following Ernie K-Doe quotations are all drawn from the *Ernie K-Doe Show*, WWOZ New Orleans, summer 1985.

136 *a really trashed-out dump*] Rick Allen, interview with author, Nov. 1, 2008.

played a juke joint] Kenny Neal interview.

I know some people thought] Herman Ernest interview.

CHAPTER 19

138 *Perhaps the most highly sought*] *Ernie K-Doe Show*, WWOZ New Orleans, June 1984.

140 *Y'know, son*] Nick Tosches, *Hellfire: The Jerry Lee Lewis Story* (New York: Dell, 1982), 255.

CHAPTER 20

141 *It wasn't as loud*] Barri Marsh, "Blues Hits the Right Note at New Sarpy Festival, *Times-Picayune* (New Orleans), July 5, 1984.

to always be onstage] Porgy Jones interview.

Martin Luther King ain't] *Ernie K-Doe Show*, WWOZ New Orleans, undated recording.

142 *It's not what you say*] Ibid.

What I'm saying is this] Commentary on Dick Clark from Ernie K-Doe interview with Palfi.

143 *I don't think it was racism*] Eddie Ray, interview with author, Oct. 2009.

K-Doe got depressed] Jessie James interview.

145 *I will never marry again!*] Ernie K-Doe interview with Palfi.

Once I had decided] Jessie James interview.

Late in 1983 I got the idea] Bill Bentley, interview with author, May 3, 2005. K-Doe is not known to have actually worked in law enforcement.

148 *I really don't remember*] Jerry Jumonville, interview with author, Jan. 2010.

I didn't think K-Doe would] Bill Bentley interview.

To me, Ernie K-Doe was] Bruce Hornsby, interview with author, Feb. 16, 2004. Other esoteric bus tapes included a long and F-bomb-laden argument among members of the British rock group the Troggs; the cirumlocutions of a preacher called Prophet Omega; and a concert tape of country singer Hank Williams Jr., apparently under the influence. When Williams garbled the phrase "country boy" so that it came out as "slumpy boy," tapes flew around the world, and a band in Nashville chose Williams's flubbed line for its name. In this skewed-humor context, Mr. Ma-Naugahyde won many new fans, indeed.

149 *The Foundation did not want*] Jerry Brock interview.

Whatever way the wind blows] *Ernie K-Doe Show*, WWOZ New Orleans, ca. 1987.

The students have been coming] WTUL New Orleans, 1990.

151 *I was unaware*] David Freedman, correspondence with author, Dec. 11, 2010.

CHAPTER 21

151 *WWOZ is the station*] *Ernie K-Doe Show*, WWOZ New Orleans, undated recording.

Because they know what] Ibid.

152 *Sitting still as a statue*] Patricia Freeman and Michael Small, "Joey Dee, Past Master of the Twist, Plans a Refuge for Those Caught Between Rock and a Hard Place," *People*, Nov. 20, 1989, 155, 159. K-Doe did, in fact, earn artist royalties on sales of his records, along with songwriter's royalties for his original compositions. At the time of this interview, however, sales would have tapered off significantly; in addition, K-Doe was transient during this time, leading to difficulties receiving mail.

154 *"Jump into Your Love" had*] Wilson Victorian, interview with author, July 2010.

Mother-in-law was always] "Father-in-Law, the Devil's Son-in-Law," lyrics by Ernie K-Doe, Milton Batiste, and Wilson Victorian, published by DuBat Music, BMI.

156 *K-Doe's powerful on-screen cameo*] As with the fabled live recording from the Houston Pladium, the author has not been able to locate film of the complete performance.

The thing about K-Doe] Kenneth "Afro" Williams interview.

157 *Milton had [already recorded] some keyboard*] Ibid.

We were looking for] Ibid.

had high hopes] Ibid.

158 *Bow down on your knees*] Ernie K-Doe, onstage commentary (Dew Drop Inn Revisited Concert, Ernest N. Morial Convention Center, New Orleans, Apr. 26, 1994).

When K-Doe was drinking] Walter "Wolfman" Washington interview.

kept up with Ernie] Lloyd Price interview.

[K-Doe] carried himself like a star] Charles Connor, interview with author, Jan. 21, 2010.

One night I was backstage] Ken Jones, interview with author, Jan. 2008.

But a lot of the cats] Charles Connor interview.

K-Doe just sitting] Jean Knight, interview with author, Nov. 3, 2010.

159 *I used to go check*] Jessie James interview.

At one point] Frankie Ford, interview with author, Oct. 5, 2006.

160 *played some of those gigs*] Amadee Castenell, interview with author, Nov. 2010.

One night I was heading home] Bobby Lonero, interview with author, Feb. 2010.

You know, we all go] Frankie Ford interview.

161 *K-Doe came to our wedding*] Mr. Cotton, conversation with author, Mother-in-Law Lounge, New Orleans, Dec. 2007.

CHAPTER 22

161 *Nobody but Milton*] Kenneth "Afro" Williams interview.

What first attracted me] Antoinette K-Doe, interview with author, May 14, 2006, Story Corps, LC classification E740.5.

I was tending bar] Ibid.

162 *I used to play*] Ernie Vincent, interview with author, Nov. 2011.

People ask me] Antoinette K-Doe Story Corps interview.

K-Doe's banker, and clothes designer] Ibid.

People always said] Jessie James interview.

That O'Doul's bottle] Kenneth "Afro" Williams interview.

Antoinette was in denial] Ken Jones interview.

166 *Me and Louis Nugent*] Doc Mancina, interview with author, Oct. 2010.

days of alcohol abuse] Reginald Owens, "Comeback Kid," *Times-Picayune* (New Orleans), Aug. 5, 1995.

I had to bring K-Doe back] Antoinette K-Doe Story Corps interview.

167 *Boy, did K-Doe burn me bad*] John Blancher, correspondence with author, Nov. 30, 2010.

Look, don't take a chance] Antoinette K-Doe Story Corps interview.

169 *Who would know*] Chris Rose, "The Artist Formerly Known as Ernie K-Doe," *Times-Picayune* (New Orleans), Dec. 17, 1998.

170 *Scholars claim that Surrealism*] S. Frederick Starr, *New Orleans Unmasqued: Being a Wagwit's Sketches of a Singular American City* (New Orleans: Édition Dedeaux, 2005), 89.

a city-wide indulgence] Ibid., 91.

171 *I grew up in K-Doe's neighborhood*] Willie Birch, interview with author, Oct. 2008.

174 *K-Doe also fits in*] Ibid.

Like gede, *K-Doe had*] Ibid.

CHAPTER 23

176 *No, I was not relieved*] Jessie James interview.

177 *back in the early '60s*] Mable John, interview with author, Jan. 19, 2010.

I was instrumental in K-Doe] Ibid.

How about a standing ovation] Ernie K-Doe, onstage commentary (Rhythm and Blues Foundation Pioneer Awards, Sheraton Hotel, New York, Feb. 26, 1998).

179 *People were amused*] Jerry Butler interview.

To see how much K-Doe loved] Eddie Levert, interview with author, July 3, 2007.

Ernie was acting] Mable John interview.

overstaying his welcome] Jon Bream, "R&B Awards Deliver what Grammys Don't," *Minneapolis Star Tribune*, Feb. 28, 1998.

Everybody was there] Ernie K-Doe, onstage interview with author, May 3, 1998.

180 *I just can't do this*] Milton Batiste, conversation with author, Apr. 28, 1997.

Over the years, K-Doe] Quint Davis, interview with author, June 26, 2009.

Last night, my wife and I] Ernie K-Doe, onstage interview with author, May 3, 1998.

181 *Strange, mysterious and bizarre*] Angus Lind, "Free Wheeling Folks: An Unusual Bus Tour Winds up at Jazz Fest," *Times-Picayune* (New Orleans), May 1, 1998.

When the day finally drew] Ibid.

183 *was the only real magnetism*] Angus Lind, "Tain't It a Shame," *Times-Picayune* (New Orleans), July 11, 2001.

CHAPTER 24

183 *I used to play in Washington*] The scene in Washington, DC, is described in Sandmel, "Mr. K-Doe Goes to Washington," *Gambit*, July 20, 1999, 25–26.

184 *In honor of Independence Day*] Ernie K-Doe with Bunny Matthews, "Ernie on Ernie," *OffBeat*, July 1999, 67.

Hopefully I'm right] Ibid.

I got a new album] Ernie K-Doe, interview with author, July 3, 1999.

What the hell is this?] Sandmel, "Mr. K-Doe Goes to Washington."

186 *Aren't you a famous singer?*] Ibid.

From a little girl] Ibid.

I thank God that Ernie] Ibid.

187 *It went good, man*] Ibid.

CHAPTER 25

187 *Coming from New York*] Michael Burke, interview with author, Jan. 2008.

189 *Not a single one of the band*] Maria Berg, interview with author, Jan. 15, 2010.

190 *a regular working cat*] Herman Ernest interview.

K-Doe picked up] Antoinette K-Doe Story Corps interview.

191 *heard Antoinette say this*] Lefty Parker, correspondence with author, June 11, 2009.

So what the children did] Antoinette K-Doe Story Corps interview.

I didn't go to my father's shows] Ernest Kador Jr. interview.

What you need to know] Ernie K-Doe, onstage interview with author, May 4, 2000.

If it's wrong] Boozoo Chavis, intro to "Forty One Days," on *Boozoo Chavis*, Nonesuch Records.

The bands have been] Ernie K-Doe, onstage interview with author, May 4, 2000.

Fun? I haven't slept] Tim Smith, interview with Courtney Egan, Apr. 2000; courtesy Courtney Egan.

K-Doe has taught us] Lefty Parker, interview with Courtney Egan, Apr. 2000; courtesy Courtney Egan.

192 *I don't never stop studying*] Ernie K-Doe interview with Egan.

One of the lessons] Bunny Matthews, "K-Doe without Tears," *OffBeat*, Aug. 1, 2001, 12.

I think the show was] Maria Berg interview.

195 *We would always visit*] Aimée Toledano, "Quintron," *OffBeat*, Sept. 1, 2000, 49.

K-Doe inspired me musically] Quintron, interview with author, July 2007.

Every Sunday, we gonna have] Sinclair, "Back Talk," 85.

K-Doe was such] Quintron interview.

196 *Ernie had a huge impact*] Lefty Parker correspondence.

the closest thing] Tondrae Kemp, correspondence with author, Mar. 3, 2011.

He was dating my mom] "Josephine Johnny" Watson, interview with author, July 2010.

CHAPTER 26

197 *Neil's a nice guy*] Antoinette K-Doe, conversation with author, May 10, 2000.

Them slick-ass people] Chris Rose, "Incident at the Mother-in-Law Lounge," *Times-Picayune* (New Orleans), May 20, 2000.

some other kind of man] Mac Rebennack interview (2002).

It was the strangest] Rose, "Incident."

198 *For six years*] Neil Strauss, "THE POP LIFE; Mother-in-Law of All Visits," *New York Times*, May 17, 2000.

199 *Uh-uh, baby*] Ernie K-Doe, onstage commentary (Mother-in-Law Lounge, New Orleans, ca. 1999).

to the Mother-in-Law] Dave Pirner, interview with author, Nov. 2010.

K-Doe wasn't real prolific] Allen Toussaint interview (2003).

White boy! Play that black boy's music] "White Boy / Black Boy," lyrics by Ernest Kador Jr.

200 Happy Here and Now] David Ng, "*Happy Here and Now*," *Village Voice*, Dec. 6, 2005.

Movies usually show us] Steven Whitty, "Before the Deluge," *Newark Star-Ledger*, Dec. 15, 2005.

Visiting New Orleans] Michael Almereyda, correspondence with author, June 7, 2007. Sun Ra (Herman Blount) was a prolific and well respected jazz pianist, composer, and poet-philosopher. A staunch individualist, his eclectic work ranged from ragtime to bebop and beyond. Sun Ra's eccentric statements included renouncing his given name because he claimed to have been born on Saturn. Following this declaration, his garb often suggested his cosmic vision.

CHAPTER 27

205 *Let's have a big round*] Ernie K-Doe, onstage commentary (Mother-in-Law Lounge, New Orleans, Dec. 9, 2000).

206 *Ever since crawling out*] "Krewe du Vieux Explores 2001: A Space Fallacy," *Le Monde de Merde* 10, no. 1 (Feb. 10, 2001): 1.

There's a thing I've dreamed] "Louis the First," *Time*, Feb. 21, 1949, 52.

208 *lampooning the white man's racial stereotypes*] James Gill, *Lords of Misrule: Mardi Gras and the Politics of Race in New Orleans* (Jackson: University Press of Mississippi, 1997), 2.

a warped picture] See Gill, *Lords of Misrule*, 208.

farcical, disgraceful spectacle] "Zulu Turns Back on Negro Community," *Louisiana Weekly*, Feb. 11, 1961.

I'm gonna be up] "K-Doe: Blazing the Trail from Emperor to King," *Le Monde de Merde* 10, no. 1 (Feb. 10, 2001): 2.

K-Doe was a guy] Antoinette K-Doe, onstage commentary (Tribute to Ernie K-Doe, Allison Miner Music Heritage Stage, New Orleans Jazz and Heritage Festival, New Orleans, May 5, 2002).

I might be old] Ernie K-Doe, onstage commentary (New Orleans Jazz and Heritage Festival, New Orleans, May 6, 2001).

one of the best shows] Red Priest, interview with author, Dec. 22, 2010.

211 *Coco Robicheaux*] Robicheaux (Curtis Arcenaux) sculpted the Professor Longhair bust at the entrance to Tipitina's. In South Louisiana folklore a Coco Robicheaux is an imaginary character whom children blame for misdeeds.

he was mostly unresponsive] Keith Spera, "Ernie K-Doe Is Dead at 65," *Times-Picayune* (New Orleans), July 5, 2001.

As far as I know] Lefty Parker correspondence.

In typical fashion] Jerry Romig qtd. in Janet McConnaughey, "'Mother-in-Law' Singer Ernie K-Doe Dead at 65," Associated Press, July 5, 2001.

The single most important] Autopsy data, correspondence from Dr. Robert A. Hammer, M.D., FACP, FACG, Tulane University Medical Center, to Antoinette Kador, Aug. 9, 2001; courtesy Antoinette K-Doe.

CHAPTER 28

212 *If they could lay out P. G. T. Beauregard*] Marc Morial, interview with author, June 8, 2009.

Ernie and Antoinette really helped] Ibid.

215 *I'm just waiting*] Marc Morial, visitation commentary (Gallier Hall, New Orleans, July 12, 2001).

There was one stunned moment] Pat Jolly, "The Story: The Wake," http://www.wwoz.org/kdoe/story.htm (accessed May 31, 2004).

216 *Ernie looked magnificent*] Ibid.

In the years since] K-Doe Publishing, *Ernie K-Doe: The Official Mother-in-Law Site*, http://www.k-doe.com/photo.shtml?funeral_outfits_w_jessie_in_coffin (accessed October 27, 2011).

217 *K-Doe would be so satisfied*] "Deacon" John Moore, funeral commentary (Gallier Hall, New Orleans, July 13, 2001).

You can feel how thick] Pat Jolly, "The Story: The Funeral," http://www.wwoz.org/kdoe/story2.htm (accessed May 31, 2004).

It's always been] Lili LeGardeur, "Young Harpist Gives K-Doe a Resting Place," *Times-Picayune* (New Orleans), July 19, 2001.

221 *some "legal dancing" followed*] Anna Ross Twichell, correspondence with author, Aug. 10, 2011.

On the morning of the funeral] Pat Jolly, "The Tomb Story: A Mother-in-Law Story," http://www.wwoz.org/kdoe/story3.htm (accessed May 31, 2004).

It was hard at first] Antoinette K-Doe Story Corps interview.

Of course I *know that K-Doe is deceased*] Ibid.

I must begin with a confession] Rose, "K-Doe Incarnate."

222 *It was a Friday*] Rose, "K-Doe without End," *Times-Picayune* (New Orleans), Mar. 3, 2002.

CHAPTER 29

222 *When my mother died*] Antoinette K-Doe Story Corps interview.

Why can't the white boy] Orissa Arend, "White Boy, Black Boy," *Louisiana Weekly*, Jan. 14, 2002, 15.

The magic of Mardi Gras] Ibid.

223 *prominent members of this krewe*] Ibid.

Ernie continues to instruct] Vivian Cahn, correspondence with author, Nov. 3, 2001.

20- to 30-something ladies] "Ready, Set, Toe!," *Bust* (Dec./Jan. 2008–09), 18.

had a picture of some pastry] Dylan James Stansbury, interview with author, Aug. 2, 2010.

224 *not only defies criticism*] David Cuthbert, "K-Doe Lives at Rock 'n' Bowl!" *Times-Picayune* (New Orleans), Oct. 8, 2004.

absurdist, slapdash, wonderful] Brian Sands, "*Burn K-Doe Burn!* at the Rock 'n' Bowl Café Theatre," *Ambush* 23, no. 6 (2005), http://www.ambushmag.com/is605/trod.htm.

I saw a play] Thurston Kelp (Chandler Harris), "Antoinette Rules," *Kelp on Kape*, March 7, 2009, www.kelponkape.blogspot.com (accessed October 27, 2011).

I didn't think a straightforward] Rob Florence, correspondence with author, Jan. 24 and Jan. 27, 2008.

226 *For too long, the South*] Bill Lavender, editor's introduction to *Another South: Experimental Writing in the South* (Tuscaloosa: University of Alabama Press, 2003), xi.

a movement beyond] Hank Lazer, "Poetry Scouting Mission: At the Intersection of Southern and Experimental," in *Another South*, xxviii.

My future wife and I] Brett Evans, correspondence with author, Feb. 16, 2008.

227 *K-Doe save me!*] Brett Evans, "K-Doe Codas," in *Another South*, 39–40, 41, 43.

228 *Now that Superdome officials*] Geoff Worden, "City Deserves a K-Dome," *Times-Picayune* (New Orleans), June 5, 2004.

Yeah, I think of Satchmo] David H. Jones, "Cyril Neville's Perfect World," *OffBeat* (June 1997), 52.

CHAPTER 30

229 *I put the statue in the closet*] Antoinette K-Doe Story Corps interview.

I absolutely need her] Quintron, correspondence with author, Sept. 3, 2005

Did you think I was] Antoinette K-Doe, conversation with author, Sept. 2005.

Eventually she was flown] Don Schanche Jr., "Rock Eagle Providing Refuge for Survivors," *Macon*

Telegraph, Sept. 7, 2005.

In a phone interview] Antoinette K-Doe, WWL-AM New Orleans, Sept. 8, 2009.

inside my budget] John Harris, "We All Gonna Have a Good Time," *Guardian*, Nov. 18, 2005.

they gave me] Antoinette K-Doe conversation with author (2005).

231 *I'm one of those stubborn*] Antoinette K-Doe, interview with Sara Le Menestrel for the Centre National de la Recherche Scientifique, Paris, Nov. 27, 2005; courtesy Sara Le Menestrel.

As long as K-Doe's been] Ibid.

232 *I never could have*] Ibid.

This is the place] Antoinette K-Doe, video interview with Mike Errico, http://www.blender.com (accessed Mar. 2008).

CHAPTER 31

235 *with K-Doe's music*] Jan Ramsey, interview with author, July 2009.

We really don't have] G. Moore qtd. in Chris Rose, "Hizzoner Ray Nagin Remains a Man of Mystery," *Times-Picayune* (New Orleans), Jan. 7, 2007.

bringing visitors to] Paul Gailiunas, "Editorial," *Times-Picayune* (New Orleans), Jan. 26, 2007.

On February 24] ("fieldsofgarlic"), "Second Line for Helen," *Livejournal*, Jan. 26, 2007, http://fieldsofgarlic.livejournal.com/29183.html (accessed Oct. 27, 2011).

236 *It's important to you*] Antoinette K-Doe, interview with Tavis Smiley, *Right to Return: New Home Movies from the Lower 9th Ward*, on *Tavis Smiley Reports*, PBS, May 28, 2007.

And joy, a Christmas ad] Claire Beale, "Beale's Best in Show: Boots (Mother)," *Independent*, Nov. 19, 2007.

Boots' new minute-long] Peter York, "Boots Puts the Sex Back into Sexism with a Cracking Christmas Tale," *Independent*, Nov. 18, 2007.

237 *a soon-to-be ubiquitous*] Alan Jackson, "Sugababes: Here Come the Girls," *Times of London*, Sept. 27, 2008.

The Ernie K-Doe statue looks] T. Gracchus, e-mail commentary, July 23, 2008, www.nola.com/news/index.ssf/2008/07/mccain_visit_details_being_wor/2986/comments-2.html.

You see that?] Antoinette K-Doe, conversation with author, Feb. 23, 2009.

241 *I'd tell them to hit*] Allen Toussaint, onstage commentary (Tribute to Ernie K-Doe, New Orleans Jazz and Heritage Festival, New Orleans, May 5, 2002).

245 *It's going to be like*] John T. Lewis, interview with Barry Yeoman and Richard Ziglar for the radio documentary *Still Singing the Blues*, http://stillsingingtheblues.org/ (accessed Sept. 22, 2010).

When my mother passed] Betty Fox, interview with Barry Yeoman and Richard Ziglar for the radio documentary *Still Singing the Blues*, http://stillsingingtheblues.org/ (accessed Sept. 22, 2010).

ANTOINETTE AND ERNIE'S WEDDING
quilted Naugahyde portrait
2010
By Annie Odell
Photo by Owen Murphy

ACKNOWLEDGMENTS

Thanks to Rick Allen, Michael Almereyda, Barry and Caroline Ancelet, Matt Anderson, archivist John Ansley from Marist College, Ana B from *Singing Bones*, Harold Bacquet, Emilie Bahr, Alan Balfour, Ron Bartholomew, Michelle Benoit, Jim Bessman, Mark Bingham, Jim Boa, Karen Brady, Brent Briggs, Douglas Brinkley, Jean-Pierre Bruneau, Bethany Bultman, Michael Burke, Graham Button, Trevor Cajiao from *Now Dig This*, Richard and Vivian Cahn, Katherine Cecil, Eileen Chapman, Anne Churchill, Tommy Cockburn, David Cole from *In the Basement*, Will Coviello, Sharon Doucet, Macreena Doyle, Thom Duffy, Robert Duncan, Blaine Dunlap, Louis Edwards, Courtney Egan, Greg Eveline, John Etter, Alison Fensterstock, John Firminger, Rob Florence, John Fohl, David and Jenn Foster, Ted Fox, Will Friedwald, Bill Friskics-Warren, Herman Fuselier, Galen Gart, Cynthia Garza, Holly George-Warren, Mindy Giles, Zack Glickman, Robert Gordon, Gail Guidry, John Harris, John Hasse, Jane Henderson, Peter Himberger, Steve Hochman, Erin Hosier, Pete Howard, Mary Howell, Joseph Irrera, Joyce Jackson, Jessie James, Ken Jones, Nalini Jones, Eugene Kador Jr., Ashley Kahn, Ashlye Keaton, Lily Keber, Jack Kresiberg (aka Jack Kay), Chris Thomas King, David Kunian, Jurgen Koop, Alyce LaBry, Sandy LaBry, Amanda LaFleur, Sara Le Menestrel, Daniel and Judith Levine, Martin Lewis, Alice Lieberman, Alan Light, Gary Lucas, archivist Rachel Lyons of the New Orleans Jazz and Heritage Foundation, Michaela Majoun, Dave Marsh, Nora Marsh, Maurice Martinez, Dominic Massa, Bunny Matthews, Kevin McCaffrey, Cree McCree, Jarrett McGehee, Glenda McKinley, Larry McKinley, Dennis McNally, Bill Millar, Rhonda Miller, Trixie Minx, Jacques Morial, John Morthland, Ingrid Multhopp, Sherry Beth Mounce, Julian Mutter, David Nathan of the UK's National Jazz Archive, Lorraine Neville, Jill Nicholls, Kathy Nicol, "Nipper" at Global Dog Productions, Nancy Ochsenschlager, Jim O'Neal, Ira Padnos, Phoebe Parros, D. Lefty Parker, Francis Pavy, Clare Beth Pierson, Tee-Eva Perry, Glen Pitre, Nicole Pouliot, Greg Preston, Angela Proctor and Vanissa Ely of the John B. Cade Library at Southern University and A&M College in Baton Rouge, Robert Pruter, Jan Ramsey, Veronica Randolph, Alex Rawls, Joe Regal, Ricky Riccardi, Altha B. Rodin, Raymond Ross, Keith Rylatt, Kalamu ya Salaam, Andrew Salinas, Joanne Schmidt, Neil Sharrow, Chuck Siler, Kent Sorrel, S. Frederick Starr, Leslie Staub, Nancy Sternberg, Billy Sturgis, Jean Sweeney, John Szwed, Elinor Tatum of the *New York Amsterdam News*, Stanley Taylor, Rico Tee, Nicolas Teurnier of *Soul Bag*, Clifton Theriot, Geannie Thomas, Dr. Gordon Thompson of Skidmore College, Tricia Tierno, Daniel Untermeyer (aka Icecube

Slim), Donna Upton, Cyril Vetter, Barbara and Walter Washington, Melissa Weber (aka DJ Soul Sister), Polly Waring, Ken Wells, Pershing Wells, Colleen Wood, Chris Williams, Jackie Williams, Wade Williams, Roger Wood, Warren Woods, Wendy Wolf, David and Kerry Yeates, Barry Yeoman, Sally Young, Gene Zacharewicz, and Richard Ziglar.

Special thanks to Steve Armbruster, Connie Atkinson, Marcia Ball, Lynda Barry, Sarah Brown, Jane Rule Burdine, Syndey Byrd, Adrianna Cador, Julia Cass, Karen Celestan, Rodney Crowell, Jo "Cool" Davis, Quint Davis, Billy Delle, Steve and Haydée Ellis, John Fox of the Henchmen, David Freedman, Edna Gundersen, Jeff Hannusch, Bruce Iglauer, Pat Jolly, Ernest Kador Jr., John and Priscilla Lawrence, Sydney Lewis, Don Marshall, Dr. Portia K. Maultsby, Andy McKaie, "Deacon" John Moore, Eric Overmyer, Mac Rebennack, A. J. Rodrigue, Kathy Sebastian, Harry Shearer, Nick Spitzer, Sonny Schneidau, Neil Strauss, and Lucinda Williams.

Eternal gratitude to Lynn Abbott, Mary Katherine Aldin, Bill Bentley, Jason Berry, John Broven, Rick Coleman, Jon Foose, David Fricke, Dan Phillips of *Home of the Groove,* Bruce Raeburn, Keith Spera, and John Wirt for graciously making research material available, making introductions, and responding to innumerable queries; designer Alison Cody, for making this book look so good; my editor, Sarah Doerries, and Jessica Dorman, director of publications at The Historic New Orleans Collection, for championing this book and then expertly bringing it into focus; Ali Duffey, for the first painstaking proofread; Peter Guralnick, for years of encouragement, help, and sage advice; Sarah Lazin, agent extraordinaire; Allen Toussaint, for patiently fielding many questions; Clarence "Reginald" Toussaint and Alison LeBeaux, for all their help over the years; and Michael Tisserand, former editor of *Gambit Weekly,* for running my first feature article about Ernie K-Doe.

Sincere apologies to any names inadvertently omitted.

Work on this book was made by possible in part by grants from the Louisiana Endowment for the Humanities—thanks to Dr. Michael Sartisky and John Kemp; the Louisiana Division of the Arts—thanks to Ann Russo and Maida Owens; the Louisiana Cultural Economy Foundation—thanks to Lisa Picone; and the Bill Muster Foundation—thanks to Nori Muster.

—Ben Sandmel

DISCOGRAPHY

At this writing, the United material is available on *Jump 'n' Shout* (Delmark DE-715), www.delmark.com; the Specialty material is available on *Creole Kings of New Orleans, Vols. 1 and 2* (SPCD-2168-25, SPCD-7038-25), http://www2.concordmusicgroup.com/labels/Specialty/; some of the Minit songs, plus other material, are available on *Here Come the Girls: Ernie K-Doe, a History, 1960–1970* (SNAX634CD); the Janus and Sansu material is available on *Here Come the Girls!* (Great American Music Company, GA-CD-942), www.greatamericanmusiccompany.com; the Fordom material is available on Threadhead, http://thrfoundation.com/ernie-vincent/.

RECORDING DATE	LABEL	RELEASE #	FORMAT	***ALBUM NAME***/Song title
November 1953	United Records (as Ernest Kador)	n/a	unreleased	Get Out of Here, Woman
				Process Blues
				Talking to the Blues
				Too Drunk to Drink
June 15, 1954	Savoy Records (as the Blue Diamonds)	Savoy 1134	45 and 78	No Money / Honey, Baby
		n/a	unreleased	She's Gone
1955	Specialty Records (as Ernest Kador)	Specialty 563	45 and 78	Do Baby Do / Eternity
		n/a	unreleased	Lay that Rock 'n' Roll Down
				So Glad You're Mine
				You Never Miss a Good Woman
1959	Ember Records (as Ernie Kado)	Ember 1050	45	Tuff-Enuff / My Love For You
	Minit Records (as Ernie K-Doe)	Minit 604	45	Make You Love Me / There's a Will, There's a Way
1960		Minit 614	45	T'aint It the Truth / Hello My Lover
1961		Minit 623	45	Mother-in-Law / Wanted, $10,000.00 Reward
		Minit 627	45	Te Ta Te Ta Ta / Real Man
		Minit 634	45	A Certain Girl / I Cried My Last Tear
1962		Minit 641	45	Popeye Joe / Come On Home
		Minit 645	45	Love You the Best / Hey, Hey, Hey
		Minit 651	45	Beating Like a Tom-Tom / I Got to Find Somebody
		Minit 656	45	Loving You / Get Out of My House
		Minit 661	45	Easier Said Than Done / Be Sweet

RECORDING DATE	LABEL	RELEASE #	FORMAT	***ALBUM NAME*/Song title**
1962 (cont.)	Minit Records	Minit 0002	LP	***MOTHER-IN-LAW*** Mother-in-Law Make You Love Me Te Ta Te Ta Ta Hurry Up and Know It T'aint It the Truth Rub Dub Dub Hello My Lover There's a Will, There's a Way Heebie Jeebies Wanted, $10,000.00 Reward Waiting at the Station She's Waiting
		n/a	unreleased	The Fight (Grandma and Grandpa)
				I Should Have Loved Her More
				What's Her Name
				Report Yourself
				Forget Her
1963	Minit	Minit 665	45	I'm the Boss / Pennies Worth of Happiness
	Instant	Instant 3260	45	Baby, Since I Met You / Sufferin' So
1964		Instant 3264	45	Reaping What I Sow / Talking Out of My Head
	Duke	Duke 378	45	My Mother-in-Law (Is in My Hair Again) / Looking into the Future
1965		Duke 387	45	Little Bit of Everything / Someone
		Duke 400	45	Please Don't Stop / Boomerang (live)
1966		Duke 404	45	Little Marie / Somebody Told Me
		Duke 411	45	Dancin' Man / Later for Tomorrow
1967		Duke 420	45	Don't Kill My Groove / Love Me Like I Wanna
		Duke 423	45	(It Will Have to Do) Until the Real Thing Comes Along / Little Marie
1968		Duke 437	45	Gotta Pack My Bag / How Sweet You Are
1969		Duke 450	45	I'm Sorry / Trying to Make You Love Me
1970		Duke 456	45	I'll Make Everything Be Alright / Wishing in Vain
No date		n/a	unreleased	All Over the World
				Back to School
				Please, Please, Please
				Doing the Blast Off
				Call on Your Love
1971	Janus	JLS 3030	LP	***ERNIE K. DOE*** Here Come the Girls Back Street Lover A Place Where We Can Be Free Whoever's Thrillin' You Is Killing Me I'm Only Human Kiss Tomorrow Goodbye Fly Away with Me A Long Way Back Home Lawdy Mama Talkin' 'Bout This Woman
		Janus 167	45	Here Come the Girls / A Long Way Back Home
1972		Janus 183	45	Lawdy Mama / Talkin' 'Bout This Woman

RECORDING DATE	LABEL	RELEASE #	FORMAT	***ALBUM NAME***/Song title
1975	Island Records	IS 031	45	Let Me Love You / So Good
ca. 1978	Sansu	Sansu 1006	45	Stoop Down / You Got to Love Me
ca. 1979		Sansu 1016	45	Hotcha Mama / (I Can't Believe) She Gave It All to Me
1986	Chiterling Circuit Society	CCS 9534	cassette	***CHITERLING CIRCUIT SOCIETY FEATURING ERNIE K-DOE AND GUITAR SLIM*** Do You Want Some? Jump into Your Love Jump into Your Love (instrumental) Don't Let Me Down Girl Father-in-Law Father-in-Law (instrumental) Saint James the Year 2000 You Did It Baby Don't Let Me Down (instrumental) Do You Want Some (instrumental)
ca. 1988	No label (probably DuBat)	n/a	CD	***ERNIE K-DOR/BLUE-EYED SOUL/BURN K-DOR BURN!*** Introduction (live) T'aint It the Truth (live) Mother-in-Law (live) Hello My Lover (live) Te Ta Ta [*sic*] (live) Certain Girl [*sic*] (live) $10,000 Reward [*sic*] (live)
ca. 1989	Syla Records	EK 120	45	Jump into Your Love / Do You Want Some
ca. 1990	DuBat	DuBat CD 51293	CD	***I'M COCKY BUT I'M GOOD JUST STANDIN' ON TOP OF 'DE WORLD*** Tain't the Truth [*sic*] Te Ta Ta [*sic*] You Did It Baby Do You Want Some? Mother-in-Law Hello My Lover Georgia on My Mind (live) Tribute to My Friend Joe Surely Gotta Woman (instrumental) Don't Let Me Down Girl
1991	Fordom Records	Fordom Records 82387	45	Night Fox II / Night Fox III
1995	No label (probably DuBat)	KD8895	CD	***FEVER!*** Only 11 Roses Your Wish Is My Command Part 1 Rock 'n' Roll U Fever When Something Is Wrong with My Baby Your Wish Is My Command Part 2 Baby Whatcha' Want Me to Do Tell Me Don't Take Me for Granted Honest I Do Love Is (The Thing We Feel) K-Doe's N.O. Groove
1999	Mardi Gras Records	MG 5016	CD	***THE BEST OF ERNIE K-DOE*** (containing 13 DuBat rereleases)
2000	No label	n/a	CD (unreleased)	Children of the World / White Boy/Black Boy

RECOMMENDED LISTENING

In addition to the Ernie K-Doe recordings listed in the discography, the following music by his colleagues is highly recommended. Although many of these artists remain active at this writing, this list focuses more on their classic than contemporary material. Over time some of these CDs may go out of print; some may be reconfigured in different packages and/or reissued by other companies. Some can be purchased as downloads. Generally speaking, European record companies show more interest in vintage New Orleans R&B than do domestic companies.

Johnny Adams: *One Foot in the Blues* (Rounder CD 2144)
James Booker: *New Orleans Piano Wizard: Live!* (Rounder CD 2027)
Fats Domino: *Greatest Hits: Walking To New Orleans* (EMI/Capitol 023512)
Dr. John: *Desitively Bonnaroo* (Atco7567-80441-2)
Lee Dorsey: "Yes We Can" / "Night People" (Raven RVCD-213, Australian import)
Earl King: *Sexual Telepathy* (Black Top BT 1052, currently available as download only)
Clarence "Frogman" Henry: *The Best of Clarence "Frogman" Henry—Ain't Got No Home* (MCA Chess CHD 9348)
Smiley Lewis: *Rocks* (Bear Family BCD 16676 AR, German import)
Lightnin' Slim: "Rooster Blues" / "Bell Ringer" (Ace CDCHD 517, British import)
Bobby Marchan: *Golden Classics* (Collectibles COL-CD-5113)
The Meters: *Look-Ka Py Py* (Rounder CD 2103)
Nat Perrilliat (featured soloist): *Boogie Live . . . 1958 featuring Ed Blackwell and AJQ-2* (AFO 92-1228-2)
Professor Longhair: *New Orleans Piano: Blues Originals 2* (Atlantic / B000002I6Z)
Shirley and Lee: *Shirley and Lee* (Collectibles COL-CD-5637 S21-18412)
Slim Harpo: *The Best of Slim Harpo* (Ace CDCHM 410, British import)
Irma Thomas: *Time Is on My Side Plus* (Ace CDKEND 010, British Import)
Allen Toussaint: *Everything I Do Gonh Be Funky: The Hit Songs & Productions 1957–1978* (Charly/Snapper Music SNAX624CD, British import)
Walter "Wolfman" Washington: *Wolf at the Door* (Rounder CD 2098)

Anthologies

Creole Kings of New Orleans, Vol. 1 (Specialty SPCD 2186-25)
Creole Kings of New Orleans, Vol. 2 (Specialty SPCD 7038-25)
The Cosimo Matassa Story (Proper, Properbox 129, British import)
Crescent City Bounce (JSP 7792, British import)
Get Low Down!: The Soul of New Orleans, '65–'67 (Sundazed SC 11094)
Gettin' Funky—The Birth of New Orleans R&B (Proper, Properbox 28, British import)
Jump 'n' Shout: New Orleans Blues and Rhythm (Delmark DE-715)
New Orleans R&B—Crescent City Classics (Acrobat ADDCD 3011, British import)
Sehorn's Soul Farm: 50 New Orleans Soul Classics (Charly/Snapper Music SNAD661CD, British import)

BIBLIOGRAPHY

Books

Abbott, Lynn. *I Got Two Wings: Incidents and Anecdotes of the Two-Winged Preacher and Electric Guitar Evangelist Elder Utah Smith*. Montgomery, AL: CaseQuarter, 2008.

Berry, Jason, Jonathan Foose, and Tad Jones. *Up from the Cradle of Jazz: New Orleans Music Since World War II*. New ed. Lafayette: University of Louisiana at Lafayette Press, 2009.

Bradley, Andy, and Charles Roger Wood. *House of Hits: The Story of Houston's Gold Star/SugarHill Recording Studios*. Austin: University of Texas Press, 2010.

Brasseaux, Carl A. *French, Cajun, Creole, Houma: A Primer on Francophone Louisiana*. Baton Rouge: Louisiana State University Press, 2005.

Broven, John. *Record Makers and Breakers: Voices of the Independent Rock 'n' Roll Pioneers*. Urbana: University of Illinois Press, 2009.

——. *Rhythm and Blues in New Orleans*. Gretna, LA: Pelican, 1974.

——. *South to Louisiana: The Music of the Cajun Bayous*. Gretna, LA: Pelican, 1983.

Butler, Jerry, with Earl Smith. *Only the Strong Survive: Memoirs of a Soul Survivor*. Bloomington: Indiana University Press, 2000.

Clifford, Jan, and Leslie Blackshear Smith. *The New Orleans Jazz and Heritage Festival: The Incomplete, Year-by-Year, Selectively Quirky, Prime Facts Edition*. Edited by Kevin McCafferey. Vol. 1. New Orleans: E/Prime, 2005.

Coleman, Rick. *Blue Monday: Fats Domino and the Lost Dawn of Rock 'n' Roll*. Cambridge, MA: Da Capo, 2006.

Davis, Stephen. *Hammer of the Gods: The Led Zeppelin Saga*. New York: Boulevard Books, 1997.

Dr. John (Mac Rebennack), with Jack Rummel. *Under a Hoodoo Moon: The Life of the Night Tripper*. New York: St. Martin's, 1994.

Evans, Freddi Williams. *Congo Square: African Roots in New Orleans*. Lafayette: University of Louisiana at Lafayette Press, 2011.

Fox, Ted. *Showtime at the Apollo: The Story of Harlem's World Famous Theater*. New rev. ed. Rhinebeck, NY: Mill Road Enterprises, 2003.

Gill, James. *Lords of Misrule: Mardi Gras and the Politics of Race in New Orleans*. Jackson: University Press of Mississippi, 1997.

Gordon, Robert. *It Came from Memphis*. Boston: Faber and Faber, 1994.

Guralnick, Peter. *Dream Boogie: The Triumph of Sam Cooke*. New York: Little, Brown, 2005.

——. *Sweet Soul Music: Rhythm and Blues and the Southern Dream of Freedom*. New York: Harper and Row, 1986.

Hannusch, Jeff. *I Hear You Knockin': The Sound of New Orleans Rhythm and Blues*. Ville Platte, LA: Swallow, 1985.

——. *The Soul of New Orleans: A Legacy of Rhythm and Blues*. Ville Platte, LA: Swallow, 2001.

Hearn, Lafcadio. *An American Miscellany*. New York: Dodd, Mead and Company, 1924.

Heilbut, Anthony. *The Gospel Sound: Good News and Bad Times*. 1971. Reprint, New York: Limelight Editions, 1985.

Hunt, Alfred N. *Haiti's Influence on Antebellum America: Slumbering Volcano in the Caribbean*. Baton Rouge:

Louisiana State University Press, 1988.

Kempton, Arthur. *Boogaloo: The Quintessence of American Popular Music*. New York: Pantheon, 2003.

Lavender, Bill, ed. *Another South: Experimental Writing in the South*. Tuscaloosa: University of Alabama Press, 2003.

Lipsitz, George. *Time Passages: Collective Memory and American Popular Culture*. Minneapolis: University of Minnesota Press, 1990.

Lois, George. *Ali Rap: Muhammad Ali, the First Heavyweight Champion of Rap*. New York: ESPB Books, 2006.

Lomax, Alan. *Mister Jelly Roll: The Fortunes of Jelly Roll Morton, New Orleans Creole and the "Inventor of Jazz."* 2d ed. Berkeley: University of California Press, 1973.

——. *The Land Where the Blues Began*. New York, Pantheon, 1993.

Murray, Albert. *The Hero and the Blues*. New York: Vintage Books, 1995. First published in 1973 by University of Missouri Press.

Murrells, Joseph. *The Book of Golden Discs: The Records That Sold a Million*. 2d ed. London: Barrie and Jenkins, 1978.

Pruter, Robert. *Chicago Soul*. Urbana: University of Illinois Press, 1991.

Ritz, David. *The Brothers Neville*. Boston: Little, Brown, 2000.

Scherman, Tony. *Backbeat: Earl Palmer's Story*. Washington, DC: Smithsonian Institution Press, 1999.

Semmes, Clovis E. *The Regal Theater and Black Culture*. New York: Palgrave MacMillan, 2006.

Starr, S. Frederick, ed. *Inventing New Orleans: Writings of Lafcadio Hearn*. Jackson: University Press of Mississippi, 2001.

Starr, S. Frederick. *New Orleans Unmasqued*. New Orleans: Édition Dedeaux, 1985.

Strauss, Neil. *Everyone Loves You When You're Dead: Journeys into Fame and Madness*. New York: It Books/HarperCollins, 2011.

Sublette, Ned. *The World That Made New Orleans: From Spanish Silver to Congo Square*. Chicago: Lawrence Hill Books, 2008.

Tosches, Nick. *Hellfire: The Jerry Lee Lewis Story*. New York: Dell, 1982. Reprinted with new preface and postscript.

Van Deburg, William L. *Black Camelot: African-American Culture Heroes in Their Times, 1960–1980*. Chicago: University of Chicago Press, 1997.

Watkins, Mel. *On the Real Side: Laughing, Lying, and Signifying—the Underground Tradition of African-American Humor That Transformed American Culture from Slavery to Richard Pryor*. New York: Simon and Schuster, 1994.

White, Charles. *The Life and Times of Little Richard*. New York: Harmony Books, 1984.

Wood, Roger. *Down in Houston, Bayou City Blues*. With photography by James Fraher. Austin: University of Texas Press, 2003.

Articles

Cooper, B. Lee. "From Lady Day to Lady Di: Images of Women in Contemporary Recordings, 1938–1998." *International Journal of Instructional Media* 26, no. 3 (1999): 353–58.

Lipsitz, George. "Learning from New Orleans: The Social Warrant of Hostile Privatism and Competitive Consumer Citizenship." *Cultural Anthropology* 21, no. 3 (2006): 451–68.

——. "Mardi Gras Indians: Carnival and Counter-Narrative in Black New Orleans." *Cultural Critique* 10 (Autumn 1988): 99–121.

Regis, Helen. "Second Lines, Minstrelsy, and the Contested Landscapes of New Orleans Afro-Creole Festivals." *Cultural Anthropology* 14, no. 4 (November 1999): 472–504.

Smith, Michael P. "Behind the Lines: The Black Mardi Gras Indians and the New Orleans Second Line." *Black Music Research Journal* 14, no. 1 (Spring 1994): 43–73.

Szwed, John. "Doctor Jazz." Essay in the liner notes to the anthology *Jelly Roll Morton: The Complete Library of Congress Recordings by Alan Lomax*. Cambridge, MA: Rounder Records, 2005.

INDEX

Note: Italicized page numbers indicate images.

Ben Sandmel is a New Orleans–based journalist, folklorist, drummer, and producer. His articles about Louisiana music have appeared in national publications, including the *Atlantic,* and have been anthologized in such collections as *Da Capo Best Music Writing 2000* and *From Jubilee to Hip Hop: Readings in African American Music* (Prentice Hall, 2010). Sandmel has written liner notes for over one hundred albums in a wide range of traditional-music genres. He is also the author of *Zydeco!* (University Press of Mississippi, 1999), a collaborative book with photographer Rick Olivier.

Since 1983 Sandmel has worked for the state-funded Louisiana Folklife Program as a field researcher and writer, documenting traditional music and occupational folklore, the latter based on his experience as a riverboat deckhand. Sandmel currently produces the Allison Miner Music Heritage Stage, an oral history/interview venue at the annual New Orleans Jazz and Heritage Festival. He has produced and played on four albums, including the Grammy-nominated *Deep Water* by the Cajun/western swing band the Hackberry Ramblers. Sandmel is currently enrolled in the masters program in musicology at Tulane University.

Special thanks to
Billy Delle, for his invaluable insight and for the use of his extensive record collection
The Hogan Jazz Archive, Tulane University

The Historic New Orleans Collection is a museum, research center, and publisher dedicated to the study and preservation of the history and culture of New Orleans, the lower Mississippi Valley, and the Gulf South. The Collection is operated by the Kemper and Leila Williams Foundation, a Louisiana nonprofit corporation.

Interview transcripts, sound recordings, and memorabilia from the Mother-in-Law Lounge are housed at The Collection's Williams Research Center, along with many of the images of Ernie K-Doe included in this volume. More images of K-Doe and of other musicians discussed in these pages can be found in various collections housed in the WRC.

SAVOY
NO MONEY
Specialty
45 R.P.M.
ETERNITY
ERNEST KADOR
And His Band
EMBER
45 RPM
MY LOVE FOR YOU
ERNIE KADO
with LEE ALLEN & His Band
E-1050
MINIT
RECORDS
WANTED, $10,000.00 REWARD
ERNIE K-DOE
REAL MAN
ERNIE K-DOE
I CRIED MY LAST TEAR
ERNIE K-DOE
GET OUT OF MY HOUSE
ERNIE K-DOE
ERNIE K-DOE
PENNIES WORTH OF HAPPINESS
ERNIE K-DOE
ERNIE K-DOE
LOOKING INTO THE FUTURE
DUKE
PROMOTIONAL RECORD NOT FOR SALE
45 RPM
ERNIE K-DOE
SOMEONE
DUKE
45 RPM
ERNIE K-DOE
BOOMERANG
DUKE
45 RPM
HOW SWEET YOU ARE
DUKE
45 RPM
ERNIE K-DOE
TRYING TO MAKE YOU LOVE ME
DUKE
ERNIE K-DOE
WISHING IN VAIN
DUKE
45 RPM
PROMOTIONAL RECORD NOT FOR SALE
ERNIE K-DOE